MW00637418

Credit Derivatives

and

SECURITIZATION

Instruments and Applications

Third Edition

Janet M. Tavakoli

Lyons McNamara LLC
Chicago

Published by Lyons McNamara LLC, Chicago, Illinois.

Limits of Liability/Disclaimer of Warranty

The Library of Congress Data (Previous hardcover edition via Wiley Finance):
Tavakoli, Janet M., 1953-
Credit Derivatives: a guide to instruments and applications /
Janet M. Tavakoli.
p. cm.— (Wiley series in Financial engineering) First edition originally published in 1998: Credit derivatives: a guide to instruments and applications. (First edition) Includes index. [ISBN 0-471-24656-5 (cloth : alk.paper)]
1. Derivative securities. 2. Risk management. 3. Credit. 4. Debt. 5. Default (Finance) 1. Title. II. Series.
HG6024.A3T34 1998 332.63'2—dc21   97-44831
Printed in the United States of America

Credit Derivatives and Securitization: Instruments and Applications (3rd Edition)
Hardcover edition, 2022

ISBN-13: 978-1-943543-32-8

Books by Janet Tavakoli

NONFICTION

Risk

Decisions: Life and Death on Wall Street

Unveiled Threat: A Personal Experience of Fundamentalist Islam and the Roots of Terrorism

Structured Finance and Collateralized Debt Obligations

Dear Mr. Buffett

Credit Derivatives and Securitization

The New Robber Barons

FICTION - MYSTERY

Archangels: Rise of the Jesuits

"Conspiracies within conspiracies, a fast-paced thriller."
—*Publisher's Weekly*

Finance Classics

The Wall Street Point of View

By Henry Clews

Annotations and Foreword by Janet Tavakoli

Twenty Years of Inside Life in Wall Street

or

Revelations of the Personal Experience of a Speculator

By William Worthington Fowler

Annotations and Foreword by Janet Tavakoli

Acknowledgements

I would like to thank the credit desks at JPMorgan Chase and Goldman Sachs for making these updates possible. I'd also like to thank Hilary Till of Premia Capital, the "crypto guys," and Jim Rogers for their broad market insights.

Fund manager Lauren Templeton, co-author with her husband Scott Phillips of *Investing the Templeton Way*, first told me of her great uncle Sir John Templeton's motto "Trouble is Opportunity."

The concept of portfolio risk came alive for me in the spring of 1981 in the late Merton Miller's corporate finance class at the University of Chicago's 190 E. Delaware building. Just before class I would comb chemical dust out of my hair and brush white powdered phosphate residue off my jeans, the result of my day job as a chemical engineer. Then I prepared for the entertaining enthusiasm of my instructor who made risk and reward the subject of imaginative financial fun.

Gimmicks and games were a key part of every class discussion in the good old days when the accrued income on zero-coupon bonds was taxed as capital gains at maturity. But times change. The IRS went on to tax implied accrued income as ordinary income on an annual basis.

Merton Miller went on to win a Nobel Prize in economics. I thanked Merton Miller for inspiring my enthusiasm for the new gimmicks and games, which inevitably evolve in the financial markets. I regret I will not have another opportunity. Merton Miller passed on June 3, 2000. He was a shining light in the world of finance.

I would like to thank others who offered their encouragement and perspective at the dawn of the credit derivatives markets when they worked at various institutions: Lauren Golden helped with early illustrations. Mox Tan encouraged me to write about credit derivatives when I preferred to go sailing. Steve Wade, then of Union Bank of Switzerland, Hei Wai Chan of

J.P. Morgan, and Stephen Partridge-Hicks of Gordian Knot ("That sounds good, but I'll have to have my lawyers study the documents.") inspired a clearheaded approach to the credit markets.

Dan Stahle and Tom Boemio at the Federal Reserve, Mu Gu at Bank of America, Randy Allison Kaufman at Bank Boston, Vivian Bronk at the Bank of England, Philip Borg and Kaye Taleghana at Bankers Trust, Carl Schuman at Westdeutsche Landesbank Girozentrale in New York, Isaac Efrat at Moody's Investors Service, Paul Varotsis at Chase in London, Kevin McGivern at Sumitomo Capital, Oliver d'Oelsnitz at DG Bank, Ethan Berman at CreditMetrics, Franklin Lee at Merrill Lynch, Ron Dembo at Algorithmics, Nancie Poulus Watson, and Patricia Sevening.

Adrian Hyde of Chase helped me correct typos and other errata for the first edition. Bin Hong of BankOne gave me technical advice on credit exposures. Sandy Sloane of Bank of America, Chris Culp of the Chicago Group, and Rupert Walsh and Chris Surr of CreditTrade helped with various insights.

Special thanks to the excellent publishing and editing staff at John Wiley & Sons, especially Claudio Campuzano, Pamela van Giessen, and Bill Falloon on the first and second editions.

J.M.T.

Contents

Introduction

The goal of this book is to help you profit from the bad financial behavior of others, or at the very least, avoid getting financially hurt by it. Two decades ago, John Wiley & Sons published the second edition of *Credit Derivatives and Synthetic Structures*, introducing the basic structures used to create tremendous hidden leverage in the global financial system. My manual on what Warren Buffett calls "financial weapons of mass destruction" included caveats about hidden risks for those who wanted to avoid disaster. Through actual market examples, it warned of information asymmetry and documentation risk—a polite ways of saying your counterparty is pulling the wool over your eyes. But my book also included ways for investors to profit from devastation that was not of their making.

This third edition, *Credit Derivatives and Securitization* gives subsequent examples of tremendous market windfalls achieved via credit derivatives during the Global Financial Crisis of 2008 and the economic crash caused by the global reaction to COVID-19 and its aftermath. It also includes tremendous losses due to carelessness or overreach: the London Whale debacle and the bankruptcy of MF Global.

In 2003, Wiley published *Collateralized Debt Obligations and Structured Finance* wherein I explained that most collateralized debt obligations (CDOs) were misrated and mismanaged.

A collateralized debt obligation is an asset backed securitization where the assets consist of a pool of any kind of debt or mixture of kinds of debt. Assets may include, but are not limited to, mortgages, corporate bonds, receivables, auto loans, student loans, credit card receivables, consumer loans, residential mortgage-backed securities, (RMBS), or tranches, i.e., bonds of other collateralized debt obligations, or credit derivatives that reference any of the former as underlying risk.

The flaws in the ratings were amplified by leverage and opacity made possible by credit derivatives technology used to transfer risk. Rent-seeking financial "professionals' used credit derivatives to introduce excess hidden risk and leverage via synthetic CDOs, securitizations that used credit derivatives to transfer risk by referencing debt obligations.

Credit Derivatives and Securitization introduces new material on how to avoid being on the wrong side of credit derivatives transactions and the types of transactions to avoid altogether. Avoiding disaster is a worthy goal. But it is not the only goal. John Templeton noted that "trouble is opportunity."

Credit derivatives skew and leverage both risk and reward. The risk/reward ratio is skewed in favor of diligent analysts who uncover material weaknesses and/or fraud. Problems are often discoverable during reasonable due diligence. If analysts find red flags for fraud, prudence mandates rigorous due diligence and a fraud audit.

Due diligence is a thankless task within banks and investment banks that are earning fees for mispriced risk. If you find yourself in such an unappreciated and undercompensated position, I offer the same advice that I gave to risk managers in 2007, eighteen months before the Global Financial crisis: "Get out and short those positions." ("Subprime Mortgages: The Predators' Fall" *GARP Risk Review*, March/April 2007 Issue 35.) This advice is as applicable today as it was then.

This edition includes most of the structures introduced in earlier editions because all the applications are either used in the same form today, can be used in the same form today, or will be used again when market conditions change. They also spark ideas for new structures.

The language in the term sheet examples is dated. You may wish to use the current language that the International Swaps and Derivatives Association (ISDA) would dearly love to make "standard." You do not have to use "ISDA standard" language; ISDA is not your counterparty.

ISDA's language is flawed, has gone through iterations, and its settlement process can be problematic. ISDA does not deal with wild card issues, such as embedded hedges in credit derivatives contracts. You may wish to adopt and modify suggestions I have incorporated in this book.

Moreover, if someone hands you a "standard" contract when you engage in an over-the-counter trade or a complex credit-linked note, compare the contract with ISDA language. It may not be "standard" at all.

The devil is in the details. Sometimes that devil aims to deceive you. A firm may recraft one or more clauses to advantage itself when selling protection and may recraft one or more clauses to advantage itself when it is buying protection—that may be the firm's "standard."

You have the choice to craft your own language, and if you are engaging in an over-the-counter (OTC) transaction, instead of an exchange traded transaction, you should negotiate and rewrite terms.

We will explore current applications of the diverse types of credit derivative products. New structures constantly appear, and printed material cannot keep up with the variations on the original theme. Nonetheless, this book presents the basic groundwork for understanding the existing and future structures in the global market.

Global banks with large balance sheets and low funding costs dominate the credit derivatives and securitization markets along with hedge funds savvy in credit and its derivatives. Investors and end users include the interbank market, corporations, insurance companies, hedge funds, private equity funds, and mutual funds. These products can be applied to credit line management, portfolio management, arbitrage opportunities, and creation of synthetic assets.

This book is accessible to the educated finance reader as it delves into the principles and processes of the credit derivatives market using only the fundamental rules of investment theory. I will point out the flaws in models and pricing theory in a general way but will not spend time on various models. There are dozens of books on models crowding technical bookshelves. None of them will help you avoid the largest losses or find the largest gains.

We will examine the limitations of mathematical models. Models cannot help one calculate unknowable unknowns; we all hope our educated guesses are lucky. Models cannot help you calculate rarely uncovered *knowable unknowns*; these are uncovered by due diligence and are the inputs—*never* the outputs—of useful models. Due diligence is your edge, and it has nothing to do with models.

For decades, quantitative modelers waxed lyrical about the cleverness of their models. But their models did not even capture basic credit risk. The only useful thing the models did was to check off a box on regulators' lists of required "tools" for regulated financial institutions. Financial institutions reserved capital based on regulators' guidelines, and everyone pretended they were managing risk. Few modelers spent time on what really matters in a credit analysis: *rigorous due diligence*.

Models miss key risks or get them profoundly wrong, even when models are used as designed. In the list below, models are only meant to address the last three.

The last item, systemic risk, is estimated based on judgment and scenario/stress test modeling. Judgment is necessary, since there is a poverty of data, and one hopes one is making lucky guesses which one will later take credit for as "good judgment." (Go ahead. I won't tell Nassim Taleb.) Despite flaws, it is a good idea to stress test based on scenarios. We will later discuss the global financial crisis and the COVID-19 market panic. There is a low-cost way to use credit derivatives to hedge oneself and skew probabilities in one's favor.

It is particularly important to look for fraud when assessing credit risk for inherently leveraged credit derivatives transactions, because the economic outcomes can be wildly skewed.

The remaining risks at the top of this list are chiefly uncovered by experience and rolling up one's sleeves to do the analysis.

- Fraud
- Information asymmetry
- Documentation risk
- Structural risk: hidden risks in deal structures
- Mergers, acquisitions, leveraged buyouts (LBOs) that change credit and cash flow priority
- Capital structure changes that alter the seniority of credit risk
- Credit risk – underlying and counterparty risk: Model
- Market Risk: Model
- Systemic risks—scenario analyses: Judgment and Model

Fraud is baked into the markets because human nature has not changed. Economic incentives in the financial industry favor those who can socialize losses and monetize gains. Enormous personal gains and net institutional profits—plus bailouts—trump institutional fines.

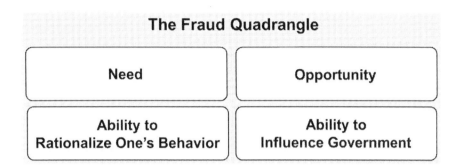

The Fraud Quadrangle

Need	Opportunity
Ability to Rationalize One's Behavior	Ability to Influence Government

The familiar fraud triangle has three elements: need, opportunity, and the ability to rationalize one's behavior. But the finance industry has a powerful *fraud quadrangle*: need, opportunity, ability to rationalize one's behavior, and influence in government so that you can get away with it.

Do you need a castle in Ireland, a villa in the South of France, a mansion in the Hamptons, the latest Tesla, or a private jet?

There is plenty of opportunity. If your bosses earn tens of millions of dollars in bonuses for looking the other way while lax risk controls and complicit regulators allow you to underreport risk, you can earn several million dollars per year. If you *are* the boss, you will earn even more.

Professor William K. Black of the University of Minnesota Law School and key regulator during the Savings and Loan crisis of the 1980s and 1990s, coined the term "control fraud" to describe frauds in which a financial institution's high-level staff use their positions within their employer as a means to defraud. Control fraud is easy to rationalize. The "in crowd" does it. There is high personal financial upside. Personal "downside" is minimal to none.

If you are the CEO of a major financial institution, crony capitalism works for you. Bundling of campaign contributions, political action committees (PACs), influencing employees' campaign contributions, hiring the relatives and friends of members of Congress, paying enormous speaking fees to people who have influence in Washington D.C. A version of this happens in every country on planet earth. Money buys you influence with "your government," and "your regulators."

Most of the financial media lionize you as a financial genius. You are! Your personal net worth is in the hundreds of millions of dollars and may exceed one billion dollars. Congress and the Federal Reserve socialize losses so that you can privatize gains for yourself, your officers, and your shareholders. Government lawyers find lucrative positions at law firms that work for you and your competitors.

If you "err," the firm you head will pay a small fine compared to the economic damage you create, and your firm's winnings in other areas will swamp the cost of the fine. You are doing "God's work"! Your massive, bundled campaign contributions and back scratching yield a thrilling return on investment, including bailouts!

Given this backdrop, using current market models to price credit derivatives is like trying to apply Euclidean geometry to describe the shapes found in nature, in this case, human nature. The formulas and curves look neat, regular, and well defined. Unfortunately, nature just does not look that way. It looks more like a Mandelbrot set, a fractal. We cannot force our observations of nature into those neat little Euclidean shapes.

The value of credit derivatives is determined by a mark-to-market, not a mark-to-model. The models currently in use have their value, but this book focuses on the assumptions which are used as inputs to these models. Assumptions are the key to understanding the risks and rewards. Yet, one cannot say it enough, models are seductive.

My advanced statistics professor, one of the world's most talented statisticians and statistical modelers, laughingly admitted to model hubris early in his career. He was asked to take part in a study to model tree trunk wood volumes.

He diligently measured the trees and recorded the wood yield data corresponding to the measured trees. He tabulated and graphed the data. He used a computer program and regression analysis. He applied modeling theory and produced a formula that was closely correlated with tree wood yields.

It was magic. Statistics worked. The formula looked very much like that for the volume of a cylinder—with a small fudge factor thrown in. Fudge factors are common. They make up for the fact that the world does not always behave the way we think it should behave. Euclidean geometry always leaves us with the need for fudge factors; we are used to it. We know the world is not made up of squares, triangles, circles, and cylinders. Nonetheless, the model was a nice, neat, and intuitive little formula. It had a high correlation coefficient.

When you plugged in the trunk width and the height of the tree, the wood volume was as predicted by the neat little formula. Statistics showed that the formula described the data and predicted future events well. That— among other things—is what makes a statistician feel satisfied.

Everyone was happy. Statistics did just what it is supposed to do. A statistician collected historical data and found a mathematical formula, which described the relationship between measurable attributes of a tree and the potential wood yield. A measurement of attributes would now allow the statistician's employer to predict wood yield of a forest.

The formula was perfect.

Well, *almost* perfect.

Little things bugged him. A plot of the residuals did not look random. The residuals, the unexplained data, appeared to have a pattern. Statisticians know that is not a good thing. That usually means the neat little formula missed something. But it was so close. The minor error seemed negligible. The budding professor was tempted to ignore these pesky residuals and declare the job done. But he kept at it, laboring away, modifying the formula, trying to make the residuals disappear. The cylinder-like formula seemed so right. It made sense. Trees look like cylinders.

The professor had a slight problem. He could not see the formula for the trees. Trees do indeed look very much like cylinders. But they look even more like cones. One day, a forester pointed this out to the professor. This is a moment statisticians and mathematicians both love and hate. They hate it because they get a churning feeling in the pit of their stomachs, which lets them know in their gut that they are wrong. They also love it because now they have hit on a better answer.

Sure enough, when the professor used the formula for the volume of a cone (with tiny modifications), those pesky residual patterns disappeared. The residuals were now random. A cone-like formula was the better answer—not a perfect answer (we were still in the world of Euclidean geometry)—but good enough for what the foresters were trying to do. That is all we really want from mathematics: utility, not perfection.

With hindsight it was easy for the professor to see that a tree trunk looks more like a cone than a cylinder. But that fact was knowable in advance. It only required objective observation. Likewise, those successful in the credit markets perform basic analysis and observation before using or writing a model. Preliminary analysis often uncovers valuable information, whereas a model may obscure credit risk. Models and their maintenance can become an expensive cost center, not a profit center.

One of the goals of this book is to prevent market practitioners from being baffled by jargon, equations, and diagrams. Before one crunches numbers like crazy, stares at a computer screen for lengthy hours, and draws dozens of diagrams, one should step back and view the problem objectively. Ask a few questions. Bring your experience to bear on the problem. What would I expect the result to look like? What do I expect to happen?

Whether I am evaluating a credit derivative, an interest rate option, an interest rate swap, or my private investment portfolio, I ask the same basic questions: How much cash will I get? When will I get the cash? How certain am I that I will get the cash? Is there a government regulation that makes me better off? Is there an accounting method that makes me appear better off? Can I use less capital to improve my rate of return? Is there a tax regulation I can use to my economic advantage? How much of the cash do I get to generate and keep?

Timing of cash flows, magnitude of cash flows, and the certainty of cash flows determine value. Relative value is further determined by regulatory, accounting, tax, and risk profile constraints. These constraints have tangible value because they affect cash.

One must firmly hold on to these concepts in any discussion of financial products. It is easy to lose sight of cash flows when the mind walks through a maze of jargon, equations, and diagrams. I cannot spend jargon. I cannot spend equations. I cannot spend diagrams. But I can spend various forms of cash. It is up to you to find opportunities. But this book provides some examples of where to look. Then you can employ credit derivatives to monetize those opportunities.

CHAPTER 1

Credit Derivatives Market Overview

Buyers and sellers of credit protection negotiate credit derivative contracts for one or more of the following motives:

- Income
- Leverage
- Speculation
- Tax benefits
- Risk management
- Accounting benefits
- Balance sheet manipulation
- Obfuscation of counterparty risk
- Regulatory and economic capital relief

CREDIT DEFAULT SWAP: THE BASIC IDEA

The classic par credit default swap (CDS) is depicted in Figure 1.1. We will first discuss the CDS as an over-the-counter (OTC) traded product. Later, we will discuss the exchange traded market "standard" for credit default swaps developed after the global financial crisis of 2008.

A credit default swap is a bilateral contract between a credit default protection buyer (seller of credit risk) and a credit default protection seller (buyer of credit risk). The protection buyer is short credit risk, and the protection seller is long credit risk. The credit protection buyers and credit protection sellers are called counterparties.

The protection seller receives a periodic premium from the protection buyer in exchange for a contingent payment if there is a predefined credit event of a prespecified reference entity.

The continent payment is determined based on prespecified settlement terms.

FIGURE 1.1   Basic Credit Default Swap (CDS)

A buyer can be a buyer of credit risk or a buyer of credit protection. A seller can be a seller of credit risk or a seller of credit protection. In this book I adopt a convention to avoid confusion. The buyer is the buyer of credit protection (a seller of credit risk). The seller sells credit protection (takes credit risk). The seller usually receives a fee for this protection.

The notional principal amount, usually called the notional amount, is the amount against which fees, interest payments, price differential, and recovery values are based in a credit default swap contract.

A $10 million notional CDS transaction, for example, is reported as one contract with a $10 million gross notional value. It is not reported as $20 million ($10 million for each counterparty).

Credit default swaps can be used as a credit risk hedges. An asset does not need to default for the buyer of credit default protection to make money. If an asset's credit quality deteriorates, the price of credit default protection on the weakening asset increases. The holder of the previously bought credit default protection can reverse the trade at a profit.

The following discussion is what every financial professional already knows about credit. Yet few have acted and profited from this knowledge. I ask you to bear with me because this approach leads to the biggest payoffs. Everyone who made well-reported huge profits in credit derivatives used this approach. They did not base their trades on conventional models. Models are necessary for regulators and risk reports, but they do little to give you the confidence to ride out a CDS trade.

CREDIT: THE BASIC IDEA

The traditional four Cs of credit are character, capacity, collateral, and capital. Of the four, character is the most important. People with character value their reputations and will do their best to pay you back.

One could develop a checklist for due diligence, but it will vary as situations change. Your burden of due diligence increases as problems are uncovered, and no list of suggestions should be viewed as comprehensive. One must use judgment in a credit analysis.

In my experience, these general guidelines are useful:

- Principals have a history of sound management. Their backgrounds and educational institutions check out.
- Cash flow does not come out of thin air. The business model is understandable. Cash flows are transparent, and one can follow them.
- Revenue growth is explainable and steady. There is not a sudden unexpected ramp up in revenue without a sound explanation of how value is being created and so quickly.
- You can verify assumptions.
- The accounting firm has a good reputation and has assigned someone with the same.
- Debt is manageable and there is no hidden leverage.
- There are multiple streams of income. The business does not depend on a single strategy, supplier, consumer, client, industry, or key man.
- Management can describe and verify its risk management controls.
- Management answers questions clearly without obfuscation.

Whether one is assessing an investment manager, a creditor, an offshore entity, a corporation's bonds, or a corporation's equity one wants to know whether the cash flow payments you expect are likely to be received by you. In the case of a corporation, payment priorities in bankruptcy are as follows. Senior debt has the lowest risk and equity has the most risk.

Hypothetical Corporate Capital Structure Priorities
Senior Secured Debt: first lien, revolving credit facilities, term loans.
Subordinated Debt aka Junior Debt aka Mezzanine Debt: second lien notes, senior unsecured debt, high yield bonds, mezzanine with/ without warrants, payment in kind bonds aka PIK bonds, obligations to vendors
Hybrid Securities: senior convertible bonds, convertible equity convertible bonds, senior convertible bonds
Preferred Stock aka Preferred Equity: nonconvertible preferred stock, convertible preferred stock. Corporation is not obliged to pay dividends. If corporation pays dividends, cumulative dividends must be paid to preferred stock investors ahead of common stock dividends.
Common Stock aka Common Equity

TABLE 1.1: Example of a "Moment in Time" Corporate Capital Structure

I labeled Table 1.1 a "moment in time" capital structure because not only do capital structures vary from company to company, but the capital structure can also materially and drastically change over time.

Many investment banks separate fixed income research from equity research. (It may make sense to have a separate department to analyze securitizations and special purpose corporations.) If one is researching a corporation, both fixed income and equity are part of the capital structure. One cannot assess equity risk without understanding the entire corporation.

If you are selling credit default protection, be aware that a company may change its capital structured if and when it raises new capital. Moreover, your counterparty may game the capital structure to deliberately trigger a technical default.

Fraud

Bonds usually come to market at par. If the security is a sound credit, it matures and pays off at par. A $10 million par bond pays $10 million of principal plus interest. Prior to maturity, the price of the security may slightly rise if credit spreads narrow or interest rates in general plummet.

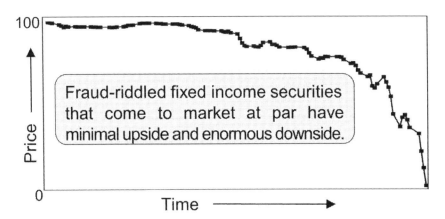

FIGURE 1.2   Fraud Price Pattern for Fixed Income Securities

Credit derivatives and fixed income securities are much more interesting when prices plummet. The price of a fixed income securities can fall below par if interest rates rise, if credit spreads widen, if ordinary defaults occur, or if there is fraud.

Fraud is a special case. It is well worth your time to look for it. If you do not look for it, you will not find it. Deception is fraud's hallmark. The price of a fraudulent fixed income security can plummet towards zero with permanent value destruction.

Figure 1.2 illustrates the fraud price pattern. This is the pattern those investors in *The Big Short* identified prior to the Global Financial Crisis. The best time to short a flawed fixed income security is when it trades at par and has nowhere much to go except down. We will discuss why this trade worked so well during the financial crisis in the final section of this chapter. But that is not the only time we have seen a similar pattern not necessarily due to fraud. Other examples include the bankruptcy of MF Global, J.P. Morgan's London Whale, and the COVID-19 market crisis of 2020. We will discuss these debacles in Chapters 2, 3 and 5, respectively.

If you are looking for security that will fall in price, finding fraud is a powerful edge. Suppose you researched corporate bankruptcies during a recession and found that for every thousand corporate bankruptcies, prudent men ran five hundred companies, and five hundred companies were run by men who were later successfully prosecuted for fraud. Does this mean that the chances of a company surviving a recession are fifty-fifty irrespective of whether there is sound management? Of course not.

Suppose the odds are that for *all* companies in this recession—not just those that fail—ninety percent are run by honest managers, and ten percent are run by crooks. Further suppose that twenty percent of the companies in this recession go bankrupt. Your analysis shows that half had honest managers and half were run by fraudsters. In other words, every company run by fraudsters went bankrupt.

This paints a different picture about fraud, doesn't it? We do not have historical data broken down this way. But experienced financiers focus on character because honest managers improve the odds of a company's success. In contrast, fraud enables permanent value destruction in both good times and bad.

One way to short a security is to buy credit default protection. If you uncover fraud and short a security at par, your cost of carry will be low. You can afford to wait for the price to fall. Moreover, unlike equities, when you short at par, the price due to credit deterioration has minimal upside with enormous downside.

Even if you cannot (or do not want to) short the security, analysis gives you the opportunity to keep it out of your portfolio.

Often when we talk about confidence intervals produced by models, we use the phrase "confidence level." But this is incorrect. The correct term is confidence interval: a range of outcomes.

If you are looking for a level of confidence, do not rely on models that crunch numbers based on suspicious data supplied by people with conflicts of interest. Confidence comes from understanding the underlying credit risk.

ESTIMATED MARKET SIZE

The estimated credit derivatives notional market size in the first half of 2021 was $24.4 trillion of which $8.8 trillion were over-the-counter contracts and $15.6 trillion were exchange traded contracts.

In the first half of 2021, the Bank for International Settlements (BIS) estimated that around 64% of credit derivatives contracts were centrally cleared, but that still leaves 36% of contracts that remain over-the-counter.

Despite trying to downsize the CDS market, in the first half of 2021, the over-the-counter credit derivatives market was almost *ten times* the size of the market in 2000, and the total credit derivatives market, including OTC and exchange traded credit derivatives, was *twenty-five times* the size of the credit derivatives market in 2000. A large chunk of this market is not used for hedging, it is used for *speculation*.

Credit derivatives contracts were originally exclusively over-the-counter (OTC) negotiated contracts. Prices were by agreement and completely opaque; today's models are at times no better.

After the 2008 global financial crisis, there was a push towards exchange traded, centrally cleared, contracts to limit counterparty risk and increase transparency. The Intercontinental Exchange (ICE) was the first exchange to centrally clear credit derivatives starting in 2009. The Bank for International Settlements (BIS) estimated that 64% of credit derivatives contracts by notional amount were centrally cleared in the first half of 2021. This is up from 56% in 2019.

As we shall see later when we discuss MF Global, central clearing does not necessarily achieve the goal of limiting counterparty risk. Even clearing houses can become capital constrained.

ICE's clearing operation breaks down chains of bilateral CDS contracts via multilateral netting of long and short positions. ICE estimates that in a normal market, reported gross notional amounts of CDS contracts net to less than ten percent of the reported amount. DTCC reported $26 trillion in gross notional value at the end of 2009. ICE opined this might net to around $2.5 trillion in notional outstanding risk.

In the second half of 2020, the BIS estimated the gross market value, sums of positive and negative positions, of over-the-counter credit derivatives alone grew 10% to $220 billion. Note that this does not track with ICEs 2009 estimates of 10%, which would make the gross market value of over-the-counter credit derivatives around $880 billion.

I have not drilled down with ICE and BIS to examine the methodologies and estimates for different time periods. But for the purposes of this book, it will not matter. Credit risk is granular. Mileage *will* vary.

Historical CDS Market

The genesis of the CDS market was in the United States. In 1996, the infant CDS market typically traded notional sizes of $10 million. As the market broadened, trades ballooned in size. Credit derivatives were privately negotiated, off balance sheet transactions. There was no way of knowing the size of the market unless participants volunteered that information. That is still true today of total return swaps.

The British Bankers Association (BBA) estimated the size of the London market alone to be $20 billion at the end of 1996, representing around 10% of the market. The global CDS market for 1996 was S100 billion to $200 billion. Those figures did not include transactions done by Japanese securities firms, which included credit default puts embedded in privately placed structures. A single Japanese firm had done about $1 billion of this type of business. Table 1.2 shows the rapid international growth of the over-the-counter credit default swap market.

In the 1990s, collateralized loan obligations (CLOs) and collateralized bond obligations (CBOs) queued in Moody's Investor Services' in box awaiting ratings. In the fall of 1997, a deal with a brand-new feature, a credit derivatives component, appeared. Soon such deals flooded the market, accelerating growth in credit derivatives. Securitizations that used credit derivatives to transfer risk are called synthetic securitizations. Credit derivatives were often equal in notional to the entire deal size. Synthetic securitization volume increased *thirty-fold* within a couple of years.

Many experts thought this rapidly growing market would double between 1996 and 1998, but it doubled in the *first six months* of 1997. Banks typically increased volume from zero to more than $10 billion inside of one year and accelerated rapidly after that. Rabobank reported $5 billion notional in credit derivative transactions by July 1997. Union Bank of Switzerland (UBS) went from zero to $4.5 billion notional in transactions in their New York branch's loan group alone for the first half of 1997. UBS estimated total 1997 transaction volume at $15 billion. That figure did not include UBS's emerging market activities or London or Asian activities.

By 2004, London traded more than 50% of the market. Europe and Asia participated with enthusiasm. The British Bankers Association (BBA) estimated

TABLE 1.2 Estimated Size of the OTC Credit Derivatives Market

Year	Notional Amount
1996	$100-200 billion
1998	$100-200 billion
2000	$900 billion
2001	$1.2 trillion
2002	$1.9 trillion
2003	$3.5 trillion
2004	$8.5 trillion
2005	$18 trillion
2006	$34 trillion
2007	$61.2 trillion
2008	$33-38 trillion
2009	$26 trillion
2015	$10-12.8 trillion
2016	$10 trillion
2017	$9.4 trillion
2018	$8.3 trillion*
2019	$7.8 trillion*
2020	8.3 trillion (estimated)
1H 2021	8.8 trillion (via BIS)

Notional amounts include single-name and multi-name CDS contracts. Notional amounts do not include exchange traded CDS or total return swaps.

Data Sources include Tavakoli Structured Finance, British Bankers Association, ICE, JPMorgan Chase, Bank for International Settlements (BIS), the International Swaps and Derivatives Association (ISDA), the Bond Market Association (BMA) the Depository Trust & Clearing Corporation, and the Office of the Comptroller of the Currency.

**BIS mid-year values reported at the end of June.

year 2000 trading volume at $900 billion. At the time, everyone thought breaking the $1 trillion barrier would be a huge hurdle. But market growth soared. Many newbies did not know what they were doing.

New participants entered the credit default protection market in both Europe and the United States. At least six brokers geared up to service this new swell of business. Credit derivatives were in high demand. The story was that they serviced an unfulfilled market need. It was not a matter of whether the broader financial community would adopt credit derivatives; it was merely a matter of how fast.

Total return swaps on loans increased dramatically in volume as market participants familiarized themselves with the documentation (See Chapter 2). Every month new entrants engaged in their first transaction.

The definition of what should be included in credit derivatives market size was and is fluid. Some firms considered—and still consider—total rate of return swaps to be a form of financing. These may be handled in a department separate from the credit derivatives department, which handles credit default swaps. Credit spread puts may be in yet another department. Currency convertibility protection, if it is traded at all, may be part of yet another group within the same institution.

Between 2000 and 2008, the credit derivatives market grew *fifty-fold*. But credit derivatives were not merely transferring risk, they were amplifying risk.

After the 2008 crisis, the credit derivatives market shrank but it never shrank to its pre-shenanigan levels. One might think that the Global Financial Crisis of 2008 put an end to gaming in the credit derivatives markets. But leverage is too seductive. We will review the 2008 crisis at the end of this chapter. Later, we will also examine some *post-crisis* debacles: the bankruptcy of MF Global in 2011, JPMorgan's London Whale in 2012, and the Archegos scandal in 2021.

CREDIT DERIVATIVES: EXPOSURE

Credit derivatives represent credit exposures that are many multiples of interest rate swaps, which have much larger notional amounts. It is impossible to estimate the difference in credit exposure between an interest rate swap and a credit default swap with the same notional size without knowing the specifics of both contracts, but the relative difference is enormous.

Consider a $100 million notional interest rate swap. As the market moves against your swap counterparty, you have credit exposure to your counterparty who owes you money if you unwind the transaction under these market conditions. A bank typically makes margin calls if exposure exceeds three percent of the contract's notional value, limiting the exposure to $3 million.

But if you have a $100 million credit default swap which references a misrated, worthless, $100 million notional "AAA rated" tranche (a bond) of a synthetic collateralized debt obligation, you have around $100 million in credit exposure to your counterparty. This is an extreme real-life example. Before the 2008 Global Financial Crisis, CDS transactions had whopping misrated exposures in the high tens of billions of dollars.

Financial professionals create hidden risk in a variety of ways: synthetic structures, short-term binary structures that knock-in to huge exposures, total return swaps, "triparty repurchase agreements"— some of which are substantively total return swaps—and more. It is dead easy to ramp up risk.

EVOLUTION: SELLING THE CDS IDEA

Warren Buffett called credit derivatives "financial weapons of mass destruction." How is it that the entire global market went nuts over them? The answer is that credit derivatives were sold as diversification tools.

The concepts of portfolio theory and risk versus reward gained popularity early in the twentieth century. Various models were developed to measure risk. The most important concept in investment theory is illustrated in Figure 1.3. This concept, developed by Jack Treynor, William Sharpe, and John Lintner, is known as the *capital asset pricing model*. It states that the expected risk premium varies in direct proportion to *beta*, the sensitivity of an investment's return to market movements. This concept can be and has been applied since human beings started thinking in terms of money and increasing their amount of money. The simple graph in Figure 1.3 is the key to all financial management.

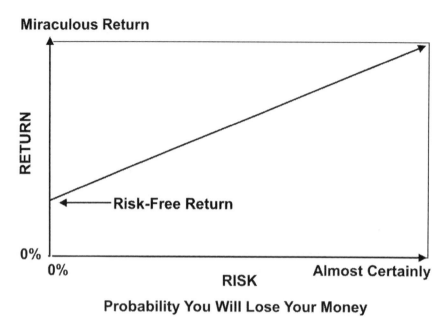

Miraculous Return

FIGURE 1.3 The Most Important Investment Graph

I deliberately made it simple because despite the simplicity of this concept, it is violated repeatedly in the financial markets. Promoters of Ponzi schemes, "respectable" investment managers, and "sane" banking executives try to promote the idea that one can earn a high risk-free return without risking capital.

The key to investment management is to minimize risk while maximizing return. In theory, for every risk appetite there is an "efficient frontier" of returns. This is the demilitarized zone (DMZ) of investment management. Below the DMZ one is safe—too safe to win the war against inflation. At the efficient frontier, one is taking the reasonable amount of risk for the desired return. Above the DMZ, the likelihood increases of having your investment shot down and taking a casualty to your principal.

Used properly, credit derivatives are a tool to move the DMZ farther into risky territory without taking more casualties. Specifically, credit derivatives can help diversify the credit risk of a portfolio to dampen the volatility of potential returns.

A key concept in risk management is the concept of diversification of assets. This includes classes of assets such as equities, bonds, real estate, and cash. It also includes diversification of the market risk of various assets through management of the sensitivity to interest rate or currency fluctuations. Risk management includes management of credit risk. Usually this means diversification through increasing the size of a portfolio. The number of obligors or the number of assets increases, although the size of the portfolio itself need not increase. But risk management can also mean reducing exposure to a weak obligor while adding exposure to a stronger obligor. The size of the portfolio remains constant, but the portfolio has less risk and a higher return.

Covariance and Correlation

When diversifying a credit portfolio, it is important to keep the correlation between assets as low as possible. This means that, to the extent possible, credit events should not affect assets in the same way. Credit quality changes of the assets should not be related. To the extent that they are related, the positive impact of diversification is diluted.

The covariance—a measure of the behavior of two random variables in relation to each other—should be as low as possible. As the number of assets in a portfolio increases, the portfolio variance approaches the value of the average covariance.

We tend to use covariance and correlation interchangeably. Correlation is calculated by dividing the covariance by the product of the standard deviations of the assets. This is useful when comparing items with different dimensions such as, say, assets denominated in Euros versus assets denominated in U.S. dollars, because correlation is dimensionless. For purposes of this section, assume that if covariance is used, dimensions are not a problem, and you can think of it as correlation.

The correlation coefficient is always between positive one and negative one. Zero correlation means assets are independent or uncorrelated. Positive one means assets have a perfect positive correlation, and the volatility of such a portfolio would be the sum of the individual asset volatilities. The best assets of all would be assets that have negative correlation: for example, in a two-asset portfolio, if one asset is adversely affected, the other asset is positively affected by the same event. A correlation of negative one means the assets are perfectly negatively correlated; for example, in a two-asset portfolio, if the price of one goes up, the price of the other goes down by the same amount, meaning the asset prices are perfectly negatively correlated. The volatility of the portfolio would be the difference of the individual asset volatilities.

Covariance matrices are used in many financial models. Sharpe's capital asset pricing model may be the most famous. But these are not the only risk metrics. Humans have evaluated credit risk ever since they started bartering goods. In Chapter 4 we will see an example of how the Maya traded and evaluated credit risk. Insurance companies have always looked at event and individual credit risks. Banks have evaluated credit risks for as long as they have been in business. Even the "new" products are not new. Options on corporate bonds have been traded since the 1970s, even before there was an option model employed by the major Wall Street firms.

Salomon Brothers (now part of Citigroup) offered total return swaps on mortgage-backed securities since the mid-1980s. Merrill, Lehman, Salomon, and others offered debt warrants on corporate debt beginning in the mld-1980s. Merrill and others stripped U.S. government risk from Latin American sovereign debt in the mid-1980s. The idea of structuring credit risk is not new, either. Banks have been doing this since the late 1970s.

Rating agencies attempt to measure credit risk: the ability of obligors to meet their obligations. Long-term ratings are based on ability to pay principal and interest and on the likelihood of not defaulting on an obligation. A chart of long-term credit ratings from highest to lowest is shown in Table 1.3. Ratings shown are from Standard & Poor's (S&P), Moody's Investors Service (Moody's), and Fitch.

A credit rating below BBB is considered noninvestment grade. In addition to the ratings in the table, the rating agencies sometimes give a plus ("+"), a minus ("−"), or add numbers to indicate additional gradations within classes. For instance, Bank of America's long-term debt is rated Aa2 by Moody's (other choices are Aa1, the highest in this class, and Aa3, the lowest in this class) and AA− by S&P. Obligors rated D are in legal or technical default or have filed a bankruptcy petition. There are other rating services besides the ones listed in Table 1.3, but the three shown are the most common in the United States and are usually a benchmark in the global markets.

TABLE 1.3   Long-Term Credit Ratings

Moody's	S&P	Fitch
Aaa	AAA	AAA
Aa1	AA+	AA+
Aa2	AA	AA
Aa3	AA−	AA−
A1	A+	A+
A2	A	A
A3	A−	A−
Baa1	BBB+	BBB+
Baa2	BBB	BBB
Baa3	BBB−	BBB−
Ba1	BB+	BB+
Ba2	BB	BB
Ba3	BB−	BB−
B1	B+	B+
B2	B	B
B3	B−	B−
Caa1	CCC+	CCC+
Caa2	CCC	CCC
Caa3	CCC−	CCC−
Ca	CC	CC
C	C	C
Default	D	D

DBRS Morningstar is the fourth largest global credit rating agency. Julian Kroll founded Kroll Bond Rating agency in 2010 to serve the global market. Japan has its own rating agencies, which tend to rate Japanese institutions higher than Moody's and S&P do. The same is true of China.

Ratings are not sufficient to define credit risk, and they are sometimes gravely misleading. Even when ratings are diligent, opinions of ratings may vary widely. In March 2007, I wrote the SEC asking it to revoke the designation of Nationally Recognized Statistical Rating Agency (NRSRO)for Moody's, S&P, and Fitch for structured products. Prior to the 2008 financial crisis, the three top rating agencies put investment grade ratings on structured credit products that should have had a junk rating.

Banks, sensitive to credit after the foreign loan debacle of the 1980s, developed their own internal rating system for their clients. The internal rating systems of banks are often much different than those for Moody's, S&P, and Fitch. Furthermore, the rating of a single security does not tell us much about the risk of a portfolio of securities and does not tell us anything about the correlation of securities, i.e., whether the values of securities move together, in a portfolio. As we shall see in the next section, there are ways to get around these deficiencies.

TECHNIQUES OF CREDIT RISK MEASUREMENT

In the global markets, statistical models have supplanted fundamental credit analysis. Models proliferate. Yet there is no substitute to understanding the granular nature of credit risk exposure. Models are ubiquitous and we are stuck with them.

Models fail when they obscure credit risk fundamentals. Models are often wrong in their initial assumptions about correlation, default probabilities, and recovery values. Models compound the error by getting *changing* correlations wrong, *changing* default probabilities wrong, *changing* recovery values wrong. Models underestimate systemic risk. We will revisit systemic risk later, but for now, since the entire industry relies on statistical models, there is no avoiding a brief discussion of general approaches.

It is a daunting task to try to model credit risk on a global scale. One of the earliest models for looking at credit risk in the United States is the Altman Z score. A high Z score implied a low probability of default on the part of a potential borrower. The Altman formula is simple, and a conventional balance sheet holds most of the information required:

$$Z = 3.3 \text{ (Earnings before Interest and Taxes [EBIT]/Total Assets)}$$
$$+ 1.0 \text{ (Sales/Total Assets)}$$
$$+ 0.6 \text{ (Market Value of Equity/Book Value of Debt)}$$
$$+ 1.4 \text{ (Retained Earnings/Total Assets)}$$
$$+ 1.2 \text{ (Working Capital/Total Assets)}$$

Much of this information is not available to foreign borrowers, particularly Asian borrowers, who may use different accounting methods and who do not disclose financial information as U.S. obligors do. For sovereigns, much of the information is not applicable. The Z score is useful for U.S. corporations.

In the 1990s, J.P. Morgan introduced its CreditManager software as an industry standard using its CreditMetrics methodology developed to evaluate credit risk. RiskMetrics Group acquired CreditMetrics and rebranded it to RiskMetrics CreditManager. MSCI Inc. (formerly Morgan Stanley Capital International) acquired RiskMetrics Group in 2010.

The methodology computes the exposure profile of each asset in a portfolio. The model also computes the volatility of value caused by upgrades or downgrades in credit quality and/or volatility due to defaults. Long-term migration likelihoods are factored into the model.

A key component of the model is to compute the correlation between assets in the portfolio. These results are then boiled down to a one-year time horizon assessment of the value-at-risk (VaR), a statistic purporting to show potential losses, due to credit risk in a portfolio using a mark-to-market framework.

The data are taken from publicly available information or from purchasable information. For example, S&P and Moody's calculate how credit quality is likely to move over time.

Initial Rating	Rating at year-end (%)							
	AAA	AA	A	BBB	BB	B	CCC	Default
AAA	88.46	8.05	0.72	0.06	0.11	0.00	0.00	0.00
AA	0.763	88.27	7.47	0.56	0.05	0.13	0.02	0.00
A	0.08	2.32	87.64	5.02	0.65	0.22	0.01	0.05
BBB	0.03	0.29	5.54	82.49	4.68	1.02	0.11	0.17
BB	0.02	0.11	0.58	7.01	73.83	7.64	0.89	0.98
B	0.00	0.09	0.21	0.39	5.98	72.76	3.42	4.92
CCC	0.17	0.00	0.34	1.02	2.20	9.64	53.13	19.21

TABLE 1.4   Hypothetical One-Year Rating Transition Matrix

Table 1.4 shows a hypothetical rating transition matrix for corporate debt for a one-year time horizon. The numbers in the table do not necessarily add up to 100 percent, because they exclude entities whose ratings were withdrawn or changed to "not rated" due to obligation payoffs or due to insufficient information after a merger or restructuring. Probabilities of default and recovery rates are similarly estimated. The probabilities of default and assumed recovery values associated with various ratings are discussed further throughout this book including comments on value, price, structural risks, language risks, and documentation risks.

Correlations between assets are often estimated using equity price correlations, where available. Fundamental data analysis or the model user's own data are alternative sources of data for correlation calculations.

Data, particularly data used for calculating correlations, are sparse. Data for Asian instruments, emerging markets, and nonpublicly traded data are difficult to obtain.

CreditManager software identifies credit risks for portfolio managers according to key parameters. Three of the most useful are absolute size, percentage level of credit risk, and absolute amount of risk. CreditManager has powerful report tools to enable portfolio managers to categorize risk. CreditManager determines the size of credit risk by maturity and by country.

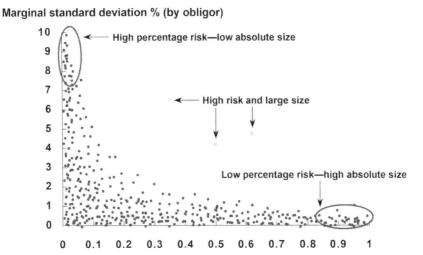

Source: J.P. Morgan CreditManagerTM

FIGURE 1.4   Exposure Size versus Risk

The power of this tool is that it also allows portfolio managers to change parameters and view by obligor industry, for instance. One of the more useful graphs shows exposure size versus risk (Figure 1.4). But the model is only as good as its input assumptions.

Risky assets and large exposures are quickly highlighted. Large-exposure-low-risk and small-exposure-high-risk assets are also highlighted, as these may be problem areas.

Another feature of this graph is that it shows the portfolio data; and if one were to draw a curve that captures most of the data points (other than the high-risk and large-size exposures), one could define the boundary condition of credit risk for this portfolio. If that boundary is consistent with the risk philosophy of the portfolio manager, that is fine. If the boundary suggests that the portfolio manager assumes too little or too much risk relative to the investment philosophy, changes can be made to shift the portfolio risk boundaries.

The key to statistical models is the probability distribution. *What is the best way to deal with skew (asymmetry of data) distributions and kurtosis (bunching or dispersion of data relative to a normal distribution)?* Simply stated: How much are the credit risk and value of the securities likely to change?

Franklin Lee, former head of the corporate bond proprietary-trading desk at Merrill Lynch, has this to say about CreditMetrics and statistical models in general:

At first glance, it looks like they use the statistical method for risk control, which I don't feel very confident about. Statistical methods that have been used in the past have never worked. However, the section on transitional probabilities is relevant in valuing credit-spread levels.

The Gaussian or normal distribution, also called a bell curve, is perfectly symmetrical. The mean, the median and the mode are the same. The arithmetic mean is the sum of the returns divided by the number of assets. The value of half of the asset returns are below the median and half are above. The most repeated return value is the mode. But of course, they are not the same value.

Credit returns tend to have skewed distributions with a long fat tail relative to market risk returns as shown in Figure 1.5.

Metrics such as mean and standard deviation are poor ways to describe risk for highly skewed distributions. Moreover, it is important to understand why the distribution is skewed. That requires understanding the underlying credit risks based on fundamental analysis such as a balance sheet for a corporation or analysis of discrete assets for an investment portfolio.

Gaussian (normal) and even lognormal distributions are merely mathematical representations designed to attempt to answer this question. There is no magic about either of them. If we know the exact probability for certain, we do not need to use a Gaussian or lognormal or other mathematical distribution. We could simply use the raw data as is. If we know the exact distribution for certain, we do not need a model. The model is mere mathematical manipulation of the result of the initial probability assumptions, and the model rises and falls on these initial assumptions. This is important to remember when looking for fraud. Fraud blows initial assumptions out of the water.

Reporting tools such as CreditManager produce lovely charts and graphs that give credit risk managers false confidence and lead them astray.

Credit Return Distribution   Market Return Distribution

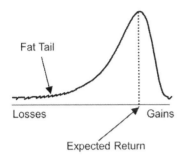
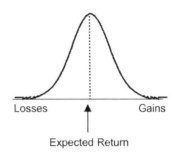

Credit returns tend to have   Market returns tend to have
skewed distributions.   normal distributions.

FIGURE 1.5   Credit Return versus Market Return Distributions

Figure 1.6 illustrates where things can go wrong. Banks tend to become complacent about high exposures to "investment grade" risks which show a low probability of default and a net "low" exposure because even though there is a huge position, models claim there is "low percentage" risk. Credits clustered in the "low percentage risk, high absolute size" area are sometimes actually high risk. It is the Bank Blind Spot. Even a so-called AAA rating is not always warranted. Those who can figure this out have a huge advantage.

When prepayment-probability distribution assumptions failed to reflect reality in the mortgage portfolios in the 1980s, Wall Street firms with sophisticated models took massive hits to their profit-and-loss (P&L) statements. The memory needed to store historical data and programming code put the Pentagon's Cray computer to shame.

The models were impressive and sophisticated, but the underlying probability distribution assumptions were fatally flawed. Mountains of historical data were precisely manipulated to give inaccurate results, on which people relied as if the models were a religion.

Investment banks took massive losses to their mortgage-backed securities (MBS) trading portfolios because of inadequately hedged positions—a classic case of more precision than accuracy.

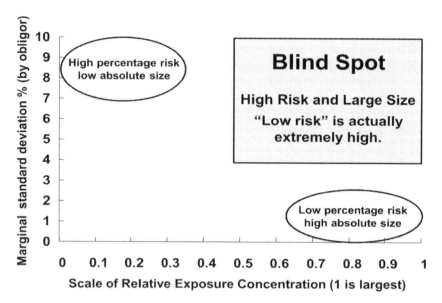

FIGURE 1.6 "Low" Risk is Actually Enormous Risk Exposure

All modern credit risk models purport to perform a horizon analysis: choose a future time and estimate a distribution of value based on various estimated credit events. It is a global requirement for risk managers who must report to the board of directors and outside regulators. But that approach has not proved helpful in identifying the largest vulnerabilities.

Instead, try this approach. Thoroughly analyze the largest positions first. It pays huge dividends to examine assumptions that suggest net risk is low for large exposures. This is true whether the assumption is about prepayment rates, probability of default, loss given default, or another parameter.

Yet this is rarely done. Even when it is done, scenarios which reveal enormous losses are often rejected as "outliers." But sometimes outright liars suppress deeply unpleasant results. This is control fraud.

Investigators uncovered control fraud during the 1980s Savings & Loan crisis. After that crisis, the Department of Justice issued thousands of felony indictments. Yet the financial industry repeated this mistake over and over for decades. After the Global Financial Crisis, there were no meaningful indictments. "Regulators" are not deterring bad behavior.

Nonetheless, historical data provide a good place to start. With some bonds or loans, there will be more history than others. But what about the future? Historical data are not always good for showing a trendline. Trendlines themselves have weaknesses. Trendlines are erroneously called "predicting the future." But they only show a trend if all conditions are assumptions are static, and they are not. Historical data do not incorporate news of current events. Credit risk does not lend itself to a Monte Carlo-type analysis in the way that interest rate risk does.

There is a market instrument, however, that incorporates current information: options. Puts and calls on underlying securities incorporate views of the future credit-influenced price moves of securities. For instance, if we want to construct a probability distribution of the terminal value of a security due to interest rate and credit moves, we could canvas the market for a menu of puts and calls in, at, and out-of-the-money for the relevant time horizon. From this we can not only back out implied volatilities, but also check the market view of the implied probability distribution of the payoff outcomes of the security and, from that, back out the market-implied probability of credit migration for the relevant time horizon. This method is a good "reality check" for the results coming out of a model that uses only historical data.

Price discrepancies should be due to market views of the influence of current events on the credit migration of the security beyond that predicted by the historical data. In an efficient market, the market should price all this information into the option premiums.

Of course, the market is not efficient, due to information and interpretation dislocations. So even the combined method won't be perfect. But that is true of any security we price, including U.S. Treasury bonds, albeit U.S. Treasury bonds until recently had one less factor: credit risk.

More simply, knowing the spread of a "pure" floater would also be a valuable benchmark. If a par floater resets instantaneously (none do), the element of price fluctuations due to interest rate moves drops from the equation. Floaters with longer periods between resets will have greater price fluctuations due to any changes in interest rates. The price move of a floater incorporates a lot of credit information, but even this market has glaring inefficiencies and inconsistencies, especially with emerging market debt. In any case, it is much easier to examine the history and the current pricing in this market than it is to try to model spreads.

I am not suggesting that portfolio managers should abandon models. Models are best for sorting, organizing, and manipulating data. But models cannot exercise judgment.

In 1989, Stephen Kealhofer, John McQuown, and Oldrich Vasicek founded KMV Corporation to focus on corporate credit risk measurement and management. KMV Corporation's credit risk model was a valuable tool. KMV had done considerable *fundamental analysis* on credits and on correlations between credits. KMV defined the benefits of "cutting off" weaker credits (as defined by KMV) of same-rated securities. Using this method, an investor could reduce the risk of default in a portfolio of same-rated securities. The strength of the KMV model was that one could improve portfolio quality at no additional asset cost: same prices, better returns.

The model's success did not contradict the efficient market statement made earlier, however. KMV was successful because most analysts did not have access to the detailed information that KMV did. There were more barriers then to obtaining it. The methodology was cumbersome. Skill and judgment were needed for some of the assessments of a corporation's balance sheet strength. The model did not lend itself to the analysis of sovereign risk without the necessity for the modeler to make some crude assumptions. KMV was less accessible to portfolio managers—other than large banks—because it was expensive. Despite these weaknesses, it was an impressive portfolio management tool for modeling credit risk—the best technology and data then available in the credit markets.

I use the past tense for the KMV model because it was acquired by Moody's in 2002. Moody's offered it as a credit risk suite that went downhill. When one analyzes securitizations, Moody's track record is shockingly bad, as I explain in detail in *Collateralized Debt Obligations and Structured Finance* (2003), and in the follow-up edition, *Structured Finance and Collateralized Debt Obligations* (2008).

Roger Ibbotson and R. Sinquefield have made a business of modeling portfolio diversification. The fundamental concepts remain exactly as they applied them. Diversification works because prices of different credit securities do not move exactly together. A decline in one credit may be partially or completely canceled out by a rise in another. The risk that can be potentially eliminated by diversification is called *unique risk,* or *specific risk.* This name stems from the fact that many of the risks that pertain to a specific credit are peculiar to that credit.

Market risk cannot be mitigated by diversification. No matter how many credits one holds, there are global economic risks that can threaten all credits or clusters of credits, and investors will always be exposed to market uncertainties.

Few models can combine credit risk and market risk. Neither CreditManager nor KMV attempted to do so. Algorithmics developed a model which provides a framework for risk management at the enterprise level. The model links market and credit exposure and has complex netting hierarchy. One can build an infrastructure to simulate a forward moment in time for the value of a portfolio. The model prices the cost of a put option on the net portfolio exposure. It minimizes the price to hedge the net exposure.

I will not suggest that you cast aside your models, but models are mere supplements to fundamental analysis and due diligence.

THEORETICAL POWER OF DIVERSIFICATION

Models require an assumption about how portfolio returns are distributed. We know that the assumption that portfolio returns form a Gaussian (normal) distribution is incorrect; returns are skewed. Simply trying to model the skew is insufficient. Yet the global financial industry fell in love with blind number modelling. Here is why.

If you have a portfolio of assets, you can weight them with fractions that add up to one. From there, you can calculate the standard deviation of the returns—also known as the volatility or variance of returns. You can also calculate the expected return of the portfolio of assets.

For simplicity, first, consider a two-asset portfolio and second, consider a three-asset portfolio. Assume a normal distribution. Calculate the parameters of the returns: the mean, variance, and correlation. (See Appendix I for traditional calculations behind the following discussion.)

Suppose you had a portfolio with exactly two equally weighted assets,

X and Y. The standard statistical result for the risk of a two-asset portfolio is the square root of the portfolio variance. Assume Asset X has an expected return of 10 percent and a variance of 0.04. Asset Y has an expected return of 15 percent and a variance of 0.05. We will also assume that the covariance of the assets, or correlation, is 0.03. The expected return of the portfolio is 12.5%, and the two-asset portfolio variance is 0.0375. The standard deviation of the variance, or volatility of our two-asset portfolio, is 19.4%. For the normal distribution, the value-at-risk (VAR) at the 99 percent confidence interval is 2.58 standard deviations from the mean. There is a one percent chance the portfolio will lose more than 37.4%. This is the value-at-risk (VaR) at the 99% confidence interval.

We want to minimize the volatility of the losses, thus minimizing the volatility of the expected return. How much will the portfolio volatility decline if we add a third asset. When we added a third asset, volatility drops from 19.4% to 12.4% versus the two-asset portfolio. The value-at-risk declines at the 99% confidence interval.

With the two-asset portfolio, at the 99% confidence interval, there was a one percent chance the portfolio would lose more than 37.4%; the model

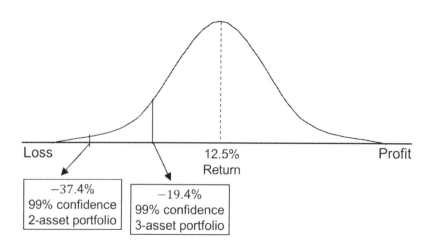

FIGURE 1.7 Value-at-Risk Confidence Intervals

shows the three-asset portfolio has a one percent chance the portfolio will lose more than 19.4% (See Figure 1.7).

This is a seductive narrative. Add the *right asset* with the same return and reduce portfolio volatility. Get the same expected upside with less expected downside. Maintain returns and reduce risk! The entire financial industry fell in love with this powerful idea. But we know the distribution of returns is not normally distributed, it is skewed. We know the model is flawed. Few examined why it is incorrect to assume a normal distribution. Instead, the entire industry employed even more sophisticated models to try to explain historically observed phenomena.

MODELS: KNOWABLE, ALLOWABLE, AND UNKNOWABLE UNKNOWNS

Prudent diversification usually benefits a portfolio. We know that some diversification is good. There is a point of diminishing returns to diversification. The optimal number of assets is a moving target, because it depends on the character, or soundness, of the assets, and the correlation between the assets. But experience showed that if assets have low correlation, with only around fifteen good assets, a manager could reduce risk by about 80%. Of course, the "results" depend on one's assumptions.

Regulators allowed such models to become "standard practice," a cover story for bad assumptions. Control fraud introduced deliberately false assumptions, and regulators did not challenge the assumptions.

Models cannot help a portfolio manager with the how and why of diversification. Diversification is a moving target. There is a point after which adding another asset provides minimal benefit. Add the wrong asset, and you can invite *permanent value destruction* of part of your portfolio.

This is where our market love story takes a tragic turn. Notice what I have done so far in this section. I put forward the narrative that most of the global financial industry uses. I produced numbers for the expected returns assets, and I assumed a correlation between those assets. I made them up. That is near to what much of the industry does: it manipulates and makes assumptions and extrapolations from an imperfect data set.

Good Luck with Your Correlation Estimates!

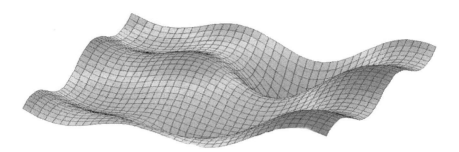

Image Credit: Mark Adelson, consultant in credit and securitization.

FIGURE 1.8   Example of a Correlation Surface

What I did not do is to talk about the various things that can go wrong with our assumptions and our models. How should one address the difference between reality and model results? The following observations may help. Notice what comes first and last on my list.

Model Fallacies

- Mathematical parametric manipulation will not uncover fraud. A model's expected return and expected loss of an asset (or assets) can be completely incorrect. This is often knowable in advance. Proper due diligence may uncover such problems, but thorough due diligence is rarely done. Credit risk is granular and losses can be extreme.
- Estimates of unexpected losses can be wildly incorrect, and this too is often discoverable in advance. We will discuss both the above points before the end of this chapter.
- Correlation (and covariance) are linear concepts, but they are not linear except for small moves, and correlations can radically change. (See Figure 1.8)
- Asset correlation data is based on prices, not default data or credit deterioration data.

- Models ignored the need to accurately estimate the probability of default. Models used historical price data and other proxies for *asset "value" correlation*, yet claimed the models used a proxy for *default correlation*.

- In cases where attempts are made to use default correlation data, the historical data is irrelevant to the character of the assets in the portfolio.

- Even default correlations are not the complete answer. Default correlations assume default probability is a *constant*, but it is *variable*.

- Models' asset correlations are a guess since there is little data on rare events, it is time-varying and regime switching, and there is a lot of risk associated with under-estimating correlation.

- *During a market panic, both sound and unsound assets become highly correlated and both good and bad assets are liquidated to meet margin calls.* Correlations based on historical data, especially irrelevant historical data, will not be helpful in determining which assets will recover and which are suffering permanent value destruction. Permanent value destruction may have been the trigger for the market panic in the first place.

- Every model ignores the need to accurately estimate recovery value in the event of default.

- It is easy for people whose bonuses depend on "performance" to hide risk and pump up "profits" by playing with correlation assumptions.

- Models use bad assumptions to calculate the shape of the probability distribution.

The entire job of credit risk analysis is to understand the underlying assets: the reasons that default might occur, and the probable magnitude of the losses when they occur. The most important step in pricing credit risk is to examine the discrete assets. This may require classic credit analysis or rigorous due diligence or both depending on the circumstances. Red flags, if any, demand increased due diligence.

You must analyze a corporate balance sheet, a bank balance sheet, a special purpose entity's assets, individual loans in a portfolio, or structured products in a portfolio—depending on the specific financial product. You must examine documentation risk of your deal for large hidden risks. There is no other way to estimate a discrete probability of default and loss given default. If possible, you should also perform due diligence on corporate officers or other financiers who can affect the credit you are modeling.

Strive to determine if there are wild cards: a corporate restructuring, a potential merger that may alter seniority, or *knowable unknowns*. Check for *allowable unknowns* such as an allowable corporate restructuring at a future date that could affect your credit exposure.

Spend most of the time analyzing underlying assets for default probabilities, recovery rates, and stress on the former two items. *Expect fraud.* Look for it. If you find red flags for fraud, perform a fraud audit. If you do not have the authority to initiate a fraud audit, document the need. Appeal to someone who does have the authority. Consider doing as much independent investigation as possible. If you uncover a bad credit, it may be a good short, meaning you may wish to be a buyer of credit default protection.

I mentioned the need for discrete analysis when I sat on a securitization industry panel to discuss the risk of synthetic corporate collateralized debt obligations backed by corporate credits. A Fitch Ratings representative protested: "You mean we have to look at every credit?" She did not appear embarrassed to say it.

"Yes," I responded, "if you have a portfolio of corporate credits, you do. There is no alternative if you want to improve your portfolio's risk profile."

Consider a different approach if you analyze a portfolio of mortgage loans backing a securitization such as collateralized debt obligation. Take a statistical sampling of the portfolio. Review the primary loan documentation. Make sure that the collateral interest has been legally perfected for a security, i.e., the loan and the underlying property have not become detached as collateral for a securitization. If you find red flags, investigate more. After that, decide whether to invest, avoid the "investment," or *short* it.

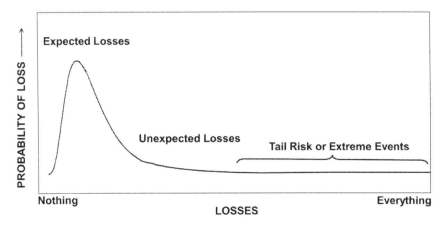

FIGURE 1.9   Expected and Unexpected Losses

A TURKEY IS NOT A BLACK SWAN

Figure 1.9 is a familiar graph to portfolio risk managers. Prudent lenders calculate expected returns that account for *expected losses*. Expected losses are calculated by multiplying the expected default rate by the magnitude of the loss that is likely in the event of default. The recovery rate is the original asset value minus the loss given default. The recovery rate is the remaining value of the asset or assets if a default occurs.

Losses larger than the expected losses are called *unexpected losses*, and lenders decide on a confidence interval for unexpected losses when determining how much capital to provision for unexpected losses. The confidence interval is meant to capture exceptionally large losses. Another way of saying this is that unexpected losses are a measure of the volatility of expected losses. At least that is the general idea.

Extreme events are supposed to happen very rarely—the rarity will depend on the soundness of your model and the confidence level you choose. This is referred to as "tail risk."

Correlation "data" is used to try to quantify portfolio risk. But these "correlations" are usually derived from market prices or market spreads instead of a fundamental credit risk analysis. The surface shape shifts, and mathematical modelers do not know why.

Use a Copula model (Gaussian, Archimedean, Student's t), or any other "sophisticated" model. Knock yourself out. The results may be useful for submitting reports, but the results won't describe the source of the real risks. Managers excuse failures with meaningless terms such as "spread convexity" to pacify regulators when it all goes wrong.

After the 2008 financial crisis, Nassim Taleb blamed the reliance on the Gaussian copula model by some financial professionals, claiming this was the reason for "black swan" events or "grey swan" extreme events. He was only partially correct. Models do not adequately capture "tail" risk so that extreme events occur much more often than models predict. But before the 2008 crisis, extreme losses were foreseeable with fundamental analysis.

Among other things, Taleb suggested industry professionals incorrectly used the normal distribution as opposed to a more skewed distribution. But credit professionals have long known credit returns are skewed as evidenced by early documentation such as CreditMetrics or even my own early books. There are ways to compensate for sloppy assumptions. By blaming models, intentionally or otherwise, Taleb was in the camp that provided an alibi for malicious mischief.

The models assumed defaults were random and not "foreseeable. I am sometimes called the "Cassandra of Credit Derivatives," but I do not have a crystal ball, and I am not in the business of making forecasts. Rather, analysis revealed that financial professionals had misrepresented the risk of the securities they were selling. *The market is not efficient. Extreme losses were knowable in advance.*

TROUBLE IS OPPORTUNITY

Fraud gives a tremendous boost to permanent value destruction in both strong and weak economies. Extreme losses due to discoverable fraud are not tail risk. Fraud will often explain the entire loss curve. Figure 1.10 illustrates the truism that extreme losses due to fraud are not "tail" risk. When fraud is involved, *extreme losses are expected losses.*

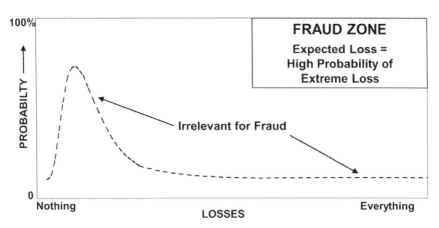

Dashed line represents irrelevant estimates, the result of using "convenient" metrics instead of fundamental credit analysis.

FIGURE 1.10   Discoverable Fraud: Expected Loss Is Extreme Loss

Global Financial Crisis of 2007/8

On April 13, 2011, the U.S. Senate Permanent Subcommittee on Investi-- gations published "Wall Street and the Financial Crisis: Anatomy of a Financial Collapse" through the Washington: Government Printing Office. The scope of the report was limited, but it characterized how malfeasance contributed to widespread systemic fraud prior to the financial crisis.

Banks and investment banks are obliged to perform due diligence. Banks knew or should have known that they financed mortgage lenders who originated fraud riddled loans that "backed" securitization portfolios. Fraudulent and predatory lending practices escalated. Variations occurred in the residential mortgage market, consumer loans, commercial real estate loans, and much more. For this discussion, we will focus on residential mortgage loans.

The following discussion is adapted from my more detailed books on the financial crisis, *Dear Mr. Buffett: What an Investors Learns 1,269 Miles from Wall Street* (Wiley, 2009) and *Structured Finance and Collateralized Debt Obligations*, Second Edition (Wiley, 2008), wherein I documented my early warnings in the face of bold-faced lies by banks and rating agencies. In real time, the *Wall Street Journal, Financial Times,* and others reported my objections to phony financial products with phony ratings. Rating agencies and investment banks pushed back to try to dismiss and discredit those objections. They were not successful. Meanwhile, those who did independent analysis, profited by shorting or avoiding the products of malicious mischief.

After the 2008 crisis, the United States Senate reported that U.S. financial institutions issued a breathtaking $2.5 trillion in residential mortgage-backed securities (RMBS), and over $1.4 trillion in synthetic collateralized debt obligations. Such debt obligations are also referred to as asset backed securitizations or mortgage-backed securitizations. Malicious use of credit derivatives technology amplified the risk.

During the crisis, bankers denied that they had jeopardized the global financial system with systemic risk. Goldman Sachs ("Goldman") was inside the tent negotiating to save itself with Treasury Secretary Henry Paulson, Goldman's former CEO. Goldman Sachs was only one of many malefactors. We will focus on Goldman because its methods were exposed in the Senate report. Moreover, Goldman was a key architect of American International Group's (AIG) distress, and thus the distress of AIG's (and Goldman's own) counterparties and colleague banks).

After AIG's bailout, apologists for Goldman Sachs and AIG's other related counterparties claimed that Goldman's (and other's margin calls on AIG kept Goldman out of danger. But an appointed bankruptcy trustee would have clawed back the money paid to satisfy those suspect margin calls. AIG's counterparties were unsecured creditors. When U.S. taxpayers bailed out AIG, they bailed out Goldman Sachs and Goldman's other trading partners, too. Briefly, here is what happened.

Mortgages As "Collateral"

Warren Buffett, CEO of Berkshire Hathaway, revealed in his 1999 annual report that the conglomerate was the largest shareholder of Freddie Mac; it owned 8.6 percent of the shares. Yet in 2000, Buffett sold nearly all the shares of both Freddie Mac and Fannie Mae.

In the 1990s, after a huge number of savings and loans throughout the United States went bankrupt, the government took a larger role in the U.S.

housing market. The Federal Housing Administration, FHA, part of HUD, insures mortgage loans made by FHA approved lenders. FHA loans are sold to Ginnie Mae, a government agency that securitizes the loans for investors. Ginnie Mae's mortgage packages are known as agency passthroughs. They pass through interest and principal payments to investors. Ginnie Mae's are backed by the full faith and credit of the U.S. government, aka U.S. taxpayers.

HUD also regulates Fannie Mae ("Fannie") and Freddie Mac ("Freddie"), privately chartered United States mortgage giants. Fannie and Freddie purchase mortgage loans from mortgage lenders and earn fees for guaranteeing payments on other mortgage loans. In this way, Fannie Mae and Freddie Mac are indirect mortgage lenders.

Fannie and Freddie's securitizations were not guaranteed by the U.S. government. But most global investors believed that the U.S. government, i.e., the U.S. taxpayer, had an implied moral obligation to bail them out and that Fannie and Freddie were too big to fail. If either one failed, the market crisis of confidence could trigger a global collapse.

Buffett later told me that both Fannie and Freddie began shooting for revenue targets of 15% per year. In 2000, the average yield on the 10-year U.S. Treasury was 6.03%. How was that double digit growth sustainable based on operating earnings alone? How much leverage did Fannie and Freddie use to inflate revenues? What else were they doing to boost revenues?

Buffett had purchased the distressed debt of manufactured housing company Oakwood Homes. Credit Suisse First Boston (Credit Suisse) gave Oakwood a line of credit to provide loans to the buyers of its homes. The home loans served as collateral for the line of credit. Credit Suisse earned fees for the loans, fees when it securitized Oakwood's loans, and fees when it sold the securitized loans to investors.

"Buyers" defaulted on the mortgage loans. Repossessions skyrocketed as sales fell. Oakwood went bankrupt in 2002. In the summer of 2008, the court issued its opinion on a lawsuit between Oakwood and Credit Suisse. Oakwood was an aggressive lender. That led to repossessions. Oakwood could not support its debt load. Credit Suisse and Oakwood engaged in business that was "value destroying." The court ruled that both Oakwood and Credit Suisse were at fault. Credit Suisse had sold investors "value destroying" securitizations backed by the bad loans for which Credit Suisse had supplied funding to Oakwood..

In his 2003 annual report, Warren Buffett wrote about manufactured housing. The industry's "business model centered on the ability…to unload terrible loans on naïve lenders." He noted that *defaults were high and, crucially, recoveries were "pitifully low."* [Emphasis added.]

Investors in the securitizations sold by Credit Suisse were too far from the loan source. They needed to drill down and examine the initial mortgage loans. There was a serious problem with some manufactured housing loans and the securitizations backed by them.

In September 2008, both Fannie Mae and Freddie Mac were placed in conservatorship. A new regulator, the Federal Housing Finance Agency (FHFA) fired the CEOs, fired the former boards of directors, replaced the CEOs, and now provides oversight for Fannie Mae, Freddie Mac, and the Federal Home Loan Bank system. The latter is comprised of eleven banks and an Office of Finance to make low-cost loans to banks and financial institutions to lend money to mortgage borrowers.

Fannie Mae and Freddie Mac were dangerously leveraged before the 2008 Crisis. If you are highly leveraged, you must keep the quality of the mortgage loans extremely high. Small decreases in value are amplified by leverage.

Predatory Lending

Traditionally, Fannie and Freddie had purchased loans originated through prudent lending practices. Loans "conformed" to lending guidelines. Politicians with an agenda pressured HUD to lower lending standards. Cheap money and lax lending bubbled the prices of homes well beyond the price of the underlying land plus cost to build plus reasonable profit. Borrowers did not own homes, they assumed mortgages they could not pay off. In the end, many borrowers were saddled with debt and without a home. But Fannie and Freddie were not alone.

Private mortgage brokers and lenders made low-standard loans with money borrowed from banks and investment banks. Mortgage brokers racked up loan fees. For example, borrowers stated their incomes and provided no documentation. Moreover, mortgage brokers had at times fabricated income numbers without the borrower's knowledge; the brokers knew borrowers could not afford the loan.

The Office of the Comptroller of the Currency (OCC), the U.S. bank examiner, subverted the states' ability to defend the rights of mortgage borrowers against predatory lenders by exercising an obscure power in the 1862 National Bank Act countermanding states' predatory lending laws over the unanimous objection of all 50 states.

Shoddy underwriting was bad enough, but some of the new risky mortgage loan products made it difficult for homeowners to pay back the loan, even if their house increased in value. If the value of the home stayed the same or declined, the homeowner had a huge incentive to default. No (or low)

TABLE 1.5 Characteristics of Prudent versus Predatory Lending

Prudent Lending	Predatory Lending
Borrower's income verified and documented.	Stated income no verification or docs.
Down payment: 20%	Down payment: None or minimal
Down payment from borrower's savings	Down payment: gift or loan via relative or friend
Total housing cost plus insurance and fees ≤ than 28 percent of gross income.	Total housing cost plus insurance and fees high percentage of gross income.
Total debt, including credit cards, auto loans, etc.: ≤ 36 percent of gross income.	Total debt, including credit cards, auto loans, etc.: unknown percent of income.
Rarely a late payment	Poor credit history.
Steady job for at least 2 years.	Day traders, et al.
Cash covers 2 months expenses.	Unverified assets.
Sound appraisals	Wildly inflated appraisals
30-year fixed rate amortizing	New risky products, incl. neg am.
First lien loan	Second lien (piggyback) loan
Sound Appraisals	Inflated Appraisals
High recovery value probable	Negative recovery value possible

down payment subprime loans (loans to borrowers with low credit scores) combined with other risky features became the new "normal." Mortgage brokers originated around 70% of subprime loans. Mortgage brokers also targeted Alt-A borrowers, those with medium credit scores, i.e., not high enough to qualify as "prime."

The loans had nicknames. *NINJA* loan: no income, no jobs, no assets and no verification by the mortgage broker or lender. *Liar loans*: borrowers stated their incomes with no documentation of income and assets. Mortgage brokers did not verify, income; as stated earlier, brokers sometimes fabricated incomes without borrowers' knowledge.

The new loans had riskier structures. Teaser coupons led borrowers to believe that payments would remain low throughout the life of the loan. Instead, within months, the coupons reset to much higher rates, and much higher monthly payments were due.

All sorts of new loan structures hit the market. Borrowers were ill-equipped to read and interpret the obscurely worded documentation. Some borrowers thought they were signing a 30-year fixed rate mortgage only to find that the loan document they signed at closing had been switched for a new risky mortgage loan product.

Forty-year or forty-five-year adjustable-rate mortgages (ARMs) built almost no equity in the loan's early years.

Interest-only (IO) loans insured that homeowner did not build equity; they were not paying down principal. Homeowners were betting housing prices would rise.

Option ARMs could have rising principal balances, i.e., negative amortization. The initial payments were so low that interest was not covered, it was added to the principal balance. When the loan balance exceeds the market price of the home, it is called an upside-down mortgage. The balance kept rising, and sometimes the home price kept falling.

"No-cost" loans stuffed closing cost fees of 2% or more into the loan's interest rate. Fees were hidden in the documents as a "yield spread premium."

"Home Equity" loans which were often second liens, were particularly risky, especially on homes where brokers had colluded with appraisers to inflate the value of homes. Mortgage brokers later called borrowers with the "news" that the appraised value of homes in the area had risen. The mortgage broker asked if the borrower would like to take out a "piggyback loan,' a home equity line of credit. The credit line could then be used to make the payments on the mortgage of the current home or *another* home, an "investment" property.

This is not an exhaustive list of mortgage market games. It is meant to give you a flavor for the danger within mortgage loan portfolios leading up to the 2008 crash.

Some borrowers engaged in fraud or knowingly took on debt they knew they could not pay in the hopes that home prices would skyrocket. But most of the fraud was fraud on borrowers, not fraud by borrowers.

Banks and investment banks, obliged to perform due diligence, lent money to private mortgage lenders who underwrote these shoddy loans. Banks purchased the mortgage loans, warehoused them in special purpose companies, and then securitized (packaged) the loans into residential mortgage-backed securities (RMBS). They sold these products to investors.

Theoretically, mortgage lenders were obliged to buy back loans that did not meet even the fashionable pre-agreed non-prudent standards. Many loans in 2006 and 2007 defaulted before an investment bank could create an RMBS and sell them to a greater fool. Mortgage lenders were strapped for cash, and banks stopped lending to them. Many investment banks were stuck with warehoused loans and toxic financial products of their own design.

Packages of residential mortgage-backed securities, have tiers of risk known as *tranches,* i.e., bonds of tiered risk (See Figure 1.11) A helpful analogy is the capital structure of a corporation. The top tier gets paid first. The equity investor, aka the preference share investor, takes the losses on the first loans to default and so on up the line.

In a hypothetical RMBS, the unrated equity investor takes the first 3.25% of losses. The lowest-rated BB tranche is protected by 3.25% subordination provided by the equity investors. The BB tranche takes the next 2.25% of losses, if any. The investment-grade rated BBB tranche is protected by 5.5 percent subordination, i.e., the total losses absorbed by the equity and BB investors. An investor in the single A rated tranche is protected by the equity, BB, and BBB investors who collectively absorb the

Some RMBSs Were Even Worse Than This Example

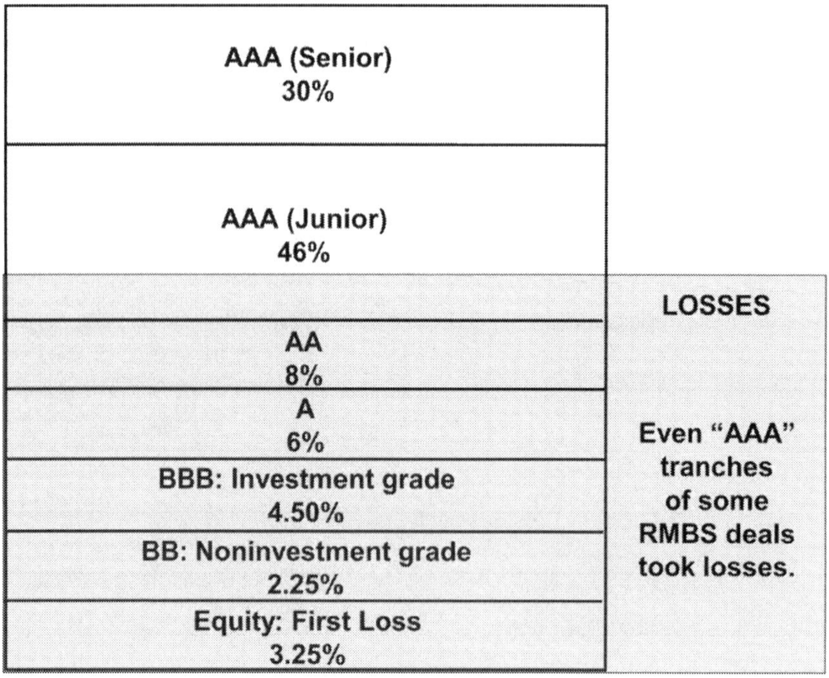

AAA (Senior) 30%	
AAA (Junior) 46%	
AA 8%	**LOSSES**
A 6%	**Even "AAA"**
BBB: Investment grade 4.50%	**tranches of some**
BB: Noninvestment grade 2.25%	**RMBS deals took losses.**
Equity: First Loss 3.25%	

FIGURE 1.11   RMBS Capital Structure with Losses at the Junior "AAA" Level.

risk of the first 10 percent of losses. An investor in the AA rated tranche is protected by the equity, BB, BBB, and A investors who collectively absorb the first 16 percent of losses.

The investor in the "junior" AAA tranche, the lowest AAA tranche, is protected by 24 percent subordination provided by the equity, B, BBB, A, and AA investors. The highest AAA rated tranche is protected by 70 percent subordination from investors in the other tranches who absorb the first thirty percent of the losses, if any.

But some RMBS products were so rotten, that losses mounted as soon as the deals closed. (See Figure 1.11.) Losses were so extreme that even so-called AAA tranches took losses. The degree of rottenness varied from deal to deal. There was no way to tell how bad a deal was without looking at the underlying mortgages.

One of many similar RMBS prospectuses that I reviewed in 2006 revealed a package of hundreds of mortgage loans including negative amortizing ARMs and interest-only loans. More than 60 percent of the loans were purchased from a subsidiary of New Century Financial Corporation. The other loans were from suspect sources, too. In February 2007, New Century announced it had to restate its financials under a cloud of fraud allegations. On April 2, 2007, it filed for bankruptcy.

By December 2007, mortgage loans that were 60 days or more late in payments or in foreclosure had climbed to 22 percent (according to LoanPerformance). Recovery rates for subprime loans were incredibly low, much lower than the rating agencies and "modelers" were assuming. Recoveries varied from pennies on the dollar to 50 percent or so for first lien mortgage loans. Second mortgage loans were often *worthless*. Collateral deteriorated rapidly.

RMBS collateralized by second lien (piggyback) loans had principal losses eating through tranches rated "AAA." Even RMBS backed by first lien loans had losses swamping AA tranches. The "AAA" tranches were eventually downgraded to junk ratings, but they should have been rated junk from the outset.

During my investigations, I spoke with servicers whose job is to collect and record loan payments. They keep the loan accounts. A major mortgage loan servicer said it was better to modify a mortgage than to recover *zero* or *negative recovery value*. These were subprime loans. They were geographically "diverse," but the risk characteristics were similar.

The servicer underreported delinquencies, late payments, which the servicer already lagged one month behind prime mortgages. As soon as a borrower missed a payment, the servicer called to work out a new deal. In the servicer's experience, most homeowners gave up after missed two payments and defaulted on the loan. The servicer's goal was to not let that happen and used a variety of ruses.

The servicer "re-aged" mortgages. It urged late paying borrowers to make even one payment to pretend the loan was still performing: "extend and pretend." Yet the servicer knew the loans were doomed. It was a stall tactic. The servicer sold such loans for three cents to six cents on the dollar. For some loans, the homeowner owed more than the underlying house, trailer, or mobile home was worth. at the time of delinquency. Legal costs exceeded what the servicer would recover. Recovery values were *negative*.

The Department of Justice (DOJ) and the Federal Bureau of Investigation (FBI) issued a press release on June 19, 2008: "From March 1 to June 18, 2008, Operation Malicious Mortgage resulted in 144 mortgage fraud cases in which 406 defendants were charged." Alleged fraud resulted in losses of approximately $1 billion in that operation. But it was a tiny portion of the total mortgage market fraud and the stupendous losses caused by fraud.

The effort should have been massive, but it was not. Moreover, there was no effort called "Operation Malicious Securitization." But there should have been. As of 2008, subprime loans were $1.3 trillion of the $11.5 trillion U.S. residential market (11-13 percent depending on how you define subprime), and subprime loans were the most troubled.

In May 2008, Standard & Poor's data showed subprime loans originated in 2005-2007 defaulted fast. Loans made in 2007 were the worst. Delinquencies for 2005 vintage subprime loans were 37.1 percent, up two percent from the prior month; 37.1 percent of 2006 vintage subprime loans were delinquent, up four percent from March; 25.9 percent of subprime loans originated in 2007 were delinquent, a six percent jump from March to April 2008. The 2007 loans defaulted right out of the box; they were already at least a couple of months late in payments.

In the second quarter of 2008, The Mortgage Banking Association reported that, according to their survey, 9.2 percent of mortgages for single family to four family homes were a month or more overdue or in foreclosure. It was the worst debacle in the survey's then 39-year history. Foreclosure filings in the U.S. rose to a record high of more than 303,000 homes in August 2008. Borrowers had trouble refinancing as lending standards tightened. Prices spiraled downward. Lending standards tightened. Estimated supply of unsold homes would take 11 months to clear.

How did banks unload the risk of toxic mortgage loans and toxic RMBS securitizations? They packaged them up in various types of collateralized debt obligations, secured wildly inflated ratings, and sold them to investors.

Structured finance provided limitless opportunities for offloading risk. Credit derivatives made it easy to add leverage to the mix. A "synthetic CDO" had a portfolio of assets comprised of credit derivatives used to transfer the risk of various reference assets. Reference assets might include tranches of RMBSs, tranches of other CDOs, or tranches of other debt securities. When a synthetic CDO had a portfolio of credit derivatives that referenced tranches of other CDOs, it was called a "CDO-squared.'

Multiple credit derivatives could be used to reference an identical asset over and over in different CDOs. Credit derivatives used by cynical control fraud experts proved detrimental to the global financial system.

Synthetic CDO Arbitrage & Super-Senior

The "CDO arbitrage" is simply the difference between the cash thrown off by the portfolio of underlying assets and the cash paid out to investors. Credit derivatives made the arbitrage for synthetic collateralized debt obligations work because of the so-called "super-senior" tranche. The latter allowed investment banks to retain a huge pool of cash which was impossible with a cash CDO. Instead of paying 50 bps to investors, banks paid around 6 bps to investors for identical risk.

The super-senior tranche was allegedly super safe. Because of this myth, the price for risk on this tranche was well below a funded "AAA" tranche. Moreover, it was by far the largest tranche in every synthetic CDO. That meant that a large portion of the CDS premiums paid on the underlying portfolio of reference assets could be held in a reserve fund. But the reserve fund was often not conserved for the benefit of the super-senior investors or any investment grade rated tranche below it. In such cases, the "first loss" tranche received such a windfall of cash, that Moody's rated it "AAA" in private rating letters. Most investors in synthetic CDOs had no idea this was happening. CDS technology enabled enormous structural risk that was invisible to investors, regulators, and Congress. Lloyd Blankfein, then CEO of Goldman Sachs, testified to Congress that Goldman had not laid off the risk of its toxic CDOs because Goldman took the first loss risk. But how many of those "first loss" tranches were beneficiaries of the cash bonanza because of the low price of super-senior tranches?

The super-senior tranche was *theoretically* protected by all the other tranches in a synthetic CDO. It was a delevered position that allegedly would only be touched by extreme credit or market events. The equity tranche, or

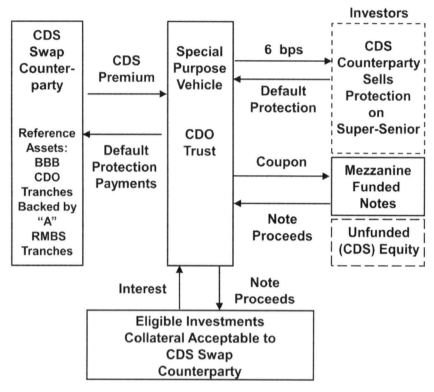

FIGURE 1.12 Synthetic CDO-Squared Backed By "BBB" Tranches of CDOs
Backed by "A" rated tranches of RMBSs

first-to-default risk, was meant to bear the name risk or the idiosyncratic risk
of the portfolio. The mezzanine tranches are between these two extremes.
Figure 1.12 illustrates a synthetic CDO-squared, a CDO backed by CDSs
which reference the BBB traches of other CDOs. The latter CDOs from
which the BBB tranches are referenced, is backed by single-A rated RMBS
tranches.

If you recall our RMBS shown in Figure 1.11, the "A" tranche was
entirely eaten through by losses. When a bank created a CDO backed by
enough of this type of "A" RMBS tranche, the "BBB" of the new CDO was
soon worthless. When a bank backed yet another CDO, a CDO-squared,
with worthless BBB tranches, the "super-senior" of the CDO-squared was
soon worthless.

Of course, it takes a while for losses to accumulate, and not all "A"

RMBS tranches and "BBB" CDO tranches were this bad. But enough were so bad that one could uncover "super-senior" tranches were in devastating trouble. That included many of the "super-seniors" of synthetic CDOs and CDO-squared deals that came to market in 2005 and 2006. It included all the synthetic CDO-squared deals that came to market in 2007.

How did the market define super-senior risk? *There was no market standard definition and no standard method of pricing super-senior risk.* The super-senior was the most important driving force in synthetic deals and the super-senior was the largest chunk of a synthetic deal. It enabled explosive growth in synthetic CDOs before the financial crisis. In mortgage backed synthetic CDOs, the super-senior tranche made up 80 to 90 percent of the securitizations. Super-seniors were the largest part of the global CDO market.

Table 1.6 shows why the super-senior made CDOs so much more lucrative. Investors in the "AAA" tranche of a portfolio of cash assets paid par upfront for a fully funded "AAA" note and wanted to receive LIBOR plus 50 bps on 85 percent of the CDO. (LIBOR was then the benchmark floating rate. Synthetic CDOs are unfunded. The AAA tranche investor would receive 50 bps on the notional amount of 85 percent of the deal. But the CDO arbitrage did not work; the portfolio of assets did not throw off enough cash, until the creation of the super-senior tranche.

TABLE 1.6 Cash CDO versus Synthetic CDO

	Cash CDO		Synthetic CDO	
GRADE	Tranche Size	Percent of Portfolio	Tranche Size	Percent of Portfolio
Super-Senior			427,500,000	80.0%
Aaa	437,500,000	85.0%	25,000,000	5.0%
Aa2	12,500,000	2.5%	12,500,000	2.5%
Baa2	15,000,000	3.0%	15,000,000	3.0%
Equity	35,000,000	7.0%	35,000,000	4.0%
Total	500,000,000	100.0%	500,000,000	100.0%

But in a hypothetical synthetic CDO, the super-senior tranche is 80% of the CDO. Banks could pay 6 basis points—sometimes less—to an outside protection provider, or the bank could simply retain the risk, claiming the enormous notional size was close to riskless. Enormous, mispriced risk hid in plain sight in the bank "blind spot." But banks were not blind to the risk. Banks created the mirage.

If a bank laid off the risk of super-senior tranches for 6 basis points, it saved 44 basis points per annum compared to a "AAA" tranche. For a $500 million CDO maturing in five years, the savings amounted to $1.76 million per annum for five years. For a $5 billion fiver-year CDO, the savings amounted to $17.6 million per annum for five years.

At first, the super-senior tranche was 100 percent BIS risk-weighted. (See "Regulatory Capital" in Chapter 8.) That meant a $1 billion super-senior was charged $80 million in regulatory capital. If a bank priced a super senor at 10 bps (when a "AAA" tranche was priced at 50 basis points), the return on regulatory capital was only 1.25 percent. At the time, if a bank found an OECD bank counterparty with a 20 percent risk-weighting, the required amount of regulatory capital was only $16 million. The return on regulatory capital for the super-senior priced at 10 bps jumped to 6.25 percent.

In the United States, the compliant Federal Reserve gave a 20 percent risk weight for super-senior risk, and even allowed "AAAs" to get a 20 percent BIS risk-weight. But 6.25 percent was not exciting enough for banks that want to wow shareholders. Banks developed models that showed the risk of a super-senior tranche was negligible and therefore the regulatory capital requirement should be miniscule. Banks persuaded regulators to allow "model-based" capital treatment. What could go wrong in producing a drastically wrong answer to seven decimal places?

Where were the regulators? In the fourth quarter of 2002, five years after the first synthetic CDO was created, I brought this abuse to the attention of a senior risk manager at the Fed. It was six years before the financial crisis. There was still time to head this off. He shrugged his shoulders claiming that it usually takes the market 18 months to catch up with new products. In the following years, rotten synthetic CDO issuance exploded.

The Fed and the BIS were useless as regulators when it came to deceptive super-senior tranches and deceptive lending. They allowed and enabled deceit. Gigantic hidden risk ran wild. Is it any wonder that culpable "regulators" denied that the financial crisis was due to hidden global systemic risk in our largest financial institutions, the beneficiaries of taxpayer bailouts?

The Short Game

Monoline and multi-line insurance companies became the credit default swap protection sellers of choice for super-senior and other "highly rated" tranches of synthetic CDOs. MBIA Insurance Corporation, Ambac Financial Group, Financial Guaranty Insurance Corporation (FGIC), Security Capital Assurance, and ACA Financial Guaranty Corp took on stupefying risk for chump change.

American International Group (AIG), a multi-line insurance company, sold credit default swap protection on "super-senior" tranches of synthetic CDOs backed by BBB rated tranches of RMBS and other CDOs. Goldman Sachs and other banks made margin calls for tens of billions of dollars before AIG went under in September of 2008.

In a bankruptcy, those margin calls would have been clawed back. Fortunately for Goldman Sachs, U.S. taxpayers bailed out AIG with cash and credit support worth more than $182 billion.

The late Senator Carl Levin reported that Goldman used credit derivatives to transfer the risk of a failing $38 million subprime mortgage bond (tranche) into more than thirty discrete debt pools backing different synthetic CDOs. The bond (tranche) was Soundview Home Loan Trust 2006-OPT5 M-8. It absorbed losses if more than 5% of the pool of mortgages backing a Soundview RMBS issued in 2006 took losses. The bond appeared in multiple CDOs. It was also a component of the ABX index which we will discuss in the next section. (See also Chapter 3, "Index Products.")

Goldman used credit derivatives to amplify the risk of this lousy bond more than thirty times. The losses on this exposure mounted to approximately $280 million. Principal was wiped out in 2008. Goldman Sachs turned

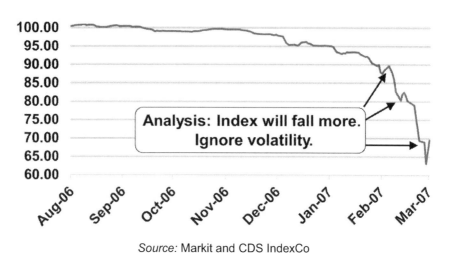

Source: Markit and CDS IndexCo

FIGURE 1.13   Bought credit default protection on the ABX.HE-BBB– 06-2 Index. Leveraged short.

a $38 million-dollar failing bond into a $280 million windfall. Goldman Sachs benefited by using credit derivatives to short lousy risks at the expense of its clients. Trades such as these were Goldman's "big short."

In 2010, the SEC sued Goldman for alleged fraud related to a CDO called Abacus 2007-1. Goldman Sachs settled for $550 million. It neither admitted nor denied wrongdoing.

In 2016, Goldman Sachs became the last bank to settle charges of improperly selling mortgage-backed securities in the run up to the 2008 financial crisis. Goldman paid $5.1 billion to settle claims for securitizing, underwriting, and deceiving investors in collateralized debt obligations backed by mortgages from 2005 to 2007. That sounds like a lot of money until one compares it with the margin calls from AIG that it kept, the damage that Goldman and other banks created, and taxpayer bailouts. In 2009, one year after the financial crisis, Goldman Sachs set aside $20 billion for salaries and bonuses.

Others, who were innocent of malfeasance, protected investment portfolios by shorting value destroying securitizations. Michael J. Burry, head of Scion Capital, Balestra, and a handful of other hedge funds *bought CDS protection* on indexes such as the price-based Asset Backed Home

Equity Index, the ABX, which referenced tranches of twenty residential mortgage-backed securities. (See Figure 1.13) When one buys CDS protection on an index, one *shorts* the index. Michael Lewis, my *Liar's Poker* classmate, dramatized the trade in *The Big Short*.

The products of top investment banks and banks that issued RMBS and CDOs were included as reference assets in the index. Those banks included Goldman Sachs, Citigroup, Merrill Lynch, Morgan Stanley, Deutsche Bank, Barclays Capital, J.P. Morgan, Bank of America, Bear Stearns, UBS, BNP Paribas and Credit Suisse.

There was no index referencing first-loss tranches. The best available short was on the next most senior tranche, backed by barely investment grade BBB– rated reference assets, for example, the ABX.HE-BBB– 06-2 index was the second index launched in 2006. This Markit administered index was launched July 19, 2006, referencing BBB– tranches of twenty home equity loan asset-backed securitizations, i.e., BBB– rated tranches of RMBSs backed by subprime mortgage loan collateral. At inception, the index was priced at 100 with a predetermined coupon. If you buy protection on the index, you pay the coupon times the notional amount of your desired contract.

Soundview Home Loan Trust 2006-OPT5 M-9 represented a $34.1 million reference component of the ABX.HE-BBB– 06-2 index. (Soundview M-8, which we discussed earlier, was a $38.75 million component of the ABX.HE.BBB.06-2 index.)

If you bought a notional amount of $10 million of CDS protection when the ABX.HE-BBB– 06-2 index launched at a price of 100, you paid the annual coupon of 242 bps upfront times the notional amount of the contract or $242,000. (The coupon varied according to the character of the collateral backing a particular index.) But subsequent to the launch date, if the index traded below par, you paid the difference between par and the then market price times the notional amount of the contract plus accrued. For example, on November 30, 2006, the price of the index had already dropped to 98.2. You would have had to pay money upfront plus accrued on the premium coupon. (See Chapter 3, "Index Products")

Here is the value of credit protection on three different dates for a $10 million notional contract on the ABX.HE-BBB– 06-2 index:

Date	Price	**Payment to Protection Seller**
November 30, 2006	98.2	$180,000 plus accrued
January 26, 2007	90.34	$966,000 plus accrued
February 13, 2007	80.36	$1,964,000 plus accrued

If you bought protection on November 30, 2006, and sold it on February 13, 2007, you found that your initial investment had increased tenfold in less than three months. You could celebrate Valentine's Day in style. But should you wait? Should you cover your short by selling your protection, or should you ride out volatility?

Alan Greenspan, a former chairman of the Federal Reserve, claimed that credit derivatives made the financial system more stable. Michael Lewis got it wrong, too. In January 2007, Lewis wrote in a commentary for *Bloomberg*:

> "[W]hen you create a derivative you don't add to the sum of total risk in the financial world; you merely create a means for redistributing that risk. They have no evidence [people such as I who not only warned but had evidence at the time of Mr. Lewis's article] that financial risk is being redistributed in ways we should all worry about."

William ("Bill") Ackman, head of hedge fund Pershing Square, bought credit default protection on MBIA and Ambac, insurers that unwisely sold protection on risks that they had not thoroughly analyzed.

Today these short trades seem obvious, but in August 2006, banks did not disclose their degree of exposure to subprime mortgage loans or other risky mortgage products and loans. After large mortgage lenders such as Ownit declared bankruptcy in December 2006, banks still lied about their exposures and accounting losses in the first quarter of 2007. In February 2007, New Century, a large subprime mortgage lender, announced it was short of cash; its share price sank. Also, in February 2007, HSBC, then the largest bank in Europe by market value, reported it had $1.7 billion in losses due to subprime lending. It sounds quaint today, but then it was a *shocking* number. MBIA, Ambac, and rating agencies denied obvious problems.

Investment banks flooded the financial media zone with the pretense that the mortgage market and associated derivatives were sound. The media accepted and elevated banks' false narratives whereas sound analysis was dismissed and "discredited."

Massive defaults and low recovery values were an open secret in the first half of 2007. But instead of halting synthetic CDO issuance, investment banks *accelerated* issuance of synthetic CDOs, especially synthetic CDO-squared products. Investment banks bought each other's losers at inflated prices, stuck them in CDOs, and tried to offload them to unsuspecting investors. The fake bids they gave each other bought them time before they had to take massive write downs. The fake bids were banks' "evidence" to support fake marks-to-market.

Banks started reporting meaningful losses in the third quarter of 2007, when they could no longer keep up the pretense. Between then and September 2008, the market suffered a series of disasters as financial institutions reported losses. The shell game finally fell apart, resulting in the global financial crisis. Afterwards, governments might have made a sound case for racketeering under the Racketeer Influenced and Corrupt Organization Act (RICO), but one must remember that the fraud quadrangle includes government influence. If at the time you were short the ABX.HE-BBB– 06-2 index, you had to wait months for the Truth Bomb.

In February 2007, sound analysis gave short investors the confidence to know that the index had further to drop due to permanent value destruction. It did not matter that banks and loan servicers played games to delay reporting losses. It was not possible to calculate the absolute bottom (the data was not good enough), but the ABX.HE-BBB– 06-2 index price of 80 on February 13, 2007, an impressive drop from 100, was still a wildly inflated price compared to what the price would have been in an unrigged market. The index's underlying reference tranches were still deteriorating. Instead of covering the short, the right thing to do was wait.

In July 2007, two hedge funds managed by Bear Stearns Asset Management had significant leveraged exposure to subprime mortgage loans and had lost most of their value. Bear Stearns took the "off balance sheet" hedge funds on balance sheet. Bear Stearns itself had a liquidity crisis in March 2008. J.P. Morgan bought Bear Stearns after Bear's stock plummeted to the single digits. Due to an internal J.P. Morgan documentation oversight, J.P. Morgan paid $10 for the shares.

On August 9, 2007, BNP Paribas, Frances largest bank, suspended redemptions in three funds ostensibly worth $1.6 billion Euros. The fund managers could not value subprime mortgage-related assets in the funds. I told CNBC: "when you get truthiness in lending you get truthiness in pricing."

The next day, August 10, I challenged AIG's accounting numbers. AIG had written credit default protection on $19.2 billion of super-senior tranches of CDOs backed by BBB rated tranches, A significant number were backed by subprime loans. AIG was obliged to mark this position to market, yet AIG claimed its accounting loss was *zero*. Moreover, that was only one of several problematic trades AIG had done.

I told *The Wall Street Journal*: "There's no way these aren't showing a loss." AIG read my comments and called me. AIG was upset. But not as upset as it was going to be. Six months later, AIG's auditor found "material weakness" in its accounting statements. Margin calls on AIG by Goldman Sachs, Societe General (SocGen), Calyon, Bank of Montreal, Wachovia, Merrill Lynch, UBS, Royal Bank of Scotland, and Deutsche Bank brought A.IG. to the brink in September 2008.

Goldman's margin calls to AIG totaled $12.9 billion. Not only was Goldman its largest trading partner for the above trades, but it was also the underwriter or co-underwriter for suspect CDOs against which SocGen and others had bought credit default protection from AIG Goldman was the largest contributor to AIG's distress.

Goldman bought credit default protection against AIG itself—about $2.5 billion in credit default protection. But without a taxpayer bailout of AIG, who was going to make good on Goldman's protection? Everyone would have been eating indigestible losses. Goldman needed AIG's bailout to bailout Goldman and its crony banks.

U.S. taxpayers via the U.S. Treasury poured $40 billion into the AIG division that did the credit derivatives trades. But if AIG had gone bankrupt, a bankruptcy trustee would have gone after all of AIG's counterparties and demanded the margin call money back. The trustee would have triggered a proper investigation into a long list of suspect securitizations and loan underwriting practices.

The Wall Street Journal printed part of my work on AIG and my above opinions on Goldman's exposure to AIG In November 2009, Goldman's spokesman called me claiming that Goldman acted only as an "intermediary" and bought protection from AIG on underlying super-senior CDO risk. Even if that partial truth were completely true, did he think that made Goldman look as if it managed risk well? Did he think this made Goldman's deals fragrant? Goldman's gaslight is not bright enough to pull that off.

I responded that the underlying so-called super-senior CDOs were at grave risk instead of "super safe." I based this on my analysis of the poor quality of the collateral backing the reference tranches and based on the structural risk of the securitizations.

Goldman's spokesman claimed Goldman could not have been aware of AIG's other positions. I pointed out that SocGen and others bought protection on some CDOs that Goldman had underwritten or had co-underwritten. Goldman's spokesman had been unaware that I possessed this information before he called me. I expressed my view that securitization professionals knew or should have known that such RMBSs and CDOs were overrated and overpriced when they came to market.

Goldman's spokesman claimed that mine was a "minority" opinion. The "majority" had a different opinion of the risk at the time. I asserted that the risks were discoverable during competent due diligence which Goldman Sachs was obliged to do. It was in the public interest not to rely on Goldman's opinion, if Goldman counted itself in what it claimed was the "majority."

That week, Countrywide, a large mortgage lender later fined by regulators, issued asset backed commercial paper (ABCP) backed by its shoddy mortgage loans. The week of August 13, 2007, nervous investors demanded higher interest rates. Countrywide told investment banks it wanted to borrow $11.5 billion. It was rumored that the banks refused to lend the money and asked the Fed for concessions.

Canadian money market funds discovered their ABCP investments were backed by risky leveraged subprime products. Prices plummeted as investors realized they would lose principal on "triple-A" rated products.

On August 17, 2007, after days of stock market turmoil, the Fed extended the "overnight" discount window borrowing rate 30 days and cut the discount rate 50 bps to 5.75% from 6.25%. Incredibly, the Fed agreed to accept investments backed with Countrywide's (and other's) mortgage loans if they had a "triple-A" rating. But the ratings were bogus.

The stock market recovered for a while. This was the beginning of a long list of stunning bailouts by the Federal Reserve Bank. In September 2008, Lehman Brothers collapsed, FannieMae and FreddieMac required support. Bank of America had to step up and buy Merrill Lynch. Citibank had huge subprime losses; its stock plummeted to single digits. Regulators shut down Washington Mutual and sold it to J.P. Morgan. The UK bailed out Lloyds and HBOS (the entity created from the merger of the Bank of Scotland and Halifax). Royal Bank of Scotland (RBS) needed support. A host of other financial institutions needed help.

Those who realized that "trouble is opportunity" had to stick with their trades while desperate financiers lied to disguise their loss-making exposures. The ABX.HE-BBB– 06-2 index continued to drift downward. It eventually bottomed out at 3. (The number three is not a typo.)

At the end of 2008, Bill Ackman reaped $1.1 billion in gains on the credit default protection he bought on bond insurers. It was enough to offset portfolio losses on other investments, some of which rebounded. The saga of Bill Ackman's tense battle over disinformation—some of us would call it lies—from MBIA and Ambac is captured in Christine Richard's excellent book, *Confidence Game*.

My friend Jim Rogers shorted shares of Citibank at the start of 2007 and made his trade public. He covered his short in January 2009 at $5 for a 1,000% return over two years. Citigroup closed at $6.623 on February 2, 2022, unadjusted for the 1 for 10 reverse stock split that Citigroup did in March 2011. The U.S. bank that required the biggest bailout was embarrassed to see its stock price in the single digits. As it did with so many other unpleasant things, Citigroup covered it up with the reverse split.

Propublica's Bailout Tracker estimates that the taxpayer disbursements for bailouts due to the 2008 financial crisis totaled $658 billion given to 989 U.S. financial institutions. Around $109 billion was still outstanding as of February 2022. But the bailout value was much more. Propublica's numbers do not include the value of subsidies, guarantees, bank charters, "asset" purchases, and cheap funding with near zero interest rates for years.

The United States enjoyed AAA ratings from all top four rating agencies: Moody's, S&P, Fitch, and DBRS. On August 5, 2011, S&P downgraded the USA's long-term credit rating to AA+.

Standard & Poor's made a salient point in its press release. The USA, in S&P's opinion, did not handle its growing "public debt burden in a manner consistent with a 'AAA' rating." In my opinion, S&P made a courageous move.

CHAPTER 2

Total Return Swaps:
Leveraged Synthetic Financing

T otal rate of return swaps (TRORS), also known as Total Return Swaps (TRS), are simply another form of financing. In this book, I will use the term Total Return Swap (TRS) to refer to the swap as most of the market does today. But I will use the term total rate of return (TROR) to refer to the timely ongoing stream of asset payments in a total return swap. One may also use total return (TR) to describe the payments, but if so, one should clarify that this is not a final total return on the asset, rather it is the total return over a specified time period. Timing, frequency, and magnitude of cash flows matter.

The following example of a modified form of a car lease illustrates the concept of the total return swap. The investor, the receiver of the total rate of return (TROR), is the lessee, the one who leases the car. In this particular lease, the investor gets all of the benefits of the car without any of the hassle. The investor gets a chauffeur. The investor does not have to worry about parking the car, putting gas in the car, maintaining the car, or servicing the car. The investor does not pay luxury tax because the investor does not own the car. At the end of the lease, the investor must pay the lessor any depreciation in the value of the car. If the car has not depreciated in value, the investor pays nothing. If the car appreciates in value, the investor gets a payment from the lessor for the value of the appreciation of the car.

For all of this, the investor pays a lease fee. There is one catch, however. If the car is damaged as defined in the lease agreement, the investor must pay the difference between the original value and the damaged value, and the lease terminates. Alternatively, the investor can take ownership of the car and pay the original value of the car to the lessor. The definition of "damage" and the determination of the value of the "damaged" car are conditions the investor and the lessor negotiate at the beginning of the lease. In some cases, the lease agreement may allow the investor to purchase the car at the market value of the car at the end of the lease agreement. The method of determination of market value of the car is negotiated by the investor and the lessor before they sign the lease agreement.

A total return swap (TRS) allows an investor to enjoy all of the cash flow benefits of a security without actually owning the security. At the end of the TRS, the investor, the receiver of the total return, must pay any decline in price to the TRS payer. If there is no decline in price, the investor does not make a payment. If the security appreciates in price, the investor gets the difference between the original price and the new, higher price. For all of this, the investor makes ongoing payments to the total return payer. The payments are analogous to the lease payments we discussed earlier. In the credit derivatives market, this payment is referred to as the floating rate payment, the financing cost, or the funding cost of the investor.

Total return swaps are off-balance sheet transactions. In the 1990s, when the credit derivatives market first took off, total return swaps were the highest volume, the most popular, and the most widespread sector of the credit derivatives market. Low-cost borrowers such as banks with large global balance sheets are naturally advantaged as payers in total return swaps. Synthetic assets are created in the process. Today, the total return swap market is probably not the most widespread product, but it is an opaque over-the-counter market that introduces hidden leverage into the financial system.

A TRS can be modified to obscure the risk. We will see an example later in this chapter when we consider the transactions that led to the bankruptcy or MF Global. A TRS can be embedded in credit linked notes or other structured financial products. The latter is invisible to global regulators who try to keep track of volume.

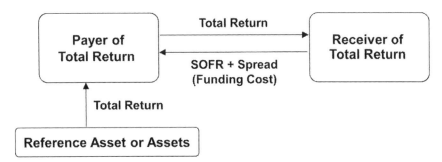

Total Return: Interest Flows + (Final Value − Original Value)
Reference Asset: Bond, Loan, Index, Equity, Commodity, and More

TRS Payer is the legal owner of the Reference Asset.

TRS Receiver is long both price and default risk of the Reference Asset(s), and positive or negatives changes in the floating rate funding cost.

FIGURE 2.1 Total Return Swap (TRS)

A TRS is a bilateral financial contract between a total return payer and a total return receiver. The total return payer pays the total return of a reference security and receives a form of payment from the receiver of the total rate of return. Often payment is a floating rate payment, a spread to the Secured Overnight Financing Rate (SOFR). But we will also see examples of legacy London Interbank Offering Rate (LIBOR) payments, and other floating rate index payments. The basic total return swap transaction is shown in Figure 2.1.

REFERENCE ASSETS

The reference assets for a TRS can be indexes, bonds (emerging market, sovereign, bank debt, mortgage-backed securities, collateralized debt obligations, credit-linked notes, corporates and more), loans (term or revolver), equities, real estate receivables, lease receivables, or commodities.

Total return swaps have been around since at least 1987 when Salomon Brothers offered the first mortgage swap agreement (MSA). Most of the total return swaps offered in the market are simpler than the MSA, which we look at later in more detail.

The total rate of return payer is the legal owner of the reference asset, just as the lessor was the legal owner of the car in our initial example. The total rate of return payer holds the reference asset on its balance sheet. For the period of the transaction, the TRS payer has a short position in the market risk (depreciation of the car), a short position in the credit risk (potential impairment) of the reference asset, and short term rate risk.

The total rate of return receiver, the investor, is not the legal owner of the reference asset, any more than the lessee was the legal owner of the car.

The TRS is an off-balance sheet transaction. The reference asset does not appear on the balance sheet of the receiver. For the period of the transaction only, the total rate of return receiver has a synthetic long position in the market risk and a synthetic long position in the credit risk (impairment) of the reference asset. At the maturity of the transaction, the total rate of return receiver may choose, but is not obligated, to purchase the reference asset at the then prevailing market price.

In the event of default of the reference asset prior to the maturity date of the TRS, the TRS usually terminates, but it need not necessarily terminate. We look at the case in which it does not terminate later; in most cases of default, however, the TRS does terminate. The total rate of return receiver bears the risk in the event of default in either case.

If the TRS terminates due to a default, the total rate of return receiver, the investor, makes the total rate of return payer "whole" for the market risk and the credit risk of the reference asset. The investor may make a net payment of the difference between the price of the reference security at the beginning of the transaction and the price of the reference security at the time of default. Alternatively, the investor may agree to take delivery of the defaulted reference asset and pay the initial price of the reference asset to the total rate of return payer. Once this has occurred, neither the payer nor the receiver has any additional obligation to the other party, and the TRS terminates.

LIBOR, SOFR, SONIA, SARON, ET AL.

Before 2021, the global market used the London interbank offering rate (LIBOR) as the chief benchmark for loans and derivatives. Counterparties were free to agree upon any benchmark, but LIBOR was ubiquitous. Rate setting was done by major global banks. LIBOR was a term rate that varies by tenor, i.e., the term, typically one month, three month, or six months. Longer terms were possible. Some legacy transitions to the new benchmarks may not be complete until 2023. LIBOR was retired at the end of 2021, and most LIBOR rates will no longer be published.

In 2022, the global market transitioned to a *theoretically* riskless rate to replace dollar LIBOR: the Secured Overnight Financing Rate (SOFR) for U.S. dollar denominated loans. The euro and yen also made the transition. SOFR is a secured rate based on overnight borrowings against U.S. Treasuries. SOFR is expected to be the most widely used index, since the dollar is, for now, still the world's reserve currency. Since this LIBOR replacement is risk free rates that reset daily, they, unlike LIBOR, do not have credit or liquidity premiums.

Switzerland uses the Swiss Average Rate Overnight (SARON), the overnight rate for secured money.

British sterling uses the Sterling Overnight Index Average (SONIA) instead of LIBOR. SONIA is an *unsecured* rate based on interbank money market rates.

SOFR includes overnight repo rates and bilateral repos cleared through the Delivery-versus-Payment (DVP) service. SOFR includes all trades in the Broad General Collateral Rate except for "Specials." If a bank is short specific Treasury securities and cannot easily find them, say due to a short squeeze, the bank may do a reverse repo. The bank reverses in the bonds. The bank accepts a special rate, a rate lower than the prevailing overnight rate. Depending on how badly the bank needs the bonds, it may agree to zero interest on its cash. The bank may even *pay* interest to get the bonds.

LIBOR was forward looking, and the rates were set for the stated tenor (term). SOFR, SONIA, and SARON are backward looking. They are daily overnight rates based on the prior day.

One of the key reasons for the transition was to prevent manipulation that had occurred when banks colluded to set LIBOR rates. Banks engaged in collusion for several decades. Since the infancy of the interest rate swap market, LIBOR rate setters engaged in interest rate horse trading based on the bias of their current trading books and daily hedges. But regulators seemed oblivious to it until ten years ago. When regulators decided it was a problem, they realized they did not know who, on balance, had been harmed, and did not know who, on balance, benefited over time.

Is the repo market free from manipulation? No rate is free from manipulation. Demand for the Federal Reserve Bank's reverse repurchase program (RPP), fueled by COVID pandemic liquidity, reached $1 trillion in August 2021, exploded to $1.76 trillion in December 2021, and was still as high as $1.5 trillion on January 3, 2022. One way to think of the RRP rate is as the Fed's interest rate floor.

When it comes to manipulation of global interest rates, Central Banks, and in particular the Federal Reserve, can give a master class.

REPO, TRIPARTY REPO, AND REVERSES

Banks may borrow to finance their positions using treasuries as collateral. A *repurchase agreement*, commonly called a "repo," is a way to borrow. Repurchase agreements allow the bank, the "seller," to sell Treasuries to the Federal Reserve Bank (Fed) with the agreement to repurchase them at a slight premium the next day. The slight premium to the previous day's price is the overnight interest rate, the repurchase rate, which is also called the repo rate for short.

The premium applies when overnight rates are positive, i.e., the bank is charged interest for the borrowed money. If overnight rates are negative, banks repurchase the securities at a discount; this is not usually the case, although we have seen negative interest rates in Europe since 2014. We will discuss this in Chapter 5.

Likewise, a bank can do a "reverse repurchase agreement," wherein a bank reverses in bonds that it needs in exchange for cash. But when the Federal Reserve Bank borrows money by doing reverses, we call it absorbing reserves.

Triparty repo, as the name implies, involves a third-party clearing bank that administers and processes the trade. The third party takes custody of the collateral and its management and manages other operations such as payment and delivery. The "third party" may even be the second party, the supplier of the securities which the first party is funding via the repo transaction.

Triparty repo is used to finance all sorts of non-U.S. Treasury collateral, and counterparties do not need to know each other's identity. In the event of a bankruptcy by a counterparty who owes money in such a transaction, the third party will seize the collateral that it holds.

Countrywide Securities, Lehman Brothers, Bear Stearns, and MF Global all engaged in triparty repo transactions, and the firms imploded. But triparty repo was not the problem, The problem was bad (to be kind) risk management and too much leverage. Triparty repo was simply their funding method.

On August 2, 2012, Jack Reed, Chairman of the Senate subcommittee on securities, said that during the 2008 financial crisis, "Triparty repos peaked at $2.8 trillion," and the triparty repo market in 2012 was $1.8 trillion in size. At the end of the third quarter 2020, the Federal Reserve estimated the total repo market at $4.6 trillion. In 2021, The Fed estimated that the triparty repo segment of the total repo market was over $1 trillion in daily transactions.

Triparty repo is not inherently riskier than two-party repo. Triparty repo has a middleman while repo does not. But one can get into just as much trouble with plain repo, especially repo-to-maturity transactions which can be identical in substance to total return swaps. You must meet margin calls if and when you get them.

In the special case of MF Global, the firm sought and got special accounting treatment for its doomed triparty repo transaction. The trade was considered off-balance sheet, which is not usual for a repo transaction of any kind. It is usual, however for a total return swap. In substance, MF Global's transaction appeared to be a total return swap. (See "The MF Global Implosion" at the end of this chapter.)

DIFFERENCE BETWEEN REPOS AND TRS

What is the difference between a total return swap and a repurchase agreement? In a repurchase agreement, also called a *repo,* the owner of an asset, the seller, sells the asset to a buyer and agrees to repurchase the asset at a fixed price on a fixed date. The asset seller agrees to pay the buyer a pre-negotiated rate of interest, the repurchase rate, also called the *repo rate.*

The buyer lends the seller money for the period of the agreement at the repo rate implied by the difference between the asset sell price and the asset repurchase price. At the maturity of the agreement, the seller is obligated to repurchase the securities at the prespecified repurchase price.

In a TRS, the total rate of return receiver is not obligated to purchase the reference asset at the maturity of the transaction, nor is there a pre-agreed fixed price for the reference asset at the maturity of the transaction. The TRS receiver is obligated only to exchange payments based on the market value of the reference asset at the maturity of the transaction.

When the maturity of the TRS is much less than that of the reference asset(s), the price risk due to market value fluctuations in the absence of default can be substantial. Some TRS receivers, the protection sellers, will not participate in mismatched maturity transactions.

How do we determine market price? In between the inception and the maturity—due to default or expiration—of the TRS, the receiver may be content with prices provided by the seller. In the event of default of the reference asset, or if the TRS matures before the reference asset, market value is often determined by a dealer poll. The calculation agent calls three to five market makers—the names are often prespecified in the documentation—in the reference asset and takes the average price. The calculation agent may be one of the dealers offering a price.

An auction method is preferable for very illiquid assets that are difficult to price. Because of the market value risk, the receiver of the TRS usually retains the option to take physical delivery of the reference asset and pays the difference between the initial price (or last reset price, if later) and the dealer poll price or auction price.

The following term sheet shows typical language for a total return swap in which the reference asset is a par bond. At the swap termination date, there is no physical delivery of the reference bond; the transaction is settled with cash.

TOTAL RETURN BOND SWAP ABBREVIATED
Indicative Term Sheet

Total Return Payer:	US Bank US Bank US Bank
Total Return Receiver:	European Bank
Reference Asset:	Reference Bond

Issuer:	US Corporate
Coupon:	7.0%
Interest Payable:	Semi-annual, 30/360
Final Maturity:	5 Years
Collateral Type:	Senior Unsecured
Settlement Price:	100
Calculation Amount:	USD 10 million
Trade Date:	Today (Insert Today's Date)
Effective Date:	5 Business Days from Today
Termination Date:	The earlier of the Effective Date plus one year or the "Early Redemption Date"
US Bank Pays:	All cash flows of the Reference Bond on the same day the cash flows the Reference Bond are paid.
European Bank Pays:	SOFR plus 25 basis points
Termination Payment:	On the Termination Date, any accrued payments due by either the total return payer or total return receiver will be paid. In addition, the following termination payment amount will be made:
	Calculation Amount × [Initial Price – Market Value]
	If positive, the TRS Receiver will make this payment to the TRS Payer.
	If negative, the TRS Payer will make this payment to the TRS Receiver.
Initial Price:	100%
Market Value:	The market value of the Reference Bond, including accrued interest, on the Termination Date. A dealer panel will determine the Market Value using the market bid price.
Early Termination:	Two Business Days following notice of a Credit Event with a Terminal Payment being made.

Credit Event:	Occurs when the Calculation Agent is aware of Publicly Available Information as to the existence of a Credit Condition.
	Credit Condition means either a Payment Default or a Bankruptcy Event in respect of the Issuer."
	Payment Default means, subject to a dispute in good faith by the Issuer, either the Issuer fails to pay any amount due of the Reference Asset; or any other present or future indebtedness of the Issuer for or in respect of moneys borrowed or raised or guaranteed.
	Bankruptcy Event means the declaration by the Issuer of a general moratorium in or rescheduling of payments on any external indebtedness.
	Publicly Available Information means information, which has been published in any two or more internationally, recognized published or electronically displayed financial news sources.
Calculation Agent:	Total return payer
Business Days	Days on which commercial banks and foreign exchange markets settle payments in London and New York.
Documentation:	Standard ISDA Master Agreement and Swap Confirmation
Law:	As per the ISDA Master Agreement

Although the preceding term sheet is typical, there is no standard transaction in the market. Some total return swaps may specify physical delivery of the reference asset as an option. Credit-event triggers may vary. Definitions may also vary. Additional clauses may be added to credit events. The sections "Defining the Event" in Chapter 3 and "Hidden Costs in Default Language" in Chapter 8 cover this in detail. Chapter 3's section "Termination Payments" offers detailed information on how to define final payments.

Total return swaps are often compared with repurchase agreements. In general, repurchase agreements allow an owner of a security, the "seller," to sell securities to an investor with the agreement to repurchase them at a fixed price on a fixed date. Repurchase agreements are financings. The seller of the security agrees to pay the buyer a negotiated rate of interest, the repurchase rate (repo rate). The buyer lends the seller money for the period of the agreement. The repo rate compensates the buyer for the financing. At the maturity of the agreement, the seller is obligated to repurchase the securities at the prespecified price.

In a TRS, the total return receiver is not obligated to purchase the reference asset at the maturity of the transaction. There is no pre-agreed fixed price for the reference asset at the maturity of the transaction. The TRS receiver is obligated only to exchange payments based on the market value of the reference asset at the maturity of the transaction.

MOTIVATION OF THE RECEIVER OF THE TOTAL RATE OF RETURN

In an important sense, total return swaps are not credit derivatives. Total return swaps, considered in their most basic form, are funding cost arbitrages. Total return swaps are applied in a variety of ways: balance sheet management, portfolio management, hedge fund leverage, and asset swap maturity manipulation.

Even though the overall effect of a TRS may have particularly important credit implications for both the payer and the receiver of the TRS, the use is primarily that of a financing. Investors hoping to boost their returns engage in financing, accept higher risk, and hope to achieve leveraged returns.

There are many reasons for both a payer and a receiver (investor) to enter into a total return swap, and there is one overwhelmingly compelling reason for the *receiver* of the total return swap. Many credit derivatives specialists who either miss the point or pander to the sensitivities of credit managers and regulators will cite reasons such as the following:

- Investors can create new assets with a specific maturity not currently available in the market.
- Investors gain efficient off-balance sheet exposure to a desired asset class such as syndicated loans or high-yield bonds, to which they otherwise would not have access.
- Investors may achieve a higher return on capital. Total return swaps are often treated as derivatives, or off—balance sheet instruments. Direct asset ownership is an on-balance sheet funded investment.
- Investors can fill in the credit gaps in their portfolios.
- Investors can reduce administrative costs via an off—balance sheet purchase (as opposed to buying loans on balance sheet).
- Investors can access entire asset classes by receiving the total return on an index.

I have been to presentations where these are the only reasons cited for the motivation of the receiver of the total return. These above reasons are often true. But it is like saying the reason you are driving a Porsche Targa around a racetrack is that it gets you around faster than walking. Although it is true, it is not the point of what you are doing.

*The key reason receivers of the total return enter into this transaction is to take advantage of **leverage**.* Investors make no initial cash payment. Cash flows are usually paid on a net basis. The investor's "payments" are subtracted in advance from the securities cash flows. The investor does nothing yet receives a positive net payment. This assumes that the funding cost of the investor remains less than the cash flows from the security. If the investor is receiving a fixed coupon and makes a floating payment, it could happen that in an inverted-yield-curve environment the investor would be in the position of having to make a net payment.

The return on capital using leverage is compelling and significant. Let us look at an example of the power of leverage. Suppose three different investors wish to receive the total return of a given asset. The asset is a BB— rated par asset with a coupon of LIBOR+250 basis points (bps), or a then current yield of around 8.30 percent. (Consider LIBOR for a moment. We will return to SOFR shortly.) Two of the investors are hedge funds and must pay a funding cost of LIBOR+100 bps. The third investor is a mutual fund, which pays cash for the investment.

The first hedge fund, hedge fund A, gets better credit terms than the other fund, hedge fund B. Hedge fund A deals with a bank eager to do business and has to put up only 5 percent collateral up front; hedge fund B deals with a more cautious bank and must put up 10 percent collateral. The banks will both pay "LIBOR flat as interest on the cash held as credit collateral for the total return swap. Table 2.1a shows the net economic return for each of the investors.

Hedge fund A, which employs a 20:1 leverage, has a net return of 35.8 percent, whereas hedge fund B, which employs a 10:1 leverage, has a return of 20.8 percent after funding costs. The cash investor has a net return of only 8.3 percent, and that does not take into account any funding costs. It is reasonable to assume that an investor with cash has an implied funding cost. If we assume LIBOR as the funding cost, the cash investor's net return is only 2.5 percent versus the double-digit returns enjoyed by the hedge funds. This is the power of leverage.

The above rates are from 1997 when LIBOR was 5.8%. The U.S. inflation rate in 1997 was around 2.29%. On January 11, 2022, SOFR was around 0.05%. The annual U.S. inflation rate for December 2021 soared to 7%, a high not seen since June 1982. The Federal Reserve Bank uses open market operations to suppress interest rates and inject money into the system, aka money printing. The manipulation in 2022 far surpasses that of the late 1990s. We will examine the implications of this policy shift in Chapter 5.

Table 2.1b shows the benefits of leverage in a low interest rate environment. One can see how leverage can appear even more enticing relative to suppressed interest rates. Real short-term rates do not keep up with inflation. Another way of saying this is that we are working in a market of *negative* real interest rates.

Leverage is the reason that hedge funds are a primary target as counterparties in total return swaps. The hedge funds are the receivers of the total return. The primary motive of the hedge funds is to exploit leverage. The participation of hedge funds and other shaky, albeit partially collateralized, credits is a critical, and not necessarily welcome, development in the credit derivatives market. Whereas the motive of the hedge fund counterparty is leverage, the motive of the payer of the total rate return in the TRS is high earnings. We examine this transaction and the quality of these earnings in more detail in the section on hedge funds in this chapter.

TABLE 2.1a   Net Economic Returns for Counterparties, Various Degrees of Leverage: Absent Rate Suppression 1997
U.S. Inflation Rate in 1997: 2.3%

	Hedge Fund A	Hedge Fund B	Cash Investor
Asset Yield	8.30%	8.30%	8.30%
LIBOR Yield	5.80%	5.80%	
Net Asset Spread	2.50%	2.50%	
Spread to LIBOR	−1.00%	−1.00%	
Net Swap Spread	1.50%	1.50%	
Collateral	5%	10%	
Leverage	20 to 1	10 to 1	1 to 1
Levered Swap Return	30.00%	15.00%	
Interest on Collateral	5.80%	5.80%	
Net Return	**35.80%**	**20.80%**	**8.30%**

TABLE 2.1b   Net Economic Returns for Counterparties with Various Degrees of Leverage: Rate Suppression January 11, 2022.
U.S. Annual Inflation Rate in December 2021: 7.0%

	Hedge Fund A	Hedge Fund B	Cash Investor
Asset Yield	2.55%	2.55%	2.55%
SOFR Yield	0.05%	0.05%	
Net Asset Spread	2.50%	2.50%	
Spread to SOFR	−1.00%	−1.00%	
Net Swap Spread	1.50%	1.50%	
Collateral	5%	10%	
Leverage	20 to 1	10 to 1	1 to 1
Levered Swap Return	30.00%	15.00%	
Interest on Collateral	0.05%	0.05%	
Net Return	**30.05%**	**15.05%**	**2.55%**

For a creditworthy bank or other creditworthy receiver, generally no upfront collateral is required. The receiver puts up no cash. The spread earned is pure spread income—the interest income on the TRS less the receiver's funding cost.

Many hedge funds will take as much leverage as they can get. In 1997, it was possible to engage in these trades with 5% collateral and 20:1 leverage. During the financial crisis, banks offloaded problematic assets by offering 10:1 leverage. Many behind-the-scenes deals can have enormous leverage even today. One hears about them when deals blow up.

ARCHEGOS CAPITAL MANAGEMENT

Archegos Capital Management reportedly engaged in total return swaps and huge concentrated positions in equities funded by eight prime brokers, the divisions within banks that provide services and funding to hedge funds. Banks are not alone in having blind spots.

Bill Hwang, head of Archegos, had around $10 billion in assets under management. *Bloomberg* reported that Archegos had $10 billion of undisclosed exposure to ViacomCBS alone, driving the price up over 300% in in just weeks. Archegos's accumulated positions were estimated at around $100 billion, implying ten times leverage on volatile equities. The prime brokers had no idea. (Erik Schatzker, Sridhar Natarajan, and Sonali Basak, "Leveraged Blowout: How Hwang's Archegos Blindsided Global Banks," *Bloomberg*, April 1, 2021.)

What was worse, Bill Hwuang's trades "forced" indexers to buy shares in Hwang's rapidly rising positions to keep up. At the time, no one knew what was behind the initial price explosions. But when Viacom announced a $3 billion stock sale—why wouldn't they? —the stock price plummeted, and Archegos faced billions in margin calls that it couldn't meet.

Despite hedge fund blowups for several decades, despite a global financial crisis related to leverage, total return swaps have little transparency and Archegos was not required to report its exposure to the underlying shares of stock, because Archegos was not the legal owner of the shares.

The situation is fluid. The reportage above is based on rough estimates and there is still no transparency on the collapse. Prime brokers are still assessing total losses in the billions of dollars. Credit Suisse is believed to have taken the biggest hit of around $10 billion in losses. In November 2021, Credit Suisse announced it was shutting down its prime brokerage business. Archegos's prime brokers included the former along with UBS, Morgan Stanley, and Goldman Sachs.

How was this possible given that the risks of these transactions have been well known for decades as evidence by the first edition of this book published in 1998, and the subsequent implosion of Long Term Capital Management in 1998 due to its high leverage?

More recent examples of hidden leverage gone wrong include MF Global's bankruptcy in 2011, and JPMorgan's London Whale debacle in 2012. We will discuss those incidents in detail later in this book.

MOTIVATION OF THE PAYER

The payer in a TRS creates a hedge for both price risk and default risk of the reference asset, although the payer in the TRS is a legal owner of the reference asset. Investors who cannot short securities may be able to hedge a long position by paying the total return in a TRS.

The TRS is an off-balance sheet transaction for the payer of the total return. A long-term investor who feels that a reference asset in the portfolio may widen in spread in the short term but then recover may enter into a TRS that is shorter than the maturity of the asset. The structure is flexible and does not require a sale of the asset. In this way the investor can lock in a return yet take a temporary short-term negative view on an asset.

In some accounting regimens, an investor who has an unrecognized loss in a bond position can defer the loss without risking even further losses on the asset. The investor can pay the total return on the asset for the period of time required to defer the loss. At the maturity of the TRS—if it is not the same as the maturity of the asset—the investor can sell the asset and recognize the loss. An investor with a gain in a security can employ the same method to defer a gain while simultaneously protecting the value of the reference asset. Although this method may work for certain accounting scenarios, U.S. taxpayers will find that paying the TROR on an asset will be evaluated as a true sale. Treatment for accounting and tax purposes varies by country, and investors must consult their own accountants and tax experts.

REGULATORY CAPITAL ARBITRAGE AND BANK MOTIVATION

The Bank for International Settlements (BIS) issued Basel I, a framework for setting minimum capital requirements for international banks, in July 1988. Since then, the BIS has issued Basel II guidelines and is now modifying Basel III guidelines. Meanwhile, each country has set up its own capital guidelines for banks, often applying inconsistent interpretations of the BIS's changing guidelines.

See the section titled "Regulatory Capital" in Chapter 8 for a more detailed discussion of regulatory capital requirements. Until then, I will state the risk weighting of assets used in discussion examples. But be aware that you should look up specific risk weights, and they are subject to change.

Regulatory capital treatment of credit derivatives is subject to change and can vary by region. Why is this important? It is important for the same reason that margin requirements are important to hedge funds and other participants in the derivatives markets. The lower the capital that banks must reserve, the higher the *leverage* banks can employ.

Both bank and nonbank participants in the credit derivatives market should have a basic understanding of the implications of bank regulatory capital, because banks make up most of the driving force of this market, and the vagaries of regulatory capital requirements affect their behavior.

After December 31, 1992, all banks were expected to meet a minimum ratio of qualifying total capital to BIS risk-weighted assets of 8 percent. The amount of capital reserved against a risk-weighted asset is not necessarily 8 percent, however. The amount of capital reserved against an asset will depend on the asset's BIS risk weighting. This risk weighting has little to do with credit quality of the risk-weighted asset; it has very much to do with often arbitrary capital standards set up for the international market by regulators who thought they were creating a framework to strengthen and stabilize the international banking community.

The well-intentioned regulators had a quaint idea. The result is that the international banking community lives with the shortcomings of an inflexible and arbitrary system. Inflexible and arbitrary rules also create perverse incentives to "optimize" according to the letter of the rules, even if common sense says otherwise. In its mildest form, a bank may enter into an economically neutral transaction to gain a regulatory capital advantage. But the rules sometimes force banks to behave like Radar O'Reilly in *M*A*S*H,* making the best of a crazy system. A bank may enter into an economically disadvantageous transaction because it improves the bank balance sheet with respect to regulatory capital treatment.

Manipulating regulatory capital is not the sole motivation of most healthy banks, but it is an important motivation. It is an even more important motivation for less healthy banks that are barely able to meet regulatory capital requirements. The game every bank plays, to a greater or a lesser degree, is to optimize return on regulatory capital.

The risk weight of a reference asset in a credit derivative transaction will generally be referred to as the "BIS risk weight." The risk weight of a reference asset may vary by jurisdiction, however. This further complicates matters because central banks and ministries of finance have the right to set local standards for assets, which are not clearly addressed by BIS.

A key reason for the 2008 financial crisis was that banks took on far too much risk. They had direct exposure to high-risk, misrated fixed income assets to which the BIS had assigned a low risk weight. Banks also had indirect exposure via counterparties who suffered from the same issue: monoline insurance companies (and others) wrote credit default protection on misrated fraud-riddled fixed income products that the banks had created.

Some of the key issues that affect bank regulatory capital with respect to credit derivatives are as follows:

- Credit derivatives had explosive growth in the 21st century. In June 1997, the Bank of England, and shortly thereafter the U.S. Federal Reserve Board, agreed that credit default swaps and options can be held on the trading book instead of on the bank book. Total return swaps had already been given trading book treatment. Capital can potentially be offset for risk assets and hedges. But this assumes trades are properly executed and counterparties are good for it. After the 2008 crisis, those assumptions proved to be flawed.

- After January 1, 1998, the Fed allowed certain banks to treat credit derivatives held on the bank's trading book the same as other derivatives in the trading book. Instruments held in the banking book are risk weighted at 8 percent of notional value, and trading book positions are usually held at much lower percentages of their notional value, so this would result in a drastic reduction of required capital. Banks would have to demonstrate that they have internal models that accurately describe the risk and add-on capital to account for counterparty risk.

- Unless a position is perfectly hedged, capital adequacy rules will not recognize offsets for credit derivatives. This means that if there is basis risk between the reference asset for the credit derivative and the asset being hedged, no risk and no capital netting will be allowed. Potentially, a bank could be charged capital for counterparty risk on an imperfect hedge and also be charged capital for the reference asset being hedged. The end result for an imperfect hedge could be a *greater* capital charge after hedging.

- After January 1, 1998, the Fed allowed certain banks to treat credit derivatives held on the bank's trading book the same as other derivatives in the trading book. Instruments held in the banking book were initially risk weighted at 8 percent of notional value. Trading book positions are usually held at much lower percentages of their notional value, so this would result in a drastic reduction of required capital. Banks would have to demonstrate that they have internal models that accurately described the risk and add-on capital to account for counterparty risk.

- By the 21st century, banks had wheedled out much lower risk weighs for financially engineered assets. Banks persuaded regulators that some of their engineered fixed-income assets, so-called Super-senior tranches, were so sound, they should get only a 20% BIS risk weight, the same as an OECD bank. We will see how that went horribly wrong later in this book. But be aware that the game to reduce regulatory capital charges is a perpetual motion machine.

- In 2022, as of this writing, banks use special purpose vehicles to move assets off balance sheet to reduce regulatory capital. But as we will see later, sometimes assets classified as "off balance sheet" have risk of coming back on a bank's balance sheet.

Figure 2.2 shows the effect of selling credit protection in the form of a TRS. The bank receives the total rate of return (TROR) on two different assets with a notional value of $10 million on the reference asset. The bank has a funding cost of SOFR flat, and both assets have coupons of SOFR+50 bps. The reference asset for one transaction (shown diagrammatically on the left in Figure 2.2) has a BIS risk weight of 100 percent. The reference asset for the other transaction has a BIS risk weight of 20 percent.

The net spread earned on the assets is identical. The net spread is unaffected by the BIS risk weight for regulatory capital purposes. If one looked at net spread alone, it appears the bank should be indifferent to selling credit protection by receiving the total return of either asset. The balance sheet analysis in Table 2.2, however, tells a different story.

Even though the return on the asset is identical in each transaction, the return on regulatory capital is dramatically different. The asset with the 20 percent BIS risk weight has a return on capital five times greater than the asset with the 100 percent risk weight. This result has nothing to do with

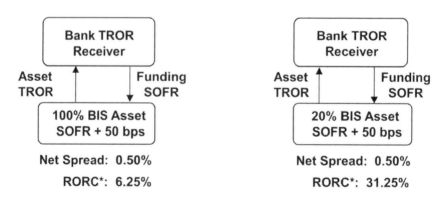

* See Table 2.2 for Calculations for Return on Regulatory Capital (RORC)

FIGURE 2.2   TROR on 100% versus 20% BIS Risk-Weighted Asset

the creditworthiness of the assets and nothing to do with the market risk of the transaction, but everything to do with the skewed effect of regulatory capital requirements.

Note that in these examples I assume my cost of regulatory capital is roughly the same as the return from investing in Treasury bills (T-bills). The cost of regulatory capital and return on investment of regulatory capital nets to zero.

The effects of the use of leverage in these examples are due to changes in economic capital and affected return on assets (ROA). The effect of differences in regulatory capital is less apparent. Actual cash inflow has not changed for a trade with the same notional amount. What has changed is the return on capital (ROC), based on an arbitrary reserve of capital.

Professionals consider three components of risk when evaluating exposures:

1. *Counterparty risk,* which is the mark-to-market exposure for the credit derivative due to the possibility that the counterparty may default on its obligation or potential obligation under the terms of the credit derivative transaction.
2. *Market risk,* which is the net exposure to interest rates, foreign exchange rates, commodity prices, and equity prices.
3. *Specific risk,* which is an adverse change in price from factors related to the issuer of the reference asset due to nonmarket movements.

One example of specific risk would be changes in the credit risk of the reference asset. This can be accounted for by scaled risk weightings of 0 percent for government risks, 3 to 20 percent for investment-grade risks, or 100 percent for noninvestment-grade and other risks. Banks have the alternative of using standard specific risk add-on factors from market—risk models.

Only banks that can prove that they have models to calculate exposures in a reproducible and consistent manner will be allowed to use this new capital treatment for credit derivatives. Much is at stake. The potential reduction in regulatory capital is great.

Risk-Based Capital Calculation			
100% Risk Weighted Asset		**20% Risk Weighted Asset**	
Asset Book Value	100.00%	Asset Book Value	100.00%
× Category Risk Weight	100.00%	× Category Risk Weight	20.00%
= % Risk Weighted Asset	100.00%	= % Risk Weighted Asset	20.00%
× Capital Requirement	8.00%	× Capital Requirement	8.00%
= % Risk-Based Capital	**8.00%**	**= % Risk-Based Capital**	**1.60%**
Notional	$10,000,000	Notional	$10,000,000
Net Income 50 BP	$50,000	Net Income 50 BP	$50,000
Capital:	$800,000	Capital:	$160,000
Return on Capital:	**6.25%**	**Return on Capital:**	**31.25%**

TABLE 2.2 Bank Balance Sheet Comparison: Bank Receives TROR, 100% versus 20% BIS Risk Weight

Consider, for example, a transaction in which an OECD bank with a funding cost of SOFR−25 bps buys credit protection on an asset with a 100 percent BIS risk weight by paying the total return on an asset to another OECD bank. The protection seller, the receiver of the TROR, is willing to pay SOFR+20 bps in this transaction. The transaction is represented as shown in Figure 2.3.

If the bank's model can show that the combined maximum exposure to the asset and to the payer of the TROR is only 30 percent of the notional amount of the transaction, the bank would get a much more favorable return on capital under the new regime. This would apply only to the trading book, however. The balance sheet summary in Table 2.3 shows the effect of buying protection under the current regime versus the capital charges under the proposed new regime.

The trading book return on capital is potentially much greater under the proposed new capital regime. Return on capital for the transaction jumps from 28.13 percent to 93.75 percent. This assumes that the bank has a model that can demonstrate the counterparty exposure as represented in Figure 2.3. If a bank does not book this transaction in the trading book or if the bank does not have a suitable model for credit derivatives, the bank will not be eligible for this potentially very favorable capital treatment.

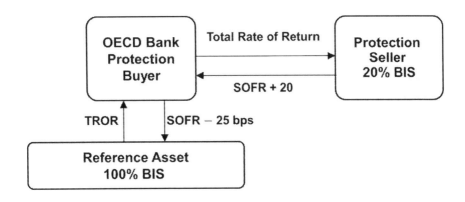

FIGURE 2.3 Buying Protection: Paying TROR

TABLE 2.3 Bank Balance Sheet Comparison under New Regime: OECD Bank Pays TROR to OECD Bank

Risk-Based Capital Calculation			
Current Treatment		**New Regime**	
Asset Book Value	100.00%	M-T-M Exposure Counterparty Credit Equiv.	25.00% 5.00%
Total Exposure x Category Risk	100.00%	Total Exposure	30.00%
Weight	20.00%	x Category Risk Weight = Relevant % Risk	20.00%
= % Risk Weight	20.00%	Weight	6.00%
x Capital Requirement	8.00%	x Capital Requirement	8.00%
= % Risk-Based Capital	**1.60%**	**= % Risk-Based Capital**	**0.48%**
Notional	$10,000,000	Notional	$10,000,000
Net Income 45 BP	$45,000	Net Income 45 BP	$45,000
Capital:	$160,000	Capital:	$48,000
Return on Capital:	**28.13%**	**Return on Capital:**	**93.75%**

CREATING SYNTHETIC ASSETS

There are several different structures beyond the plain vanilla one in which the TRS maturity matches that of the underlying asset. The following list summarizes some of the most common features:

- Investors can receive the total return for a shorter period of time than the maturity of the reference asset.
- For the first time, a financial institution can short credits even in maturities for which no reference asset exists.
- The return of the underlying asset can have a cap or a floor.
- The financing can be capped or floored to better control the financing cost on the floating rate payment.
- Investors can lock in a market level for the underlying asset or for the financing rate by specifying a forward start date. This is particularly useful for investors who will have cash to put to work in the future.
- Investors can receive the total return on a basket of assets and can possibly reduce collateral requirements and net financing costs.

MISMATCHED MATURITIES

The most significant development, besides financing, in the TRS market is the ability to change the maturity of the credit exposure. This is touted as a tremendous benefit to the TROR receiver, the investor, but I offer some important caveats to this structure. The term sheet shown earlier for the bond total return swap referenced a five-year maturity, fixed-coupon asset, but the term of the swap was for only one year. The returns for total return swaps are generally greater than for a credit default swap with the same maturity. This is because the return to the protection seller incorporates compensation for a combination of default risk and price risk. Price risk is particularly important when the maturity of the reference asset is greater than the term of the TRS.

When the maturity of the TRS is less than that of the fixed-coupon reference asset, the receiver of the TROR has a great deal of price risk at the end of the transaction. Many protection sellers—investors who are receiving the TROR on a fixed-coupon reference asset—do not like to engage in unmatched maturity transactions. The benefit to the investor of the unmatched maturity is the ability to invest in a reference asset for a period of time that is shorter than what is available in the market. The risk to the investor now includes an additional element of market risk.

The TRS will end before the maturity of the reference asset, even if there has been no default event on the reference asset. This means that the price of the reference asset may fluctuate due to market interest rate moves. If interest rates rise relative to the start of the transaction, the price of the reference asset may decline. The receiver of the TROR must pay the difference between this new market price and the price at the start of the TRS transaction. This price may have declined purely due to interest rate moves, even in the absence of any deterioration in the credit quality of the reference asset. It is even possible that the reference-asset credit quality can improve while the final market price declines due solely to a general rise in interest rates.

How much can this price risk be? Consider the case for a one-year period in which the price of the reference asset declines by one point. The total return on the transaction will decline by 100 basis points. If the net spread earned by the investor for the one-year time period is only 50 basis points, the investor must now make a termination payment of one point, or 100 basis points, to the total return payer. This means the net margin on the trade is now a *negative* 50 basis points for the investor, the total return receiver.

TRANCHED ASSET SWAP VERSUS TRS

Tranched asset swaps look remarkably similar to mismatched maturity TRS, but there are some important differences. Tranched asset swaps have been around for several years, but only recently have they been classified by some market professionals as credit derivatives.

A tranched asset swap is an asset swap package, which can be put back to the asset swap package "seller" provided the reference bonds are not in default. The put is usually a European put, exercisable one time only, on the specified put date. The investor purchases the asset swap package. This consists of the reference asset combined with a swap of the fixed coupons for floating rate (or floating coupons net of the investor's funding cost). The investor usually pays par for the shorter maturing asset swap position and earns a reduced spread relative to the longer asset swap position from which it was tranched. The investor is the legal owner of the asset swap package.

If there is no default on the reference asset and if the investor exercises the put, the seller of the asset swap package is obligated to purchase the asset swap package at par. The seller is immunized from the default risk of the reference asset, but the seller has the market-price risk and credit-spread widening risk of the reference asset if the put is exercised under adverse market conditions. Figure 2.4 shows the cash flows of this transaction.

The net asset swap return is determined by the spread over SOFR paid on the investment less the funding cost of the investor. The *tranched* asset swap return is further determined by the relative maturity of the tranche to the longer underlying asset swap. The spread difference between the underlying asset swap and the shorter tranche is similar in concept to a loan facility fee.

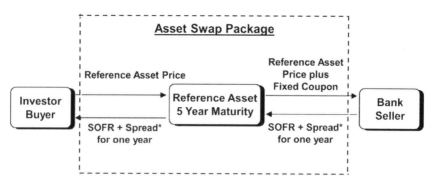

* Any discount or premium to par of the reference asset is incorporated in the spread.

At the end of one year, the investor (buyer) has the right to put the asset swap package back to the Bank (seller) at par, provided the reference asset has not defaulted. The investor receives a spread near the one-year asset swap spread, not the five-year asset swap spread.

FIGURE 2.4 Tranched Asset Swap: Five-Year Maturity Asset, One-Year Maturity Tranche

A TRS with a shorter maturity than that of the reference asset is economically different than a tranched asset swap. In this case, the seller—the TROR payer—is the legal owner of the reference asset. The seller passes the cash flows of the reference asset to the investor, the receiver of the TROR. The investor has the market risk and the credit risk of the reference asset as if the investor owned the asset, albeit the investor does not own the asset.

The seller is immunized from price risk and credit risk—including default risk—of the reference assets.

Unlike the asset swap, a TRS *is* sensitive to the investor's credit quality. If the reference asset experiences a credit event, the investor, the TROR receiver, must make a payment to the TROR payee. Posting collateral mitigates this risk, but it does not eliminate the risk for unexpected (or ignored) extremes. The credit rating of the investor and the correlation of the investor to the reference asset being hedged are key considerations in determining the spread to the investor.

For OECD banks, the investor BIS risk weight is also important. This spread is determined by the contingent payment, so calculation of this spread is not always straightforward, as we shall see in Chapter 4. Simplifications abound, and for publicly well-traded assets with investment-grade rated counterparties, simple assumptions, usually related to the funding cost, and broad guesses of correlation between the investor and the reference asset usually suffice to make a market level.

FUNDING ARBITRAGE AND THE JOINT PROBABILITY OF DEFAULT

One of the primary reasons that total return swaps are so popular is that they are a form of financing and thus banks can employ a perceived funding cost arbitrage. A higher funding cost bank can receive the total return on an asset from a lower funding cost bank and take advantage of a favorable financing rate. The lower cost bank benefits from the lower joint probability of default from the combination of the reference asset and the receiver of the total return.

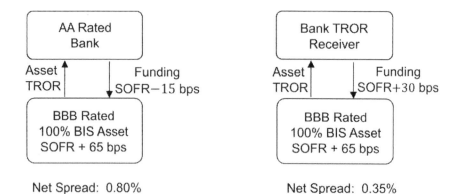

Net Spread: 0.80%   Net Spread: 0.35%

This Is an On-Balance Sheet Transaction for Both Banks

FIGURE 2.5 Outright Purchase: 100% Risk-Weighted Asset

Consider the case for an AA rated bank with a funding cost of SOFR−15 bps and an A− rated bank with a funding cost of SOFR+30 bps. If each bank were to purchase a BBB rated asset with an asset swap coupon of SOFR+65 bps for a five-year maturity outright, the net investment might be as shown in Figure 2.5.

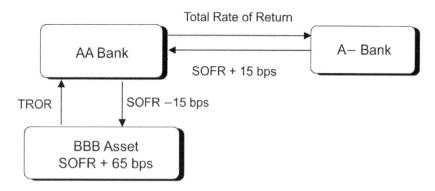

The maturity of the TRORS matches the five-year maturity of the BBB Asset. If the Asset defaults, the A− Bank makes a payment to the AA Rated bank.

The A− rated bank has the same risk as if it purchased the BBB asset outright and locks in a five-year funding cost of LIBOR+15 basis points versus a funding cost of LIBOR+30 basis points.

FIGURE 2.6 TRS Transaction Flows

If the AA rated bank enters into a TRS with the A− rated bank, the AA rated bank may be able to give the A− rated bank a slightly more favorable funding cost. If both banks are OECD banks, the AA rated bank hedges the market risk—the credit risk (both the default risk and the credit-spread widening risk)—and can reduce the capital charge of the transaction from 100 percent to 20 percent. The AA bank can offer more favorable funding terms to the A− rated bank and still be better off. If the AA bank offers a five-year financing cost to the A− rated bank of SOFR+15 bps—a 15 basis-point reduction in its normal funding cost—the transaction flows will be as shown in Figure 2.6.

The AA bank benefits from the lower joint probability of default between the A− rated bank and the BBB rated reference asset. Based on Standard & Poor's (S&P) tables, if there is no correlation between the A− rated bank and the BBB rated reference asset, the implied rating on the effective credit risk to the AA rated bank is a rating of A+. S&P and Moody's publish jointly supported ratings for non-correlated assets and guarantors. Table 2.4 shows S&P's jointly supported ratings.

The AA bank has created a *synthetic* asset with an implied credit rating of A+, a 20 percent BIS risk weight versus the 100 percent risk weight before the TRS and is able to reduce credit-risk and market-risk exposure to the reference asset on its books. In fact, both institutions are economically better off after the transaction, although the A− rated institution is in exactly the same regulatory situation as when it purchased the asset outright as opposed to receiving the TROR.

The A− rated bank locks in a favorable financing rate for five years. The A− rated bank does not have to put up any economic capital and receives net flows on the transaction off balance sheet. The A− rated bank is able to leverage its position even if it is temporarily short of investment cash. The new position of both banks after doing the TROR is as shown in Figure 2.7.

Even if the AA bank found a counterparty, such as a 100 percent BIS risk-weighted investment banking firm, the AA bank still benefits from the lower joint probability of default, even though the regulatory capital charges will remain the same. All other things being equal, however, the AA bank will prefer to do this transaction with another OECD bank.

Notice that this transaction works because of the difference in the funding costs of the two institutions. For some assets, and for some institutions where the funding cost differential is less, the funding cost arbitrage may not look as good, and it is sometimes impractical to structure this sort of transaction.

BALANCE SHEET MANAGEMENT

Besides using total return swaps for financing and for gaining the benefits of leverage, there is another key use for total return swaps. Financial institutions often use total return swaps as a balance sheet management tool. For example, an institution with a relatively high cost of funds, such as the U.S. branch of a Japanese bank, Lehman Brothers, or Salomon Brothers, will want to get assets off its balance sheet. It may want to do this for a long period of time or for a short period of time. Most of these transactions are thinly disguised balance sheet dressing when done for short periods of time, such as two weeks to three months. Nonetheless, the higher funding cost institutions wishing to get assets off their balance sheet by using this technique have a true economic risk as if they own the asset for the term of the transaction.

TABLE 2.4   S&P Jointly Supported Ratings as of August 1997

	AAA	AA+	AA	AA–	A+	A	A–	BBB+	BBB	BBB–
AAA	AAA	AAA	AAA	AAA	AAA	AAA	AAA	AAA	AAA	AAA
AA+	AAA	AAA	AAA	AAA	AAA	AAA	AAA	AAA	AAA	AA+
AA	AAA	AAA	AAA	AAA	AAA	AAA	AAA	AA+	AA+	AA+
AA–	AAA	AAA	AAA	AA+	AA+	AA+	AA+	AA+	AA+	AA
A+	AAA	AAA	AAA	AA+	AA+	AA+	AA+	AA	AA	AA–
A	AAA	AAA	AAA	AA+	AA+	AA	AA	AA–	AA–	A+
A–	AAA	AAA	AAA	AA+	AA+	AA	AA–	A+	A+	A
BBB+	AAA	AAA	AA+	AA+	AA	AA–	A+	A	A	A–
BBB	AAA	AAA	AA+	AA+	AA	AA	A+	A	A–	BBB+
BBB–	AAA	AA+	AA+	AA	AA–	A+	A	A–	BBB+	BBB–

Note: The way to read this table is to choose either the row or the column for the A– rated bank and the other for the BBB rated reference asset. Reading across and down, they intersect at A+, the implied effective credit risk for the joint credits.

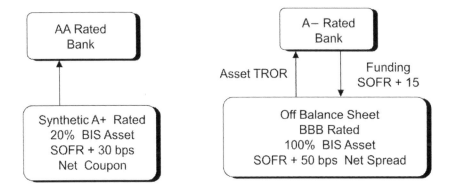

FIGURE 2.7 Net Position After TRS

For example, suppose a BBB rated securities firm with the higher cost of funds sells securities to an AA rated bank with a lower cost of funds. The AA rated bank pays the TROR on the securities to the securities firm, and the securities firm simultaneously pays SOFR plus a spread to the bank. The bank finances the position for the securities firm. From the point of view of the securities firm, this is a true sale of securities as long as the securities firm is not obligated to repurchase the securities. The securities firm will take the mark-to-market risk at the end of the transaction and may repurchase the securities; but the key is that it is not obligated to do so. The bank earns the income from the short-term transaction. At the end of the transaction, it can sell the securities in the market at the market price without taking price risk on the securities. The bank earns income, which is immunized from price risk. The gain or loss in price at the maturity of the TRS is borne by the securities firm.

ADVANCED BALANCE SHEET MANAGEMENT

Many banks have set up conduits as fee-earning vehicles to accommodate balance sheet transactions. One creative use of these conduits is as a vehicle to pass through risk. Banks enter into a Sale/TRS transaction with the conduit. The conduit purchases the bonds and funds this purchase via its commercial paper (CP) program. The conduit then transfers the risk. If the risk is merely being passed through the conduit, it must eventually end up somewhere. It usually ends up back where it started. The conduit pays the total return on the assets to the derivatives trading desk internal to its mother bank. The derivatives trading desk then passes the risk by paying the total return on the assets to a subsidiary of the bank that originally sold the assets to the conduit in the first place. This circular transfer of risk sounds confusing at first. The basic transaction is illustrated in the following scenario:

> You run the corporate bond trading desk for Bank A. Bank A has a variety of subsidiaries and other entities. Your trading desk has taken down a $100 million position of very illiquid bonds, and you are having no success in selling them. You want to get these bonds off the trading book balance sheet for a period of at least one year. It would be ideal if you could get rid of the bonds altogether. Bank A is willing to continue to bear the market risk and the credit risk of the illiquid bonds, which have a highly positive carry; but you do not want the risk to appear in the trading book. For all intents and purposes, you want it to appear as if you sold the bonds to a customer.

Figure 2.8 shows the cash flows of the transaction. You sell $100 million of bonds to Bank B's conduit. Notice that by setting up a conduit

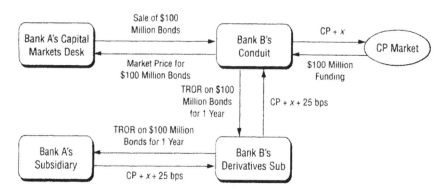

FIGURE 2.8 TRS for Balance Sheet Management

for this purpose, Bank B avoids having the bonds hit its balance sheet. Bank B's conduit pays you the market price for these bonds. Bank B's conduit obtains $100 million in funding from the CP market in order to purchase the bonds. The conduit lays off the market risk of the bonds for one year by paying the TROR to Bank B's derivatives subsidiary. Bank B's derivative subsidiary lays off the market risk by paying the TROR on $100 million notional of the bonds to Bank A's subsidiary. Bank A's subsidiary pays Bank B's derivatives desk CP plus a spread plus a fee. The spread is denoted in Figure 2.8 as *"x."* This spread is equal to the spread required for the conduit to fund itself. The fee is consideration for the use of Bank B's conduit and the derivatives subsidiary to pass through the risk. Bank B's derivatives subsidiary pays CP plus the spread plus the fee (minus a small consideration) to the conduit. The net cash flow to the conduit is the fee. Fees vary. This is a negotiated market. In 2000, banks charged 12.5 to 26 bps and more to allow other banks to rent their balance sheet in this fashion.

At the end of the year, how does Bank B make sure that the bonds are sold? Because these bonds may still be very illiquid, they want to be sure to have a way of disposing of these bonds. Furthermore, the bonds may have deteriorated in value, and that is the scenario that most concerns Bank B. Documentation usually calls for an average of several dealer quotes to determine the market value of the bonds at the end of the one-year TRS. Bank B can ask for a bid on these bonds. If the bid price is too low, Bank A has an incentive to buy the bonds because they have to pay the difference between the original market price and the current market price at the end of the TRS. If the TRS called for a mark-to-market on a periodic basis, the final exchange of value would be based on the market price at the beginning of the period, versus at the end of the year. Some documents have a provision that if they cannot get a dealer bid at the end of the TRS, the assumed mark-to-market price of the bonds is zero. The language is careful not to require Bank A to repurchase the bonds in this scenario, but the economic incentive of Bank A to make a bid is overwhelming. Naturally, this documentation is controversial, and one must check with accountants and lawyers to make sure that Bank A gets the required true sale treatment while Bank B gets its required flexibility at the end of the TRS.

RELATIVE PERFORMANCE TRS

Two investors may manage the balance sheet by paying the total return of one asset in exchange for receiving the total return of another asset. This is a relative performance TRS and theoretically should help investors diversify credit risk using an off-balance sheet tool. In practice it is not seen often in the market. Most banks, for instance, want to pay the total return as a means of getting credit protection, but they are less eager to take on credit risk. It is also difficult to get two institutions to agree on the proper ratios of payment for the relative performance of two different credits.

Nonetheless this underused transaction may become more popular in the future among low funding cost banks wishing to free up overused credit lines of investment-grade credits. Banks may become more willing to swap low-margin returns to free up lines for the opportunity to book higher-margin business with targeted clients. This transaction is a means of expanding credit lines. This concept has been slow to grow among banks, but for transactions in the banking book, the favorable capital treatment enjoyed by some banks supports continued exponential growth.

HEDGE FUNDS AND LOAN TOTAL RETURN SWAPS

Until recently, most financings were done through repurchase agreements. Most repurchase agreements are short term, but some can be longer. In the United States, mortgage-backed securities dealers, eager to sell risky inverse floaters combined with interest-only tranches ("inverse/IO" product) in the early 1990s to drive collateralized mortgage obligation (CMO) deals, offered repurchase agreements for as long as two years to buyers. Buyers eagerly sought leveraged financing for their already very risky purchases. The financing rate is known as the "repo rate." The repo rate took into account the creditworthiness of the repurchase agreement "seller" as well as the creditworthiness of the "buyer." The repo rate also took into account the riskiness of the asset. In this case the riskiness of the asset arose from its prepayment sensitivity to interest rates. Therefore, the dealers asked for upfront collateral, usually 10 percent or 20 percent of the initial value of the securities. This upfront collateral compensated for the unusual price volatility of these securities.

The upfront collateral was also meant to compensate for the fact that many of the institutions buying these "high yielding" risky assets were risky institutions. The reason for the financing, of course, was leverage. Most of the institutions asking for financing were either hedge funds or lower-rated Japanese trading and leasing companies.

In the early 1990s, David J. Askin managed a fund of very risky CMO tranches. Askin thought he had a model that could predict an unknowable unknown—the prepayment behavior of the U.S. mortgage holder. His firm, Askin Capital Management, bought these securities using dealer-provided financing on margin. Unfortunately, the prices predicted by his models did not agree with the market quotes he got from the dealers who sold him those securities, *the same firms making margin calls on Askin*. As buyers for esoteric mortgage-backed securities withdrew from the market, liquidity disappeared. Market prices diverged even farther from model prices as fundamentals gave way to supply-and-demand forces in the market.

As prices dropped, Askin was asked to put up more collateral. Askin, with insufficient liquidity (and some said insufficient solvency), was unable to meet margin calls. He was forced to liquidate fund positions at distressed prices and finally to file for bankruptcy protection. Askin Capital. Kidder Peabody had financed sales of many of these CMO tranches to Askin. It lost around $25 million.

How did this happen? It is the old story. If the returns seem miraculously high, the probability that you will lose your money is just about as high. Askin reportedly claimed he could achieve return of 15 percent on their investment with minimal risk. *The New York Times* quoted one regretful investor: "Maybe this sounds too easy to say now: If it looks too good to be true, maybe it is." Investment banks were eager to extend financing because they wanted to get rid of the "nuclear waste" tranches of CMOs. Once then investment banks sold the risky piece, they could underwrite more transactions and book attractive underwriting fees. When liquidity for these instruments dried up, risk managers started asking tough questions, but much too late.

David Askin believed in his ability to perform. He developed models, graphs, and investment literature to support his claim that he could deliver well above market returns with low risk—or so clients claimed when they were dazzled by the numbers; documents may have included disclaimers.

But "garbage in" equals "garbage out," even if the garbage is wrapped in gold foil. This is especially true for illiquid products where market forces can cause a firm with insufficient capital to fold, even when the assets perform as predicted. In Askin's case, that firms providing market prices were the same firms that were lending money on these products. They had the ability to squeeze investors such as Askin whether it was warranted or not. Askin had bought illiquid assets, and those who made the margin calls had the most influence over prices in this privately traded market. Whether Askin's model was correct or not, he was at their mercy.

Imagine a scenario wherein firms that engineer financial products have all the pricing clout in an opaque market; a firm claims assets dropped far in price; the firm makes a huge margin call; the firm buys the assets you were forced to liquidate; and the firm soon after sells these same assets at a higher price after pocketing your margin call money. Models do not account for such devious shenanigans.

Remember the "most important investment graph." If it sounds too good to be true, it probably is. Askin's plight was similar to AIG's many years later. But during the financial crisis, many bankers deliberately obscured risks and knew or should have known they sold misrated products.

Investors want high returns. They will borrow money to buy CMOs, tulip bulbs, or shares of stock. The lenders "know" their client is good for the money because prices are rising and will continue to rise. In the end everyone learns the lesson for the umpteenth time. The only sure thing is that there is no such thing as a sure thing.

What do market professionals learn from these experiences? Not a great deal.

The early TRS market showed interesting parallels with the hedge fund/ mortgage debacle in the early 1990s. Several banks fell over themselves to provide financing for hedge funds. Hedge funds purchased highly leveraged transactions (HLTs). The leveraged loans originated from bank loan groups eager to open up a new investment base for their products. Banks paid the total return on these loans to hedge funds.

Hedge funds and mutual funds gained new access to the bank loan market. Prior to this, banks syndicated and underwrote loans. Most of the loans were (and often still are) held in bank portfolios. Loans have higher recovery rates than bonds and often have high returns relative to similar risks in the bond market. Banks, eager to broaden HLT market liquidity, found yield-hungry investors.

By receiving the total return in a loan swap, an investor creates a synthetic lending facility (SLF). The maturity of the SLF may not match that of the reference loan. SLFs may use either an investment-grade loan or an HLT as a reference asset. Hedge funds, with their high implied funding costs, participate in total return swaps using HLTs as the reference asset. The appealing features of a TRS referencing HLTs include the following:

- Loans are senior secured assets for the most part with high estimated recovery rates, which contributes to low price volatility.
- The transaction is off-balance sheet.
- HLTs are floating-rate instruments, so the netting is simple to calculate.
- Investors avoid the high administrative costs associated with direct management of a loan portfolio, such as tracking funding of revolving credit facilities or prepayments and amortization on term loans.
- As an investor books a collection of transactions, overall risk may decline. Diversified loan portfolios tend to have low volatilities.
- The TRS structure enables investors to use *leverage*.

LOAN TRS MECHANICS

The hedge fund investor receives all loan payments, including interest, commitment fees and all pro rata amortization (subject to adjustment for price changes). Fees may be split between the total return payer and the investor, however. The hedge fund pays SOFR plus a margin on the notional principal. As the loan amortizes, any period gain in price on the amortized amount relative to the initial loan price is paid to the investor. The investor pays the decline from the initial price on the amortized amount. This price adjustment may be netted with amortization, interest, and fee payments. At maturity or default, the reference loan is marked to market. Any gain in price on the remaining notional amount is paid to the investor. The investor pays any decrease in price.

The SLF or TRS on loans is similar to an investment in a sub participation in a loan while funding the purchase on a SOFR basis. The bank payer of the total return is the legal owner of the loan. The investor receiving the total return does not have voting rights and, therefore, does not have a say in potential loan restructuring. This can be a disadvantage; therefore, some banks have a "gentleman's agreement" that they will consult and vote according to the wishes of the total return receiver. An advantage to the investor is that this is an off-balance sheet transaction.

The terms of loans are different from those for bonds. Periodic amortization, tranching of loan maturities, and the combination of revolvers and term loans in a loan syndication can be confusing to novices. The following term sheet is a generic example of a one-year-maturity total return swap on all of the tranches of a newly syndicated loan for one-fourth of the entire loan. In this case, a bank is paying the total return to an investor. The investor essentially takes the risk on this package for one year, a period of time shorter than the term of the underlying loans. This idea can be adapted for just the revolver or for any of the tranches of a term loan, whether newly syndicated or traded in the secondary market.

This term sheet is for an investor with a high cost of funds. The spread of 100 basis points required as payment by the investor may be reduced if the investor agrees to give the payer of the total return swap upfront collateral. If the investor were more creditworthy and had a lower cost of funds, then the required spread might be greatly reduced, and no collateral required.

*****

TOTAL RETURN SWAP LOAN REFERENCE ASSET
Indicative Term Sheet

Transaction Overview: The Bank will pay the total return on 25 percent of the full commitment amount on the following basket of high yield loans (the "Reference Asset(s)") to the Total Return Receiver as consideration for receiving the payments shown below.

Reference Obligation(s)

Type of Borrowing: High Yield Borrower Senior Bank Facilities

Credit Agreement Dated: To be determined.

Senior Bank Facilities: Collectively the Revolving Credit Facility, a Term Loan A Facility, a Term Loan B Facility, a Term Loan C Facility, and a Term Loan D Facility.

For Each Loan Facility:

Principal: Up to USD XXX million as in credit agreement

Interest Rate: 1. Contract Rate plus x.xx% per annum or   2. SOFR plus x.xx% per annum

Final Maturities for Each Loan Facility:

Revolving Credit Facility: Six Years from closing date

Term Loan A Maturity: Six Years from Closing Date

Term Loan B Maturity: Seven Years from Closing Date

Term Loan C Maturity: Eight Years from Closing Date

Term Loan D Maturity: Nine Years from Closing Date

Initial Prices for Each Loan Facility:

Revolving Credit Facility: Par

Term Loan A: Par

Term Loan B: Par

Term Loan C: Par

Term Loan D: Par

Total Return Payer: The Bank

Total Return Receiver: Investor Hedge Fund

Closing Date:	As Soon As Practical
Trade Date:	Today
Effective Date:	Closing Date (Usually within five business days)
Termination Date:	The earlier of

1. One Year from the Effective Date; *or,*

2. Date of cancellation or permanent settlement in full of principal and interest on the Revolving Credit Facility, Term Loan A and Term Loan B and Term Loan C and Term Loan D; *or*

3. The Non-scheduled Termination Date, if any.

Investment Participation:	25%
Notional Amount:	The sum of the average daily Funded Commitment Amount of the Reference loan times 25% (the Investment Participation) times the Initial Price, where: Funded Commitment Amount as of any date is the Total Amount of Borrowings, the principal amounts of any drawings, outstanding under the Reference Loan. The Notional Amount may be reduced by mandatory and voluntary prepayments as outlined in the Credit Agreement.

Amortization based upon full Commitment (The Investor receives 25% of full Commitment):

Year	Term Loan A	Term Loan B	Term Loan C	Term Loan D
1	$0	$0	$0	$0
2	$6,000,000	$780,000	$780,000	$780,000
3	$30,000,000	$780,000	$780,000	$780,000
4	$36,000,000	$780,000	$780,000	$780,000
5	$36,000,000	$780,000	$780,000	$780,000
6	$36,000,000	$780,000	$780,000	$780,000
7	—	$74,100,000	$780,000	$780,000
8	—	—	$73,320,000	$780,000
9	—	—	—	$72,540,000
Totals	$144.000.000	$78.000.000	$78.000.000	$78.000.000

Prepayments:	Mandatory and voluntary prepayments may exist on the Senior Bank Facilities as discussed in the Credit Agreement

The Bank Total Return Payments:

On the Payment Date, The Bank will pay the Investor an amount equal to 25% × (The sum of any Interest Amounts, Commitment Fees, L/C Amounts, and the Ongoing Fee Amount, on the Reference Assets)

Additional Amounts:	On each Payment Date The Bank shall pay to Investor the positive amount, if any, equal to the sum of each Reference Loan of:
	Period Principal Prepayment for each Reference Loan × 25% × (100% - Initial Price for the Reference Loan)

Investor Payments:

Floating Payment:	On the Payment Date for each Period Investor pays an amount equal to:
	(Notional Amount - all Prepayments) × Floating Rate Index **plus 100 basis points** × A/360 where A is the actual number of days in The Period.
Additional Amounts:	On each Payment Date Investor shall pay to The Bank the positive amount, if any, equal to the product of:
	(Period Principal Prepayment for each Reference Loan) × 25% × (Most Recent Mark-to-Market − 100%), if positive.
Floating Rate Index:	Identical to Reference Obligation interest rate
Spread:	**100** basis points per annum
Period End Dates:	Reference Obligation Period End Dates
Payment Dates:	Two Business Days after Period End Date
Compounding Rate:	Investor Floating Rate Index plus **100 basis points** for the appropriate accrual period
Final Termination Payment:	Two New York Banking days after the Termination Date, at the option of The Bank the final exchange will consist of either:
	1. Physical Settlement:

The Bank makes Physical Delivery of the Reference Obligation equal to the Notional Amount to Investor.

Investor pays the sum of:

(Notional Amount of each Reference Loan) × Initial Price).

or

2.   Cash Settlement:

Investor pays The Bank the sum the Amount for each Reference Asset calculated as follows:

Notional Amount × (Most Recent Mark-to-Market − Initial Price), if positive;

or

The Bank pays Investor the sum of the Amount for each Reference Asset calculated as follows:

Notional Amount × (Initial Price − Most Recent Mark-to-Market), if Positive.

Non-scheduled Termination:

Date:

Two business days following the Notification Date, if any.

Payment:

As described in Final Termination Payment.

Notification Date:

If a Credit Event or Merger Event occurs during the term of this transaction, the Agent shall have the right to designate a Non-scheduled Termination Date by delivering notice (even if such notice occurs after the Maturity Date) to Investor of the occurrence of such Credit or Merger Event. Such notice must contain a description, in reasonable detail, of the facts giving rise to the Credit or Merger Event. Total Return Payment accruals shall terminate on such Notification Date, if any.

Credit Event:

Means with respect to the issuer of the Reference Obligation ("Reference Credit") any of the following which occurs on or prior to the Maturity Date:

1. A failure by the Reference Credit to make when due any payment under any Financial Obligation.

2. A default, event of default, or other similar condition or event occurs on the part of the Reference Credit under any Financial Obligation.

3. A waiver, deferral, restructuring, rescheduling, exchange, or other adjustment occurs in respect of any Financial Obligation and the effect of such adjustment is overall materially less favorable from a credit and risk perspective to the relevant creditor.

4. Bankruptcy.

5. Any violation of the Credit Agreement.

6. Downgrade.

7. Credit event upon merger.

8. Repudiation.

Merger Event:	An actual or publicly announced intended consolidation, amalgamation, substantial transfer of assets, or merger of the reference credit with another entity.
Financial Obligation:	With respect to the reference credit, any senior unsecured financial obligation incurred by the reference credit in any capacity.
Market Value:	On any day, with respect to the relevant reference obligation, the percentage equal to the unweighted arithmetic mean of the firm USD denominated bid prices (exclusive of any accrued but unpaid interest and expressed as a percentage of principal amount) for such reference obligation provided to the calculation agent on such day by not less than one and not more than five referenced dealers, including the bank, as such prices are available.
Suitability:	This transaction will be executed with an investor having such knowledge and experience in financial and business matters that he or she is capable of evaluating the merits and risks of the transaction.
Documentation:	Standard ISDA master agreement and swap confirmation.

Liquidity:	There may be no, or only a limited, secondary market for a transaction of this type.
Firm Unwind Prices:	The bank may quote (but is not legally obligated to quote) a firm price that the bank would pay or charge to unwind the transaction prior to maturity. A firm unwind price for a transaction of
	this type will be affected by the then-current level of the market, but it may also be affected by other factors A firm unwind price for a trans-action of this type can change significantly from day to day over the life of the transaction.
Periodic Pricing:	It is the current practice (but not a legal obligation) of the bank to provide to its client in a transaction of this type information in writing about the value of such transaction, upon request of the client
Calculation Agent:	The bank
Business Days	Days on which commercial banks and foreign exchange markets settle payments in London and New York.

The preceding term sheet is not a confirmation. Confirmations are up to 30 pages long and are modeled after the ISDA standard. The ISDA does not actually have a current standard for total return swaps or for loans as reference assets. Therefore, documents are negotiated in the spirit of ISDA guidelines. The confirmation is the document which counterparties regard as their legal agreement. These are usually couched in language much more precise and technical than the language in the term sheet. The confirmation will usually contain information not referenced in the term sheet. Detailed credit terms, including required upfront collateral, are generally included in the confirmation, not the term sheet.

The TRS is a convenient and efficient way for financial institutions to lay off the risk of existing loan portfolios. The borrower need never know that the bank is laying off its risk, and the bank can continue to have a profitable relationship with the borrower. In the event of an actual borrower default, if the TROR receiver takes delivery of the loan, the borrower would know at that time that the bank no longer held its loan. In that event, however, the bank will probably not be as concerned about the relationship implications of laying off the borrower's credit risk.

HEDGE FUNDS AND LEVERAGE

Total return swaps open up distribution in the loan market, and the TROR receiver continues to be an important element in the structure. When a bank lays off the credit risk of a loan by paying the total return to a hedge fund, how much risk does the bank reduce?

Figure 2.9 shows a total return swap using a B+ rated loan as the reference asset for a hedge fund investor. Let us look at potential one-year returns for a hedge fund that puts up 10 percent collateral to receive the total return of a $10 million principal amount of an HLT. The initial price of the HLT is par (100). Let us assume that the collateral is invested at 6 percent per annum. Table 2.5 shows the one-year total return for different loan prices ignoring potential margin call adjustments to the upfront collateral. The coupon amount shown in the table is the net spread earned by the hedge fund after financing costs. The gross coupon is assumed to be SOFR+325 bps, and the hedge fund is required to pay SOFR+75 bps with 10 percent upfront collateral. The total return for the hedge fund is calculated based on the actual cash collateral amount posted, $1 million. The hedge fund enjoys the positive effects of leveraged high returns when the asset performs well or increases in value. When the asset declines in value, however, the hedge fund returns feel the negative effects of leverage.

Credit managers face a dilemma. Banks are in the business of providing finance and generally want to lay off risk in a cost-effective manner. Credit derivatives traders, eager to book income, want to lend money to hedge funds because the spread of SOFR+75 basis points, and sometimes as high as SOFR+100 basis points, is a greater spread than the banks can get from other counterparties, such as U.S. banks, insurance companies, or investment banks.

There is a reason for the high funding cost demanded of the hedge funds, however. Hedge funds do not disclose other assets on their balance sheets.

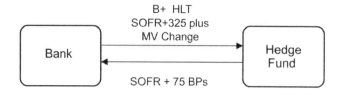

Total Return* = Interest + % age of Commitment Fees
+ (Final Value* - Original Value)

Hedge Fund Posts 10% Collateral on a $10,000,000 loan balance.

* Total Return is paid on remaining balance.
** Final Value at amortization is the current Market Value calculated on the
amortized amount.

FIGURE 2.9   TRS – Reference Asset Is a Loan

The credit manager evaluating the credit of a hedge fund has nothing
to go on. There is no way of knowing how many of these transactions have
been done by the hedge fund. On the one hand, more transactions imply
greater diversification. On the other hand, the credit manager has no way to
determine how much leverage the hedge fund employs. Some hedge funds
are required to put up only 5 percent upfront collateral.

Banks demanding 20 percent upfront collateral often find that hedge
funds will do the TRS with another bank who will give more favorable
collateral terms. Banks will often require a daily mark-to-market on the
underlying asset, and often there is a "cure" period, which allows the hedge
fund time to come up with additional collateral. Not every bank requires a
daily mark-to-market, however.

If a bank enters into a transaction with a hedge fund, what benefit, if
any, does the bank get from a reduced joint probability of default? Is there
a reduced probability? Does the upfront collateral suffice to enhance the
credit quality of the hedge fund counterparty to compensate the bank in the
event of default? If the HLT defaults, is the price volatility low enough so
that the upfront collateral will cover the decline in value?

A hedge fund counterparty seems to be a perversion of the concept of credit
derivatives. Do I view the hedge fund as a single A? Most banks would
emphatically say not. Do I view the hedge fund as BB+? The problem is, no

TABLE 2.5 HLT TRS: Rate of Return Scenarios After One Year,
$10,000,000 Notional, 10% ($1,000,000) Collateral

Loan Price in One Year	Loan Coupon LIBOR + 250 bps	Gain (Loss) on Loan	Interest on Collateral (at 6% per annum)	Rate of Return (% per annum)
102	$250,000	$200,000	$60,000	51.0%
100	$250,000	0	$60,000	31.0%
96	$250,000	($400,000)	$60,000	(9.0%)
92	$250,000	($800,000)	$60,000	(49.0%)
88	$250,000	($1,200,000)	$60,000	(89.0%)

one really knows. Hedge funds do not disclose enough information to make this evaluation.

If I want to lay off risk in the portfolio, to what degree am I hedged when the counterparty is a hedge fund? What sort of assumption can I make for a jointly supported rating?

I believe that there is no benefit from a jointly supported rating when a hedge fund is the "guarantor." The protection provided by the hedge fund is phantom protection. The only benefit is from the upfront collateral, which reduces my exposure in the event of a default on the underlying asset. If a hedge fund puts up only 5 percent collateral, that is not much of a reduction in my overall exposure. The unfortunate truth is that in the event of default of the reference asset, I do not know whether the hedge fund will be in a position to come up with the additional money. Will the hedge fund seek comfort in bankruptcy?

The fact that banks are willing to do this business with hedge funds illustrates how difficult it is for banks to generate income from their traditional investment-grade loan business. Investment-grade loans show a dismally low return on capital. Unlike the CMO scenario, banks do not need to provide financing in order to find buyers for their loans. There is high demand for HLTs from investors and banks seeking collateral for collateralized loan obligations. The primary goal is not increased distribution. The primary goal is to book higher spread income. The question remains whether the enhanced spread income of SOFR+75 bps and more that hedge funds are willing to pay as a funding cost is enough to compensate banks for the credit risk.

HEDGE FUNDS AND LEVERAGED EXPOSURE TO SPREADS

When hedge funds engage in fixed-income arbitrage transactions, they often attempt to create leveraged exposure to asset swap spreads by buying an asset, financing the asset, and paying fixed in an interest rate swap transaction. The combination of the long position (buying the fixed-coupon asset) and the short position (paying fixed in an interest rate swap to receive floating) creates a market-rate, asset swap package. By financing the asset, the hedge fund then creates a leveraged exposure to asset swap spreads.

Let us look at an example of this transaction. A hedge fund buys a 30- year German-government Bund and pays fixed in a 30-year euro swap. If interest rates increase, the hedge fund will have a gain in the swap position and an equivalent loss in the bond position, the difference being the gain or the loss on the swap spread. The fixed coupon on the bond offsets the payment of the fixed

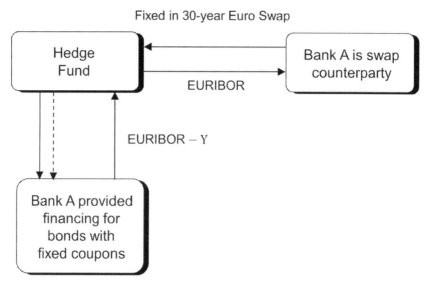

Fixed in 30-year Euro Swap

Example for a rising-rate scenario: If rates rise, the price of the Bunds declines, but the market value of the swap increases. The hedge fund would owe the bank Final Value – Initial Value on the bonds for the TRS (represented by the dashed arrow), but this credit risk is offset by the hedge fund's gain in swap market value.

FIGURE 2.10 Hedge Fund Spread Play: Rising Rate Scenario

leg of the swap. The floating leg of the swap offsets the financing cost of the bond. The financing of the bond could be done with term repurchase agreements or a bond forward; but because we are concerned with a total return swap, we will assume that that is how the hedge fund will finance the asset. The hedge fund will usually obtain funding at some discount to EURIBOR, which I will define as Y. Figure 2.10 illustrates the cash flows.

The bank's credit exposure to the hedge fund on the 30-year euro swap is huge. Many banks will decline to do this swap even with a collateral agreement and mutual termination provision. The TRORS seems to mitigate most of this credit risk. Because total return swaps are usually executed under an ISDA master, this transaction can be combined in one confirm. The credit risk on both the long and the short sides of this transaction offset each other.

The bank would take further steps to ask for frequent mark-to-market periods on the asset swap package (often daily, but at a maximum of every three months), for initial margin on the asset swap package, and for a one-day "cure" period on the collateral to further minimize risk.

This is a risky transaction from an operational point of view. The bank has risk if the hedge fund tries to unwind any leg of this transaction. This is known as "fire hydrant" risk, or the risk of "lifting a leg." For instance, if the hedge fund lifts the TRS leg of the transaction, the bank will have no offset for the credit risk on the swap. The bank should attempt to get the hedge fund to agree that the entire transaction must unwind in entirety. This condition should be explicitly spelled out in the confirm, and risk management must have a means of monitoring and enforcing this condition.

RELATIVE VALUE AND BALANCE SHEET MANAGEMENT

Often a mispricing exists between loans and debt markets. In the mid-1990s, for instance, banks lent money to Italy at a rate of SOFR+45 bps, whereas Italian government dollar-denominated debt traded at SOFR+25 bps. This is a dislocation in the pricing of capital structure.

Often subordinated debt may trade at a tighter spread than loan yields do. Subordinated debt is generally more volatile than loan pricing. It is generally nonamortizing and has a much longer maturity than loans do. The price of subordinated debt will therefore be much more volatile than that of a loan. It is possible, however, to construct an asset swap from subordinated debt to make this debt a synthetic floating rate note (FRN). The synthetic FRN has much less price volatility than a fixed rate bond because the coupon resets frequently and the price hovers near par. In the absence of a general change in market credit spreads and in the absence of a change in the credit spread of the issuer, the synthetic FRN will have the same price characteristics as a par floater. Counterparties interested in receiving the total return on subordinated debt will probably be much more willing to do this if the price volatility due to a change in market interest rates is dampened by the creation of the synthetic subordinated debt FRN.

If an investor, such as an insurance company, owns subordinated debt trading at spreads tighter than the same issuer's bank loans, the insurance company can arbitrage the credit risk. The transaction to do in this case is to pay the total return on the subordinated-debt, asset swap package.

The insurance company lays off the subordinated credit risk of the issuer. The insurance company then simultaneously receives the total return on a bank loan to the issuer. The credit quality of the bank loan is higher than that of the subordinated debt, and the insurance company can therefore receive the total return on a higher notional amount. For instance, for every $20 million of subordinated debt, the insurance company may be willing to receive the total return of $30 million of the bank loan debt. The insurance company may view the net credit risk position as equal; however, the insurance company can enjoy a pickup in income.

Figure 2.11 shows a transaction in which an insurance company pays the total return to a high-credit quality bank, which funds at SOFR-20 bps. The bank receives the total return on the $20 million subordinated-debt, asset swap package and receives a payment stream of SOFR$+200$ bps until the maturity of the transaction if there is no default on the subordinated debt. The insurance company then agrees to pay SOFR$+25$ bps to the loan desk of another bank and receives the total return on a term loan with an initial balance of $30 million. The insurance company receives a payment stream of SOFR$+300$ bps until the maturity of the transaction if there is no default on the bank loan.

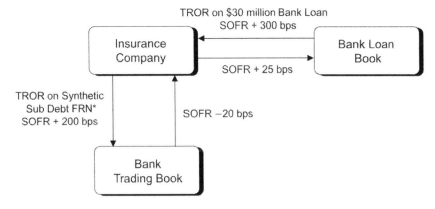

* This is the total rate of return on a par asset swap package consisting of the subordinated debt and a swap of the fixed coupons for floating.

FIGURE 2.11 Subordinated Debt / Bank Loan Arbitrage

Although the insurance company pays a higher cost to receive the bank loan total returns, the higher spread of the bank loan more than makes up for this. In addition, the insurance company levers the return by receiving the total return on a higher notional amount. In this case, before taking into account the higher notional amount of the bank loan, the insurance company has a net positive spread of 55 basis points. Taking into account the notional of the bank loan, which is 1.5 times higher than that of the subordinated debt, the insurance company earns a net spread of 192.5 basis points.

Bank loans are prepayable, amortized, and often have final maturities and average lives shorter than the remaining maturity of subordinated debt. The insurance company can mitigate this maturity mismatch if it is willing to accept a reduced payment from the bank trading book in order to have the right to periodically adjust the notional of the TRS on the subordinated-debt synthetic FRN.

Total return swaps also give investors the ability to take views on entire sectors of the market. Investors can receive the total return of an equity index, the technology sector of an equity index, a high-yield bond index, or any sector of the market for which an index is available and a counterparty is willing to pay the total return.

Investors can take views on the relative value of different sectors of the market as well. Figure 2.12 illustrates how an investor can short the 10-year constant maturity treasury (CMT) and go long a broad-based high-yield index to take a view on the relative performance of the high-yield index and the U.S. 10-year treasury. The investor has the view that the high-yield index will outperform the 10-year CMT. The bank payer of the high-yield index may want to reduce exposure to the high-yield market or may be laying off the other side of a transaction in which it receives the high-yield index.

The bank in the above example may have used the TRS as a balance sheet management tool. In general, total return swaps are underused as balance sheet tools when banks swap credit risk. Banks are more than happy to offer bonds for purchase to another bank and then receive the total return on the swap. This is a method of financing a position and getting bonds off the balance sheet. Banks are less willing to swap risks, however, as there is no permanent net reduction in credit exposure for a transaction that is shorter than the maturity of the reference assets. Nonetheless, this method of cooperating to diversify credit exposures is a transaction that makes sense for banks. Figure 2.13 illustrates an underused market transaction in which a European bank reduces credit concentration to a low-yielding investment grade European corporate bank loan and a U.S. bank reduces exposure to a low-yielding investment-grade U.S. corporate bank loan.

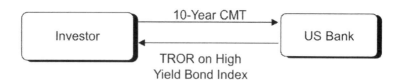

Investor can increase exposure to high-yield spreads and benefit from a tightening versus the ten-year US treasury by paying the 10-year Constant Maturity Treasury and receiving the total rate of return on a high-yield bond index.

FIGURE 2.12 Spread Play: High Yield Index versus 10-Year Treasury

The market is not as willing to recognize the value of transactions in which no money changes hands but portfolio risk is diversified. One of the barriers to this recognition is that on a portfolio basis, it is difficult for banks to see the small incremental benefit. The interest in the case-by-case transaction from banks is almost exclusively a one-sided sale of exposure to gain relief from a full credit line.

CREDIT EXPOSURE AND THE CONDITIONAL PROBABILITY OF DEFAULT

If a bank owns a reference obligation on the bank book, it might use a TRS to reduce both market risk and credit exposure to an underlying obligor. The internal debate will usually center around how much credit exposure the bank has after doing the TRS. In addition, the bank must determine to whom the bank has this credit exposure. This is not obvious to the internal credit-and-risk committees of many banks. In particular, management of the credit exposure lines of the bank book and recognition of the benefit of the conditional (also sometimes erroneously called the "joint") probability of default are still debated among banks that rank among the top five in size in their respective countries.

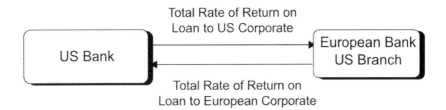

Banks can reduce over concentration of credit risk by swapping exposures off-balance sheet. Notional may or may not be one to one depending on perception of credit risk and compensation for credit exposure.

FIGURE 2.13 Balance Sheet Exposure Management

I will digress for another word on market terminology, although non theoreticians may want to skip this paragraph. Consider the purchase of credit default protection in which Bank A buys credit default protection from Bank B on the loan obligation of Reference Obligor, R. If only R defaults, Bank A is still protected by Bank B. If Bank B defaults but R has not defaulted, Bank A can theoretically replace the credit default protection with another protection seller. Bank A is concerned about the scenario in which R defaults, given that Bank B has defaulted. It may be a source of annoyance to statisticians that the credit derivatives market often refers to the former scenario as the *joint* probability of default when in reality we mean the *conditional* probability of default. Throughout this book, I have generally adopted the market terminology. The J.P. Morgan CreditMetrics Monitor published in the third quarter of 1998 gave tables of joint credit transition probabilities and conditional probabilities. Assume Bank B has a probability of default of 0.04 percent. The probability that R migrates to default is the marginal probability of default of 0.17 percent. For a correlation of 0 percent, the joint probability of default is 0.0001 percent. For a correlation of 30 percent, the joint probability of default is 0.0011 percent. The conditional probability given a default of Bank B for zero correlation is 0.17 percent. For 30 percent correlation, the conditional probability is 2.69 percent. The conditional probability is higher than the joint probability for a given correlation. The bank book assumes that 100 percent of the loan value is applied against a credit line, so applying credit for the lower conditional probability of default is a tremendous benefit versus the current bank book treatment.

Although there is still no market standard, I sense a trend. Most banks for bank book purposes will show $100 million of credit exposure for a loan to a reference obligor. How much should a bank reduce this exposure when a bank buys credit default protection on a loan to the reference obligor?

I believe most banks will eliminate the entire exposure for the $100 million loan from the credit line of the reference obligor. The credit line of the counterparty, which receives the TROR, is then reduced by the amount of credit exposure resulting from the TRS. But this credit exposure is significantly lower than the original $100 million credit exposure charged to the line of the reference obligor who issued the original reference obligation.

This is because many banks recognize a much-reduced credit exposure because the conditional probability of default between the reference obligor and the counterparty is much lower than one.

The challenge of calculating the conditional probability of default is finding data that are acceptable to all the internal committees who want to have a say in your calculation method. While you may never reach an agreement, if you did have the data, the following approach is usually viewed as reasonable.

Let us review some of the features of a TRS that will affect any calculation approach. First, you can decide either to accept the counterparty and the underlying credit risk, the obligor, or to reject the transaction. This means you must have some view on the default probability of the reference obligor, on the default probability of the counterparty, on the correlation of the default probability of the reference obligor and the counterparty, and on the market risk or market volatility of the reference obligation. Considering a basket of reference obligors instead of a single asset can further complicate the transaction. If you choose to do a basket transaction, correlation is an important consideration, and you will try to create the most diverse basket possible to minimize specific risk.

Besides your choice in doing the transaction at all, you have further input to the structure of the transaction. You can minimize credit exposure and risk by increasing the frequency of the mark-to-market periods in the TRS. This increase in frequency will decrease the joint probability of default, the event risk, and the market risk, or price risk, of the transaction.

The joint probability of default describing the event risk is defined by the following equation. Note that we are actually calculating the conditional probability of default of the asset, given the probability of default of the counterparty. It is only under this scenario that risk exists. If the counterparty alone defaulted, you could replace the counterparty with another—at least that is the theory.

This formula is easy to understand but producing formulas is not the main issue in determining the value of credit risk. The main issue is the data. Where do you get the data for the default probability of the assets, the default probability of the counterparty, and the default correlations between the assets (also between assets if it is a basket structure) and the counterparty?

$$P_{(u|c)} = P_{(u)} + \rho_{u,c} \sqrt{\frac{(P_{(u)})(1 - P_{(u)})(1 - P_{(c)})}{(P_{(c)})}}$$

where $P_{(u|c)}$ =   Conditional Default Probability of underlying Asset
                         Dependent on default probability of counterparty
        $P_{(u)}$ =   Probability of default of underlying asset
        $\rho_{u,c}$ =   Correlation of default between asset and counterparty
        $P_{(c)}$ =   Probability of Default of Counterparty

As we said before, ratings agencies such as Moody's and S8cP provide default probabilities per ratings class, though they lack firm specific data. Alternatively, you can use estimates provided by experts in your own institution. That presupposes you can get experts to agree on the treatment of the data, itself a major undertaking.

Data from the firm founded by Stephen Kealhofer, John McQuown, and Oldrich Vasicek (KMV) is gaining wide acceptance. KMV has data on more than 17,000 firms. KMV generates default probabilities and default correlations by modeling asset values against the relative level of debt for a firm. KMV assumes that when the asset value falls below that debt level, the firm defaults. The distance away from that point is measured and expressed as the expected default frequency (EDF; we will discuss this further when we address capital issues).

If you get to the point that your data are accepted and your institution adopts a formula such as the one given for $P(u, c)$, you have another decision to make. For what time period is the formula valid? Most default frequency data are available for periods no shorter than six months or one year. Is it proper to scale this by the square root of time? Should you use a different time factor, depending on the frequency of resets of your TRS? There is no evidence to support scaling by the square root of time. Indeed, for credits below investment grade, scaling with the square root of time can be very misleading because noninvestment-grade credits near bankruptcy may actually improve with time if their credit difficulties were due to factors that resolve with business success and time. Nonetheless, for investment-grade credits the temptation is great to scale with the square root of time, and several banks currently do this. Once you have decided on your calculation of the joint probability of default, you will want to calculate the credit expo-sure. The following equation describes the credit exposure one would apply to the notional amount of the swap. This is the event risk associated with the swap. Because you have already calculated the conditional probabilities and default correlations across all the assets and the counterparty, you can use these results to compute the exposure of the swap.

$$UL_{(u,c)} = \sqrt{\sum \rho_{ij} n_i n_j \sqrt{\frac{(P_{(ui \mid c)})(1 - P_{(ui,c)})(P_{(uj \mid c)})(1 - P_{(uj,c)})}{(1 - P_{(c)})}}}$$

where $UL_{(u,c)}$ = Unexpected Loss or Credit Event Risk (Default)

$\quad P_{(ui \mid c)}$ = Probability of default of asset i

$\quad P_{(uj \mid c)}$ = Probability of default of asset j

$\quad P_{(ui,c)}$ = Joint probability default of asset i and counterparty

$\quad P_{(uj,c)}$ = Joint probability default of asset j and counterparty

$\quad P_{(uj,c)}$ = Probability of counterparty default

$\quad P_{(c)}$ = Probability of default of counterparty

$\quad n_i$ = Asset i's weight in the portfolio

$\quad n_j$ = Asset j's weight in the portfolio

Now that you have calculated the exposure, you can multiply the exposure by the notional amount of the swap. You have now established the credit exposure for the swap with respect to event risk.

MARKET RISK/PRICE RISK

Although market price risk is the other credit exposure component, it is often tracked separately and reported for regulatory and internal management purposes as value-at-risk (VaR). We need the volatility of the asset or the basket of assets in order to calculate VaR.

Let me generalize this approach for a fixed-income asset and then ad-dress the special case of the TRS, which can be viewed as a collateralized FRN. First you must choose the time horizon over which you want to calculate the volatility and the VaR. These time horizons are drastically different. For the volatility calculation, you need a time series of data for the calculation. We will get back to that in a moment. You also need to decide the confidence level for your VaR. Notice we are talking not about confidence *intervals* but confidence *levels*. Furthermore, we generally make the assumption that we are using a lognormal distribution, an assumption that may cause you further unease. After you determine the volatility and the confidence level, you plug them into the following equation:

$$\text{Confidence level percentile} = e^{-\sigma\sqrt{t}*c} -1$$

where σ = Volatility of Assets
           t = Time between resets
           c = Factor corresponding to the chosen confidence level

For the 95th percentile (1.645 SD), the result implies that your price movement would exceed this value on the loss side only 1.645 times, or twice if you round up, for every 100 trading days. Your formula would look as follows:

$$95^{th} \text{ percentile} = e^{-\sigma\sqrt{t}*1.645} -1$$

Where σ =   Volatility of Assets
           t =   Time between resets

For the 99th percentile (2.33 SD), the result implies that your price movement on the loss side would exceed this value no more than once for every 100 trading days. Your formula would look as follows:

$$99^{th} \text{ percentile} = e^{-\sigma\sqrt{t}*2.33} -1$$

where σ = Volatility of Assets
           t = Time between resets

We still have not calculated the volatility of the assets, however. While there are many ways to calculate the volatility, it is probably a good idea to step back for a moment and review the general approach. Your specific approach will depend on the amount and the frequency of the data available to you and on the application.

Volatility as a Risk Measure

We tend to retreat to familiar mathematics when trying to describe risk. Because variance and volatility are such key concepts in any discussion of risk, it may be useful to step back and review a general method for calculating these risk parameters. Variance of an asset's or a portfolio's return or price change is usually used to describe the price risk of a portfolio. You may recall that *variance* is simply a statistical measure of the dispersion of a return from its average return level for a specific period of time. We generally make an assumption about the probability distribution. Most practitioners assume a normal distribution because the mathematics is well known.

For a given probability density function *f(x)*, variance is defined as follows:

$$\sigma^2 = \int_{-\infty}^{+\infty} (x-\mu)^2 f(x)dx$$

where μ is the distribution's mean. If I had all of the data and the actual distribution, I wouldn't have to approximate the distribution. I could just examine the actual distribution and draw my conclusions from that. Of course, we usually never have the actual distribution *f(x)*, so we must use that actual sample data to try to approximate the distribution. For some time series o of returns $(R_1,...,R_n)$, sample variance is:

$$s^2 = \frac{1}{n-1} \sum_{i=1}^{n} (x_i - \mu)^2$$

where μ is now the sample mean, or the average return over time periods 1 to *n*. The square root of the variance is the standard deviation of the returns. The market usually refers to this as the volatility. This is most properly symbolized as σ, but we will use the more common symbol for volatility, σ.

TABLE 2.6   Weekly Prices

Week	Underlying Price	$\ln(P_i/P_{i-1})$	Mean	Deviation from Mean	Deviation Squared
0	102.00		0.0009756		
1	103.00	0.0097562		0.0087806	0.0000771
2	100.00	-0.0295588		-0.0305344	0.0009324
3	100.50	0.0049875		0.0040119	0.0000161
4	100.70	0.0019881		0.0010125	0.0000010
5	104.00	0.0322451		0.0312695	0.0009778
6	99.00	-0.0492710		-0.0502467	0.0025247
7	99.50	0.0050378		0.0040622	0.0000165
8	99.90	0.0040120		0.0030364	0.0000092
9	104.00	0.0402212		0.0392456	0.0015402
10	103.00	-0.0096619		-0.0106375	0.0001132

Example: You have 10 weeks of bond price data and want to calculate the annualized price volatility. (In practice, you would have much more data and probably use daily closing prices, but I'm using a small sample to make this example easier to follow.) How would you determine the annualized price volatility?

You might first calculate the natural log of the daily price changes. If your current price is P_i, and the previous week's price is P_{i-1}, the natural log of the daily price changes is $\ln(P_i/P_{i-1})$.

From these price changes, you calculate the mean, or μ. For n observations, this is simply:

$$\mu = \sum_{i=1}^{n} x_i$$

Now you calculate the square of the deviation from the mean and the variance from the formula for variance stated earlier. Table 2.6 shows the results you will get for the weekly prices given in the table.

The sum of the squares of the deviation from the mean is 0.0062082. The variance is simply 0.0062082/9, or 0.0006898. The standard deviation, or volatility, is the square root of the variance, or 0.02626399. We recall that annualized volatility is simply the standard deviation times the square root of the time period.

Because we used weekly prices, the time interval between prices is 7 and the time interval is 365/7, or 52.14. The annualized volatility is $0.02626399 \times (52.14)^{0.5}$. Therefore, the annualized volatility is 0.1896, or 18.96 percent. Some assets, such as investment-grade floating rate loans, will generally have lower annualized implied price volatilities because volatility for periods shorter than a year can be calculated from annualized volatility by multiplying by the square root of time. For instance, if the mark-to-market is weekly, we would use 0.02626399, or 2.6 percent. This is why frequent mark-to-market periods are often used for total return swaps.

Now that you have all of the components, you can calculate the credit exposure due to both price risk and event risk using the following formula:

$$\text{Credit Exposure} = \text{Notional Amount} \times$$
$$(\text{Price Risk at your chosen confidence level}) + \text{Event Risk}$$

This is the amount of credit exposure one would apply to the line of the counterparty, which is the credit protection provider.

The reduction of credit line for the assets in the basket is another matter. Many banks apply a credit exposure reduction to the worst credit in the basket only. If one is using investment-grade credits, however, it is often difficult to distinguish the "worst" credit in the basket. Banks have a lot of discretion on how they handle their internal credit lines with respect to basket transactions, and as yet there is no market consensus.

The preceding analysis does not take into account the possibility of credit spread migration. You may have the view that the market prices the possibility of credit spread migration into the price risk. Currently, most practitioners do not seem to share this view. They feel that models such as CreditManager account for this possibility over a time horizon of three months or more, but market price volatilities do not seem to imbed this information in short-term price moves. Most practitioners are willing to ignore this problem for regulatory reporting purposes that typically have a one-day or a ten-day time horizon for reporting VaR. For credit exposure purposes, if the reset of the TRS is monthly, the possibility of credit spread migration is usually ignored. For longer reset periods, some practitioners attempt to account for credit spread migration, but many do not.

MATURITY MISMATCHES: LOANS AND SYNTHETIC CLOS

When financial institutions begin using credit derivatives, they often claim that they do not have maturity mismatches when they do a TRS or a credit default swap. "While that may be the intent, maturity mismatches may occur due to the structure of the underlying reference obligation. For instance, if a bank buys two years of protection in the form of a credit derivative against a two-year loan, in the beginning the reference asset and the credit default hedge are matched in maturity. After one year, it is remembered that the issuer of the reference asset has the option to extend the loan for an additional year. If this is done, the final year of the loan will not have credit default protection. The loan originally had a two-year maturity, but now the loan has a three-year maturity. The credit default protection had no feature to allow extension of the protection. A maturity mismatch is the result. This poses a problem for credit line managers. Do you credit the remaining first year (originally the second year) with credit protection knowing that you have default risk in the final year? How do you reserve capital for this credit risk? Could you look at this as a forward credit obligation? None of these questions have been satisfactorily resolved by most financial institutions. It is worth addressing these issues early on as the issues become even more pressing later. Once an institution engages in a synthetic CLO, it may find that protection is provided for a fixed period of time; but credit obligations may be added that exceed the maturity of the original protection.

A side effect of the issue of the structural issue mentioned earlier in the case of the extendable loan is that banks are starting to think more seriously about how they price these imbedded options in their loans. Today, most lenders do not attempt to rigorously price these features, albeit they have real economic value. The cost of purchasing credit protection shines a bright light on the value of the ability to extend a loan. This may force banks to use option pricing models to justify the costs they assign to the imbedded options in loan documentation. Although it is not an accounting requirement, there is a growing trend to mark to market loan portfolios. J.P. Morgan currently marks its loan portfolio to market, and many U.S. banks are attempting to follow suit. In a short period of time, this will be deemed a bank best practice. But what do we mean by marking to market? To do this properly, one must be able to assign a price to the imbedded options in loan documentation. I predict increased demand for quantitative skills and for better models in loan portfolio pricing and in loan syndications.

MF GLOBAL'S TRIPARTY REPO-TO-MATURITY: TRS

The Federal Reserve Bank of New York announced that it suspended MF Global Holdings, the largest non-bank Futures Commission Merchant, as a primary dealer in U.S. Treasury securities the morning of Monday, Halloween, October 31, 2011. Trading in MF Global shares were halted. MF Global had just declared bankruptcy. It was the biggest financial collapse since Lehman Brothers imploded in September 2008.

Futures traders were aghast; the exchange-traded futures markets were in turmoil. MF Global's customers were stunned to discover their accounts frozen; nearly $1 billion of their money had been impermissibly transferred from their accounts to meet margin calls on triparty "repo-to-maturity" (RTM) trades crafted by Jon Corzine, MF Global's Chairman of the Board and CEO since March 2010. Corzine resigned on November 4, 2011.

Good God! How did MF Global, with a multi-year history of scandal win the coveted role as a primary dealer of U.S. Treasuries, part of the Fed's Open Market Operations, in the first place? The answer is that Jon Corzine, recruited to save money-losing MF Global, knew the Fed's William Dudley, a key member of the Fed's Open Market Committee, from their days at Goldman Sachs. The Fed approved MF Global's status as a primary dealer, a participant in the Fed's Open Market Operations, less than one year after Jon Corzine arrived on the scene with government influence (Figure 2.14). Jon Corzine was the former CEO of Goldman Sachs, former U.S. senator (Democrat, New Jersey), and 54th governor of New Jersey before losing re-election and joining MF Global. Crucially, he was a "bundler," a huge fundraiser of aggregated political contributions for Democrats.

FIGURE 2.14 MF Global Bankruptcy October 31, 2011

According to the Center for Responsive Politics, altogether, he and his first and second wives contributed $917,000 to Democratic committees and candidates over a 20-year period. He rallied his Wall Street friends in 2011 to bundle $500-600 thousand dollars for then President Obama's re-election campaign.

Three months after MF Global's bankruptcy, Jon Corzine and his fellow MF Global officers testified that they did not know what happened to customers' money, assets that they were obliged to keep in segregated accounts, away from MF Global's greedy paws. *The Wall Street Journal* wrote that the money "vaporized."

Bankruptcy trustees threatened MF Global's intermediary counterparties, JPMorgan—MF Global's largest secured creditor—and Bank of New York Mellon, with litigation. The banks negotiated settlements with the bankruptcy trustees. It took the trustees two years to make MF Global's customers whole. Farmers and ranchers use futures to hedge their products. For some of MF Global's 26,000 customers, it was too late; their businesses were ruined. Many more hung on but endured financial hardship. Independent brokers and other clients and traders who did business with MF Global had to scramble for credit, since they did not have access to the assets that MF Global had transferred away.

In December 2011, then President Obama reportedly returned direct contributions from Corzine and his second wife: $70,000 to the Democratic National Committee and Obama's campaign. Democrats kept the big bundle.

Why didn't the Commodities Futures Trading Commission (CFTC) act to protect MF Global's customers as it had protected customers of other firms in the past? The CFTC "always" moved customer money before a Futures Commission Merchant (FCM) declared bankruptcy. But not this time. Gary Gensler, Jon Corzine's former Goldman Sachs colleague and then head of the CFTC knew MF Global had a history of rogue trading. Its risk management history was poor. Moreover, MF Global disclosed the off-balance sheet trades and the risks in its 10K of March 31, 2011. Since then, the trades had moved against a financially weak MF Global, and that meant MF Global had to meet margin calls.

MF Global's margin calls were a chief factor in its report of a record loss of almost $192 million for the quarter ending September 30, 2011. By the end of October, the combination of a $90 million August legal settlement against MF Global coming due, increased capital calls by the Financial Industry Regulatory Authority (FINRA), and margin hikes from counterparties worried rating agencies.

On October 24, 2011, seven days before its Halloween bankruptcy declaration, MF Global's chief financial officer sent a letter to S&P with the claim: "MF Global's capital and liquidity has never been stronger." No one sensible would accept that statement at face value. S&P said it might cut MF Global's ratings.

On Thursday, October 27, 2011, The New York Times' Dealbook published an article by Mikehal De La Merced and Kevin Roose titled: "MF Global Fights to Stay Afloat After Two Credit Downgrades." It might as well have been an engraved invitation to the CFTC to act. That day, Moody's downgraded MF Global from Baa2 to Baa3, the lowest investment grade rating, and that rating was still too high. A further downgrade would have triggered greater margin calls for MF Global and it was already desperate, drawing every credit line it could. Gary Gensler, where were you when MF Global's customers needed you?

On Sunday, October 30, 2011, Corzine sat down with Interactive Brokers to negotiate a sale. In the days before and during the weekend, money impermissably flowed out of the accounts of MF Global's customers to satisfy MF Global's creditors. Suspecting something was horribly wrong, Interactive Brokers walked away from the negotiating table.

After using his personal email account to "monitor" MF Global with CFTC employees up until the banruptcy, after MF Global became a global scandal, two days after the bankruptcy Gary Gensler suddenly felt the need to consult with ethics advisors and commissioners. Only then did he recuse himself. The Inspector General's report of May 2013, faulted him for it.

On December 14, 2011, Representative Marcy Kaptur (Democrat, Ohio) read a special order into the U.S. Congressional Record:

> The fact that "customer accounts were not intact," as [CFTC] Commissioner Sommers described it, means that someone took other people's money. I believe most of us would call that theft. Even if some of the money is recovered by the bankruptcy process, that does not alter the fact that the process by which customer accounts were violated broke the law.

Kaptur's fellow Democrats gave Corzine an easy time in Congressional hearings about the MF Global collapse. Then President Obama had stumped for Jon Corzine before Corzine lost his 2009 gubernatorial re-election bid. Obama's then vice president Joe Biden did, too. Biden joined Corzine on stage and gushed, "he's the smartest guy that I know in terms of the economy and on finance, I really mean this."

Corzine's Hail Mary trade didn't work out because his firm didn't have enough capital to carry the trade to maturity. It is not enough to be right. One must meet interim margin calls before one can reap the winnings of this type of leveraged trade. Corzine knew or should have known this. He once ran the fixed income trading desk at Goldman Sachs.

A total return swap looks nearly identical to Corzine's triparty "repo-to-maturity" except for some fudging around the end dates (see Figure 2.15).

You'll recall that repo transactions are on balance sheet and total return swaps are off balance sheet transactions. The softheaded accountants and regulators who allowed off-balance sheet treatment for Corzine's triparty repo transactions had egg on their faces when MF Global imploded. At the time, credit derivatives with labels such as total return swaps spooked regulators.

It was cynically politic to give Corzine's trades the form-over-substance label of "repo-to-maturity."The assets that Corzine leveraged and funded were treated as a sale to his counterparty. MF Global retained the price and default risk of $6.3 billion (later reported as havnig grown to over $7 billion)

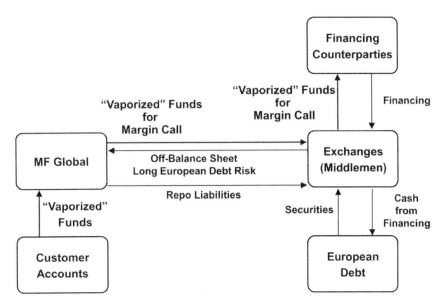

Adapted and simplified from Morrison & Foerster LLP, Attorneys for the Chapter 11 Trustee, 2013, "Report of Investigation of Louis J. Freeh, Chapter 11 Trustee of MF Global Holdings Ltd., *et al.,*" *In re MF Global Holdings Ltd., et al.,* Debtors, United States Bankruptcy Court for the Southern District of New York, Case No. 11-15059 (MG), April 4. P. 33.

FIGURE 2.15 MF Global's Triparty Repo-to-Maturity Gone Wrong

of the sovereign debt of Belgium, Italy, Spain, Portugal, and Ireland.

Prices of these securities were highly volatile in 2011 due to an increase in the perceived credit risk of this debt. MF Global was reportedly leveraged between 35:1 to 40:1 against the sovereign portfolio. That's a whopping amount of leverage.

Corzine may have hoped that he could somehow meet margin calls and ride out the volatility to maturity. At maturity, he would "buy back" the bonds with the par amount the bonds paid at maturity—if they didn't default in the meantime. That was unlikely, since they were guaranteed by the European Financial Stability Facility. This final formality of "buying back" the bonds with the money he received at maturity would have no material economic consequence.

The problem was that Corzine didn't have enough capital to last to maturity. But this is the entire point of risk managemnet. A key principle of leveraged finance has become a mantra: *The markets can stay irrational longer than you can stay solvent.* If one puts on a leveraged trade, one must have enough capital or be prepared to unwind the trade, often at a loss.

But MF Global's customers had money in their "segregated" accounts. Did MF Global think it could replace the funds before anyone noticed? Had it already transfered funds from customer accounts to meet margin calls made that summer? Perhaps it had.

MF Global likely had several trading days in 2011 with moves of 5% to 10% against it on the bond prices alone—before taking leverage into account. MF Global's positions were highly correlated. It probably had several negative equity days in 2011, before its official bankruptcy.

MF Global Holdings paid a $100 million fine to the CFTC plus settlements for other various civil claims. Jon Corzine and nine other officers settled a class-action claim for $64.5 million. Corzine settled with regulators for $5 million and a lifetime ban from leading a futures broker or registering with the CFTC.

The SEC approved Jon Corzine's newly launched hedge fund in 2019. President Biden nominated Gary Gensler to head the U.S. Securities and Exchange Commission, and the U.S. Senate approved him. Gensler was sworn into office on April 17, 2021. As of this writing, no information is available as to whether Mr. Gensler will use his personal email account to communicate about Corzine's hedge fund.

CHAPTER 3

Credit Default Swaps and Options

A credit default swap or option is simply an exchange of a fee for a payment if a credit default event occurs (see Figure 3.1). Credit default swaps differ from total return swaps (TRS) in that the investor does not take price risk of the reference asset, only the risk of default. The investor receives a fee from the seller of the default risk. The investor makes no payment unless a credit default event occurs.

If the fee is paid up front, which may be the case for very short-dated structures, the agreement is likely to be called a credit default option. If the fee is paid over time, the agreement is more likely to be called a swap. Unless two counterparties are actually swapping and exchanging the credit default risk of two different credits, I prefer to call the former structure a credit default "option." Cash flows paid over time are nothing more than an amortization of an option premium. Because the documentation references International Swaps and Derivatives Association, Inc. (ISDA) master agreements, however, swap terminology has crept into the market. Because the credit derivatives business at many commercial and investment banks is often run by former interest rate swap staff, the tendency to use swap terminology dominates. Therefore, I most often refer to these transactions as credit default "swaps."

The credit default premium is usually paid over time. For some very short-dated structures, the credit default premium may be paid up front. For over-the-counter par swaps, there is often no upfront premium.

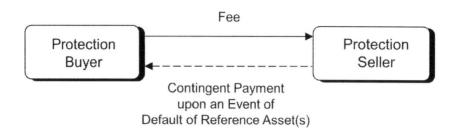

Fee

Protection Buyer

Protection Seller

Contingent Payment
upon an Event of
Default of Reference Asset(s)

FIGURE 3.1   Credit Default Swap

Exchange traded CDS require payments over time but also require an upfront payment calculated based on the difference between the credit quality of a benchmark and the actual credit quality of the particular credit that is the reference credit of the CDS.

The premium can be thought of as the credit spread an investor demands to take the default risk of a given reference asset. If the investor bought an asset swap, the investor would earn a spread to his funding cost. This spread represents the compensation, or the premium, the investor needs in order to take the credit default risk of the reference asset in the asset swap. (See "Comments on Pricing CDS" later in this chapter.)

The credit default swap or option is a *contingent option* and not to be confused with an American option. A termination payment is made only if a credit event occurs. If the credit event does not occur, the default protection seller has no obligation.

For an American option, the premium is paid up front (or over time with the proviso that the total premium is owed, even if exercise occurs before the expiration date). The American option can be exercised any time that it is in the money. The holder of the option does not have to exercise, however, and can wait and hope the option will go further in the money. If the market reverses direction, the American option can again become out of the money, and the holder who failed to exercise the option when it was in the money cannot then exercise it. With a credit default option, once the trigger event has occurred, the holder must exercise, and the option stays exercisable.

Default protection can be purchased on a loan, a bond, sovereign risk due to cross-border commercial transactions, or even credit exposure due to a derivative contract such as counterparty credit exposure in a cross-currency swap transaction. Credit protection can be linked to an individual credit, to a basket of credits, or to a structured credit product such as an asset backed security.

At first glance, a credit default swap or option looks structurally simpler than a total return swap. We already know that a total return swap is simply a form of financing. In this chapter, we explore the complex, various, and interesting features of the credit default swap and the credit default option market. *Complex? Various?* Wait a minute. Didn't I mention that a total return swap already has a credit default swap imbedded in its structure? After all, if my counterparty is taking the default risk of a bond or a loan, I have reduced my credit exposure to that reference asset. We understand everything there is to know about credit default swaps already, don't we?

Those are the questions most practitioners ask themselves the first time they enter into a credit default contract. The first key difference is that although the price or premium of a credit default swap or option may increase, it is never actually in the money until a credit default event as defined by the confirm language has occurred. That seems like a knock-in option or a knock-in swap, which is a type of barrier option. Knock-in options have been around since the 1960s. When a market price reaches a predetermined strike price—the barrier—the knock-in option comes into existence. But *this* "knock in" is not linked to traditional market factors. It is linked to either a credit default or a credit event/s, or both. The counterparties are free to specify the triggers of the credit knock-in. If the option "knocks in," then and only then is the option in the money. The termination payment is usually not binary or predefined, but it can be if the counterparties so specify. We explore those exceptions later in this chapter. The termination payment is usually linked to a recovery value or a recovery rate for the reference credit or credits involved.

The terminology is further complicated by the U.S. market's use of the word *swap* to refer to an exchange of one bond for another (usually accompanied by a cash payment to make up for any discrepancy in relative values) and the U.K. market's use of the word *switch* for the same transaction. U.S. market practitioners are often mystified when they first hear of "asset swap switches," an exchange of one asset swap package risk for another asset swap package risk. We discuss this product later in this chapter.

As we see in this chapter, a variety of structures have evolved in this market. The risk characteristics of these structures are different from the structures discussed so far and merit close scrutiny. One structure, known by such names as digital, binary, all-or-nothing, and the zero-one structure, has a substantial amount of risk. The investor loses the *entire notional amount*—not merely coupon and some principal loss—if there is a default event.

Other structures, such as the par value minus recovery value structure, can leave a position of premium bonds partially unhedged or can over hedge a position of bonds trading below par. Exposure management officers evaluating the suitability and the appropriateness of such deals must be fully aware of the total exposures implied in these transactions.

The credit swap becomes even more interesting when one realizes that the term *default event* does not even apply to many credit agreements. The event, which triggers a termination payment under the terms of the credit default swap confirmation, is negotiable. The event may be defined as a spread widening, an event in a foreign country that may cause its sovereign debt to decline in price, or just about any event on which the two parties can agree and define a price. Even the termination payment is negotiable. It may be preset at a fixed amount or based on the recovery value of a reference asset, to mention only two structures.

Some credit "default" options, those linked to spread widening, for instance, sound very much like put options that are struck out of the money.

Example: A German bank's emerging-markets trader discovered he had exceeded his Russia position limit, an offense for which he could have been fired. He approached a large U.S. bank and asked to buy credit protection on Russia for one month. To accomplish this, the German bank's trader paid a high premium for a one-month, 35-point, out-of-the-money put on Russian Vanesh. The U.S. bank happily pocketed the fat premium for an option it considered virtually worthless. There was no pricing model, no calculation of recovery values, and no analysis of asset swap spreads. The price the German bank's trader was willing to pay was an obvious windfall for the U.S. bank. The need defined the price.

Was this transaction a credit derivative, or was this merely a bond option? This question often stymies people who are new to this market.

This reminds me of a commodity conference attended by a number of bright derivative specialists who were relatively unfamiliar with the commodities market. It was the end of a very long day marked by a series of monotone speakers. Louise Rowsell Crean, a petite British oil trader, bounded up to the podium trailed by a veil of long brown hair. She briefly paused, looked at her mainly male audience, and said, "All right chaps! Who knows the difference between a future and a forward?"

She paused again. "Let me find a volunteer." Crean picked up a seating chart and began examining it.

Philip Basil, a structuring specialist at Royal Bank of Scotland in London, recalled a sense of panic and dread as he came to attention and hurriedly sifted through his notes.

Mrs. Crean called out to a "volunteer" (actually a prepared colleague planted in the audience) and asked again, "You there, in the second row at the left aisle, what is the difference between a future and a forward?"

The answer, of course, is that a future is an exchange-traded contract and a forward is an over-the-counter contract.

Of course. Everyone in the room probably intuitively knew the answer. Nonetheless, when confronted with an unfamiliar product, we tend to be thrown by unfamiliar terminology.

The credit derivatives market has adopted similar over-the-counter versus exchange-traded terminology, which makes it difficult to define the size of the credit derivatives market. Virtually any credit-related, over-the-counter option could be defined as a credit derivative. Generally, however, credit derivative contracts are further distinguished from other over-the-counter options on bonds by the fact that they are negotiated transactions.

Was the Morgen Grenfell trade a credit derivative? It certainly helped a bank free up credit lines. It was a negotiated transaction. I would say, yes, the transaction was a credit derivative, albeit the circumstances created an urgent and odd negotiation, which suited both parties.

A recurring theme in the CDS market is that terms can change even after a trade closes. For example, risky debt can be inserted into a corporate capital structure, triggering a default, unless contract language prohibits it.

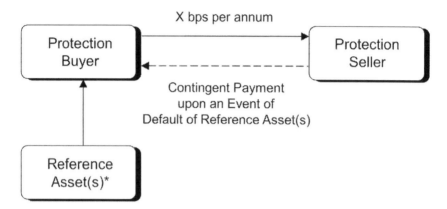

*Seller receives a fee in return for making a Contingent Payment if a predefined Credit Event occurs to the Reference Assets(s). Underlying exposure can be single credits, baskets of credits, or indices.

FIGURE 3.2 Plain Vanilla Credit Default Swap

This chapter examines the not so plain "plain vanilla" structures and explains in greater detail the difficulties of defining credit events, hedging default risks, basis risk between the reference asset and the risk, and mutually agreeable methods of exchanging payments if a credit event occurs. It investigates the difference between par and reference asset price-adjusted structures. We will cover the basic building blocks of complex structures: knock-in options, first loss-protected options, asset swap switches, geared default options, options on credit spreads, callable step-up structures, basket default options, and pro rata default structures.

TRADITIONAL CREDIT DEFAULT SWAP

The traditional, or plain vanilla, credit default swap is a payment by one party in exchange for a credit default protection payment if a credit default event on a reference asset occurs (see Figure 3.2). The amount of the payment is the difference between the original price of the reference asset and the recovery value of the reference asset.

Let us look at an example in which the reference asset is a bond. If the issuer of the bond fails to make coupon interest payments when due and other conditions of a default event exist, then the buyer of the credit default protection option has the right to notify the seller of the option to make a payment.

As we shall see, even for plain vanilla credit default protection, there are a variety of choices in creating a credit default protection agreement. The following term sheet presents an example of a formerly common structure in the over- the-counter credit default protection market.

ONE-YEAR BRAZIL CREDIT DEFAULT SWAP
Indicative Term Sheet

Default Protection Buyer:	Default protection buyer.
Default protection buyer.	Default protection seller.
Transaction Type:	Credit default swap
Trade Date:	As soon as practical
Effective Date:	Three days after the trade date
Early Termination Date:	With three business days' notice *following* a credit event with a terminal payment being made.
Calculation Amount:	USD 25 million

Payments of the Default Protection Buyer:

Payment Amount and Dates:	XXX basis points on a semiannual A/360-day basis (where *A* is the actual number of days in
	the period) calculated from the effective date to the earlier of:
	1. one year after the trade date, *or*
	2. the early termination date.

Payments of the Default Protection Seller:

Termination Payment:	The default protection seller pays to the default protection buyer the following amount:
	(Calculation Amount $\times$ Par $-$ Market Value)

	Accrued but Unpaid Interest on the Reference Obligation
	where a dealer panel using the market bid price will determine market value.
Credit Event:	When the calculation agent is aware of publicly available information as to the existence of a credit condition and at the same time materiality exists.
Credit Condition:	Either payment default or a bankruptcy event in respect of the issuer.
Payment Default:	Subject to a dispute in good faith by the issuer, either the issuer fails to pay any amount due of the reference asset when due; or any other present or future indebtedness of the issuer for or in respect of moneys borrowed or raised or guaranteed, in an amount in aggregate of not less than USD 25 million (or its equivalent in other currencies), becomes due and payable prior to its stated maturity otherwise than at the option of the issuer, or any such amount of indebtedness is not paid when due or, as the case may be, within any applicable grace period.
Bankruptcy Event:	The declaration by the issuer of a general moratorium in or of a rescheduling of payments on any external indebtedness in an aggregate amount of not less than USD 25 million (or its equivalent in other currencies).
Materiality:	The price of the reference asset after price adjustment is 90 percent or less relative to the initial price as reasonably determined by the calculation agent.
Publicly Available Information:	Information that has been published in any two or more internationally recognized published or electronically displayed financial news sources. Nonetheless, if either of the parties or any of their respective affiliates is cited as the sole source for such information, then such information will be deemed not to be publicly available information.
Price Adjustment:	The price of a reference U.S. Treasury security on the valuation date less the price on the effective date. The reference U.S. Treasury security will be selected by

the calculation agent to match, as far as possible, the maturity and other features of the reference asset.

Market Value:

On any day, with respect to the relevant reference security, the percentage equal to the unweighted arithmetic mean of the firm USD-denominated bid prices (exclusive of any accrued but unpaid interest and expressed as a percentage of principal amount) for such reference security provided to the calculation agent on such day by at least two but not more than five referenced dealers.

Dispute:

If there is a dispute between the parties as to the occurrence of a credit event unresolved on the maturity date, a credit event will be deemed to occur on that date.

Notification Date:

If a credit event occurs during the term of the transaction, the default protection buyer shall have the right to designate a protection seller payment date by delivering notice (on the notification date) to the default protection seller of the occurrence of such credit event. Such notice must contain a description in reasonable detail of the facts giving rise to the credit event.

Business Days:

Days on which commercial banks and foreign exchange markets settle payments in London and New York.

Business Day Convention:

Modified following.

Calculation Agent:

Default protection seller.

Documentation:

Per the existing ISDA master agreement between the default protection seller and default protection buyer.

Law:

Per ISDA master agreement.

Suitability:

The notes will be sold to an investor with such knowledge and experience in financial matters to assure capability of evaluating the merits and risks of the prospective investment.

Default Protection Buyer Risk:

The default protection buyer is exposed to the default protection seller for its payment if there is a credit event for the Republic of Brazil. The maximum amount of this payment is the calculation amount.

Reference Obligation:

Issuer/Borrower:	Federative Republic of Brazil ("the Republic").
Rating:	B1 Moody's, B+ Standard and Poor's.
Type:	Global.
Currency Denomination:	USD.
Coupon:	8 7/8 percent payable semiannually.
Maturity:	November 5, 2001.
Reference Issue Date:	November 5, 1996.
Reference Amount Issued:	USD 750 million
Substitution:	If the amount of the reference asset (or a substitute) is materially reduced, the calculation agent shall reasonably select a substitute issued or guaranteed by the reference name that is of the same credit quality as the reference asset and with a maturity at least that of the reference asset and shall notify the counterparties. If no substitute can be found, the swap will terminate with no further payments on either side.

Notice that, except for the definition of the credit event and some additional defined terms, there is really not much to this term sheet. One counterparty agrees to pay the other a fee in exchange for a payment equal to the par amount minus the market value of the reference asset plus accrued interest due on the reference asset in the event of a default. In actual practice, the negotiation of all of these terms can be a drawn-out and protracted process. Each of these terms potentially has an economic value to the buyer and the seller of default protection; we examine them in more detail later in this chapter.

IMPORTANCE OF THE DEFAULT PROTECTION SELLER

If an investor is purchasing credit default protection, what kind of credit default protection seller is most desirable? If prices were the same, a default protection seller with a triple A credit rating and a zero percent correlation with the asset that the investor is trying to hedge would be the most desirable. But as we saw in the sections on total return swaps in Chapter 2, a default protection seller with these characteristics will probably sell very expensive protection. Therefore, it is beneficial to relax the criteria and find another provider. The investor should be aware that there are unsuitable providers, however.

There are unsuitable applications, too. One must ask the right questions before trying to apply a solution. Credit derivatives are sometimes seen as the panacea, the answer to any finance problem that cannot be solved by conventional market strategies. Although this is often true, the following example shows an instance in which a "credit derivative" is not the answer.

Example: In the summer of 1997, a newly hired salesman in Bank Arranger's Asian office wanted to get cheaper funding for one of his customers. One of the top Korean commercial banks, Hanil Bank (BBB), wanted to raise USD 100 million to 200 million one-year money in the floating rate note (FRN) market at a rate below six-month London interbank offering rate (LIBOR) plus 40 basis points(bps).

Unfortunately, Hanil Bank's outstanding issues traded at around six-month LIBOR+45 bps. This was at least 5 bps cheaper than the new issue market. Further, Hanil Bank did not want to issue an interest-rate-related structured note to lower its cost of funds. The salesman was positive that a credit derivative could lower the cost of funds for Hanil Bank. He suggested that Bank Arranger's Asian office should underwrite USD 100 million at around six-month LIBOR+45 bps. He further suggested that Bank Arranger do a credit default swap with the issuer, Hanil Bank. Bank Arranger would pay a premium of 10 bps at the end of one year, only if Hanil Bank repaid its principal. With the 10-basis-point rebate, Hanil Bank would achieve a funding cost of six-month

LIBOR+35 bps. The salesman thought that by buying credit default protection in the form of a credit default swap from the issuer, he could transfer underwriting credit risk from Bank Arranger's Asian syndicate group to the swap book.

The salesman discussed this concept with his managers and sent e-mail to Bank Arranger's credit derivatives group. Everyone with whom the salesman spoke agreed this was a good idea. No one challenged the salesman's assumptions for two weeks. Finally, one of the credit derivative specialists carefully read the e-mail and debunked this notion.

What was wrong with the salesman's logic?

Ignoring credit derivatives for a moment, consider if a bank offered an after-the-fact rebate to *any* issuer who performed under the terms of their agreement to pay back principal and interest as promised. The bank could pay a rebate to a credit-card holder who pays the entire balance on a credit card. The bank could pay a rebate to an auto-loan holder who pays back the entire auto loan. The bank could pay a rebate to an issuer who pays back the entire amount of principal borrowed plus interest.

Why stop at a measly 10 basis points? After the borrowers have actually paid back the entire amount of principal and interest, they are better credit risks than a *proposed* AAA borrower.

Why is this?

It is due to the fact that after the borrower has actually repaid principal and interest, the bank has 100 percent *certainty.* Value is based on the timing of cash flows, the magnitude of cash flows, and the certainty of cash flows. Even a proposed AAA borrower cannot give a bank 100 percent certainty *before* the AAA borrower has repaid the obligation.

Following that logic, why not give Hanil Bank a rebate of 65 basis points. At the time, an AAA issuer had a proposed funding level of around LIBOR−20 bps. Hanil Bank's funding level of LIBOR+45 bps versus LIBOR−20 bps would have suggested a 65-basis-point rebate. It seems only fair in the calculation of crazy rebates. As we saw earlier, after repayment Hanil Bank is *better* than an AAA proposed issuer.

The reason banks do not hand out rebates is that in advance the bank does not have the certainty, so the bank needs to be compensated for the uncertainty, for the risk. It is these risk premiums that over time compensate a bank for the occasions when one of the issuers actually does default. Therefore, the bank doesn't give back any part of these risk premiums.

Perhaps an easier way to come to this conclusion is to notice that the joint probability of default of Hanil Bank versus Hanil Bank is 100 percent, so no one should pay a premium for credit default protection for Hanil Bank to Hanil Bank. *The whole point of using credit derivatives is to diversify credit risk.*

Asset swap spreads are independent of the credit quality of the investor. A market asset is swapped to a LIBOR-based floating coupon, for instance. The market is indifferent to the credit quality of the investor, who pays cash up front for the asset swap package. Unlike an asset swap, the premium paid to the investor—the credit default protection seller—is sensitive to the credit quality of the investor. The premium is further sensitive to the correlation between the investor and the reference asset on which one is buying the credit default protection. Depending on the structure, the credit default swap contract may require an uncollateralized payment by the investor if there is a credit default event.

Around three months after I fielded the question about Hanil Bank, but before the fall 1997 crisis, I took a call from a trader at a securities firm formed by a French bank. The trader told me that several Korean banks were willing to offer credit default protection on other Korean names. In order to bolster up their own credit perception, they were willing to post 30 to 40 percent of the notional amount with G7 (Group of Seven) collateral.

One bank was even willing to post 100 percent G7 collateral if it went below investment grade. That sounded mildly interesting, although I had no interest in taking on more Korean credit risk. The trader then went on to tell me that Commercial Bank of Korea would sell credit default protection on bonds issued by the Commercial Bank of Korea.

"That's very interesting," I countered, "but that credit default option is worthless."

"But people are doing it," persisted the trader.

"That's because they don't know what they are doing," I affirmed. "The correlation between Commercial Bank of Korea and itself is 100 percent. I would pay nothing for that credit protection. It is worthless for this purpose."

The trader mustered his best grammar, chilliest tone, and most authoritative voice: "There are those who would disagree with you."

That is what makes a market.

Example: An investor has a choice of buying credit default protection from one of two counterparties to hedge a single-A rated asset. One counterparty is rated BBB with a zero percent correlation with the A credit. The second counterparty is rated single A but is ninety percent correlated with the single-A rated asset, which I am trying to hedge. Which counterparty is the better choice?

Counterintuitive as it may seem, it is better to buy credit default protection from an uncorrelated lower-rated credit default protection seller than from a credit protection seller that is highly correlated-with the reference asset one is trying to hedge. Again, the benefits of diversification, as we saw in the Standard & Poor's (S&P) table earlier, weigh in favor of the BBB counterparty. The joint probability of default between the A rated asset and the BBB counterparty might merit an implied credit rating of AA for the credit default protected asset. The combination of the 90 percent correlated A rated names would probably merit a rating no higher than A.

Determining correlation, then, would seem key. The data break down when we look at sovereign credits and at foreign credits, however. For example, let us look at a U.S. commercial bank that hedges a Hyundai (Korean corporate) asset swapped position with credit default protection purchased from Korea Exchange Bank (see Figure 3.3). Notice that the U.S. commercial bank may pick up some benefit from protecting the credit default risk of Hyundai with credit protection from Korea Exchange Bank. But the question is: "How much additional protection?" What is the correlation between these credits? The difficulty is that no one knows. The U.S. commercial bank in this example assumed a low correlation. That is why the U.S. commercial bank was willing to pay 40 basis points for the credit protection. But the degree of correlation is debatable. I personally feel the correlation is high—at least 50 percent. Political risk, restructuring risk, and the risk of possible future war merit a number at least that high for a two-and-one-half-year period.

Why not just purchase an asset swap on Korea Exchange Bank? At the time of this transaction, the U.S. commercial bank could have saved itself a lot of paperwork and earned LIBOR+45 bps. How much does the reduction in the joint probability of default enhance the value of the synthetic Korea Exchange-Hyundai package? Remember the Moody's and S&P credit rating enhancement tables? They assumed that the correlation of the rated assets was zero. If there is a 100 percent correlation, there is no rating enhancement benefit. If the correlation is high, the enhancement will be very slight. Does this enhancement justify the reduction in spread of 15 basis points versus the stand-alone purchase of Korea Exchange Bank?

The head of one U.S. bank's New York Emerging Markets Derivatives Group thinks not. "I've heard about those trades, but I don't do them. It is a little crazy to do a trade like that." He feels the correlation between Korean banks and Korean corporates is extremely high.

The head of a U.S. bank's London office credit derivatives department sees this differently. He feels that the international banking community

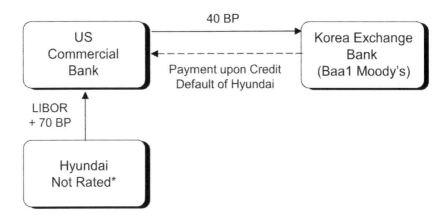

Net spread to the US commercial bank is LIBOR + 30 bps. Korea Exchange Bank at the time traded at LIBOR + 45 bps.

* In 2021, Hyundai was rated Baa1 by Moody's, BB+ by S&P, and BBB+ by Fitch. This example is from the late 1990s.

FIGURE 3.3 Korean Bank Corporate Credit Default Swap, 2.5-Year Maturity

could not tolerate an upset in the Korean banking community and would step in to see that there was not a series of defaults in Korea. The reflection and panic in the international banking community would be too horrible to contemplate if Korea were allowed to sink. Korea is viewed as part of the mainstream global banking network. He argues that Korea presents a much different situation from *Latvia,* for instance, where a default domino effect wiped out debt obligations in a series of defaults.

An emerging markets economist feels that the first tier of Korean banks will not have a problem. The merchant banks, however, have zero free capital of their own. Their funding costs reflect this at levels of LIBOR+100 bps to LIBOR+120 bps. He points out that in Vietnam, state-owned banks have defaulted. There have been defaults on private market debt service.

I personally would feel much better if the default protection seller were a European bank, for instance. I think European banks and Korean corporates have a very low correlation. *

This is why we rely on other experts, economists, and traders who closely follow the markets, and we rely on our own staff close to credit situations to provide guidance. The more information one has about correlation and credit risk, from whatever the source, the better. In the end, the differences in interpretation of information make a market.

This conversation took place in the summer of 1997. By October 1997, Thailand's midsummer decision to allow the baht to float severely weakened several Asian currencies, among them the South Korean won, resulting in a severe dollar crunch. The sinking won mushroomed foreign debt. Interest rates soared and banks curtailed lending. At least nine Korean corporations declared bankruptcy in 1997. At the end of 1997, other major Korean corporations, the chaebol, indicated they might have problems repaying debt. The Korean Composite Stock Price Index closed down 42 percent for 1997, and banks and corporations neared default on their debt.

The International Monetary Fund (IMF) announced a conditional $40-57 billion bailout for the region in December 1997 and imposed restrictions. By the end of 1997, the United States and the IMF announced $10 billion in new credit (part of the bailout plan) for South Korea. Major banks in the United States, Europe, and Japan were exploring ways of rolling over Korean debt rather than attempting to force repayment on loans that could likely default. At the end of 1997, Moody's lowered Korea's rating to junk bond status. By 1999, the region's economies began to recover. In January 2012, Moody's rated South Korea's sovereign credit at Aa2 with a stable outlook.

Correlation and credit quality of the credit default protection seller are the key issues. One head trader's biggest concern is that the credit default protection seller has a zero or low correlation with the reference asset. Often this trader does deals in which an Asian bank provides credit default protection for a Latin American credit risk. If the credit default swap economics move more than USD 3 million to 4 million in exposure against the protection seller, Bankers Trust exercises a collateral call against the default protection seller.

Over-the-counter credit default swaps are negotiated transactions, and although there is some agreement on plain vanilla structures, there is very little agreement on anything else. No standard practice exists in the credit derivatives market, so just about any contract imaginable can be created. The key issues in the credit default swap market revolve around the following parameters:

- Defining the event.
- Determining the default protection fee.
- Determining the reference asset.
- Determining the default payment.

The issues may vary by structure, and as we continue through this chapter, we encounter these issues in many forms.

DEFINING THE EVENT

The plain vanilla credit default market ceases to appear vanilla after we deviate from the most basic definition of credit default. Defining the event for a sovereign debt denominated in dollars, for instance, seems pretty straightforward. One reasonable way to define the default event would be to look at the language in the prospectus. The following language from the prospectus for the 100,000,000 British sterling (GBP)-denominated

Federative Republic of Brazil, 9.75 percent due June 11, 1999, is an example of default language. Default, or acceleration of maturity, occurs if any of the following events occurs:

- Default in any payment of principal or interest on any of the Notes and the continuance of such default for a period of 30 days; or
- Default that is materially prejudicial to the interests of the Noteholders in the performance of any other obligation under the Notes and the continuance of such default for a period of 30 days after written notice requiring the same to be remedied has been given to the Fiscal Agent by any Noteholder; or
- Acceleration of in excess of USD 25 million (or its equivalent in any other currency) in aggregate principal amount of Public External Indebtedness of the Republic by reason of any event of default (however described) resulting from the failure of the Republic to make any payment of principal or interest thereunder when due; or
- Failure to make any payment in respect of Public External Indebtedness of the Republic in an aggregate principal amount in excess of USD 25,000,000 (or its equivalent in any other currency) when due (as such date may be extended by virtue of any applicable grace period or waiver) and the continuance of such failure for a period of 30 days after written notice requiring the same to be remedied has been given to the Fiscal Agent by any Noteholder; or
- Declaration by the Republic of a moratorium with respect to the payment of principal of or interest on Public External Indebtedness of the Republic that does not expressly exclude the Notes and that is materially prejudicial to the interests of the Noteholders; or
- Denial by the Republic of its obligations under the Notes. Then each Noteholder, so long as such event is continuing, may, by written demand given to the Republic and delivered to the specified office of the Fiscal Agent, declare the principal of and any accrued interest on the Notes held by it to be due; and such principal and interest shall thereupon become immediately due and payable, unless prior to receipt of such demand by the Republic all such

defaults have been cured; provided that, in the case of any event described in subparagraph (a), (e), or (f) entitling holders to declare their Notes due has occurred and is continuing, become effective only when the Fiscal Agent has received such notices from the holders of at least 10 percent, in principal amount of all Notes then outstanding. Notes held by the Republic or on behalf of the Republic shall not be considered outstanding for purposes of the preceding sentence.

If any event described in subparagraphs (a) to (f) gives rise to a declaration that is effective and such event ceases to continue following such declaration, then such declaration may, in the case of any event described in subparagraph (a), (e) or (f) be rescinded and annulled by the Noteholder that has made such declaration and, in the case of any event described in subparagraph (b), (c), or (d), (unless at the time any event described in subparagraph (a), (c), or (f) has occurred and is continuing) may be rescinded and annulled by an affirmative vote of the Noteholders in accordance with the procedures set forth in Condition 13.

In short, if there is a credit default event as defined in the prospectus and if 10 percent or more of the noteholders notify the Republic in writing that they want their principal and interest back, the Republic must pay it, unless it already did so before receiving the written notification. If the Republic has already agreed to pay back principal and interest as reflected in the prospectus, then why buy credit default protection?

Recall the joint probability of default discussed in Chapter 2. For example, example Oresundskonsortiet, rated AAA by S&P in the late 1990s. This is the entity responsible for building a bridge between Copenhagen and Malmö. Oresundskonsortiet's debt obligations were jointly guaranteed by the Kingdom of Denmark (then Aa1/AA+) and the Kingdom of Sweden (then Aa3/AA+). Neither the Kingdom of Sweden nor the Kingdom of Denmark then had triple-A ratings. Oresundskonsortiet achieved a rating higher than either of its guarantors because *both* the Kingdom of Sweden and the Kingdom of Denmark would have to default before an investor holding an obligation issued by Oresundskonsortiet would fail to get paid. The Venn diagram in Figure 3.4 represents the benefit of the joint probability of default.

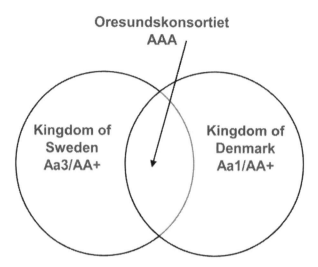

In 2022, both the Kingdoms of Sweden and Denmark have AAA ratings, but in the late 1990s they did not. Oresundskonsortiet achieved a AAA rating due to the kingdoms' joint guarantees.

FIGURE 3.4   Benefit of the Joint Probability of Default

If an investor purchases debt of the Federative Republic of Brazil (Bl/B−) and wants added credit protection, the investor can purchase a credit default swap from a default protection seller. If that default protection seller is not in default, the investor has added protection in the event that the Federative Republic of Brazil defaults. The investor can demand a cash "make whole" payment from the default protection seller. Alternatively, the investor can deliver the defaulted bonds to the default protection seller and demand the principal plus accrued interest from the default protection seller. The default protection seller would then try to recover the maximum possible amount on the defaulted bonds. Payment calculations and methods of settlement are discussed later in this chapter.

DEFAULT LANGUAGE FOR NONSOVEREIGN DEBT

Corporate default language varies considerably from sovereign credit default language. The following term sheet is typical of structures offered where the reference obligation is corporate debt.

CREDIT DEFAULT SWAP
RJR NABISCO, INC.
Indicative Term Sheet

Default Protection Buyer:	Default protection buyer.
Default protection seller.	Default protection seller

Reference Obligation:

Issuer:	RJR Nabisco, Inc.
Coupon: 8.625%.	
Interest Payable:	Semiannual.
Reference Obligation:	December 1, 2002.
Moody's/S&P:	Baa3 / BBB—
Cusip Number:	74960LAX4.
Initial Price:	To be determined.
Calculation Amount:	USD 50 million.
Trade Date:	To be determined.
Effective Date:	Trade date + two business days.
Maturity Date of the	
Credit Default Swap (CDS)	The earlier of:
	1. the reference obligation maturity date, *or*
	2. the nonscheduled termination date, if any.

Default Protection Buyer:

Payment Date:	Each reference obligation coupon payment date.
Payment Amount:	XX basis points per annum.
Day Count Convention:	Payments are made in USD based on a semiannual 30/360 day count.
Payment Calculation:	Calculation Amount × Payment Amount × Day Count Convention

Nonscheduled Termination:

Date:	Two business days following the notification date, if any.

Payment:

At the option of default protection buyer, either:

1. Default protection buyer makes physical delivery of the reference obligation with face value subject to this transaction to default protection seller. Default protection seller pays default protection buyer the calculation amount plus accrued but unpaid interest. Default protection buyer pays default protection seller the accrued payment amount up to the date of the earliest credit event, at which time the credit default swap is terminated with no further obligation to either counterparty.

2. Default protection seller makes a cash settlement payment to default protection buyer in an amount equal to:

Calculation Amount × (Initial Price − Market Value)

Default protection buyer pays default protection seller the accrued payment amount up to the date of the earliest credit event, at which time the credit default swap is terminated with no further obligation to either counterparty.

Notification Date:

If a credit event or a merger event occurs during the term of this transaction, the default protection buyer shall have the right to designate a nonscheduled termination date by delivering notice (even if such notice occurs after the maturity date) to the default protection seller of the occurrence of such credit or merger event. Such notice must contain a description, in reasonable detail, of the facts giving rise to the credit or merger event.

Credit Event:

Shall include, with respect to the issuer of the reference obligation (reference credit), any of the following, which occurs on or prior to the maturity date and at the same time materiality exists:

1. Bankruptcy.

2. Credit event upon merger.

A default, event of default, or other similar condition or event occurs in respect of such reference credit under any financial obligation that has resulted in such financial obligation becoming, or being capable at such time of being declared, due and payable before it would otherwise have become due and payable.

3. Cross-acceleration or cross-default.

A waiver, deferral, restructuring, rescheduling, exchange, or other adjustment occurs in respect of any financial obligation, and the effect of such adjustment is overall materially less favorable from a credit-and risk-perspective to the relevant creditor.

4. Downgrade.

5. Failure to pay.

6. Repudiation.

7. Restructuring.

Such reference credit (a) is dissolved; or (b) becomes insolvent or is unable to pay its debts; or (c) makes a general assignment, arrangement, or composition for the benefit of its creditors; or (d) institutes a proceeding seeking a judgment of insolvency or bankruptcy; or (e) has a resolution passed for its winding up, official management, or liquidation; or (f) seeks or becomes subject to the appointment of an administrator; or (g) has a secured party take possession of substantially all of its assets. (See also Chapter 8, "Hidden Costs in Default Language.")

Merger Event: An actual or publicly announced intended consolidation, amalgamation, or merger or a transferal of all or a substantial amount of assets from the issuer to another entity.

Financial Obligation: With respect to the reference credit, any senior unsecured financial obligation in an aggregate amount of not less than the threshold amount incurred by the reference credit in any capacity.

Materiality:
The price of the reference obligation less the price adjustment is 90 percent or less relative to the initial price as reasonably determined by the calculation agent.

Price Adjustment:
The price of a reference U.S. Treasury security on the notification date less the price on the effective date. The reference U.S. Treasury security will be selected by the calculation agent to match, as far as possible, the maturity and other features of the reference obligation.

Market Value:
On any day, with respect to the relevant reference obligation, the percentage equal to the unweighted arithmetic mean of the firm USD-denominated bid prices (exclusive of any accrued but unpaid interest and expressed as a percentage of principal amount) for such reference obligation provided to the calculation agent on such day by not more than five referenced dealers as such prices are available.

Business Days:
Days on which commercial banks and foreign exchange markets settle payments in New York and London.

Business Day Convention:
Modified following.

Calculation Agent:
Default protection buyer.

Documentation:
This transaction will be documented on a confirmation linked to the existing **ISDA** master agreement between the default protection seller and the default protection buyer.

Early Termination/Assignment:
An over-the-counter derivative transaction of this type may not be assigned, transferred, or terminated prior to its stated termination date by either party without the consent of the other party except as stipulated in the terms of the transaction.

Liquidity:
There may be no, or only a limited, secondary market for a transaction of this type.

Transactions of this type are not standardized or fungible. A seemingly identical transaction with another over-the-counter party will not automatically act as a perfect hedge for an existing transaction.

It is impossible to cover every contingency. Deteriorating creditworthiness can be a continuous process. A holder of default protection can watch in frustration as the value relentlessly yet slowly slides to credit default. Sometimes payment default is a minor problem compared to other potential problems. The manufacturer of aircraft carriers can be current on debt but fail to make a delivery of the carriers under the terms of a trade agreement. An automobile manufacturer can be current on debt but forced to recall a line of automobiles for safety reasons. A drug company may be current on debt but find that a newly launched flagship sedative causes birth defects. A chemical company may be current on debt but face class action lawsuits when the silicone implants it manufactured are leaking material into the chest cavities of thousands of women. An investment banking firm may be current on debt but fail to deliver bonds following the exercise of an option. An investment bank may be current on debt but suddenly face trading scandals enmeshing its management, which cause the exodus of its most productive employees.

None of the suggested events is commonly provided for in the standard credit default agreements in the market. Language referring to possible restructuring, bankruptcy, judgment of insolvency, and mergers is common. Common, too, is language referring to a secured party taking possession of substantially all assets. This language is absent from sovereign credit default language. On the other hand, one rarely sees war referred to as an event in corporate default language, although the example in the following section provides an exception.

REDEFINING THE CREDIT DEFAULT EVENT AS A CREDIT EVENT

All is well and good when the event of default is easily agreed on, as when trade counterparties are referencing a prospectus. But what about situations in which the default event is not as well defined? One U.S. corporate client, a producer of technology products, was interested in providing a hedge for its investment in a $100 million-factory in Mexico. The corporation was concerned that political risks, such as war, hostilities, labor strikes, confiscation of nonlocal assets, or a coup d'état, might disrupt business. Insurance seemed too expensive. A tax-advantaged lease-leaseback structure would take a long time to evaluate. Credit derivatives seemed less expensive and could be executed more quickly.

One solution was to reference a USD-denominated United Mexican States global bond (Ba2 by Moody's) 9.75 percent of 2001. Then the U.S. corporation defined the default conditions to include war, hostilities, and confiscation of nonlocal bank assets. The following abbreviated term sheet reflects those changes. Future term sheets will be abbreviated to illustrate key points with the assumption that term sheets will have the key definitions, subject to dealer variations, shown in earlier term sheets.

UNITED STATES OF MEXICO CREDIT DEFAULT SWAP ABBREVIATED TERM SHEET

Default Protection Buyer:	U.S. corporation.
Default Protection Seller:	Seller.
Calculation Amount:	USD 100 million.
Reference Security:	United Mexican States (Ba2)
	United Mexican States, global bond.
	Maturity: February 2001.
	Currency Denomination: USD.
	Coupon: 9.75%.
Trade Date:	As soon as practical.
Maturity Date:	One week from trade date.
	The earlier of:
	1. one year from effective date, *or*
	2. the default protection seller payment date, if any.
Default Protection Buyer:	Default protection buyer.
Payment Dates:	Every reference security coupon payment date.
Payment Amount:	75 basis points for one year.

Day Count Convention:	Payments are per annum paid on a semiannual N360 basis, where A is the actual number of days in the period.
Nonscheduled Termination Date:	With five business days' notice (even if this date is after the maturity date) following a credit event with a termination payment being made.
Termination Payment:	Seller pays *only* upon a credit event:
	Calculation Amount × (Par − Market Value).
	where Market Value means the USD-denominated market value of the reference security on the notification date determined by the calculation agent with reference to a dealer panel.
Credit Event (abbreviated):	Credit condition means either a payment default or a bankruptcy event in respect of the issuer; any war, revolution, insurrection, or hostile act that interferes with foreign exchange transactions; or the expropriation, confiscation, requisition, or nationalization of nonlocal banks, the declaration of a banking moratorium, or suspension of payments by local banks.
	Payment default means ... issuer fails to pay any amount due of the reference asset ... of not less than USD 10 million.
	Bankruptcy event means ... declaration by the issuer of a general moratorium amount of not less than USD 10 million.

Notice that each of the term sheets presented so far differs in several details. This is typical of the proposals circulating in the credit derivatives market and is a reflection of the lack of standardization in the market. Notice that this term sheet uses a termination payment formula based on par instead of on initial price. Market value is determined by at least two but not more than five reference dealers. These terms are negotiable. The RJR Nabisco term sheet allowed for either physical delivery of the defaulted security or a payment calculated on the initial price. The RJR Nabisco term sheet also allowed a net cash settlement. The term sheet for Mexican risk is cash settle only, based on a payment calculated using par, not initial price. For the first time, we see a section allowing substitution of the reference obligation. We examine the issues surrounding calculation of the termination payment using par versus initial price and also examine substitution later.

Even if the bond has not defaulted according to the terms of the prospectus, if any of the credit events as defined clearly in a final confirmation has occurred, the U.S. corporation has remedies. The U.S. corporation must notify the default protection seller in writing that one of the credit default events has occurred. Once that happens, the U.S. corporation has the right to receive a payment according to the formula:

$$\$100 \text{ Million} \times (1 - \text{Market Value at the Tune of}$$
$$\text{the Occurrence of the Credit Event})$$

Notice that the U.S. corporation never actually purchases the global bonds issued by the United Mexican States, the 9.75 percent due 2001. The reasoning is that if such a credit event has occurred, even though the global bonds of the United Mexican States may not be in default, the bonds will probably decline in value. The potential payment under the terms of the credit default swap agreement would then partially hedge the loss in asset value of the Mexican factory.

BASIS RISK: IMPERFECT CORRELATION BETWEEN REFERENCE ASSET(S) & SPECIFIC RISK

Once again, we are plagued by correlation. One cannot write all of the desired terms into the contract. In a perfect world, the U.S. corporation could specify a termination payment as follows: "If the credit event occurs, pay me the decline in value of my Mexican operations due to depreciation in the value of my factory and interruption in income stream due to lost production." Credit derivatives are not designed to protect against this kind of risk. In the absence of a better hedge, it is not unreasonable to take some basis risk to get cash payment, which has some correlation to a drop in asset value in the face of a credit event.

A better hedge might be to reference bonds issued by a Mexican subsidiary of a U.S. corporation. If business of the referenced subsidiary is disrupted due to a credit event, the debt of the subsidiary should trade down in sympathy, reflecting a decline in the value of the subsidiary assets. This would apply only if the subsidiary were highly correlated with the original U.S. corporation seeking the hedge.

Coca-Cola Femsa, a subsidiary of Coca-Cola Bottlers in Mexico, issued 10-year maturity bonds in 1996 (see Figure 3.5). The number of bonds outstanding is only $200 million, and it is difficult to get a market price on these securities because bonds are rarely seen trading in the market. Unfortunately, the lack of liquidity and the lack of ability to fix a reference price make this bond unsuitable as a reference asset. Even if these bonds were relatively traded in the market, however, is this reference asset highly correlated with a producer of technology products? What if a credit event occurs, a national strike in midsummer, for instance, and Mexicans buy more Coca- Cola as an inexpensive source of consolation?

The questions must come before the model. The U.S. corporation must satisfy itself that the price of the protection justifies the residual intangible correlation risk. All events cannot be hedged, just the major events in this case. Because the sovereign debt is more liquid, the U.S. corporation concluded it is the more suitable benchmark for this application.

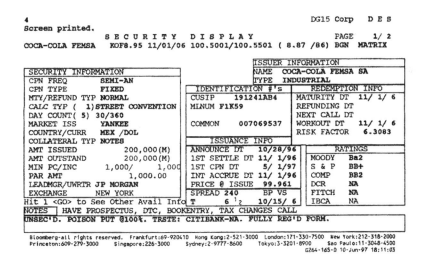

FIGURE 3.5 Security Display for Coca-Cola Femsa (1997)

VARIATIONS IN SOVEREIGN DEFAULT LANGUAGE

The definition of credit events for sovereign names is not standard, even though sovereign default language is readily available from the prospectus. All terms are negotiable. The investor also needs to be aware that aside from negotiated nonprospectus language, the prospectus language itself may vary for two different sovereigns.

The language used in the prospectus for the United Mexican States global bonds differs very slightly from the language shown earlier for Brazil. The threshold amount for nonpayment is $10 million for Mexico, whereas for Brazil the threshold amount is $25 million. As we see next, for high credit quality sovereign borrowers in the loan market, the language describing credit conditions is much less stringent than that for less credit-quality sovereigns.

The higher an issuer's credit rating, the more aggressively it can push to have favorable credit event language in its prospectus. A single issuer could have significant differences in credit default language, depending on when the debt was issued.

It is even possible for a single issuer to use different language when issuing different instruments. A private placement loan placed in the Japanese market may have different language than a euro medium-term note intended for the European market. The following is an excerpt of a September 1996 loan agreement for loans from Japanese insurance companies to the Riksgaeldskontoret, the Swedish National Debt Office (Kingdom of Sweden) then rated Aa3/AA+ (Aaa/AAA as of this writing).

11.1 Occurrence of Events of Default Subject to Clause 11.2, it shall be an Event of Default if:

(1) the Borrower fails to pay on the due date any principal, interest, or other sum due and payable . . .

(2) the Borrower commits any breach of or omits to observe any of its obligations or undertakings under this Agreement. . .

(5) the Borrower declares a general moratorium on its External Indebtedness.

Notice that language referring to negative pledges and cross-default is absent from this loan agreement. The Kingdom of Sweden as borrower is demand in Japan. Sovereign debt and long-dated debt are very popular with Japanese insurance companies, who are content with the credit risk and with the sparse language.

In general, loan documentation is even less standardized than bond documentation. Each bank and legal firm have developed their own favorite clauses. Loans are "inside debt," defined as a loan for which the lender has access to information about the borrower that is not otherwise publicly available. This is true for the interbank loan market in particular. Bank officers may be on the board of directors of a corporation, for instance. For loans privately placed into another country, a loan may not be classified as inside debt and may appear to be like any other senior-secured obligation of the issuer. Bond private placements are loan like transactions with a limited number of investors. "Outside debt," on the other hand, would be publicly traded instruments such as bonds or commercial paper.

In the United States, corporations borrow primarily in the commercial paper market and in the commercial and industrial loan market. The comercial paper market is usually limited to the large, well-known corporate borrowers. Most medium-size and smaller corporates rely on the commercial bank loan market. Borrowers are subject to periodic review by the lenders.

INFORMATION ASYMMETRY
& DOCUMENTATION ASYMMETRY

This brings into focus the issue of "information asymmetry." Bank relationships with the borrower frequently result in a greater variation of terms and conditions than in the publicly traded bond market. Specific terms and conditions may be known by banks but may not be reflected in credit derivatives confirmations.

If one is using a credit derivative to hedge a loan or a bond, the protection buyer is using the credit derivative to protect against the breach of the terms of the original credit document. Documentation asymmetry can occur if the terms are not matched.

If a protection buyer is using a commoditized credit derivative purchased in the broker market to hedge a bond or a loan position, there will very likely be basis risk. This basis risk arises from documentation differences. We see later how commoditized credit derivatives can also result in price risk. This seems to be a compelling reason to avoid the broker markets and to directly negotiate terms and conditions with the direct provider of the credit default protection.

How important are these language differences? When the market thinks the default probability is low, there is very little focus on these differences. When a credit event occurs, swarms of lawyers pore over nuances in the language. Loans can be delinquent for years without being called into default. The need to declare default is usually obviated by intermediate steps such as rescheduling and restructuring. The key is to understand the references in advance and negotiate any additional terms and conditions desired for the final default protection. The price for these additions or deletions may change, but the investor will pay the agreed price for the agreed conditions.

An additional caveat is that there is debate over disclosure issues when banks offer total return swaps and when banks purchase credit default protection, in the form of credit default swaps and options, on loans. How much financial information is the bank required to disclose to its counterparties in these transactions? Does the lending bank have insider information that unfairly advantages it in these transactions? Does the lending bank have an obligation to the original borrower to keep confidential its knowledge of the corporation's nonpublicly disclosed financial information?

When a bank pays the total return on a loan or when a bank buys credit default protection on a loan, the voting rights remain with the bank. There is usually a "gentleman's agreement" that the bank will vote according to the wishes of the total return buyer, or the credit default protection seller. If the bank cannot contact the counterparty, however, it is usually assumed that the bank will vote with the majority of the other lenders.

This may not be in the best interests of the bank's counterparty in the credit derivative transaction, however. There is the further issue that the lenders may have better information than the credit derivative counterparty, which may influence the majority vote.

These are all difficult issues and, as of this writing, have not been satisfactorily resolved. There is no standard in the market. For this reason, it is wise to carefully choose a counterparty based on reputation, expertise, grasp of the issues in the credit derivatives market, and willingness to negotiate terms.

BASIS RISK: MATERIALITY, PRICE ADJUSTMENTS, & SUBSTITUTION

Imbedded in the preceding term sheets were some clauses referring to materiality and price adjustments. Let us examine these clauses more closely:

Materiality: The price of the reference asset less the price adjustment is 90 percent or less relative to the initial price as reasonably determined by the calculation agent.

Price Adjustment: The price of a reference U.S. Treasury security on the notification date less the price on the effective date. The reference U.S. Treasury security will be selected by the calculation agent to match, as far as possible, the maturity and other features of the reference asset.

Materiality clauses are often inserted into credit default swaps to ensure that the credit event is indeed linked to a potential default of the reference bonds. The intent is to prevent exercise of the option merely because of a temporary negative view on the credit or a temporary market dislocation in the price of the bonds due to supply-and-demand factors.

As we see later, materiality clauses are absent from knock-in credit spread default options because a price decline due to a credit spread event is meant to trigger the option. A general increase in interest rates could cause a decline in the price of the bond. For bonds of the same issuer and the same maturity, the coupon makes a difference in the potential price move of the bond. The higher the coupon on the bond, the less sensitive it will be to this price decline. The lower the coupon of the reference bond, the more sensitive it will be to a change in interest rates.

To illustrate why this is the case, it is useful to quickly review what we know about duration. Duration is a shorthand method in the bond market for evaluating the change in the full price of a bond as interest rates rise and fall.

A noncallable bond trading at par has a Macaulay duration of 4.0 and a yield of 10 percent. If interest rates rise so that the bond is repriced to yield 10.1 percent, we can use a quick duration calculation to estimate the new price of the bond. To do this, however, we need to use modified duration, not the Macaulay duration.

Modified Duration   = Macaulay Duration / {(1 + (Yield/2)}
        = 4.0 / {(1 + (0.1/2)}
        = 3.809

What does this 3.809 represent? It represents the percentage price change in the price of the bond for a 100-basis-point move in rates. As rates move up 100 basis points, the price of the bond will move down approximately 3.809 percent, ignoring convexity effects. On a par bond, this represents 3.81 points. Therefore, the repriced bond will have a price of approximately 96.19.

Another security with a coupon of 8 percent, a full price of $70, and a modified duration of 8 would have a very different sensitivity to a change in interest rates. For this bond, the price move for a 100-basis-point increase in rates would be $70 × 0.08 = 5.6 points. This means the new price of the bond would be $64.40.

The relative difference in the price change in these two bonds for a 100-basis-point move in rates is 1.79 points. The bond trading at a discount with a lower coupon and a longer duration has a larger percentage price change than the bond trading near par with the higher coupon.

If the materiality clause did not have a price adjustment feature, the reference asset price could be 90 percent of the initial price due just to a general shift in market interest rates. For a security that is more sensitive to rate moves, this effect would be seen more quickly. The price move could be entirely unrelated to a credit event.

The price adjustment feature attempts to correct for this effect. Although it is impossible to find a Treasury security that will exactly match the price characteristics of a reference asset as interest rates move, a

Treasury security with the closest possible characteristics is chosen. The price move of the Treasury security is then used to normalize, or adjust, the price of the reference asset. If the reference asset moved 7 points downward in price and the Treasury security moved down 7 points in price, the adjusted price would be exactly the same as the initial price. This is because the negative 7-point price move of the Treasury security is subtracted from the downward price move of the reference asset. This negative subtraction results in a positive price adjustment to get back to the initial price. Every effort is made so that market price factors do not trigger a credit event.

If the price of the reference asset drops 20 points and the price of the Treasury security drops 4 points, the normalized price of the reference asset would be deemed to have declined 16 points. If the original price was par, this 16-point price decline would constitute materiality. If a credit condition has not occurred, however, there would be no trigger of a termination payment. Only if a credit condition has occurred and materiality exists will a termination payment be triggered under the terms of an agreement that includes a materiality clause.

There are several other issues involving materiality that will not be obvious in a term sheet but should be specified in the confirmation. The market can use an averaging method in which the average price for a period of 10 days must be 90 percent of the initial price or lower for materiality to exist. Another method is the simple method in which materiality exists if on any one day the price is 90 percent of the initial price or lower. This is a matter of personal preference. Not surprisingly, the default protection buyer may want a simple test, and the default protection seller may want an averaging method.

Another issue may crop up when a credit condition exists but the materiality test is not met. How long must one go on testing before rejecting the credit condition as a credit event? This is entirely negotiable. Most default protection sellers will want a limited time period, such as 10 days. A default protection buyer may wish to insist on an unlimited number of days.

Even the frequency of evaluation to determine materiality is negotiable. One can evaluate daily or weekly, for instance. Because materiality is a necessary but not sufficient condition to determine whether a credit event has occurred, it is not necessary to make calculations to determine materiality until notification of a credit condition has occurred. After the notification, however, a default protection buyer may want a daily evaluation as opposed to a weekly evaluation. A default protection seller, on the other hand, may wish to have the longest possible time period between evaluations.

None of the preceding may be obvious from the term sheet. As we saw from the earlier term sheets, length of testing time, average versus simple determination, and frequency of evaluation are usually absent from term sheet language. These features are usually negotiated in the confirmation and there is no standard. Credit default protection buyers and sellers must negotiate the final document together.

BASIS RISK AND SUBSTITUTION

Substitution is another clause that may be present in some term sheets and absent in others. Going back to the plain vanilla, or traditional, term sheet earlier in this chapter, let us take another look at the substitution language:

Substitution: If the amount of the reference asset (or a substitute) is materially reduced, the calculation agent shall reasonably select a substitute issued or guaranteed by the reference name that is of the same credit quality as the reference asset and with a maturity at least that of the reference asset and shall notify the counterparties. If no substitute can be found, the swap will terminate with no further payments on either side.

If the reference asset is no longer priceable in the market, if the reference asset can no longer be produced, or if the reference asset has been paid down, then it makes no sense to have that specific security as a reference asset. In that case one would want to substitute another reference asset while keeping the credit risk identical. Often the maturity of the reference asset and the maturity of the credit default swap differ, but the maturity of the reference asset must be as long as or longer than the maturity of the credit default swap.

The maturity of the reference asset may make a difference in the determination of the termination payment in the event of default. If the agreement calls for physical delivery of a reference asset, the maturity can make a difference as well. A U.S. investment bank gave an Israeli bank a proposal that called for delivery of either a short-dated bond with a maturity near the maturity of the credit default swap or a long-dated bond with a maturity five years longer than the maturity of the credit default swap. This optional delivery was separate from the substitution clause, and the reason for it may have been different.

A bond-trading house may want to hedge more than one security, but the credit default protection seller should not be indifferent. In the event of default, bond prices typically become depressed. In the early 1980s, Latin American debt traded at severely depressed levels, and bonds of different maturities traded at different levels. The payment in the event of default for two bonds with maturities five years apart could very well trade at different levels, with the longer maturity bond likely to trade at a default market price well below the shorter-dated bond.

There is nothing wrong with the Israeli bank agreeing to this proposal, but the cost of the perceived difference between this proposal and a proposal that suggests delivery of a bond with a maturity near the maturity of the credit default swap should be factored into the decision-making process.

OTC TERMINATION PAYMENTS

There are several different methods of calculating credit default swap termination payments. Counterparties should know the differences among the methods. In a February 1997 cover story article of Emerging Markets Investor, the following definition was given for a *credit default swap:*

A transaction where a protection-buyer pays an upfront or annual premium to a protection-seller (an investor willing to take that exposure at the right price), in return for protection against default of some underlying reference credit. If default occurs during the life of the swap, *the protection seller pays the par value of the asset, minus recovery value.* (Italics mine.)

This is the structure with which most newcomers to the credit derivatives market are most comfortable. This structure has been touted in numerous articles published on credit derivatives over the past couple of years. But it is only one of several structures in the market. In some instances, the structure is actually inappropriate for certain reference assets.

There are three common types of credit default termination payments in the market and a fourth type that is being employed by counterparties who want to hedge nonpar assets:

1. Digital cash payment.
2. Par minus post-default price method,
3. Initial price minus post-default price method.
4. Normalized price minus post-default price method.

Digital Cash Payment

The digital cash payment structure has a termination payment based on a fixed percentage of the notional principal. Usually there is no physical delivery of the reference asset to the default protection seller. The default protection seller, however, makes the pre-agreed payment in the event of default. There are also two types of pre-agreed termination payments.

The first is a binary payment equal to the entire notional amount. For instance, if the notional amount of the credit agreement is $50 million, the payment if a credit event occurs is $50 million. This digital payment carries a great deal of risk to the default protection seller. The probability of default is combined with an *all-or-nothing* payment on the notional amount. The premium for giving this type of protection should be greater. The default protection seller should consider whether this structure makes sense for the application. These structures are also known as *zero-one structures*. I do not recommend them. The risk is not strictly related to credit default risk. Rather a credit default event is an event trigger, which causes the investor to lose the entire investment.

Although credit derivatives are not insurance products, perhaps an insurance analogy would be useful here. "Would you write a fire insurance policy that allowed you to recover the entire cost of a home if the fire damage were limited to the kitchen? If it appears that I am not a fan of the all-or-nothing termination payment structure, it is because I am not. I encourage investors to avoid this structure. I see very little need to offer credit protection on the entire notional amount when recovery rates are usually greater than zero.

The second type of pre-agreed termination payment requires a fixed cash payment in the event of default. This might be set at 50 percent of the notional amount in the event of default, for instance. Many of these structures seem arbitrary but may be linked to a percentage recovery rate to credit enhance another piece of a complicated structure. If the structure is linked to historical recovery rates for the reference asset credit, the pre-agreed payment method may make sense. The determination of which method to use, however, is up to the default protection seller.

Another case in which the pre-agreed fixed cash payment makes sense is one in which the buyer of the default protection estimates a recovery value or a default price for a security but feels that market volatility after a default event may cause the reference asset to temporarily trade below its true value. Daily price volatility can be enormous. As most credit default contracts look for settlement within a month of an event, a daily price fluctuation can work against the default protection buyer. If the protection buyer wants protection against this possibility, it can make sense to agree in advance on a fair default payment.

Par Minus the MV of the Reference Asset

The most common termination payment calculation in the market today uses the following formula:

$$\text{Calculation Amount} \times (\text{Par} - \text{Market Value})$$

where the calculation amount is equal to the face value of the reference asset. This method was used in the vanilla term sheet at the beginning of this chapter. The market value is the post default price of the reference asset and is usually determined by a dealer poll. This method may be fine when there is no physical delivery involved and the default protection buyer is merely trying to hedge a country risk or a general credit risk, as opposed to a specific asset. This method may not be acceptable, however, when the reference asset is trading well above or well below par. When the credit default protection buyer is trying to hedge an actual position and the reference asset is trading above or below par, this method is simply incorrect.

Initial Price Minus the Market Value

The third common type of structure is a payment of the initial price of the reference asset minus the post default price. The credit default protection buyer receives this payment and, in return, must make physical delivery of the reference asset. If the credit default protection buyer does not own the asset, the asset theoretically can be purchased in the market at the post default price, which should be equal to the market value.

But what if the credit default protection buyer does own the asset? What if the asset is trading above par? What if the asset is trading below par? The initial price minus the post default price method was meant to somehow make up for this. That structure is shown in the next abbreviated indicative term sheet.

Notice that the structure in the term sheet does not take into account accrued interest on the coupon of the reference asset. But if the credit default protection buyer owns the reference asset, the buyer should naturally want to hedge the loss of this potential coupon as well. The potential accrued coupon loss will vary. For instance, three bonds with the same credit and the same maturity will have different prices for different coupons. For higher-yielding bonds, the difference can be significant, as shown by the different initial prices and coupons for three different bonds with the same assumed credit and maturity.

Initial Price	Coupon
105	10.9%
100	9.5%
95	8.6%

Nonpar bonds pose a problem. If the bond is trading above par, the default protection seller does not want to receive the same premium as for

UNITED STATES OF MEXICO CREDIT DEFAULT SWAP
Abbreviated Indicative Term Sheet
Initial Price Is Used to Calculate Payment

Calculation Amount:	USD 10 million.
Reference Security:	United Mexican States, global bond. Initial price of the security: **105.**
Nonscheduled Termination Date:	With five business days' notice (even if this date is after the maturity date) following a credit event with a termination payment being made.
Termination Payment:	Default protection seller pays only upon a credit event: **Calculation Amount × (Initial Price – Market Value)** where market value means the USD-denominated market value of the reference security on the notification date determined by the calculation agent with reference to a dealer panel

a bond trading at par. The default protection buyer wants a termination payment linked to the above-par initial price of the bond and should also ask for accrued but unpaid coupon interest at the time of the credit event.

The problem with making a termination payment based on the initial price is that as the bond approaches maturity, the bond decretes to par. The default
protection seller is actually paying out more than the loss on the reference asset.

One bank's credit derivatives desk in New York said that they do not try to make an adjustment for the price of the bond because that is "too complicated." Rather, they adjust the calculation amount of the transaction. This compensates the default protection seller for the additional termination payment because the default protection buyer pays a fee based on a calculation amount adjusted to reflect the initial price of the bond. The following term sheet shows how the calculation amount is adjusted to

UNITED STATES OF MEXICO CREDIT DEFAULT SWAP
Abbreviated Indicative Term Sheet
Adjusted Calculation Amount Above Par Price

Calculation Amount:	USD 10.5 million.
Reference Security:	United Mexican States, global bond.
Initial price of the security:	105.
Nonscheduled Termination Date:	With five business days' notice (even if this date is after the maturity date) following a credit event with a termination payment being made.
Termination Payment:	Default protection seller pays *only upon* a credit event:
	Calculation Amount × (Par – Market Value)
	where market value means the USD-denominated market value of the reference security on the notification date determined by the calculation agent with reference to a dealer panel.

$10,500,000 to account for a bond with $10,000,000 face amount trading at a price of 105.With bonds trading below par, the par minus post default price method will overstate the termination payment for the bond if the bond defaults prior to the bond's maturity date. Yet this is the way most of the credit default agreements are written for bonds trading a few points below par. Furthermore, for bonds trading below par, the initial price minus post default price method understates the termination payment for a default protection buyer trying to hedge a bond position.

These methods have led to much confusion. One large U.S. commercial bank underhedged a position in an Argentine bond trading at a price of 110. The bond was asset swapped using a par asset swap package. The U.S. commercial bank then purchased credit default protection on the Argentine bond from another bank using the par minus post default price calculation method for the termination payment.

What if the bond defaulted after day one? What would have happened? Assuming interest rates had not moved, the U.S. commercial bank would have a defaulted Argentine bond and would have an open swap position. The U.S. commercial bank's swap position would be 10 points under water because the 10-point bond premium was to have been paid over time as an above-market fixed coupon on the swap. The credit default premium calculated based on par, rather than on the actual 110 price of the reference asset, would leave the U.S. commercial bank with a 10-point loss after the credit event.

Normalized Price Method

To be fair to both the default protection buyer and the seller, one should account for the initial price of the reference asset and recognize that the price of the reference security will change over time. The price will decrete to par if the reference asset is initially trading above par. The price will accrete to par if the reference asset is initially trading below par. Naturally, the reflected price should be adjusted to screen out price changes due to market moves and changes in the term structure of credit spreads.

Creating a fictitious asset with the same maturity and coupon as the reference asset can normalize the price of the reference asset. The spread of the *reference* asset to a "risk-free" asset, such as an AAA Treasury security, is input into a bond pricing calculator. That way, as the reference asset approaches maturity, the price of the shorter maturity proxy bond can be used as the reference price to calculate the termination payment owed under the credit default agreement.

The following term sheet shows how this might work in practice. This can work for both dollar and nondollar assets but let us look at a U.S. dollar-denominated asset and choose a U.S. Treasury security as a risk-free reference. This term sheet, although not as detailed as a confirmation, addresses the issues discussed earlier and summarizes them on one term sheet.

*****

BRAZIL CREDIT DEFAULT SWAP
Indicative Term Sheet

Default Protection Buyer:	Default protection buyer.
Default Protection Seller:	Default protection seller.

Reference Obligation:

Issuer/Borrower:	Federative Republic of Brazil (the Republic).
Rating:	B1/BB—.
Type:	Eurobond.
Currency Denomination:	USD.
Coupon:	8.875% (payable annually 30/360).
Maturity:	November 5, 2001.
Initial Reference Price:	To be announced (approximately 104.125).
Initial Reference ISMA Yield:	To be announced [ISMA is the International Securities Market Association].
Initial Risk-Free Bond:	U.S. on-the-run Treasury with a maturity closest to that of the remaining maturity of the reference obligation.
Initial Risk-Free Bond Price:	To be announced.
Initial Risk-Free Bond	
ISMA Yield:	To be announced.
Initial Reference Yield Spread:	To be announced.
Trade Date:	As soon as practical.
Effective Date:	One week from trade date.
Termination Date:	November 5, 2001.

Payments of the Default Protection Buyer:

Calculation Amount:	USD 20 million.
Payment Amount and Dates:	XXX basis points per annum calculated from the effective date to the earlier of
	1. November 5, 2001, *or*
	2. the termination payment date.

| Day Count Convention: | Payments are made in USD based on an A/360day count, where A is the actual number of days in the period. |

Payments of the Default Protection Seller:

Calculation Amount:	USD 20 million.
Condition to Payment:	If the calculation agent receives notice of credit event prior to the termination date.
Calculation Date:	The date on which the termination payment is calculated.
Termination Payment Date:	Three business days following the valuation date.
Termination Payment:	The default protection seller pays to the default protection buyer the following amount:
	(Calculation Amount × Calculation Price) +
	Accrued but Unpaid Interest on the
	Reference Obligation
Calculation Price:	Equal to the price of a bond with the same coupon, coupon dates, and maturity as the reference obligation yielding the calculation yield.
Calculation Yield:	The yield according to the ISMA yield of the initial risk-free bond at the calculation date using the risk-free-bond settlement price plus the initial reference yield spread.
ISMA Yield:	Yield calculated on a 30E/360 basis following the method of the ISMA.
Risk-Free-Bond Settlement Price:	The default protection buyer and the default protection seller will agree on a midmarket price for the initial risk-free bond on the calculation date. If they cannot agree, then a dealer poll will be made to obtain the risk-free-bond settlement price.
Obligation of the Default	The default protection buyer will deliver the
Protection Buyer:	aggregate principal amount of the reference obligation equal in value to the calculation amount. The bonds will be delivered versus payment on the termination payment date, if any.

Notification of Calculation Date: Upon a credit condition, the default protection buyer shall have the right to designate the calculation date by delivering notice to the default protection seller.

Credit Event: Occurs when the default protection buyer is aware of any credit conditions supported by publicly available information and at the same time materiality exists. Credit condition means an event of default as defined in the confirmation. The language of the agreed confirmation will supersede any deviations from that language in the following summary. In summary, a credit condition occurs if any of the following events occurs:

1. Default in any payment of principal or interest on any of the notes (reference obligations) and continuance of such default for a period of 30 days; *or*

2. Default that is materially prejudicial to the interests of the noteholders in the performance of any other obligation under the notes and the continuance of such default for a period of 30 days after written notice requiring the same to be remedied shall have been given to the principal paying agent by the holder of any note; *or*

3. Acceleration of in excess of USD 25 million (or its equivalent in any other currency) in aggregate principal amount of public external indebtedness of the Federative Republic of Brazil by reason of any default (how-

ever described) resulting from the failure of the issuer to make any payment of principal or interest thereunder when due; *or*

4. Failure to make any payment in respect of public external indebtedness of the Federative Republic of Brazil in an aggregate principal amount in excess of USD 25 million (or its equivalent in any other currency) when due (as such date may be extended by virtue of any applicable grace period or waiver) and the continuance of such failure for a period of 30 days after written notice requiring the same to be remedied

shall have been given to the principal paying agent by the holder of any note; *or*

5. Declaration by the Federative Republic of Brazil of a moratorium with respect to the payment of principal or interest on public external indebtedness of the Federative Republic of Brazil that does not expressly exclude the notes and that is materially prejudicial to the interests of the noteholders; *or*

6. The Federative Republic of Brazil shall deny its obligations under the notes.

Materiality:	Occurs when the price of the reference obligation less price adjustment is 90 percent or less relative to the initial reference price. The default protection seller and the default protection buyer will agree on the price of the reference obligation at the calculation date. If they cannot agree, a dealer poll will be made to obtain the price of the reference obligation at the calculation date.
Publicly Available Information:	Information that has been published in any two or more internationally recognized published or electronically displayed financial news sources. Nonetheless, if either of the parties or any of their respective affiliates is cited as the sole source for such information, then such information will be deemed not to be publicly available information.
Price Adjustment:	The risk-free-bond settlement price less the initial risk-free-bond price.
Business Days:	Days on which commercial banks and foreign exchange markets settle payments in London, Frankfurt, and New York.
Business Day Convention:	Modified following.
Calculation Agent:	Default protection seller, whose determinations and calculations shall be made in good faith and in a commercially reasonable manner and which shall be binding in the absence of manifest error.
Documentation:	This transaction will be documented as a confirmation under the existing ISDA master agreement between

	the default protection seller and the default protection buyer.
Law:	Per the ISDA master agreement.
Suitability:	This transaction will be executed with a counterparty with such knowledge and experience in financial matters to be capable of evaluating the merits and risks of the prospective transaction.
Early Termination/Assignment:	An over-the-counter derivative transaction of this type may not be assigned, transferred, or terminated prior to its stated termination *date* by either party without the consent of the other party except as stipulated in the terms of the transaction.
Firm Unwind Prices:	The default protection seller may quote a firm price that the default protection seller would pay or charge to unwind the transaction prior
	to maturity. A firm unwind price for a transaction of this type will be affected by the then current level of the market, but it may also be affected by other factors. A firm unwind price for a transaction of this type can change significantly from day to day over the life of the transaction.
Periodic Pricing:	It is the current practice (but not a legal obligation) of the default protection seller to provide in a transaction of this type information in writing about the value of such transaction upon request of its counterparty. A routine periodic pricing may be different from a firm unwind price for the same transaction.

This term sheet gets us a lot closer to our ideal of the fair price in the market. Even this term sheet, however, ignores the term structure of the credit spreads of the reference asset. This term sheet creates a fictitious bond using the credit spread of the reference asset to the risk-free bond at the trade date, the beginning of the transaction. Most securities, however, have a term structure of credit spreads, and often the credit spread narrows as the bond approaches maturity. This effect is ignored. One way to adjust for this effect is to use the credit default offer spreads on the trade date to specify spreads to be used for years one through four. Spreads for intermediate time periods can be interpolated.

Market Value and Termination Payments

The time to negotiate the mechanism for determining the termination payment and market price of the reference asset is before the close of a transaction. This detail should not be left to lawyers drafting confirmation language after the transaction has closed. There is no standard language, so counterparties should be aware of the available choices. Reference asset market price determination is not always straightforward, and additional negotiated payments may be folded into termination payments if a credit event occurs.

The default protection seller may agree to pay accrued, but as yet unpaid, interest on the reference asset. This point must be negotiated up front. The payment or nonpayment of accrued interest is not "understood" between dealers, because there is no set rule. Therefore, if payment of accrued interest after the occurrence of a credit event has not been specifically mentioned, the default protection buyer cannot add it to the terms of a confirmation after the close of the transaction. If a default protection buyer requires this payment, the buyer must explicitly state that as one of the terms of the transaction and should insist on a term sheet that reflects this condition. If there is no term sheet and the transaction is a verbal agreement, save the recorded phone conversation until the final confirmation that reflects all of the required transaction terms has been signed by all parties. For any complex transaction, it is a good idea to insist on final term sheets because final confirmations may not arrive for a couple of weeks from understaffed legal departments. Furthermore, it is also a good idea to note the day and the time of a transaction in case you must refer to a tape recording of the transaction conversation. Human memories cause honest mistakes, and misunderstandings are quickly resolved in the face of good documentation.

Hedge costs are the wild card in credit default swaps. Often hedge costs are folded into termination payments. This is most common when a buyer of protection asks for credit default protection on a par asset swap package. The buyer will usually get a par-market value payment plus accrued interest plus hedge costs. The hedge costs are the costs of unwinding the swap in the asset swap package. Because the reference asset is often not priced at par; the price difference from par is reflected in the hedge cost. It is important to note that the seller of protection does not usually get a rebate if there is a net market gain in the hedge. If there is net market loss, however, the hedge cost will most likely reflect all costs to make sure the buyer is made completely whole. In credit-linked note structures (we will see an example later), issuers often incorporate the hedge costs of a swap from fixed to floating coupons as part of the termination payment. This is tricky for the seller because the theory is that the hedge costs make up for any price difference from par of the reference asset. This practice is even used in multicurrency structures in which an issuer may hedge a nondollar asset to dollars. This is fine if the intention of the default protection seller is to hedge all of the risks for the buyer on a dollar basis, but that cost should be factored into the seller's price of protection.

Market price determination can be tricky even for a TRS. TRS structures referencing liquid assets often use a cash settlement at the maturity of the TRS with an option for physical delivery of the reference asset. The option to switch from cash to physical delivery may be the right of either the TRS receiver or the TRS payer. In the event of default of the reference asset in the TRS, the mechanism for determination of market value is often a dealer poll. A calculation agent would typically call three to five dealers and take the average price. The calculation agent is very often one of the dealers offering a price.

Very illiquid assets may require measures other than a dealer poll. High-yield assets in the United States, for instance, can be very difficult to price. Many securities do not trade often, and dealers do not stand ready to help out competitors by providing pricing. For cases such as this, an auction method is preferable. The deal confirmation may call for an auction set at the maturity of a TRS for a total return transaction or after a credit event in the case of a credit default option. The receiver of the TRS or the seller of credit default protection who is not happy with the results of the auction can retain the right to take physical delivery of the reference asset.

As we saw in the case of digital payments, a reference asset may not be available, or physical delivery may not be an option. Some structures may simply reference the "senior unsecured" obligation of a reference credit. There may be no stated reference asset at all; a protection buyer may simply wish to hedge general balance sheet exposure. In the event of default, the payout may be the Moody's standard recovery rate for senior unsecured debt—the recovery rate is 51 percent.

Buyers and sellers of credit default protection and counterparties in total return swaps must be sensitive to the nuances of termination payments. If necessary, one can agree in principle to a transaction subject to a review of all of the conditions. That way, a buyer or a seller who is unsure or who needs to review information can take the time to do this and then go back and negotiate a final transaction. There is no need to rush into a trans-action. Heading off a potential misunderstanding saves a lot of time in the long run.

PRICING AND APPLICATIONS

The Funding Cost Advantage

Credit default protection should logically trade at the spread of the refer-ence security to a risk-free asset. For instance, if a 10-year maturity bond trades at a spread of 100 basis points to the 10-year U.S. Treasury, the amount of spread due to credit risk is about 100 basis points. Some of the 100 basis points may be due to liquidity. Credit default swaps, however, tend to trade at a level that is benchmarked to the asset swap market. This is because most banks benchmark their funding costs based on a spread to SOFR or other floating rate and look at the net spread they can earn on a given credit relative to their funding costs.

Now that we have some familiarity with basic structures in the credit derivatives market, let us take another look at how a bank might put together a credit default swap while hedging the credit default risk by buying protection from another bank (see Figure 3.6). The commercial bank entering into this transaction has a funding cost of SOFR−15 bps per annum. The net spread earned by the commercial bank in this transaction is 90 bps minus the 50 bps the commercial bank pays for the credit default protection. That is a total of 40 basis points. But there is an additional benefit. Because the commercial bank borrows at a sub-SOFR rate, SOFR −15 bps, the bank realizes an additional 15 basis points in spread. The commercial bank's advantage is actually 55 bps per annum.

Although it is always true that a lower funding cost is better, notice that if the commercial bank had a funding cost of 45 basis points per annum,

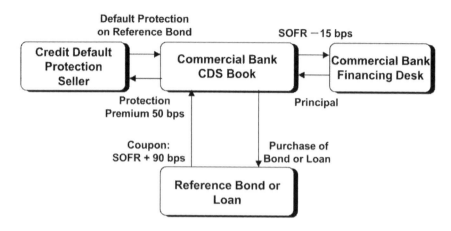

FIGURE 3.6 Credit Default Swap Application: Commercial Bank Purchases a Bond and Arranges a Hedge

his trade would not even be possible. The 40 bps per annum spread between the reference bond and the cost of the credit protection would have been inadequate. The high-cost borrower bank would have to pay SOFR +45 bps to raise the money to borrow the bond in the first place, leaving it with an all-in net spread of −5 basis points.

The high-cost borrower, however, is happy to receive the credit protection premium of 50 basis points to take the credit of the reference bond. That is a net spread of 50 basis points, which would have been unattainable for the bank if it had purchased the reference bond outright.

Often professionals new to the market ask why a bank would sell credit default protection when it could just buy the asset outright. The answer usually comes down to the funding cost of the bank. Other reasons include the opportunity to earn off—balance sheet income and the lack of need to use actual economic capital to earn income.

COMMENTS ON PRICING CDS

Although this book is not intended to provide a methodology for pricing credit derivatives, there are certain features of credit default protection that are worth pointing out before delving into new structures.

As one U.S. bank credit derivatives department head said, in talking about some of the more exotic credit default structures: "The spread is where it is because that's where the market says it is." What he was referring to is that the models for certain types of credit derivatives either do not exist or require assumptions about unknowable unknowns. Earlier we discussed unknowable unknowns, such as the U.S. homeowner's prepayment rate on mortgages when interest rates decline. Investment banking firms kept archives of historical data, researchers created sophisticated models to match the data, but the U.S. homeowner prepaid faster than the models expected. The U.S. homeowner did not care about models, did not care about data, but did care about favorable refinancing terms and shocked the market to its senses.

The equation on the following page is an example of how the unknowable unknowns in the credit derivatives market can lead to gross oversimplifications. One of the most common equations used in this example equates the probability of default (an unknowable unknown) to the credit swap spread divided by the expected loss rate, which is expressed as one minus the recovery rate of the obligor.

We are guessing at default probabilities, and we are guessing at recovery values for the issuer. There is a great degree of variance in both of these values. The lower the credit quality of the issuer, the more dramatic the variance.

This is why global banks invest in computers, people power, and money to try to analyze financial data to come up with better estimates of default probabilities and recovery rates for companies. Right now, these data inputs are still unknowable unknowns, so we make our best-informed guesses given the economic resources, time, and intelligence available to us.

This is why the market relies so heavily on asset swap spreads. The theory is that if the market prices information efficiently—a big "if"—we will have the best information possible already imbedded in market levels.

There is value in the market observation approach. We trade the market; we do not trade the models. Also, if we all suffer from the same hallucination about credit spreads, we can trade on the basis of this common hallucination. I cannot trade uncertainty. I can trade certainty, however, even if the certainty is based on a common hallucination.

$$P_{(default)} = \frac{\text{Credit Spread}}{1 - R_{(obligor)}}$$

where

$$\text{Credit Spread} = \frac{\left[\Sigma_i\, D_{i+1} - \text{Cum}P(ND_{i+1}) \right] \times \left[(1 - R_{obligor}) \times \text{Marg } P(Def_{i+1}) \right]}{\Sigma_i\, D_{i+1} - \text{Cum}P(ND_i)}$$

and

$$\frac{\Sigma_i\, D_{i+1} - \text{Cum}P(ND_{i+1})}{\Sigma_i\, D_{i+1} - \text{Cum}P(ND_i)} = 1$$

Credit Spread $\quad$ = Credit Swap Spread
$R_{(obligor)}$ $\qquad\qquad$ = Obligor recovery rate in the event of default
Cum $P\,(ND_i)$ $\quad$ = Cumulative probability of no default at time i
Marg $P\,(Def_{i+1})$ = Marginal probability of default at time $i + 1$
D_{i+1} $\qquad\qquad$ = Risk-free discount factor at time $i + 1$
Cum $P\,(ND_{i+1})$ = Cumulative probability of no default at time $i + 1$

Lest market participants get too concerned about this ambiguity in the data, we need to remind ourselves that banks have always lent money on this basis, often using no data whatsoever. Often banks have lent money for even worse reasons.

Savings and loan associations in the United States nearly went under in the 1980s due to the losses suffered from real estate loans made on the basis of assurances by fast-talkers. The capital, the capacity, and the character of the borrower were brushed over in favor of whether the borrower was a "friend of the bank" or, worse, a contributor to the private pension funds of key officers of the financial institution. After the fact, due diligence some-times revealed that there was no underlying building whatsoever. U.S. banks rushed to lend to Latin America in the 1970s to their regret in the early 1980s. Loan rates in Europe are ridiculously slim. Lending rates are often justified with the phrase: "That is how we have always lent money." The decision is whether to lend to the corporation, not what spread should we charge if we decide to lend the money. Generally, the level is based merely on what the bank feels the market will bear. The decision isn't based on a rigorous fundamental analysis of the balance sheet for well-known credits. The credit spigot is either open at broad-brush market levels, or the credit spigot is closed because the bank does not want any more of that type of credit. Global and European banks have billions of dollars' worth of loans put on at levels that do not justify their current return on capital.

Taken in this context, credit derivative swap spread pricing starts to look like nuclear physics. I am not trying to make a case for complacency, however. We need to do better than we have done in the past, and we need to do better than we are currently doing in the pricing of credit derivatives.

Credit default protection has many features, which makes it difficult to model. For one thing, it is "sticky." This is primarily because human beings are "sticky." We tend to stick to one location. We have a need for stability. Most of us are homebodies. We claim we have efficient markets, electronic transfer of data, and instantaneous access to knowledge. But this is a myth.

Banks tend to lend money to people who are close to them. The credit concentration of a typical bank's portfolio tends to be concentrated among credits in their own country or neighboring countries. Often, bank credit concentrations will reflect the region of the country closest to them. That is natural. Banks tend to understand the credit risk of businesses that operate on their doorstep. We humans tend to feel we understand things that are familiar. We have only so much time and so much life in which to evaluate data and make our decisions. Although it is true that banks will buy foreign bank debt and foreign assets, the credit concentration buildup is most often to credits close to home.

Asset managers do their best to diversify risk. But over time they too see a buildup of well-known credits as they make the easy decision to concentrate in assets for which they have the most data and the most research. Although this is not universally true, it is often true. Investment banks provide research on the credits they sell, and the market—although professionals hate to admit it—has a herd mentality.

This is where credit derivatives can be helpful because the main reason for the existence of credit derivatives is to diversify credit risk in a portfolio of assets. Purchasing credit default protection is one way to reduce exposure to a credit in a portfolio of assets. Many capital-rich entities, such as economic development corporations (EDCs), find themselves with a high degree of credit concentration in a few credits. These are the credits that borrow money to develop business, which supports the economy of the home country. The EDCs do not want to be seen selling off portions of their loan portfolio. At the same time, they need to diversify risk. A credit default swap is the ideal vehicle for removing this exposure from the EDC's balance sheet. An EDC can purchase credit default protection in the form of a credit default swap, or it can do a TRS to remove this risk from its balance sheet. The EDC can then further diversify credit risk by purchasing other assets in the cash markets that meet the criteria of being related to the economic development of their home country.

The question is: How much should the credit default protection cost? There are inefficiencies in the credit derivatives market, which generate nonrational prices. Supply and demand drive this market. Nonetheless, it is useful to know when one is paying too much or when one is getting a better price than rational models will allow.

There are other factors that drive the market beyond supply and demand and can create nonrational pricing. Evaluation of credit default pricing requires several assumptions, as we shall see in a moment. It is a useful exercise to stress test these assumptions.

Most modelers of credit derivatives build models to predict the possible payoffs. If I were to buy credit default protection, I would build a model and make some assumptions. This model might be no more than looking up a few key variables and putting pen to paper, but I would still use an algorithm to produce an answer that I find defensible and replicable. Key inputs include the following:

- Credit quality of the issuer (or issuers, in the case of baskets) as defined by my internal credit committee.
- Correlation among the issuer(s) and the correlation of the issuer(s) with the credit protection seller.
- Credit quality of the default protection seller as defined by my credit committee.
- Probability of default of the issuer(s) and the credit default protection seller.

- Joint probabilities of default in the event that the issuer(s) and credit default protection seller are correlated.
- Assumed recovery rates in the event of default as defined by my exposure management group, and the leverage of the structure.
- Maturity of the deal and any provisions I have made regarding settlement.
- Supply and demand for the credit default protection.
- Economic research, which may change my view of the credit quality.
- Urgency of the need to reduce my credit exposure.
- Special documentation considerations.
- The BIS risk weighting of the default protection seller (this last one because I work for a bank).

Notice that most of the inputs to the model require some assumptions. The internal-credit-quality perception of the issuer is distinct from the probability of default and the recovery rate in the event of default. Although I may assess a low probability of default, my internal bank-credit people may have a view of an improving or a deteriorating credit based on fundamental analysis, which is not reflected in data tables for a given name. Supply-and-demand considerations are also based on market observations and assumptions.

Key variables, which also require assumptions, are probability of default, the recovery rate, and the correlation between the issuer(s) and the credit default protection seller. In the following discussion, I generally refer to the default risk of an issuer, but it should be understood that this also applies to the default risk of the default protection seller, the counterparty.

The probability of default and the recovery rate are based on historical data, and estimates are available from databases kept in the public market as well as from proprietary databases. The major rating agencies maintain tables that show the probability of default for bonds with given ratings. These data are based on historical data, which includes mainly U.S. and European credits. These data are often used to estimate default probabilities for any bond with the same rating.

The market extrapolates data to include Asian and sovereign bonds.

There is limited information on sovereign default probabilities which tend to be both event and credit related. There is no way to refine the data, except to pay attention to global economic and political events.

Several characteristics of probability of default are worth noting. There is a low joint-default frequency among asset classes. Whereas credit spreads will be highly correlated for asset classes, default probability is not, except for systemic risk. Trading and hedging are much more difficult for default risk than for market risk. It is difficult to find a highly correlated—much less fungible—security in the same asset class to use as a hedge. All is not lost, however. It is the very absence of strong correlation that allows a portfolio manager to benefit from diversification.

Another characteristic is that default risk may vary over time. Rating agencies keep data that measure the cumulative risk of issuer default over the term of an obligation. For discrete time periods within the term of an obligation, rating agencies also measure the marginal risk of default, which shows the change in the default probability of the issuer over time. During the term of an obligation, it is wise to refresh these data to incorporate current data and revised predictions on the credit prospects of an issuer. Tables 3.1 through 3.4 show Moody's and S&P's cumulative and marginal default rates for a wide range of rated assets.

Recovery rates pose another problem. Credit officers at many institutions may do individual name analysis based on their experience and on the fundamentals of the company. A bank with a long lending relationship may have access to data that are difficult to obtain in the public market and may be the best source of a recovery value estimate.

The major rating agencies keep extensive databases on recovery rates for individual names, which can be used in a credit default price analysis. They also compile data on rated securities and their recovery rates. But the best way is to estimate recovery rates based on individual balance sheets.

The rating of the security is backward looking. Current financial information is crucial. Seniority of the obligation (see Table 3.5) and the capital structure of the issuer(s) are key factors in recovery rate estimates. Senior secured debt has a much higher average recovery rate than even

TABLE 3.1 Moody's Marginal Default Rates (%), 1970–1994

	\multicolumn{10}{c}{Years}									
	1	2	3	4	5	6	7	8	9	10
Aaa	0.00	0.00	0.00	0.00	0.10	0.10	0.10	0.10	0.10	0.20
Aa	0.00	0.00	0.10	0.10	0.10	0.10	0.10	0.10	0.10	0.20
A	0.00	0.10	0.20	0.10	0.20	0.20	0.20	0.20	0.20	0.30
Baa	0.20	0.30	0.40	0.50	0.50	0.40	0.60	0.70	0.60	0.50
Ba	1.70	2.40	2.40	2.40	2.20	1.80	1.50	1.40	1.30	1.30
B	7.90	6.30	5.10	4.00	3.20	3.20	2.10	2.00	1.50	1.40

TABLE 3.2 Average Marginal Default Rates (%), S&P, 1981–1996

	\multicolumn{10}{c}{Years}									
	1	2	3	4	5	6	7	8	9	10
AAA	0.00	0.00	0.06	0.07	0.08	0.18	0.19	0.34	0.13	0.16
AA	0.00	0.02	0.09	0.11	0.16	0.21	0.18	0.15	0.09	0.16
A	0.05	0.09	0.10	0.16	0.20	0.19	0.23	0.29	0.30	0.31
BBB	0.17	0.25	0.26	0.54	0.50	0.56	0.53	0.46	0.37	0.33
BB	0.98	2.21	2.35	2.32	2.08	2.05	1.11	1.08	0.96	0.75
B	4.92	5.40	4.66	3.24	2.27	1.54	1.30	2.22	0.95	1.03
CCC	19.29	7.29	5.05	4.31	4.12	0.98	0.89	0.35	0.86	0.58

Source: Derived from *Ratings Performance* 1996, Standard & Poor's.

TABLE 3.3 Moody's Cumulative Default Rates (%), 1970–1994

	\multicolumn{10}{c}{Years}									
	1	2	3	4	5	6	7	8	9	10
Aaa	0.00	0.00	0.00	0.00	0.10	0.20	0.30	0.40	0.50	0.70
Aa	0.00	0.00	0.10	0.20	0.30	0.40	0.40	0.50	0.60	0.80
A	0.00	0.10	0.30	0.40	0.60	0.80	1.00	1.20	1.50	1.80
Baa	0.20	0.50	0.90	1.40	1.90	2.30	2.90	3.60	4.20	4.70
Ba	1.70	4.10	6.50	8.90	11.10	12.90	14.40	15.80	17.10	18.40
B	7.90	14.20	19.30	23.30	26.50	29.70	31.80	33.80	35.80	36.70

TABLE 3.4 Static Pools Average Cumulative Default Rates (%), S&P, 1981–1996

	\multicolumn{10}{c}{Years}									
	1	2	3	4	5	6	7	8	9	10
AAA	0.00	0.00	0.06	0.13	0.21	0.39	0.58	0.92	1.05	1.21
AA	0.00	0.02	0.11	0.22	0.38	0.59	0.78	0.93	1.02	1.18
A	0.05	0.14	0.24	0.40	0.60	0.79	1.02	1.31	1.61	1.92
BBB	0.17	0.42	0.68	1.22	1.72	2.28	2.81	3.27	3.64	3.97
BB	0.98	3.19	5.54	7.86	9.94	11.99	13.10	14.18	15.14	15.89
B	4.92	10.32	14.98	18.22	20.49	22.03	23.33	24.55	25.50	26.53
CCC	19.29	26.58	31.63	35.94	40.06	41.04	41.93	42.28	43.14	43.72

Source: Derived from *Ratings Performance* 1996, Standard & Poor's.

TABLE 3.5 Moody's Recovery Rates (1% of Par)

Seniority Class	Mean (%)	Standard Deviation (%)
Senior secured	53.80	26.86
Senior unsecured	51.13	25.45
Senior subordinated	38.52	23.81
Subordinated	32.74	20.18
Junior subordinated	17.09	10.90

senior subordinated debt: 53.8 percent with a standard deviation of 26.86 percent versus 38.52 percent with a standard deviation of 23.81 percent. The relatively high standard deviations indicate, however, that there is much overlap in the recovery values among the various classes of debt. Among senior secured debt, there is a strong argument that loans may fare better than bonds. Moody's data show that for a limited time period,
1991 to present, loans tend to have a higher recovery value than bonds. The average recovery value estimate was $71 for loans versus $57 for senior secured bonds, and loans have a much higher median value of $77. The caveat in pricing credit default remains, however. The 95 percent of the loan price observations fell in a band from $15 to $97 for loans; so although recoveries are skewed higher for loans than for senior secured debt, there is a great deal of overlap.

Even for the same classes of debt, average recovery rates vary dramatically. For senior secured debt, recovery rates in the 10th percentile are only 18.5 percent, versus 85.32 percent in the 90th percentile. There is a "binaryness" about recovery rates. This is the nature of default. One must make an assumption, and it is entirely fair to have an informed view that differs from the market consensus for a given credit or group of credits.

In general, loans tend to be more price robust than fixed rate bonds because loans have a floating rate coupon. If the coupon could adjust instantaneously and if credit spreads remained constant throughout the life of the loan agreement, the loan would always trade at par. As market rates moved, the loan's coupon would instantly readjust. In reality, there is some lag in the loan coupon adjustment, but this market price readjustment tends to be small compared to that for bonds. In a default situation, the price adjustment market coupon readjustment of defaulted bonds adds another element of confusion to the price of defaulted bonds.

The major advantage for the price robustness of loans is that loans are negotiated agreements between banks and borrowers. The bank may have a long-standing business relationship with the borrower and have access to extensive financial data. Often banks are advisers, and bank officers may be on the board of directors of the borrowing institution. Loans are often restructured with customized work-out periods.

The following table from the Moody's Investors Service November 1996 report, *Defaulted Bank Loan Recoveries,* compares data for defaulted loans and bonds.

Average Defaulted Bank Loan and Bond Prices
One Month after Default
(September 1989 to September 1996)

Bank loans	$71
Senior secured bonds	$57
Senior unsecured bonds	$46
Subordinated bonds	$34

Loan prices one month after default were on average 14 points, or nearly 25 percent, higher than prices for senior secured bond debt. The explanation seems to be related to the "inside" nature of loans. It should be noted, however, that even loans have a hierarchy. Loans secured by current assets have higher average recovery values than loans secured by plant and equipment.

Once the default probability and loss in the event of default, or the recovery value, has been determined or "guesstimated," the next step is to calculate the expected loss for the issuer. In its simplest form, expected loss is defined by the following formula:

$$\text{Expected Loss} = \text{Default Probability} \times (1 - \text{Recovery Rate}) \times \text{Loss Exposure}$$

It is important to stress that this is an average expected credit loss. If one wanted to examine a worst-case scenario, one could look at the worst-case default probability and worst-case recovery rate for a given loss exposure to calculate the expected loss.

If the security has been placed in a structure, the loss on the structure may have a different expected loss than that of the underlying issuer(s). The key expected loss variables remain the default probability and loss in the event of default for the issuer, however. The expected loss on the structure then follows from the cash flow characteristics of the structure.

Another note on structures is worth mentioning at this point. The expected loss on the structure can be compared with a senior unsecured bond that has the same expected annual loss rate as the structure. The implied rating on a structure will be the same as the rating of the senior unsecured bond. Rating agencies determine ratings on tranches of asset securitizations,
collateralized loan obligations, and collateralized bond obligations in this fashion.

By now it should be easy to see that default risk has some unique characteristics that can cause pricing to vary significantly based on input assumptions. The following summary recaps the most important points:

1. Default risk is dynamic. Events and market conditions can cause risk to change suddenly and dramatically irrespective of historical data.

2. Correlation between default risks is low. Note, however, that although the *probability* of default for riskier credits can suggest that two risky credits simultaneously default, coincidence does not necessarily mean correlation.

3. Default probabilities in a portfolio have a very high variance. There is a large difference between the highest and the lowest default probabilities.

4. Recovery rates have a very high variance. There is a large difference between the highest and the lowest recovery rates.

5. Very little data exist to support correlation assumptions in the emerging market sector.

6. Diversification suggests that credit default losses will be lower than expected, but diversification cannot remove the probability of an infrequent catastrophic loss on an individual credit.

7. Portfolio loss distributions are skewed due to correlation effects.

8. There is no substitute for experienced active portfolio management.

9. Default protection prices are often distorted by tax, accounting, and regulatory considerations.

Several sophisticated pricing models have popped up in the marketplace. But most of the market trades credit default swaps off of asset swap levels. Traders look at the asset swap levels for a given credit and hypothesize that an investor should be happy to earn the same spread on a credit default as the investor would have earned had they invested cash in the asset itself. Traders take into account the funding cost of the institution.

The Funding Cost Arbitrage

Funding cost arbitrages drive much of the mainstream credit default business. Take the case of an AAA rated institution that funds itself at SOFR−25 bps and an institution with a weak single A rating that funds itself at SOFR+20 bps. Further, assume that the AAA institution wants to lay off the credit risk of a BBB rated bond trading at SOFR+30 bps. Before laying off the credit risk, the position of the AAA bank is as shown in Figure 3.7.

The AAA institution must reduce its risk to this particular BBB asset on which the AAA institution earns 55 bps per annum. The AAA institution may be full on this particular credit, may be reducing risk to BBB rated

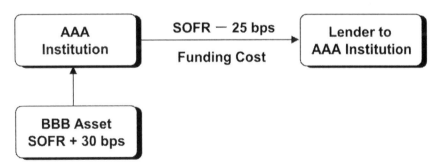

The AAA Rated Institution earns a net spread of 55 bps on the BBB Asset. The AAA Institution must layoff the risk of the BBB Asset.

FIGURE 3.7 AAA Institution owns BBB Credit Risk

institutions in general, or may need to expand credit lines to do more business with this particular BBB entity. Furthermore, the AAA institution may not want to be seen selling this risk in the public market. To accomplish this reduction in credit exposure, the AAA institution enters into an off—balance sheet agreement with a single A rated institution in which the single A rated institution agrees to accept a fee to take the credit default risk of the BBB rated institution.

If the single A rated institution were to purchase this bond outright, it would fund itself at SOFR+20 bps and earn SOFR+30 bps on the BBB asset. The A rated institution would have to put up the full cost of economic capital, and the asset would be booked on the A rated institution's balance sheet. The A rated institution would earn a net spread of 10 basis points per annum as shown in Figure 3.8.

In the case where an AAA rated institution pays the A rated institution 20 basis points per annum to take the credit risk of the BBB asset, however the transaction would look as shown in Figure 3.9.

Both the AAA rated institution and the single A rated institution are better off. After the transaction, the single A institution earns a net spread of 20 basis points per annum off—balance sheet. The AAA institution has a credit-risk-protected asset at a net spread of SOFR+10 10 bps. Assuming there is no correlation between the A institution and the BBB issuer credit, the synthetic asset created by the combination of the BBB asset and the

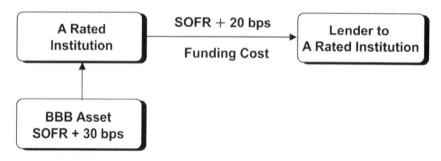

The Single A Rated Institution purchases a BBB Asset on balance sheet. It puts up full economic capital and earns a net spread of 10 bps per annum.

FIGURE 3.8   Single A Rated Institution Purchases BBB Asset

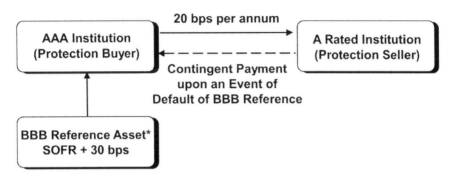

* Single A Rated Institution receives a 20-basisi-point fee in return for making a Contingent Payment if a predefined Credit Event occurs to the BBB Reference Asset.

FIGURE 3.9 Credit Default Swap to Offset BBB Risk

credit default protection of the A rated institution would have an implied credit rating of AA−.

The major rating agencies publish their views of credit ratings of jointly supported obligations for various credits. Table 3.6 shows an excerpt from Standard and Poor's data. This S&P table (Table 3.6) assumes that the two credits are unaffiliated and uncorrelated, which is the condition specified earlier for this transaction. The AAA institution creates a synthetic AA asset with a coupon of SOFR+10 bps, and the A rated institution takes on acceptable credit risk for a spread otherwise unattainable for the same credit risk in the market. Both the AAA rated institution and the A rated institution are better off. The net positions of the AAA rated institution and the A rated institution are shown in Figures 3.10 and 3.11, respectively.

The AAA rated institution does not necessarily need to own an underlying asset to purchase credit default protection. The AAA rated bank

TABLE 3.6 Standard & Poor's Ratings for Jointly Supported Obligations, November 1995

	A+	A	A−	BBB+	BBB	BBB−
A+	AA+	AA+	AA+	AA	AA	AA
A	AA+	AA	AA	AA−	AA−	A+
A−	AA+	AA	AA−	A+	A+	A
BBB+	AA	AA−	A+	A	A	A−
BBB	AA	AA−	A+	A	A	BBB+
BBB−	AA−	A+	A	A−	BBB+	BBB

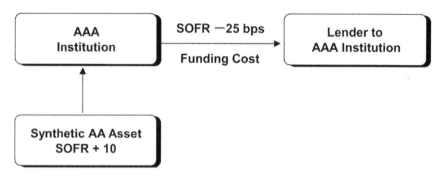

The AAA Rated Institution earns a net spread of 35 bps on a Synthetic AA Asset.

FIGURE 3.10   AAA Institution Final Position

might be in a position of managing a credit line due to foreign exchange or interest rate swap exposures, for instance. In a public, well-traded market, both counterparties will look at the asset swap market as a benchmark price and begin negotiations from this point of reference.

A credit default protection buyer can have another reason for purchasing credit default protection independent of hedging an asset position or managing overall credit exposure. The credit default protection buyer can take a view on a given credit and inventory the protection or look for appreciation in the price of the protection. A buyer may view the premium as payment for cheap protection on a deteriorating credit. The credit default protection buyer can pay the default premium to create a short position in a credit.

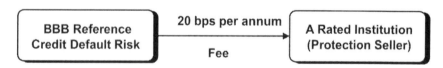

The Single A Rated Institution earns a 20 bps fee in return for making a Contingent Payment if a predefined Credit Event occurs to the BBB Reference Asset.

The Single A Institution is 10 bps per annum better off than if it had purchased a BBB asset outright.

FIGURE 3.11   Single A Rated Institution Final Position

Likewise, a credit default protection seller can receive the credit default premium and go long the credit exposure to fill in credit gaps in a diversified portfolio. Similarly, the credit default protection seller may be taking a long position in a given credit because of a positive view on the credit.

Credit default swaps can be used to create long or short positions in credit exposure to a given credit or credits just as total return swaps can be used to create long and short positions in given assets.

The credit quality of the credit default protection seller is important for all of the reasons mentioned earlier: correlation, absolute credit risk, Bank of International Settlements (BIS) risk weight, and so forth. But there is another factor implied in the credit quality of the default protection seller. In order for the preceding credit arbitrage to work, the funding cost of the default protection seller must be higher than the funding cost of the default protection buyer. I believe this is the fundamental reason that many banks were keen to overlook possible high correlations of Korean banks, for instance, in order to do more credit derivatives business. Korean banks such as Hanil Bank and Shinhan Bank look on selling credit protection on Korean corporate names as "found money."

Of course, trades are done where the credit quality of the default protection seller is as high as or higher than that of the default protection buyer. When it is necessary to free up a credit line, supply-and-demand conditions may dictate paying up for credit protection. In the context of a larger business view, this can be a sensible transaction. This is particularly true among banks where buying credit protection on a 100 percent BIS risk-weighted asset from a bank can lower regulatory capital from 100 percent to 20 percent, as we saw in Chapter 2 on total return swaps.

From the funding cost arbitrage, we can see that key factors in pricing credit default swaps are the funding costs of the counterparties and the cost of capital for the credit default protection buyer. The likelihood of default and the likely recovery value for different counterparties and assets are also important; but in the given example, it was assumed that the market factored this information into the credit spread of the asset and the funding costs of the counterparties. Calculations were a matter of simple addition and subtraction.

The funding arbitrage transaction works well for public debt where there is a defined asset swap market and a general market consensus view on credit risk. Complications arise in nonpublic or controversial markets. If there is no asset in the desired maturity, or no public market, the task is more difficult. This is particularly true in emerging markets and in the Latin American markets.

In May 1997, I tried to purchase sovereign credit protection on Brazil for a five-year maturity. At the time, the Brazilian reference Eurobond was trading at a spread of 220 basis points to the five-year U.S. Treasury. That would have been an implied asset swap level of approximately 180 basis points. The range of quotes for the credit protection varied as follows:

Credit Default Protection Referencing a
Five-Year Brazilian Eurobond (May 1997)

Chase Manhattan Bank	240 basis points per annum
Broker Market	285 basis points per annum
J.P. Morgan	325 basis points per annum

It is possible that the broker reflected Chase's price plus the broker's markup. This range in price is typical of what one finds in the credit derivatives market. Supply and demand for this type of credit protection drives prices. It may be that Chase had just created a hedge whereby it was long credit default protection and did not want to inventory the protection but was willing to make a good offer.

Credit protection on Russian sovereign risk (then Ba2/BB—) referencing a Eurodollar bond exhibited similar characteristics. It is extremely difficult to find sellers of protection in large size. This is partly because it is difficult to find bonds with which to hedge in large block sizes and because it is difficult to sell credit-linked notes, which create a hedge, in large block sizes. The Russian Eurobond, the 9.75 percent of 2001, asset swapped to a level of LIBOR + 252 bps per annum for a 4.5-year maturity.

The following levels were offered as good indications of where three large commercial banks would sell credit default protection referencing this Eurobond. The offer size was for a principal amount of $50 million.

Credit Default Protection Referencing a
4.5 Year Russian Eurobond (July 1997)

1-year protection	230 basis points per annum
2-year protection	270 basis points per annum
4-year protection	320 basis points per annum

Notice that in each case, as one moves to a longer maturity, credit default protection is more expensive than owning the reference asset. There is no arbitrage possibility. An investor cannot purchase the underlying Brazilian debt or Russian debt and then purchase credit default protection and still earn a positive spread. It is also typical of emerging-market debt that the farther out an investor goes in maturity, the more expensive it is to purchase credit default protection. Much of the price structure has to do with the "specialness" or scarcity of the bonds as one moves farther out along the curve. This has to do with the fact that the supply of offers for large-size and longer maturities is limited.

There are a variety of reasons for this limitation. Among the most important is the exposure number. Bank of America estimated the following exposure numbers for a 1-year maturity credit default swap on Russia and for a 4.4-year maturity credit default swap referencing the Russian Eurobond (then rated Ba2/BB—) just cited.

Bank of America's Exposure Estimates for
Credit Default Swaps on Russian Debt

1-year maturity	4.86% × Notional Amount
	(4.86% × $50 million = $2.43 million)
4.4-year maturity	52% × Notional Amount
	(52% × $50 million = $26 million)

The Risk Management Analytics group at Bank of America makes the assumptions regarding recovery rates. For this BB credit, they assumed the exposure was huge. For a shorter maturity, the exposure number is not too onerous, but the exposure number jumps dramatically, *more than 10 times for an extension in the maturity of the credit default swap of 3.4 years.* This means that the credit risk of a credit default protection buyer to a credit default protection seller is also huge. Again we see that the counterparty matters, not just from a correlation point of view and not just from a regulatory capital point of view, but critically from a credit quality point of view. This means a large number of credit default protection sellers may be disqualified as credit lines are used for other business.

How does one create a model to deal with supply-and-demand conditions such as these? How does one reconcile a credit default protection pricing model with some of the intangibles we discussed earlier? Models are a good place to start, but they are not the complete answer. The fact of the matter is that no economic model can take into account all of the technical factors involved in credit default pricing.

The spread is where it is because that's where the market says it is.

EXCHANGE PRICING, ASSET SWAPS & THE BASIS

Ye olde classic single name par credit default swap required no upfront payment. If you bought credit default protection for five-years on $100 million notional for 100 bps, you paid $1,000,000 per year in quarterly installments. You could enter into the swap at any pre-agreed time. If you bought protection on a liquid name, you could exit quite easily. If you bought protection on an illiquid name, you would have to put it out for bids in competition. If there was a credit event, it could get messy as discussed elsewhere in this book. But you did it to enjoy the leverage combined with hedging or speculative opportunities depending on your risk appetite.

Before we can discuss exchange pricing, we need to review the concepts behind traditional par swap pricing (See Figure 3.12), par and nonpar asset swaps in the cash markets, and the basis, the difference between the premium of credit default swaps versus credit spreads in the cash markets. Here is a painless (I hope) review.

Theoretically, the pricing of a five-year maturity credit derivative was similar to the price of a five-year maturity par asset swap. One can construct a par asset swap using a fixed coupon security whether the security is trading at par, a discount to par, or a premium to par. If you think of the

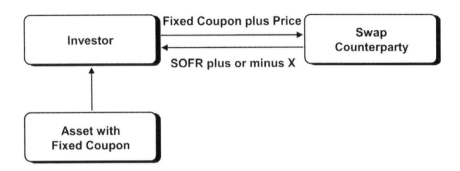

The asset may be trading at a premium or discount to par, or at par. The difference from par, if any, is amortized over the life of the swap and incorporated into the floating rate coupon.

Note that an asset swap can also swap floating coupons to fixed. The swap can be single-currency or from one currency to another currency.

FIGURE 3.12 Generic Par Asset Swap

coupon of a five-year maturity bond as the premium investors demand for the underlying credit risk, by swapping the fixed coupons to frequently resetting floating rate coupon, it is easier to compare spreads and credit risks between different bonds.

Suppose you own a five-year maturity USD-denominated corporate bond. The bond is trading at par with a semiannual coupon of 1.85 percent. You want to do a par asset swap and you want to swap the coupon to three-month SOFR. The five-year swap is trading at 15/25 versus three-month USD SOFR, and the five-year Treasury is trading at 1.6 percent. The swap quote means that if the interbank dealer market is going to pay a fixed rate versus receiving three-month SOFR, they will pay the five-year Treasury rate plus 15 bps. In this case the fixed rate the swap dealer would pay versus receiving three-month SOFR is 1.6 percent plus 15 bps, or 1.75 percent. This is the *bid side* of the market.

For our asset swap, we will *pay* a fixed rate versus receiving USD SOFR. The trader will quote us the *offer side* of the market, which is 1.6 percent plus 25 bps or 1.85 percent. The trader wants to receive 1.85 percent versus paying three-month SOFR. Conveniently, our bond pays a 1.85 percent semiannual bond-equivalent-yield coupon, and this is the same way that the U.S. market quotes its interest rate swaps.

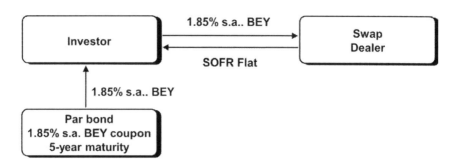

FIGURE 3.13 Par Asset Swap Cash Flows with Par Asset

Furthermore, let us assume our bond pays its coupon on the exact day the trader wants the first fixed swap payment on the swap. The cash flows are shown in Figure 3.13, where we are the investor and the owner of the bond. From the investor's point of view, this is similar to owning a par floater with a coupon of USD SOFR flat. Notice that in this example, the swap provider faces the investor who owns the bond, so the rating on the bond is irrelevant from the point of view of the investor's swap counterparty. Only the creditworthiness of the investor matters for our example.

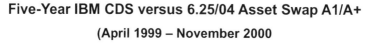

Five-Year IBM CDS versus 6.25/04 Asset Swap A1/A+

(April 1999 – November 2000

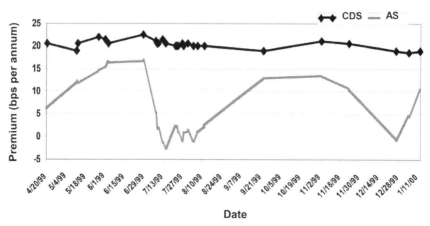

FIGURE 3.14 CDS vs Asset Swap Spreads for IBM

Consider IBM's credit risk. Figure 3.14 captures the five-year CDS premium versus the five-year asset swap spread for IBM for the period April 1999 to November 2000. The top line is the CDS spread. For this period, the CDS spread was close to constant while the asset swap spread showed some volatility. Despite the asset swap spread's volatility, the CDS spread was always wider.

Is this still typical in 2022? Do CDS spreads always trade wide relative to the cash markets? Unless a new convertible or large bond issue is involved, there is always a tendency for CDS spreads to trade wider. But we will examine some exceptions when we discuss negative basis trades in the next section.

Figure 3.15 shows typical behavior of the CDS market versus floating-rate spreads for the same credits. CDS spreads tend to be wider and more volatile than asset swap spreads or floating-rate note spreads. Moreover, the credit default swap market a high beta market. Technical factors and faster reaction to rumors and market data often drive credit default swaps to be much more volatile than the cash market.

Even in a calm market, the credit default swap market tends to be slightly more volatile than the cash market, although the correlation between the markets is estimated to be around 90 percent for the few years

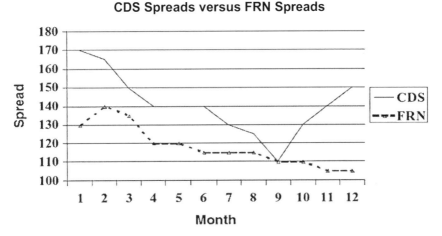

CDS Spreads versus FRN Spreads

CDS spreads tend to be wider and more volatile than FRN or asset swap spreads.

FIGURE 3.15 Typical Pattern of CDS versus FRN Spreads

in which credit default swap prices have been tracked relative to the cash markets. The difference between the spread of credit default swaps over the spreads in the cash markets, or the *basis*, is also correlated with market direction. As credit spreads widen, the basis widens. As credit spreads narrow, the basis narrows. Of course, there are exceptions in which the basis becomes negative due to supply and demand pressures.

Supply and demand often drive credit default swap prices. Models do a lousy job of capturing this effect. Journalists rediscover this fact every time there is stress in the market. Models cannot predict the whims of corporate officers who may change the capital structure of their organizations, for example. New issuance of convertible bonds creates demand for credit default protection. Arbitrageurs buy protection in anticipation of this issuance. This new demand raises the price of credit default swap protection, i.e., the premium increases.

Even if the balance sheet is rock solid and there is no change in the corporation's credit risk, do not be surprised to see OTC premiums increase 50% within a week (on exchanges, the increase may be reflected in the form of an upfront payment which we will discuss in a moment). While this may not happen, be prepared.

Meanwhile cash instruments that are locked up in buy-and-hold portfolios will have their spreads remain the same. The *positive basis* between the corporation's bonds and credit default swaps widens solely due to supply and demand pressures. If the balance sheet is not rock solid, and the capital structure changes due to new issuance, you will see much more volatility and spread widening before analysts can figure out the new lay of the credit land.

Supply and demand effects depend on the specific situation. Some convertibles have short-dated puts or maturities shorter than five years. The most actively traded and most liquid credit default swaps have five-year maturities. When arbitrageurs buy large notional protection in the short end of the curve (for example, two-year protection), the credit default swap curve tends to *invert* for this reference credit. For example, before the demand rise, the two-year CDS traded at 130 pbs per annum and the five-year CDS traded at 150 bps per annum. Arbitrage demand widened two-year protection to 200 bps per annum while the five-year CDS remained at

150 bps per annum. If all other terms are equal, one can buy five-year protection, sell two-year protection, and lock in a gain. Anomalies disappear quickly but the important thing to remember is that they do appear.

Furthermore, it is sometimes possible to create a five-year par asset swap in the cash market, purchase five-year credit default protection, and lock in a positive spread. In other words, one can put on a *negative basis trade*.

EXCHANGE TRADED CDS & THE "BIG BANG"

In response to the 2008 financial crisis and the mayhem around unwinding credit default swap positions, the credit derivatives market 'reformed." Instead of investigating fraud, the credit derivatives market decided that the problem was "systemic risk." The way to mitigate it was via central clearing of credit derivatives on exchanges. Prior to this, the credit derivatives market consisted of over-the-counter bilateral contracts. If one unwound a position on an illiquid name, liquidity and transparencies were huge issues. The exception was the indexes which were transparent and standardized.

With a central clearing facility, dealers trade with dealers. Dealers post collateral with the central clearing facility. Theoretically, the central clearing facilities are well-capitalized. If one wants to offset a trade, dealers' trades are novated, a dealer's counterparty is replaced by the central clearing facility so that the dealers face the central clearing facility as their new counterparty. The dealer and non-dealer counterparty, i.e., the dealer's customer, have a bilateral contract, but if the dealer implodes, systemic risk is mitigated by the fact that the other dealers face the central clearing facility. In a huge crisis, it will be much more convenient for the Fed to bailout out the central clearing facility, since that way it will not look as if it is bailing out dealers again.

The International Swaps and Derivatives Association's (ISDA) response was called the "Big Bang," a new protocol, issued in a 2009 supplement, to avoid settlement mayhem. The ISDA "Determination Committee" determines whether a credit event has occurred per ISDA language. Restructuring is no longer a "standard credit event" for CDS contracts that reference U.S. investment-grade credits. The latter use fixed "coupons" of 100 or 500 bps depending on the strength of the credit with accrual to the previous coupon payment date. The theory seemed to be that calling premiums "coupons" made it sound more like bond trading and less like risky *derivatives*. When you want to look as if you have accomplished something, rebrand and relabel. Cash settlement is achieved via an auction process.

Today, about two-thirds of credit derivatives contracts by notional amount are centrally cleared, and one-third are traded over-the-counter. (See Chapter 1, "Estimated Market Size.")

Standard North American Corporate (SNAC)

An exchange traded single name credit default swap on North American corporate names is priced using a 100/500 fixed coupon for a specific maturity date and is based on the current exchange contract language. The fixed coupon includes accrued from the previous coupon date. These are the terms for the Standard North American Corporate (SNAC).

The CDS contract calls for upfront points that reflect the present value of the difference between today's market price and the fixed coupon on the exchange traded credit default swap contract, if any, for the remaining length of the particular contract. If credit spreads have widened from the date of the exchange contract's inception, the credit is perceived as weaker, and the protection buyer will pay the upfront points. But if credit spreads have tightened, the credit is perceived as stronger, and the protection seller will pay the upfront points to the protection buyer.

Although upfront payments were adopted for SNAC, credit default swaps on tranches of CDOs used upfront payments prior to the 2008 financial crisis. The upfront payments then as now are meant to reduce ex

When a credit protection buyer enters the trade after the start date of the exchange traded contract, it is as if a credit protection buyer is assuming a pre-existing credit default swap contract, including any accrued on the premium from the prior premium date. If the credit has deteriorated on either an absolute or relative basis to the market, then the protection buyer must pay something more for protection, since the original fixed coupon credit default swap was based on a stronger credit.

An analogy is the par swap market wherein an original par bond is trading at a discount due to a weakening of the underlying credit.) That something more, is the present value of the spread differential between today's spread and the spread of the credit default swap. The present value of the spread differential is called "points upfront." But if the credit has strengthened, then the protection seller must make the "points upfront" payment to the protection buyer.

The idea behind this is to make cash flows more predictable, more management and more nettable, i.e., one can cancel out long and short positions on the exchanges. It is easier to offset positions that have the same payment dates. Moreover, an index may be offset in part or in its entirety by the single names, single tranches, or single entities making up the index. It is much easier to program netting when the cash flow dates are known and uniform.

"BIG BANG" SETTLEMENT AND "LANGUAGE ARBITRAGE"

Throughout this book you will find examples of the vagaries of cash and physical settlement in over-the-counter credit default swap contracts. Cash settlement has become the most popular means of settling contracts for both OTC and exchange traded contracts. Investors betting on credit spreads are not trying to hedge a specific bond or a specific loan.

Since the inception of the CDS market, getting bids on reference assets from multiple dealers—whether settlement was cash or physical—was the norm. ISDA introduced a global protocol for a credit event auction in 2005. ISDA's 2009 "Big Bang" language calls for cash settlement with the choice to opt in for physical settlement.

Counterparties electronically submit an adherence letter to ISDA agreeing to settle via the auction. Today, most contracts are settled via a credit event auction due to the volume of exchange trading. This auction fixes the price for all counterparties who choose cash settlement.

As was true before for most over-the-counter CDS contracts, cash settlement requires the seller of protection to pay the buyer or protection the difference between the notional minus the price of the Reference Obligation. Past disputes were about the nature of the reference obligation, the legitimacy of it, and the price and method of determination of the price. The new auction process is supposed to make this process smooth and fair.

This process for indexes and the most liquid top fifty single name credits is likely to work well. There is price transparency. The problems have always been with illiquid names which is why I focus on them in this book. If a couple of large influential dealers have a net lopsided position and have a key role in setting prices on illiquid Reference Obligations, what do you think is likely to happen?

The size of speculation in the CDS market has made physical settlement difficult for most names. It is impossible to find bonds to satisfy the terms of contracts. Even when physical settlement is effective, this book shows examples of gaming the delivery, even with pre-specified Deliverable Obligations. Nonetheless, physical settlement is a crucial opt in. A credit default protection buyer who owns Deliverable Obligations with a face amount equal to the notional amount of the contract will be eager to opt in for physical settlement. The credit default protection buyer will deliver the obligation/s to the seller of credit default protection, will be paid the notional amount of the contract, and thus be made whole.

One does not have to use ISDA language or adhere to the auction process in over-the-counter contracts. Likewise, one does not have to use ISDA's Credit Derivatives Determinations Committee to decide whether a credit event has occurred. ISDA may stall in declaring a credit event as it did to the ire of those who bought credit default protection on Greek sovereign debt. ISDA "deliberated" its "standard" documentation for at least four months.

But if you want to use the auction, here is how it works. Counterparties who adhere to the credit event auction may choose cash settlement or a new form of physical settlement. If one chooses physical settlement, it is on the net buy. Dealers determine the mid-market price, i.e., the inside market midpoint (IMM). They place orders for the affected company's debt. (This works more smoothly for corporate names than anything else, and even then, there are hiccups) The range of prices received is used to calculate the

IMM via a preset calculation methodology and the size and direction of open interest is determined. This information is published.

This information is used to decide whether to submit auction limit orders If you use ISDA "standard" language you must opt out of the credit event auction protocol to settle using a preapproved list of deliverable obligations.

But as you see throughout this book, you are free to do that with your own over-the-counter contracts, and you do not need to as ISDA or its "Determinations Committee" to do it. It is your choice.

In future, there will be more SNAFUs, and there will be a new and improved "standard." But you may choose to use your own language, since credit risk is granular. Credit events and settlements are situational.

PAY-AS-YOU-GO (PAUG)

ISDA introduced the pay-as-you-go (PAUG) template in 2005 for amortizing asset backed securities such as RMBS, and CMBS. It introduced a template for CDOs in June 2006. The ISDA PAUG standard template is an attempt to replicate the cash flow profile of the cash bond with a CDS contract. One can modify these terms, and that may make the contract less liquid. The ISDA contract can be problematic when it comes to asset-backed securities (ABSs).

For example, an RMBS with tranche risk backed by mortgage loans, interest is paid sequentially to the most senior bond in the deal first, and so on down the line. The ultimate amount of interest paid is capped at the weighted-average mortgage rate net of expenses. This is also known as the net WAC, or the available funds cap (AFC).

Unlike other CDS contracts, the protection seller makes floating payments if there is an RMBS reference obligation interest shortfall, called the AFC shortfall; or if there is a CMBS reference obligation interest shortfall, called a WAC shortfall; or, if the reference obligations are CDOs, the interest shortfalls are called pay-in-kind (PIK-ing) shortfalls. The protection buyer may reimburse these payments if the interest shortfall is ultimately recovered. Protection buyers usually have an option whether to call a credit event or a floating amount event.

Some investors are not satisfied with this contract, in particular PIK-ing, and prefer to rewrite the language depending on the assets and the structure. Language that allows restructuring of mortgages is problematic because it is difficult to determine whether the restructuring is noneconomic and simply a delaying tactic to avoid recognizing losses. Furthermore, the PAUG introduces substantial basis risk, and the market may demand further changes.

PAUG credit events for pay-as-you-go contracts are defined as follows:
- Failure to pay (FTP) principal.
- Write-down.
- Distressed rating downgrade (CCC or below).
- Failure to pay (FTP) interest for CDO reference obligations only.

PAUG floating amount events are:
- Interest shortfalls.
- Principal shortfalls.
- Write-down amounts.

PAUG settlements are trickier than for other CDSs. The secondary market for structured finance securities is illiquid. It is difficult to obtain objective valuations. Floating payments are designed to replicate the actual loss amounts, but it is possible to manipulate those amounts. That was an issue in the subprime market and its related CDS indexes prior to the financial crisis, and one should watch out for this in today's deals. Old dogs play old tricks.

If a credit event occurs—or, more accurately, is *deemed* to occur—then the protection buyer has the option to physically deliver all or part of the notional amount to the seller. If the entire notional is physically settled then the CDS is terminated. If a portion of the notional is settled, then the CDS continues on the remaining amount.

There are several interest shortfall cap options:

- *Fixed cap*. Floating payments are limited to the amount of the CDS premium.
- *Variable cap*. Floating payments are limited to LIBOR plus premium.

- *No cap.* No limit to the floating rate payments. This option completely replicates the payments of the cash bond or total return swap; it may require principal to be liquidated to pay interest shortfall.

REMIC law limits a floating rate RMBS bond pass-through rate to the lesser of the bond spread plus a predefined index—one-month or three-month SOFR, for example—or the net WAC, the underlying mortgage collateral pool's weighted average coupon, net of expenses. Whether the cap is reached depends on the actual prepayment speeds of underlying mortgages, the effectiveness of interest rate hedges in the RMBS structure, and the short-term interest rate increases before hybrid ARM mortgages switch to floating interest rate payments.

INDEX PRODUCTS

IHS Markit administers a variety of credit default swap indexes ranging from the iTraxx indexes on any cluster of CDSs and even structures made from the iTraxx (Europe, Australia, Japan, non-Japan Asian and emerging market indexes) to a menu of CDX indexes (single name credit default swap baskets, typically of 125 single names) including investment grade and high yield reference assets.

Corporate bond indexes have been used as reference portfolios to create bespoke (custom-made) tranches of CDOs and as a reference for other new products.

Earlier we discussed the decline of an Asset Backed Home Equity index, ABX.HE-BBB– 06-2 index. But the first such index was the ABX.HE 06-1 launched in January 2006 referencing a basket of twenty subprime residential mortgage-backed securities. Ratings added to the index indicated which rated tranches were tracked by the index. Each index had five tranches each: AAA, AA, A, BBB, and BBB–. Each of the five indexes linked to specific rated tranches had its own predetermined annual coupon paid at the beginning of the year. For example, for the ABX.HE-BBB– 06-2 index, the preset coupons were: AAA: 11 bps; AA: 17 bps; A: 44 bps; BBB: 133 bps; and BBB–: 242 bps.

The indexes were launched twice per year at par. A protection buyer paid the first annual coupon upfront.

Who provides the information on the underlying securities to the administrator? Answer: the major banks who structure and underwrite these securities and who get the ratings from the rating agencies. They also report any interim amortization, missed interest payments, or defaults which affect the protection seller's floating rate payments to the protection buyer.

During the unfolding financial crisis, demand for subprime market hedge indexes was so high that the TABX was launched on February 14, 2007. It was composed of standard tranches on the ABX.HE Index.

Any index can be created or recreated at any time if there are enough banks providing reference assets and information about those reference assets. Moreover, one can create one's own over-the-counter bespoke basket of reference assets with willing counterparties.

Bespoke Baskets, Tranches, and Indexes

Recall Figure 1.12 (p. 52), our illustration of the Synthetic CDO-Squared. The collateral was a collection of credit default swaps that referenced single-A rated tranches of CDOs. You may also recall the senate findings on Goldman Sachs. The bank used the same impaired mortgage-backed security as the reference asset for multiple credit default swaps to amplify risk. These are examples of using credit default swaps to transfer risk.

This flexibility makes it easy to create a bespoke single tranche of a CDO to match an investor's risk appetite (when done with integrity). The investor can purchase a cash note (for example, the mezzanine note investor in Figure 1.12) or the investment can be unfunded (for example, the credit default swap on which the super-senior counterparty in Figure 1.12 sold protection, i.e., went long the risk).

A bank can create a customized index from single name credit default swaps or from other structured financial products on a bespoke basis for customers. Those CDS contracts can serve the portfolio for a structured credit investment. The index can easily be sliced and diced.

Basket credit default swaps are usually bespoke. Investors choose the assets in the basket and choose which default risk(s) they will accept. Investors may choose the "nth to default," such as the fifth name to default in a portfolio of thirty names. An investor may choose to accept the risk of the first three names to default in a portfolio of thirty names. In Chapter 4, I show a simplified example of a three name basket credit default swap and how to think about the pricing. (See Chapter 4, "Basket Credit Default Swaps," and "Pricing Basket Credit Default Swaps.")

THE "LONDON WHALE"

Jamie Dimon, Chairman and CEO of J.P. Morgan Chase (J.P. Morgan) spent the end of 2011 and beginning of 2012 campaigning against the Volcker Rule. The new rule was meant to restrict banks' proprietary trading because proprietary trading might be speculation in disguise. Dimon asserted J.P. Morgan did not engage in proprietary trading and only traded on behalf of customers.

Meanwhile, J.P. Morgan's London based Chief Investment Office (CIO) engaged in speculative credit derivatives trading, and the bets were in trouble. The CIO reported directly to Dimon. At the end of 2011, Peter Weiland, then the unit's chief risk officer, was alarmed. On a *large net basis*, traders collected small premiums to provide credit default protection on indexes of credit risk, including the CDX NA. IG9 10 year index ("IG9 10Y") that tracks 125 companies. Just three years after the financial crisis, a unit in J.P. Morgan that reported directly to Dimon was doing an AIG It took huge risk for chump change.

One does not need a model to uncover *qualitative* risk. The bank was the wrong way around on the pattern that I keep asking you to find. One wants limited downside with maximum upside with a small initial outlay and the potential to make multiples of that outlay. J.P. Morgan found the opposite. Tight credit spreads are more likely to gap out than to contract. J.P. Morgan did large size but received small premiums on that large side to take enormous risk.

Spreads widened, i.e., prices of the underlying reference credits backing the credit derivatives trades fell. This is exactly what J.P. Morgan did not want to happen. Instead of closing out or reducing the positions, J.P. Morgan *increased the size.* Someone leaked. Reporters smelled trouble and branded J.P. Morgan's trader, Bruno Iksil, the "London Whale."

J.P. Morgan's risky credit derivatives trade reportedly had a net notional exposure of $157 billion with huge basis risk. The London Whale trade was large and risky. It's $6.2 billion of losses swamped years of the CIO unit's earnings. (WSJ Staff, "Tracking the Trade: Timeline on J.P. Morgan's London Whale," *The Wall Street Journal*, July 13, 2012.)

The eventual SEC cease and desist order stated that the CIO's Structured Credit Portfolio had no notional risk limits. J.P. Morgan tried to blame its models, but the bank had marked some of the largest notional positions outside the bid/ask spread, meaning the values were divorced from defensible mark-to-market values.

On April 13, 2012, during its quarterly earnings conference call, Chief Financial Officer Douglas Braunstein claimed the Structured Credit Product's speculative trade was an approved long-term investment. He said the bank's risk managers approved it; the bank was transparent to regulators; and the trade lowered risk. He claimed it was consistent with the proposed Volcker Rule. None of it was true.

In March 2013, Braunstein admitted to Congress that he hadn't been forthright with shareholders. Regulators did not receive granular information about J.P. Morgan's trades on a "regular and recurring," basis. Moreover, a Senate report pointed out that there was more than one serious issue with the firm's regulatory reporting. (Carl Levin and John McCain, "J.P. Morgan Chase Whale Trades: A Case History of Derivatives Risks and Abuses," P. 10. *United States Senate Permanent Subcommittee on Investigations, Committee on Homeland Security and Governmental Affairs*, March 15, 2013.)

Ina Drew, the CIO unit's Chief Investment Officer, emailed Dimon and Braunstein on April 12, 2012, that the mark-to-market loss was $412 million for the day, an "8 standard deviation event." But it is not a black swan or an 8 standard deviation event when you amass an illiquid position that has a miniscule margin of safety. This is called shooting oneself in the foot. What do you expect when your trembling hand holds a loaded gun, and you point it at your feet?

Drew suspected the market anticipated J.P. Morgan's liquidation of its large position. She was correct. It did, She noted that no other high grade or high yield index had moved so much. The cumulative loss for the book was already $1.2 billion, and it was the first time the unit's losses had ever been that high. The market smelled J.P. Morgan's blood in the water. The late Senator Carl Levin asked Drew whether Jamie Dimon, her direct boss, was informed about the units "investments," she responded, "Yes." (Levin and McCain, Pp. 134-135.)

On J.P. Morgan's April 13, 2012, first quarter earnings conference call, an analyst questioned Jamie Dimon about media reports of large risky derivatives trades and mounting losses. Dimon claimed it was "a complete tempest in a teapot." The Senate's investigation revealed that Dimon knew the portfolio had been bleeding for three months before the conference call. He knew losses increased exponentially in March, and the London CIO unit was in trouble; it couldn't exit its huge positions without being the cause of widening spreads and making the losses even worse. Dimon's performance during the conference call was an attempt to put a Band Aide on a burst artery.

Dimon delayed the 10-Q's scheduled release. Even with the delay, the first quarter earnings were later restated. At the time of the call, losses were over $1-2 billion. On May 11, 2012, J.P. Morgan launched a surprise conference call. Dimon said, "It was a bad strategy. It was badly executed. It became more complex. It was poorly monitored." That was an extraordinary statement since the financial crisis was still branded in our brains. On May 13, 2012, Dimon admitted to David Gregory on NBC's "Meet the Press" that the "teapot" statement was a "terrible, egregious mistake." Losses ultimately rose to more than $6.2 billion — at least, that is the official number.

FIGURE 3.16 J.P. Morgan's Quadrangle

In 2012, J.P. Morgan gave Dimon an $11 million pay package (down from $23 million in 2011). He remains Chairman and CEO of J.P. Morgan Chase as of this writing in 2022. Who wouldn't need that? (See Figure 3.16)

J.P. Morgan Violated Securities Laws

Levin and McCain found: "The Structured Credit Portfolio's trades comprised "at least $62 billion in holdings in a U. S. credit index for investment grade companies; $71 billion in holdings in a credit index for European investment grade companies; and $22 billion in holdings in a U. S. credit index for high yield (non-investment grade) companies." There were more than 100 different credit derivative instruments, including both "short and long positions, referencing both investment grade and non-investment grade corporations, and including both shorter and longer-term maturities."

J.P. Morgan's risk management was unsound. The London CIO was speculating. When the bets went wrong and losses climbed, traders doubled down. J.P. Morgan's personnel knew they were speculating and described "'perilous size' since a small drop in price could quickly translate into massive losses." (Levin and McCain, Pp. 134-135.)

J.P. Morgan admitted to violating federal securities laws and paid a $920 million fine to resolve claims by the Federal Reserve, the Securities and Exchange Commission (SEC), the U. S. Comptroller of the Currency (OCC) and the U. K. Financial Conduct Authority (FCA, which got a $220 million payout).

The SEC reported that J.P. Morgan admitted that those losses occurred "against a backdrop of woefully deficient accounting controls" in the CIO unit. The bank was guilty of "misstating" its financial results in its public filings for the first quarter of 2012.

But the SEC did not allege that J.P. Morgan's officers were guilty of failure to supervise for which the SEC would have to take action. The SEC spun it as "failed to keep watch over." Jamie Dimon's name did not appear in the report even though he was on tape and the financial press reported his actions. The SEC merely noted that senior officers kept the board in the dark. They "broke a cardinal rule of corporate governance." The SEC has a sense of humor. Jamie Dimon was Chairman of the Board.

The SEC's September 19, 2013, release states that J.P. Morgan's management did not uphold its SOX responsibilities regarding corporate governance and disclosure. But the SEC did not recommend charges to the Department of Justice. So much for Sarbanes Oxley's effectiveness. (Securities and Exchange Commission, "Securities Exchange Act of 1934 Release No. 70458, Accounting and Auditing Enforcement Release No. 3490, Administrative Proceeding File No. 3-15507" September 19, 2013.)

The Commodity Futures Trading Commission's enforcement order showed J.P. Morgan admitted to "reckless conduct." On a single trading day, February 29, 2012, J.P. Morgan's IG 9 10Y trades were greater than 90% of that day's net volume traded by the entire market and "nearly 11 times the Structured Credit Portfolio's average daily volume in February." The CFTC alleged J.P. Morgan violated Dodd Frank's "prohibition against manipulative conduct." J.P. Morgan admitted to "certain facts" that the CFTC disclosed in the order, but the bank neither admitted nor denied wrongdoing.

The CFTC alleged J.P. Morgan manipulated a global market. J.P. Morgan settled with the CFTC for $100 million. (CFTC Press Release 6737-13, "CFTC Files and Settles Charges Against J.P. Morgan Chase Bank, N. A., for Violating Prohibition on Manipulative Conduct in Connection with 'London Whale' Swaps Trades," October 16, 2013.)

The Department of "Justice"

The Department of Justice charged "London Whale" Bruno Iksil's direct boss, Javier Martin-Artajo, and Julien Grout, who recorded the position values for Iksil, for allegedly covering up losses. Martin-Artajo fought extradition from Spain. Mr. Grout, a French citizen, resides in France. France does not extradite its citizens. Bruno Iksil agreed to cooperate in exchange for immunity.

But after reading Levin and McCain's report, Iksil revised his thinking, and changed his story. Prosecutors dropped the criminal case against Martin-Artajo and Grout. In 2017, Iksil wrote in an email: "I mostly inferred that Dimon and his close lieutenants were responsible much, much more than my two colleagues could ever be." (Lucy McNulty, Gregory Zuckerman, and Rebecca Davis O'Brian, "'London Whale' Has a New Target: J.P. Morgan's Top Brass," *The Wall Street Journal*, August 3, 2017.)

Dimon knows his math. The bank paid legal fees and fines. The bank had litigation reserves to defend itself against allegations of illegal behavior. Regulators rarely pressured banks to admit to criminal behavior. But regulators made an exception for the London Whale case. J.P. Morgan admitted wrongdoing. I believe it was because the $6.2 billion loss was so large, the timeline of events was widely documented and reported. Dimon's quotes in conference calls were colorful and widely quoted. Yet, Dimon came out ahead. He knows his quadrangles, too.

CHAPTER 4

Exotic Structures

U p until now, we have looked at plain vanilla structures and the various features of plain vanilla credit protection. Although we saw a variety of term sheets and looked at a variety of ways to hedge risk, we did not look at structures that were exotic. The points of negotiation centered mainly on fairly straightforward structures. A series of complicated structures has appeared on the market. The market's ability to create structures has outstripped the market's ability to price these structures. That makes these structures less liquid than the plain vanilla structures we have discussed.

Credit spreads are very narrow versus historical levels, and investors who want to enhance return must either be willing to invest in lower-credit-quality assets or to take other risks. Other risks can include event risks and market-contingent risks. Market-contingent risks related to credit spreads or credit default events are becoming increasingly popular in the market. We will return to this theme repeatedly. Market-contingent risks appear to be credit risks that financial institutions understand and deal *with* daily. Banks, for instance, have often made credit decisions without rigorous models to support credit decisions. This was not unusual because relationships, future business prospects, and past lending rules of thumb dictated lending behavior. Often there were market-contingent components of the lending decision.

Although lenders were aware of these components of risk, not much was done to model or to quantify these risks. For a large commercial bank, it was important to be right more often than one was wrong. The risk most dreaded by commercial bankers and portfolio managers was not the "invisible" market-contingent risk, but rather the catastrophic loss of a default on a lending position.

New credit default and credit spread products have cropped up in the market that incorporate features of this invisible market-contingent credit risk. Often the price risk is not rigorously analyzed. But the market is paying more attention to these structures; and as the demand for better methods of pricing this risk increases, more attention in portfolios will be focused on market-contingent risk that is not transparent at first glance.

The following section discusses many of the new structures that have appeared in the market, but because this is an evolving market, new structures will continue to appear. A firm grasp of the fundamentals will guide anyone through the shoals of new structures. The three key components of value remain (1) the timing of the cash flows, (2) the magnitude of the cash flows, and (3) the probability of receipt of the cash flows.

ASSET SWAP SWITCHES

One way of increasing spread on an asset swap is to exchange a current on—balance sheet asset swap package for another asset swap package contingent upon a change in market conditions. In Europe, this is called a switch asset swap. In the United States, it is sometimes called an asset swap.

A brief word on terminology may be useful here. The U.S. bond market has historically used the word *swap* for the sale of one security and the purchase of another. These swaps are sometimes further described as credit swaps (exchanging lower-rated for higher-rated bonds), yield pick-up swaps (exchanging a lower-yielding for a higher-yielding bond), or maturity swaps (exchanging a shorter-dated for a longer-dated bond), and so on. In the United States market, *switching* is often used as a pejorative term for "bait-and-switch" sales techniques, in which a customer is baited by a tempting offer of an unavailable bond and switched to a less attractive but conveniently available bond.

The European market—and often the Asian market—has traditionally used the term *switch* to denote the sale of one security and the purchase of another security, the same way that the U.S. market uses the word *swap* to denote a bond swap.

Markets globally also use the word *swap* for interest rate swaps, currency swaps, and credit default swaps. The exchange of one asset swap package for another asset swap package can correctly be called a swap of asset swaps or a switch of asset swaps, depending on where the market professionals learned their craft. To avoid confusion it is best to immediately reiterate the terms of the transaction. I know several seasoned market professionals who have run into difficulty as a result of not clarifying terminology.

Salomon Brothers has a long-standing anecdote, probably apocryphal, in its Corporate Finance Department. One of its U.S. investment bankers wanted to check the creditworthiness of an equity issuer and called a colleague in the London office. The British colleague told his U.S. counterpart that the equity issuer was "on his uppers." On the strength of this recommendation, the U.S. investment banker accepted the equity as collateral. After all, if the equity issuer was "on his uppers," then the equity issuer's credit quality was improving, the American thought. The only problem was that the equity collateral was nearly worthless. In England, the expression "on his uppers" means that someone is broke. The individual has no soles on his shoes because he is too poor to replace the shoes or to get them resoled and is literally left with only the upper part of the shoes.

I had a similar misunderstanding with a British colleague when I said that someone was "tap city." My British colleague took this to mean that the client was doing well. Fortunately, I headed off the misunderstanding. This is actually a typically American expression referring to Depression-era shantytowns in which unemployed men tap-danced for money.

These are classic misunderstandings illustrating the old joke that the United States and England are two nations divided by the same language. Unfortunately, that is often true in the global marketplace, where two counterparties can be divided by the same market jargon.

For the purposes of this section I use "asset swap switches" to refer to a transaction in which one counterparty exchanges a current on—balance sheet asset swap package for another asset swap package contingent on a change in market conditions. The asset swap switch can also apply to an exchange of floating rate notes.

In an asset swap switch, an investor purchases an asset and agrees to deliver the asset in exchange for another, usually uncorrelated asset, if the new asset's spread widens to a prespecified level. For instance, an investor purchases an Italian bank asset swap at the London interbank offering rate

(SOFR) plus 20 basis points (bps). A commercial bank offers to pay the investor an additional 20 basis points if the investor will agree to exchange the Italian bank asset swap for a Korean bank asset swap. The exchange is market contingent. The Korean bank asset swap is currently trading at SOFR+45 bps. If the spread widens to SOFR+65 bps, then the commercial bank has the right to deliver the Korean bank asset swap to the investor in exchange for the Italian bank asset swap. Diagrammatically, the transaction is as shown in Figure 4.1.

For both counterparties to feel better off in an asset swap switch trans-action, the investor and the commercial bank must have slightly different points of view. In this example, the investor must have the view that Korean bank debt is a good investment even if the asset swap spread widens to SOFR+65 bps. The investor might feel, for example, that Korean debt is priced too rich at SOFR+45 bps for the credit risk under current market conditions. If the spread widens to SOFR+65 bps, however, the investor might feel that that is the credit spread at which he is willing to own an asset linked to the credit risk of a Korean bank. The investor must have the further view that the credit spread widening is due more to market levels coining in line with the true credit risk than to a credit spread widening that indicates that Korean bank debt will slip into default.

The commercial bank must have the view that Italian bank asset swap spreads will not widen in sympathy with or more than Korean bank spreads. In other words, this transaction works best when both counterparties feel that the asset swap spreads have a low correlation. Further, the commercial bank must have the view that it is unwilling to own the Korean bank asset swap at a spread wider than SOFR+65 bps. This may be either because the commercial bank cannot tolerate a further widening in this asset position or because it feels the asset swap spread widening is symptomatic of fundamental underlying credit problems. Notice that the commercial bank bears the risk of a credit spread widening of the Korean bank asset swap package up to the point that the asset swap widens to SOFR+65 bps. The commercial bank is hedged for a credit default event, however.

Another variation on the asset swap switch is known as a credit exchange agreement or a credit risk switch. This looks similar to the asset swap switch trans-action but has some important differences. The investor is generally paid a higher premium to compensate for the credit risk. The credit risk switch occurs only in the event of default of the reference credit. The transaction is as shown in Figure 4.2.

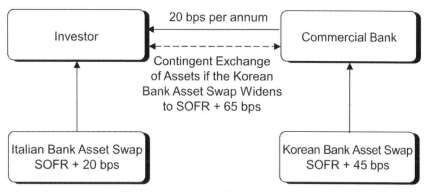

Investor earns an enhanced yield of SOFR + 40 basis points on the Asset Swap Switch (aka Asset Swap Swap) transaction.

FIGURE 4.1 Asset Swap Switch (UK) aka Asset Swap (USA)

In this transaction, the investor purchases an Italian bank asset swap package at SOFR+20 bps. The investor also earns a premium of 55 basis points to take the credit default risk on a BBB asset. In the event of default on the BBB asset, the investor delivers the Italian bank bond to the counterparty and takes delivery of the defaulted BBB asset. Often the investor will be held responsible for potential adverse costs associated with unwinding the swap in the asset swap package. As we see later, the costs of unwinding this swap can be significant for longer maturities and especially for cross-currency swaps. The mark-to-market for these swaps does not necessarily have to be negative; the investor may have a gain in the swap. Nonetheless, the potential adverse cost is a real one, which is rarely factored into the premium earned by the investor.

KNOCK-IN OPTIONS, CREDIT SPREAD OPTIONS, AND FORWARDS

The asset swap switch in the previous section had an interesting feature. The exchange took place based on a change in market conditions, not based on an actual default event. This market-contingent feature can be viewed as a knock-in structure. This is familiar to users of derivatives as a "barrier option."

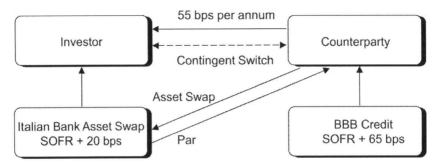

Investor earns an enhanced yield of SOFR + 75 basis points on the Credit Switch transaction.

FIGURE 4.2 Credit Risk Switch

The option becomes active only when the preset barrier is reached. The credit spread of a reference asset must widen to a preset barrier level before the option becomes active. The commercial bank does not have the right to demand delivery of the Italian bank asset swap package in exchange for the Korean bank asset swap package until the Korean bank asset swap spread widens to SOFR+65 bps. Of course, the commercial bank also has a form of default protection on the Korean bank because it is unlikely that the Korean bank would be in default if its asset swap spreads were SOFR+65 bps or less.

Credit spread options are more conventionally used in one of two ways: (1) to hedge index-related basis risk and (2) to hedge credit default risk. An insurance company or a fund manager can purchase an option on the credit spread between a single-A corporate bond index and an index on similar duration and maturity U.S. Treasuries. As we saw earlier, the same kind of credit spread protection can be accomplished using the index swap market.

Credit spread options have been around for approximately 15 years in various forms. One of the classic spread options is the mortgage/Treasury spread option. This market started with a simple strategy in which investors sold calls on mortgage-backed securities (MBS) and bought calls on Treasuries. This protected mortgage investors against a widening in yield spreads between mortgages and Treasury securities. This strategy was unsatisfactory, however, because it did not provide spread protection in all interest rate scenarios. When spreads widened as prices of both security classes fell, both options expired out of the money. This scenario was unhedged.

Salomon Brothers, Merrill Lynch, and others began selling mortgage/ Treasury spread options to correct the flaw in the hedging strategy. The holder of the spread option has the right to buy MBS and sell Treasuries (or the opposite if the investor is hedging a spread-narrowing scenario) at prespecified prices and a prespecified ratio of face amounts. The hedge ratio accounted for spread changes due to price-level changes, and any residual spread change was due to a true widening or narrowing of MBS/Treasury spreads.

Investors can also simply purchase a call option on a spread. For example, an investor could purchase a call option on the spread between Mexican and U.S. Treasuries. If the spread widens, the investor receives a payment based on the new spread versus the initial strike spread. In this way, an investor long a portfolio of Mexican government bonds can protect the investment in the event that the credit of the Mexican government bonds weakens relative to U.S. Treasuries. These contracts are usually structured with a one-time exercise. For ongoing protection, an investor might want to structure the hedge as a credit spread forward (or credit spread swap).

If an investor wants to target a purchase of a security at a wider level than today's market spread, the investor can write a credit spread option. The investor can earn an upfront premium and must purchase the bonds if the spread widens to the pre-agreed level. The investor has written a credit spread put on a bond. This strategy is generally used in the emerging and the high-yield markets, but it is not limited to these markets. Several European banks are writing these options on investment-grade debt. Some European banks receive favorable capital treatment for selling credit spread put options versus selling credit default protection.

Credit spread forwards, also known as credit spread swaps, are similar to credit spread index swaps. Credit spread forwards are indexed to an identified security or an index of securities. The investor pays a per annum fee and receives the credit spread. The credit spread is calculated as the yield of the security minus the yield of a reference risk-free rate. An investor who wishes to have an ongoing hedge for a long position can receive a periodic payment based on the credit spread to a risk-free reference yield. The investor pays an ongoing premium. This can be structured as a swap, with a continuous exchange of net payments, or as an option for which the investor pays an upfront fee.

The second use of credit spread options incorporates elements of a credit default swap. The motives of the counterparties in a credit spread option agreement are necessarily very different. For instance, a bank may wish to sell credit spread protection for a fee because it feels the asset is undervalued at current market levels and further feels that a credit spread widening is not a leading indicator of a default event. The buyer of the protection is willing to take some risk of credit spread widening. At a certain trigger level, the buyer must either reduce credit exposure or hedge a potential default.

Notice that the buyer and the seller of a credit spread option never reference a default event, only a widening in credit spreads. If the reference for a credit spread option is a floating rate note or an asset swap, it is very easy to tell if the option is in the money or not. If the discount margin has increased, the credit spread has widened; if the discount margin has decreased, the credit spread has narrowed.

If the reference security is a fixed-income instrument, however, then we
must use another methodology for determining whether the credit spread has widened or narrowed. The spread to a reference Treasury may not be enough. As a bond ages, it becomes shorter in maturity. We call this "rolling down the yield curve." The spread to the Treasury curve using a similar duration risk-free reference Treasury rate may narrow as the implied risk of the credit declines the closer the bond gets to maturity. In this case, one can use a risk-free reference Treasury (see also the Brazil credit default example in the section on the normalized price method in Chapter 3) combined with a credit spread curve for the reference asset. One can also use asset swap spreads and compare the spreads to a reference asset credit spread curve constructed at the time the credit spread option transaction was initiated.

Credit spread options can take the form of puts or calls. If credit spreads tighten, a call on credit spreads becomes more valuable. If credit spreads widen, credit spread puts become more valuable.

Just as with all options, volatility of the credit spreads is an important input into pricing. In addition, recovery rates and credit spread curves are important inputs. The pricing methodology difficulties incorporate all of the difficulties we discussed earlier.

Credit spread options can take on as many variations of form as interest rate options, including knock-in structures, knock-out structures, levered structures, and more. An example of a knock-out structure is one in which a credit spread put becomes null and void if credit spreads tighten to a certain level, say by 10 basis points. This would indicate that the credit quality of the reference asset improved, possibly even upgraded; and the perceived need for the credit put disappears. The resulting credit spread put would be cheaper than the conventional put. Current demand for this structure is low. Credit spread differentials between various rated credits are at historically low levels. It is possible that more applications will arise linked to highly leveraged transactions and to high-yield bonds.

A knock-in credit spread put does not become active until spreads widen to a certain level. When that happens, the investor will take delivery of an asset at a much wider credit-spread level. The counterparty essentially has credit default protection. One German bank enters into this transaction in the one-to-five-year maturity range. They reference assets trading around SOFR+20 bps and write the protection for a spread widening to SOFR+250 bps. If the spread widening occurs, the German bank has a commitment to purchase the assets at pat They carefully review the underlying credits and demand a premium equal to the full asset swap spread of the reference
asset, the same premium demanded for credit default protection. The German bank gets unfavorable capital treatment for selling credit default protection. The German bank experiences favorable capital treatment, however, for selling credit spread puts because they never reference a credit default event.

BALANCE SHEET SWAPS AND EXPOSURE MANAGEMENT

Most of the calls I receive in the U.S. market are from counterparties wishing to buy and sell credit risk for the purposes of balance sheet management. Often a bank will call looking to sell credit default options for lower A rated credits, hoping to book acceptable credit risks. In most cases they are looking to reference a drawn term loan and to take delivery of the loan in the event of default. Unfortunately, these credits usually yield only 5 to 8 basis points for an undrawn back-up commercial-paper revolver. Often I will receive calls in which counterparties want to purchase a credit default option to lay off credit default risk. In this case, the counterparty agrees to pay a full commitment fee on a loan in order to deliver the loan in the event that it is drawn.

These are logical uses of bank balance sheet capacity and will eventually change the way banks do business globally. Figure 4.3 shows an example of a consolidated portfolio composition of a hypothetical U.S. bank with a branch in the United Kingdom. The bank's assets are concentrated in U.S., British, and German assets, due to the bank's marketing reach. Although the bank has credit capacity for other-country risk, most risk concentration is low in areas where the bank has poor marketing reach.

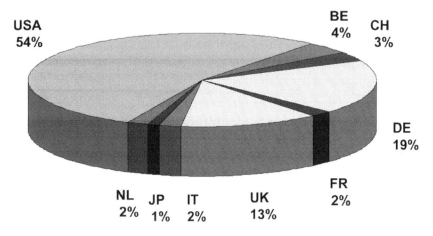

BE (Belgium): Euro; CH (Switzerland), CHF (Swiss Francs); DE (Germany): Euro; FR (France): Euro; UK (Great Britain/United Kingdom): GBP (Pound Sterling); IT (Italy): Euro; JP (Japan): JPY (Yen); NL (Netherlands): Euro; USA (United States): USD (US Dollar)

FIGURE 4.3 Portfolio Distribution of Bank Percentage Assets by Region—

It may not be cost-effective to add marketing staff to attempt to generate assets in a variety of under concentrated countries. One solution might be to offer credit default protection to other banks that are overconcentrated in those countries. Approaching regional banks in desirable countries is one way to diversify risk. The bank could offer credit default protection to banks in Holland, Belgium, France, and Switzerland on local assets.

Banks buy and sell credit risk. Banks lend money. Banks provide financing and make assumptions about the credit risk of their customers. This is the nature of what banks do. The buying and selling of credit risk between global banks is a natural extension of the banking business.

Another area in which banks can enhance business is in providing credit protection for credit exposures between banks and customers of banks. Banks often have unused exposure lines, which can be bought and sold,. For instance, trade lines or exposures in interest rate swaps can be exchanged between banks. Exposures on interest rate swaps can be very large. Table 4.1 shows potential exposures and potential interest rate line usage for U.S. dollar interest rate swaps for various maturities.

Using this chart, how does one look up the exposure for a $100 million notional interest rate swap in which a bank will pay the fixed rate and the counterparty will pay SOFR? Looking down the column labeled "5 years" in which the bank pays fixed in an interest rate swap, one can see that the maximum exposure (14.44) occurs in 2.5 years. This maximum exposure is read as a percent of the total swap notional amount. For a $100 million notional interest rate swap, the peak exposure would be approximately $14,440,000. For a swap with a longer maturity, a 15-year swap, for instance, one would look down the column labeled "15 years" and read down the column for which the bank pays fixed in an interest rate swap. The peak exposure (46.05) is in 8.5 years, and the total exposure is $46,050,000. The longer the maturity of the swap, the greater the exposure.

The exposure numbers tell us that we have a great deal of exposure to a counterparty in a long-dated swap and that we also have it for a long time. In addition, if the bank does a great deal of business with a counterparty, the accumulation of exposure, even for short-dated swaps, can quickly add up. One way to lay off some of this risk is to buy a credit exposure option.

TABLE 4.1 Credit Exposure for U.S. Dollar Interest Rate Swaps (Hypothetical. Varies by market conditions.)

Maturity	1 Year		5 Years		10 Years		15 Years	
Time	Fixed	Floating	Fixed	Floating	Fixed	Floating	Fixed	Floating
0	0.00	0.00	0.00	0.00	0.00	0.00	0.00	0.00
2 weeks	0.32	0.30	1.85	1.79	2.95	2.92	3.89	3.92
1 month	0.47	0.43	2.74	2.62	4.35	4.29	5.70	5.77
2 months	0.68	0.59	3.99	3.72	6.28	6.13	8.17	8.29
3 months	0.84	0.71	4.99	4.57	7.79	7.56	10.08	10.24
4 months	0.96	0.79	5.83	5.27	9.07	8.74	11.67	11.85
5 months	1.08	0.87	6.63	5.90	10.27	9.82	13.15	13.34
6 months	1.18	0.93	7.37	6.46	11.35	10.77	14.48	14.66
9 months	1.30	0.84	9.52	7.39	14.57	12.65	18.44	17.36
1.0 year	1.33	0.85	11.24	8.51	17.16	14.73	21.55	20.28
1.5 years	—	—	13.22	9.18	20.82	16.92	26.22	23.77
2.0 years	—	—	14.23	9.24	23.47	18.29	29.79	26.26
2.5 years	—	—	14.44	8.88	25.39	19.16	32.60	28.14
3.0 years	—	—	14.20	8.23	26.98	19.66	35.12	29.62
3.5 years	—	—	13.15	7.19	28.09	19.80	37.21	30.68
4.0 years	—	—	11.11	5.77	28.73	19.62	38.88	31.36
4.5 years	—	—	8.04	4.06	29.04	19.20	40.30	31.76
5.0 years	—	—	4.27	2.05	29.07	18.40	41.57	31.76
5.5 years	—	—	—	—	28.94	17.47	42.83	31.63
6.0 years	—	—	—	—	28.29	16.36	43.76	31.30
6.5 years	—	—	—	—	27.32	15.15	44.54	30.89
7.0 years	—	—	—	—	26.01	13.80	45.21	30.36
7.5 years	—	—	—	—	24.11	12.26	45.57	29.63
8.0 years	—	—	—	—	22.24	10.69	45.98	28.75
8.5 years	—	—	—	—	19.46	8.87	46.05	27.71
9.0 years	—	—	—	—	15.97	6.86	46.00	26.54
9.5 years	—	—	—	—	11.53	4.69	45.75	25.24
10.0 years	—	—	—	—	6.03	2.34	45.42	23.79
11.0 years	—	—	—	—	—	—	43.34	20.76
12.0 years	—	—	—	—	—	—	35.44	17.29
13.0 years	—	—	—	—	—	—	26.85	12.97
14.0 years	—	—	—	—	—	—	18.75	7.92
15.0 years	—	—	—	—	—	—	7.24	2.67

Conversely, if another bank wants to use some of the excess line capacity of another bank, it can purchase a credit exposure option. The credit exposure option is an exchange of a fee for a guarantee on the swap line credit exposure for a given transaction. Because these exposures may vary over time as market conditions and yield curves change, the credit exposure option can be linked to a given transaction. More simply, however, the credit exposure option can also be sold as exposure coverage for a fixed amount for a fixed time period. The latter method will cover a number of swaps to a given counterparty to provide a broader hedge for the swap line. In this way, a bank can avoid assigning a swap to another bank, which could make a counterparty aware of what it is doing and possibly damage a business relationship.

How much will banks charge each other for these credit exposure options? The answer depends on each individual bank's appetite for more business with a given counterparty. For instance, if bank A needs to free up swap lines so that it can provide an interest rate swap linked to a profitable bond underwriting, it may be willing to pay more than the net spread earned on the interest rate swap itself. Bank B, as provider of the exposure protection, will look at its opportunity cost of selling part of its swap line capacity to bank A. If bank B only does interest rate swap business with the counterparty, it should be happy to earn the swap spread plus a small fee for the potential—however small—shrinkage in its ability to do business with the client counterparty.

Another instance is one in which a bank wants to do lucrative business with a counterparty but has no credit line to the counterparty. Recently, a U.S. bank asked for credit exposure protection for a French bank that was an equity derivatives client. If the U.S. bank could offset the credit exposure risk of the French bank, it would earn 150 basis points on an equity derivatives transaction with the French bank. The total calculated exposure was a maximum of $50 million for one year. Normally, one would expect to earn a level commensurate with a commitment fee on an unfunded loan, which would be only 6 to 8 basis points in the Euromarket—hardly worth the trouble, given the number of banks wanting to offset risk in their unprofitable European loan portfolios. Because the equity derivatives specialist was in great need of locating a hedge for the credit risk, however, the specialist paid 25 basis points for the credit hedge. The U.S. bank used a credit derivative to facilitate a profitable equity derivative transaction, and the provider of the credit protection earned a spread on its credit line that was unattainable in the conventional market.

As banks review their concentration of credit risk in portfolios, they may do swaps of credit risks in which banks offer an exchange of default protection. This is under discussion with several large commercial banks in the United States; and in the future, bank portfolio managers may routinely swap credit risks in a growing interbank market.

Figure 4.4 illustrates an example of a credit event exchange swap. Two banks, the U.S. branch of a European bank and a U.S. bank, wish to free up credit lines on their balance sheets. As in the previous example, the two banks may want to increase their capacity to lend money to these credits or to participate in loan syndications or revolvers. The two banks agree to exchange credit risks. The credit event can be defined as an undrawn revolver becoming drawn. In the case in which the U.S. bank holds the drawn revolver, one of two things can happen: (1) The U.S. bank can deliver the drawn revolver to the European bank and take delivery by assignment of the undrawn revolver owned by the European bank, as shown in Figure 4.5. (2) The U.S. bank can deliver the drawn revolver and begin receiving a credit protection fee for the as-yet-undrawn revolver held by the European bank, as shown in Figure 4.6.

The major challenge that banks face to the efficient management of exposures is bank managers. I once lost a deal when a AAA/AA+ rated U.S. bank gave me an exclusive to consider selling credit protection on a pool of letters of credit (LOCs) having underlying U.S. corporates with an average rating of single A. The average life of the pool of LOCs was 8.5 months. All of the final maturities were under one year. The pool's notional size was more than $1 billion. The proposed fee was 12 basis points per annum. At the same time, the bank for which I was working was trying to

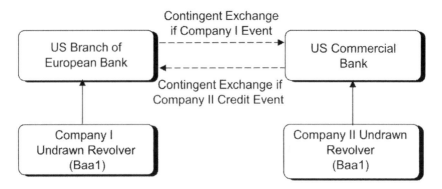

The US Branch of the European Bank and the US Bank swap credit risks with no up-front or ongoing exchange of payments. An exchange occurs only if there is a Credit Event.

FIGURE 4.4 Exchange of Credit Event Protection

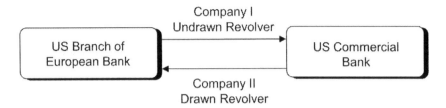

The US Branch of the European Bank and the US Bank swap the drawn
and undrawn revolvers. The exchange occurs only if there is a Credit Event.

FIGURE 4.5 Exchange of Credit Event Protection: Workout Method One

sell $30 million of loan risk on a single-A corporate name. The maturity
was two years, and we proposed paying 12 basis points to purchase
protection for our risk. Note that the maturity was more than a year longer
than the risk we were being asked to take on board.

Because the bank did not wish to take on more category I (loan and
LOC exposure) at the time, we turned down more than $850 thousand in
fees on very short dated risk. Fee income was not the real issue here. We
did not object to the level; we did not attempt to negotiate for a higher fee;
we didn't even consider the fee. The fact of the matter was that we were a
seller of risk, and we were a buyer of credit protection. We were not a buyer
of risk; we were not a seller of credit protection. We did not even consider
the alternative idea of identifying exposures we wanted to sell and
swapping them for the exposures the U.S. bank wanted to sell.

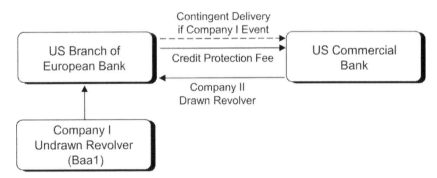

The US Bank delivers the drawn revolver to the European Bank. The European
Bank begins paying a credit protection fee on its undrawn revolver to the US Bank.

FIGURE 4.6 Exchange of Credit Event Protection: Workout Method Two

This is typical of banks starting out in the credit derivatives market. The market is one way. Bank managers are quite happy to sell their exposure, but not to purchase exposure. The demand for credit protection outstrips the supply. Reasons cited include spread (but as I mentioned, that is not the key issue), the fact that we are not doing "relationship" business when earning fees off balance sheet, and the fact that multiple credit managers must be consulted when more than one credit is considered.

It is difficult for banks to make a decision, at least initially, to take on a large exposure, even when it makes good business sense. Mental kluge sets in.

The head of credit derivatives at a U.S. bank expressed a similar frustration to me. She said that the bank would readily book low-fee loans, citing relationship building, but would not do more profitable credit derivatives business because it is off balance sheet. She put it this way: "We're in the business of taking on risk for the wrong fee for future business we're never going to get." She coined this amusing exaggeration to make a point. There is no reason to leave good money on the table when often the premise of lending is a false one. Often there is no future business garnered by the bank. But that is not the main issue here, as the credit derivatives head also pointed out.

Banks are in the business of buying and selling risk. The management of balance sheet risk via the credit derivatives market cannot be a one-way market. Banks need to sell risk and banks need to buy risk. The petrified mind-set of having one-way market risk and failure to use corporate credit lines other than to make direct loans will necessarily change over time. A large part of the future flow business in the credit derivatives market will be driven by large credit line swaps in the credit derivatives market.

CALLABLE STEP-UPS

The callable step-up structure is a balance sheet transaction designed to reduce regulatory capital requirements. This credit derivative transaction opportunity was popular for large commercial banks in the late 1990s and may enjoy resurgence in popularity as more banks feel the pressures of regulatory capital constraints. Participants who sell credit protection usually book income in their credit derivatives trading books where returns on both regulatory and economic capital look attractive. The following example illustrates the motivation of both the buyer and the seller of credit default protection in a callable step-up structure:

Example: You are the risk manager for a Japanese bank. Your bank has accumulated a $3 billion position in loans to several investment-grade U.S. corporations. The per annum coupon on these loans averages LIBOR+25 basis points. You wish to reduce the regulatory capital required for this position and thus report a higher return on capital for year-end reporting purposes. You feel that buying a credit default option from a bank would reduce your required regulatory capital from 100 percent to 20 percent and that your return on capital would increase fivefold. You wish to purchase the default protection for a short period of time, ideally just over your quarter-end, so that you can pay the smallest possible premium for this protection.

You are faced with a dilemma. Most of the loans have maturities of five or more years. Although there are no explicitly stated guidelines, you believe the Japanese Ministry of Finance (MOF) will not recognize a regulatory capital reduction unless the credit default protection is purchased for the maturity of the underlying asset.
What do you do?

Suggestion: The Callable step-up structure was designed in response to this dilemma. It works as follows: The Japanese bank purchases protection for three months at an agreed premium for this initial time period. The premium for this initial period is in the neighborhood of the return on the underlying assets. The market usually commands a slight premium to the three-month implied yield of the underlying loans, chiefly due to supply and demand but also due to documentation and regulatory risk. After the initial period of three months, the premium steps up dramatically. This gives the Japanese bank a compelling economic incentive to call back the risk, thereby terminating the contract. In this way, the seller of the protection is reasonably certain that the Japanese bank will terminate the contract. If for some reason the Japanese bank does not terminate the contract, the protection stepped-up premium is large enough to satisfy the protection seller's internal approval board that they are getting a superior deal for the potential use of their credit lines. Based on the given pricing, a protection seller might pay approximately 5 to 6 bps flat (20 to 24 bps per annum) for the first 90-day period. Thereafter the premium would step up to 100 bps or 125 bps per annum unless the protection seller terminated the transaction at the end of the 90-day period.

Deals in the market place have been for time periods as short as a week. Initial premiums have been as low as 2 basis points with a step up to several hundred basis points if the deal is not terminated at the end of the week. Although 2 basis points does not sound like much, on an annualized basis a protection seller with a funding cost of LIBOR flat is earning much more than the net 25 basis points on the underlying asset. Because these deals are usually done for $1 billion to $3 billion, the fee income is worth the trouble of the detailed documentation required for a successful deal.

Typically, underlying assets for these transactions have been U.S., investment-grade, corporate-unfunded commitments. Ratings are generally BBB or better, with an average rating of A to A—. The maturity of the reference obligations is usually approximately five years. Potential protection sellers usually are asked to sign a confidentiality agreement before they can examine the underlying reference credits.

The motive of the protection buyer is to reduce U.S., investment-grade, corporate credit exposure reported in their U.S. Federal Reserve Board call reports over a quarter-end. This reduces regulatory capital requirements for the commitments.

The notional size varies but is typically $2 billion to $3 billion, with each reference credit approximately $25 million to $100 million in size. The deal should be structured so the protection buyer must pay all protection premiums at the beginning of each relevant protection period. Therefore, the protection seller has no credit risk to the protection buyer.

The protection seller assumes the credit default risk of the underlying unfunded commitments of the U.S., investment-grade, corporate obligors. The protection seller is not responsible for funding. The protection buyer assumes responsibility for funding of commitments, if any. Funding of an unfunded commitment would *not* be a credit-event trigger. A credit default event would occur only if a commitment funds *and* there is failure to pay.

There is no balance sheet impact for the protection seller. Exposure is usually footnoted. If the protection seller were a U.S. bank, regulatory capital as reported in the Fed call reports would increase by 4 percent times the notional amount of the transaction.

The protection seller usually increases credit exposure to the reference obligors by the full notional amount of the unfunded exposures. For the short time periods involved, this is usually not a problem. The legal lending limit of the protection seller is unaffected as long as the credit default option remains unexercised.

Many banks acting as protection sellers view this transaction as similar to a standby letter of credit. They would hold regulatory capital of 8 percent on the notional amount of both unfunded and funded (if any) assets in the transaction. For example, if the protection seller earns 5 bps for a 90-day period, the return on regulatory capital for the initial 90-day period would be approximately 0.625 percent for the 90-day period, or approximately 2.5 percent on a per annum basis.

There is no market consensus on how to calculate the rate of return on economic capital for these transactions. Ideally, one would calculate the credit exposure for the investment credits for a 90-day period (a very small number) and from that the required economic capital required and a return on economic capital.

One approach is to consider the return on capital without accounting for expenses or taxes based on internal-bank-developed economic capital factors. Internal capital charges vary widely from bank to bank, so it is difficult to generalize. For example, assume the economic capital factor required for an unfunded commitment is 0.29 percent, and the operating capital factor for a derivatives transaction is 0.486 applied directly to revenues. If the protection seller earns 5 bps for a 90-day period, the return on capital is 15.9 percent for the 90-day period, or approximately 63.63 percent on a pretax, pre-expense annualized basis. This estimate is pretaxes and pre-expenses. The protection seller could then factor in expenses for its credit derivatives operations and compare the result with its internal pretax, post expense hurdle rate on an annualized basis.

This transaction has further challenges. It is extremely difficult to determine a fair price on very short-dated credit risk. Assume KMV shows a one-year probability of default of around 0.15 percent. A protection seller might translate this to an estimated probability of default (EDF). Assume a median EDF of 11 bps, or 0.11 percent. The premium for the first 90 days of the structure is 5 to 6 bps for 90 days, or about 20 to 24 bps per annum. Theoretically the premium more than covers the likely default risk as reflected by EDF

But there is a problem. Assume that the five-year and one-year probabilities of default for the credits are on average 0.17 percent and 0.15 percent, respectively. The probability of default for the 90-day period is probably lower than the one-year rate of 0.15 percent, but it is difficult to exactly determine how much lower. Martha Seller of the former KMV commented on this. KMV points out they really do not know anything about 30-, 60-, or 90-day default probabilities; there just is not enough default data. There are few observations of default (roughly 15 in 10,000 for a one-year time period). A reasonable approach might be to assume that it is a function of the square root of time, so one might expect that the 90-day probability of default is *higher* than one-quarter of 0.15 percent. On the other hand, there is no evidence that credit default probabilities vary with the square root of time. It is simply a convenient fiction. Although this might be allowed for investment-grade credits, for noninvestment-grade credits this is actually a dangerous and usually false assumption. To date, I do not know of any agreed method to estimate default probabilities for short discrete time periods.

Nonetheless, using a common sense approach, J.P. Morgan, Citibank, Deutsche Morgan Grenfell, Svenska Handelsbanken, Wachovia (to a more limited extent), Toronto Dominion, and CIBC, among others, have been participants in these transactions.

Participants in these transactions view the income as more than fair compensation for their assessment of the risk. These transactions are booked in credit derivatives trading books, and the regulatory and capital charges are much smaller when viewed from the perspective of the trading book as opposed to the bank book. Most of these competitors use a value-at-risk (VAR) model, or a modified VAR model. The corresponding return on capital for both regulatory and economic capital is much higher for the trading book than comparable calculations made for the bank book.

Protection sellers must decide whether they want to participate in transactions that are motivated by regulatory capital management to enhance reported performance over quarter-end or year-end reporting periods. Suitability is usually an internal bank decision.

SYNTHETIC LENDING FACILITIES

Synthetic lending facilities (SLFs) are often used to describe loan total return swaps. More typically, SLFs refer to forward commitments to purchase revolvers and loans. Investors can gain exposure to credits that otherwise would be unavailable.

Maturity, fees, and sometimes credit enhancements can be customized. For example, an investor can synthetically create a participation in an unfunded revolving loan. As long as the loan remains unfunded, the investor receives a commitment fee. If the loan remains unfunded throughout the period of the SLF agreement, the investor's commitment terminates or converts into a term loan at the option of the borrower. If the unfunded commitment converts into a term loan, it converts at a predetermined credit spread agreed on at the start of the transaction.

Investors receive a fee for providing—via an asset swap transaction—a forward commitment to purchase a security. This is not the same transaction as a credit default swap. In this transaction, the trigger event is not a default. The trigger event is usually the funding of the revolver. The investor does not make a termination payment if a funding event occurs. The investor allows the borrower to convert to a term loan at a predetermined credit spread.

The synthetic credit facility (SCF) is the sister product to the synthetic lending facility. SCFs are sometimes used for general debt obligations. For instance, a German bank currently participates in an SCF linked to the debt obligations of the Republic of Ireland, rated AA. The German bank earns 4 basis points per annum. In exchange, the German bank's counterparty has the right to put Irish debt obligations to the German bank for a period of three years. This is an American-style put, exercisable at any time over the three-year period. The debt obligations can have a final maturity no longer than 2007, and the level at which the counterparty can put the obligations is LIBOR+8 bps. The German bank feels that LIBOR+8 bps for the zero percent, Bank for International Settlements (BIS), risk-weighted obligations of Ireland is a fair level. Meanwhile, the German bank earns 4 basis points just for standing by to purchase something it is happy to own at a price at which it is happy to own it. The counterparty has an outlet for its Irish government risk at a price of 4 basis points per annum.

GEARED DEFAULT OPTIONS

Many banks, reaching for more fee income, will accept a geared, or leveraged, credit default structure. This structure has enjoyed popularity in the United Kingdom and Asia in particular. These structures are sometimes confused with basket structures, which we discuss later. Geared structures are linked to only one name credit risk. If credit default occurs, however, the seller of the default protection pays a multiple of the loss.

One AA rated bank provided a geared credit default swap for a five-year maturity on an unfunded Philip Morris loan. Instead of earning the expected fee of 25 basis points for a five-year maturity credit default swap, the AA bank earned a fee of 40 basis points. The loss severity would be twice the default loss exposure. The bank that hedged its Philip Morris position reduced the Philip Morris exposure by $20 million and took exposure to the AA rated bank for only $10 million, the notional amount of the geared credit default swap, albeit leveraged to hedge the loss of $20 million worth of the Philip Morris loan. The AA bank had the view that the Philip Morris credit would improve rather than decline. Both banks felt they were better off in this transaction.

We look at credit-linked notes in more detail in Chapter 6, but at least one structure is worth mentioning now. The following term sheet shows a three-year maturity credit-linked note linked to Mexican sovereign credit risk. Note the boldface type, which highlights some key points.

*****

MEXICO CREDIT-LINKED NOTE
Indicative Term Sheet

Issuer:	AA rated European bank, Indonesian branch.
Investment Amount:	USD 5 million.
Calculation Amount:	USD 5 million.
Trade Date:	To be determined.
Issue Date:	Trade date plus three weeks.
Maturity Date:	The earlier of:
	1. issue date + three years, *or*
	2. early termination date, if any.
Interest Payments:	**Six-month USD LIBOR + 215%** paid semiannually on an Act/360 basis modified following with no adjustment for period end dates.
Interest Payment dates:	Semiannually. If a credit event occurs, accrued interest will not be paid.
Redemption Amount:	The note will be redeemed at 100 percent of the investment amount on the scheduled maturity date provided that a credit event with respect to the reference credit has not occurred on or prior to such date; provided, however, that if a credit event with respect to the reference credit has occurred on or prior to such date, the note will be redeemed on the early termination date by **delivery of a portfolio of securities selected from the list of reference obligations. The amount of securities will be such that the current market value is equal to the cash redemption amount. The calculation agent will determine the composition of such portfolio.** The issuer or any of its affiliates will make the delivery of such portfolio.

Cash Redemption Amount =
Face Amount of Reference Security
× MV − Hedge Costs

where MV equals the market value of the relevant reference security on the notification date.

Hedge costs are the sum of the mark-to-market value of the swap that swaps fixed-rate cash flows to floating-rate cash flows that are paid on the note *plus* the product of 30 percent and the calculation amount.

Early Termination Date;	In the event that a credit event occurs during the term of the transaction, the issuer shall have the right to designate an early termination date that is not less than 10 business days from the delivery of notice to the investor of the occurrence of the credit event.
Credit Event:	The occurrence of any of the following events with respect to the reference credit:

1. The reference credit fails to make when due any payment under any financial obligation, and such failure continues for more than 10 days.

2. A default, event of default, or other similar condition or event occurs in respect of such reference credit under any financial obligation that has resulted in such financial obligation becoming, or being capable at such time of being declared, due and payable before it otherwise would have become due and payable.

3. A waiver, deferral, restructuring, rescheduling, exchange, or other adjustment occurs in respect of any financial obligation, and the effect of such adjustment is overall materially less favorable from a

	credit and risk perspective to the relevant creditor.
Reference Credit:	United Mexican States (UMS).
Reference Security:	United Mexican States, global bond. Maturity: February 6, 2001. Currency Denomination: USD. Coupon: 9.75%.
	Face Amount: USD 6.5 million (Calculation Amount $\times$ 1.3).
Financial Obligation:	With respect to the reference credit, *any financial obligation in an aggregate amount of not less than the threshold amount incurred by the reference credit in any capacity.*
Threshold Amount:	**USD 3 million.**
Market Value:	On any day, with respect to the relevant reference security, the percentage equal to the unweighted arithmetic mean of the bid prices
	(expressed as a percentage of principal amount and exclusive of any accrued but unpaid interest) for such reference security provided to the calculation agent on such day by at least two but not more than five dealers in the market for such reference security; **provided, however, that if only one or if no such bid prices are so provided, the market value shall mean the market value as determined by the calculation agent.**
Reference Obligations:	UMS 9.75% of February 6, 2001
	UMS FRN of February 6, 2001.
	UMS 9.875% of July 15, 2007.
	UMS 11.375% of September 15, 2016.
	UMS 11.5% of May 15, 2026.

	In addition, if in the future the reference credit issues obligations that rank equal in priority of payment with the above list of reference obligations, then those obligations will be included in the list of reference obligations.
Business Days:	**Days on which commercial banks and foreign exchange markets settle payments in Tokyo, London, New York, Labuan, and Mexico City.**
Calculation Agent:	**AA or better rated European bank, Indonesian branch (the issuer).**

At first this appears to be very similar to the other term sheets we have seen. The issuer, a AA rated bank, would otherwise have paid about 200 basis points per annum for protection. The investor is purchasing a note issued by a AA European bank branch—one that has the same credit standing as the main bank. The bank would normally fund at around LIBOR — 25 bps—but the investor should disregard this. The credit risk is Mexican sovereign credit risk, not the credit risk of the AA rated issuer. The bank should not get a discount for its Mexican protection just because it lends its name, and only its name, to the issuance of a credit-linked note with underlying Mexican sovereign risk. But it appears this has been taken into account. The issuer is not getting a discount. In fact, at first glance it appears the bank may be paying the full offer side of the market, perhaps even a bit more. The bank is paying a coupon of LIBOR+215 bps.

Caveat emptor: Let the buyer beware.

BASIS RISK: DELIVERY, HEDGE COSTS, AND CALCULATIONS

This brings us back to the sections in boldface type. Eight key points create value for the issuer of the credit-linked note but are potentially to the advantage of the issuer and not the investor:

1. The calculation agent is the issuer of the note.

2. The issuer has the right to deliver any one of several securities with various maturities in the event of default. The calculation agent, the issuer, determines the composition of the portfolio.

3. The issuer has the right to add more securities to the list of deliverable securities if Mexico issues more obligations in equal rank to the reference obligations.

4. The value of the delivered securities must be equal to the cash redemption amount. The issuer has the final say in the determination of the value of the delivered securities. If only one or if no bid prices are available with which to determine market value, the calculation agent, the issuer, determines the market value of the securities in the issuer-designated portfolio.

5. Default means default on *any financial obligation of Mexico incurred in any capacity* not less than the threshold amount.

6. The threshold amount is only $3 million.

7. The materiality clause is absent.

8. The usual cash redemption amount is reduced by *hedge costs.* The calculation agent, the issuer, determines the value of the hedge costs.

By now it is easy to see that there are several new key issues we have not seen before. In fact, only the first key issue, the issuer as calculation agent, is one we have seen before. Using the issuer as calculation agent is quite usual. This is fine as long as the investor has some objective recourse for the note calculations and as long as the investor has some remedies if the investor feels the calculations are arbitrarily disadvantageous. But that is not the case here. Let us examine this in more detail.

The calculation redemption amount is calculated using the defaulted market value of the United Mexican States 9.75 percent of 2001. This is not what the investor will necessarily receive in the event of default, however. The calculation agent, the issuer, can deliver securities ranging in maturity from the year 2001 to the year 2026. In a default situation, prices on several securities may not be readily available, especially for longer-dated securities. Further, the pricing may be more volatile for longer-dated maturities. A number of factors contribute to this. One is the uncertainty of what may happen in a workout situation with longer-dated paper. There may be re-structuring of longer-dated securities, whereas shorter-dated paper may be paid down at least partially. Longer-dated paper with the loss of a long coupon stream may trade at deeper discounts and experience price volatility for a small change in rates, similar to a zero-coupon bond, while speculation rages over whether the sovereign will resume payments or restructure its debt.

The investor should not be indifferent to the composition of the portfolio of securities. Furthermore, as more Mexican debt is issued with the same credit standing as the reference pool of securities, the issuer can add these securities to the list. The investor, however, has no choice. Worse, the investor has no recourse other than an expensive and difficult-to-win after-the-fact litigation if the investor is unhappy with the final result.

Not only does the investor not have the right to choose or to veto de-liverable securities, the investor does not have the right to designate a disinterested third party to oversee the process. The same is true of pricing. In the event of default, it would not be surprising if one or more of the reference pool securities had no bid. This leaves the investor at the mercy of the issuer to determine the price of the reference pool securities. In that instance, the market value would be whatever the issuer says it is. In this way, the issuer can potentially manipulate the cash redemption amount owed the investor. From the investor's point of view, this is a potentially dangerous situation.

Of course, neither the investor nor the issuer believes that Mexico will default within three years on its sovereign debt obligations. I do not believe that will happen, either. The investor certainly would not enter into this transaction if the investor thought Mexico would default on one of its sovereign obligations.

But wait just a minute! The reference credit is the United Mexican States. The reference security for purposes of calculation of the cash redemption amount is the UMS 9.75 percent of 2001. The reference credit for purposes of defining the default event, however, is *any financial obligation of Mexico with a value no lower than $3 million.* Notice that this is the lowest threshold value we have seen so far. This means any obligation that ranks in seniority with the UMS global debt, even over-the-counter transactions, could potentially be cited for a default event. The conveniently low threshold makes it even easier for the issuer to declare a default event. Easier still is the complete absence of any materiality clause. The materiality clause is meant to avoid spurious declarations of default events when there may be merely a legitimate dispute over a payment. For a sovereign, a dispute amounting to only $3 million leaves room for a declaration of a default event even when the principal and interest payments on global debt are not in jeopardy. We saw some potential problems in the calculation of the cash redemption amount owed to the investor in the form of the determination of the market value and the determination of the market value of the reference securities that can be delivered in satisfaction of the cash redemption amount. Looking back, we see the following:

$$\text{Cash Redemption Amount} = \text{Face Amount of Reference Security} \times \text{MV} - \textit{Hedge Costs}$$

There is more to this formula than the previous formulas we have examined. There are other problems as well, from the point of view of the investor. For example, there is the little matter of subtracting off the hedge costs.

Hedge costs? This is the first time we have seen hedge costs thrown into a redemption amount calculation. There are two components to the hedge cost calculation, as previously discussed. The hedge costs is the sum of (1) the mark-to-market value of the swap that swaps fixed-rate cash flows to floating-rate cash flows that are paid on the note and (2) 30 percent of the calculation amount.

In the first component of the hedge cost calculation, the issuer is asking the investor to bear the brunt of the mark-to-market value of an interest rate swap in which fixed-rate cash flows are swapped to a floating-rate coupon. That does not sound unreasonable. The swap is a fixed-dollar for a floating-dollar swap. After all, a swap can have a gain as well as a loss in the event of default, depending on prevailing market conditions in the U.S.
interest rate market unrelated to a Mexican default. This is possible, but in the case of this particular swap, not probable. The reason is that the reference bond is originally trading above par, and the coupon on the bond

is higher than the prevailing fixed-rate market. The fixed payment owed on the interest rate swap is well above market. Therefore, it is very likely, even if there has been a substantial rise in U.S. interest rates, that the mark-to-market value of the swap will be against the investor. According to the payoff structures discussed earlier, the investor is essentially giving the issuer a payoff based on the initial price, an above par price, instead of a par minus market value structure. The hedge costs compensate the issuer for the initial price risk of the reference security plus swap package. This is fine, provided the investor realizes that the implied payoff formula is essentially a payoff based on a premium price for the reference asset, as the premium price of the reference asset is imbedded in the swap payments. In addition, the investor is also hedging for market risk on the swap. Nowhere is this clarified in the term sheet, so the investor must be clear on the initial cash flows of the transaction. How many investors actually look at this and are capable of pricing the value?

The second component of the hedge cost calculation is more subtle. The issuer subtracts 30 percent of $5 million from the cash redemption amount. At first this seems reasonable, given that the cash redemption amount calculation includes the face amount of the reference security. The face amount of the reference security, we recall, is as follows:

$$\text{Calculation Amount} \times 1.3 = \$5,000,000 \times 1.3 = \$6,500,000$$

The 30 percent differences should offset one another—or do they? A closer look shows us they do not. Whether by omission or by design, the only reference to the calculation amount in the term sheet is in the definition of the face amount, which leaves us to imply a value of $5 million for the calculation amount. In the cash redemption amount, we must first multiply this number by the market value of the reference security (either the UMS 9.75 percent of 2001 or an appropriate substitute) and then subtract off the hedge costs.

Notice that no matter what the market value of the UMS reference security is, we are always subtracting off a fixed value of:

$$\$5,000,000 \times 30\% = \$1,500,000$$

The investor should insist that instead of subtracting off a fixed amount, the face amount of the reference security should equal $5 million, the calculation amount, in the cash redemption amount calculation.

How much can this potentially hurt the investor? Let us take a look at some sample calculations assuming market values of 40, 60, and 80 for the UMS reference security, and let us ignore the mark-to-market on the swap, setting this to zero for now. If we compare the cash redemption amount calculation as it now stands in the term sheet with the suggested revisions, we see the following results:

Cash Redemption Amount Difference Using Term Sheet Formula versus Revised Formula (Setting swap mark-to-market to zero)

	Market Value of Reference Security		
	40	60	80
Term Sheet Amount	$1,100,000	$2,400,000	$3,700,000
Suggested Revision Amount	$2,000,000	$3,000,000	$4,000,000
Difference	($900,000)	($600,000)	($300,000)
Percentage of Initial Investment	(18%)	(12%)	(6%)

The difference in cash redemption amount is significant. If after a default event the market value of the UMS global bond drops to 40, the investor's cash redemption amount is $900,000 lower than by using the suggested revised formula. That is a difference of 18 percent of the initial investment amount. Even at a price of 60, the difference between the two formulas is 12 percent of the initial investment amount. The lower the market values, the greater the difference in the calculated amounts. This kicks the investor when he or she is down. It may not even have been the intention of the issuer to create this anomalous result, but under the term sheet conditions, the formula works to the advantage of the issuer and not the investor. So it is up to potential investors to ask for clarification and modifications to the term sheet if there is any doubt.

If that were not bad enough, there is also the matter of the swap mark-to-market, which we temporarily set to zero for purposes of the preceding calculations. This can also be a significant number. Because the swap coupon payment is an off-market coupon payment, the mark-to-market value could be over 10 percent of the $5 million notional amount, or an additional $500,000. Let us plug in this number and see how much that changes the difference:

Cash Redemption Amount Difference Using Term Sheet Formula versus Revised Formula (Setting swap mark-to-market to $500,000)

	Market Value of Reference Security		
	40	60	80
Term Sheet Amount	$600,000	$1,900,000	$3,200,000
Suggested Revision Amount	$2,000,000	$3,000,000	$4,000,000
Difference	($1,400,000)	($1,100,000)	($800,000)
Percentage of Initial Investment	(28%)	(22%)	(16%)

The swap mark-to-market can be lower than $500,000, of course, depending on the time remaining to the maturity of the swap and on the prevailing market conditions. I am using this number as an illustration without calculating sensitivities. The point is, however, that investors need not suffer the swap mark-to-market at all unless they are getting compensated for the risk. At the levels offered in this particular credit-linked note, however, that additional risk does not seem to be factored in to the spread offered to the investor.

This particular credit-linked note looks as if it is a geared structure offering a slightly above-market spread. If fact, the coupon offered is just about at the market. The term sheet is rife with hidden risks to the investor. The term sheet seems unclear on terms such as calculation amount, and the term sheet interpretation does not work in favor of the investor. Investors must carefully examine terms and conditions and ask for modifications to term sheet language. If necessary, investors may wish to restate calculations and to ask for different pricing if they find they are taking more imbedded risk than they realized at first glance. Further, investors must carefully scrutinize confirmation language to make sure it agrees with the terms and conditions as they understand them.

Unfortunately, the credit derivatives market is flooded with this kind of paper, and most of it is offered in the Asian markets, where there seems to be less regulatory scrutiny of structured product. It is this kind of structure that gives derivatives market professionals a bad name. I do not think it is an accident that this particular note was offered to a Japanese leasing company.

Japanese leasing companies are looking for securities with high spreads because their funding costs are high, in the area of LIBOR+100 bps. The AAA issuer credit makes it appear, for booking purposes, as if the creditworthiness of the offered security is also high. Unfortunately, this investor base is also new to the credit derivatives market and less sensitive to the subtleties of structures. My intention is not to characterize Japanese leasing companies as victims, but rather to point out that any investor lured by high yield should take a hard look at a deal that appears to be too good to be true. As the saying goes, it usually is.

BASKET CREDIT DEFAULT SWAPS

Just as a portfolio manager can purchase protection on a single credit, a portfolio manager can purchase protection on a basket of credits. If a portfolio manager chooses four credits with an asset value of $100 million each, the portfolio manager can purchase credit protection in a first-to-default structure. For example, if one of the credits experiences default on any of its debt, which remains uncured for five business days, the credit default swap terminates. The default protection seller will pay $100 million to the portfolio manager, who will deliver to the default protection seller the asset of the credit that has experienced the credit default event.

One can think of the first-to-default basket structure as similar to a senior/ subordinated collateralized bond obligation (CBO) or as a senior/subordinated collateralized loan obligation (CLO). The credit default protection seller is like an investor in the subordinated tranche of a CBO or a CLO. The default protection seller takes the risk of the first loss in the structure. The remaining credits in the basket are similar to the senior tranche of a CBO or a CLO. The holder of these remaining credits, the senior position, has been protected from the first loss by the default protection seller, the holder of the subordinate position.

Although this comparison is often made in the marketplace, there are very important differences between first-to-default baskets and senior or subordinated CBOs and CLOs. The risk of the default protection seller is an off—balance sheet risk as opposed to an on—balance sheet risk for the buyer of a subordinated tranche of a CBO or a CLO. Furthermore, the default protection seller does not invest capital but earns a fee. It is also important to note that the assets that compose a first-to-default basket are generally small in number and not necessarily well diversified. The construction of a first-to-default basket does not meet the same rigorous tests that rated CBOs and CLOs must meet in determining the composition of assets, which make up the collateral for these instruments.

The following is an abbreviated term sheet for a bespoke (custom-made) basket credit default swap referencing three credits.

BASKET CREDIT DEFAULT SWAPS
Indicative Term Sheet

Default Protection Buyer:	Portfolio manager.	
Default Protection Seller:	Default protection seller.	
Reference Credits:	**Issuer**	**Maturity**
	Merita Bank (A2)	June 2004.
	Philip Morris (Moody's A2)	September 2004.
	IcelandAir (NR)	February 2005.
Merita Bank	USD 25 million.	
Philip Morris	USD 25 million.	
IcelandAir	USD 25 million.	
Trade Date:	To be determined.	
Effective Date:	One week after the trade date.	
Maturity Date:	Five years after the effective date.	
Notional Amount:	USD 25 million.	
Adjusted Notional Amount:	If any of the issuers prepays an underlying loan, another loan of a maturity not longer than seven years from the effective date may be substituted for the relevant credit. If none is available, the notional	

	principal will be reduced on the next payment date to reflect the lowest outstanding value of the remaining loans.
Credit Default Fee:	Portfolio manager will pay to the default protection seller a fee of 30 basis points per an-
	num on an actual/360-day basis on a notional amount of USD 25 million.
Termination Payment:	If there is a credit event, the credit default protection seller will pay the notional amount to the portfolio manager. The portfolio manager will deliver the underlying credit asset for the credit that experienced the credit event with a face value equal to the notional amount. If there is no credit event up to and including the maturity of the basket credit default swap, the credit default protection seller makes no payments.
Credit Events:	A filing for bankruptcy protection by any one of the underlying credit issuers or a payment default on any debt that remains uncured for five business days.

There is something different and unique about basket credit default swaps, which we have not seen before. Figure 4.7 shows the exchange of contingent and actual flows in such a swap. If there is a credit event on one of the reference credits, for instance, Philip Morris, the portfolio manager delivers the underlying Philip Morris asset and receives the notional amount of $25 million (if there have been no notional amount adjustments) from the default protection seller. The swap then terminates, and the portfolio manager remains unhedged on the remaining credits, Merita Bank and IcelandAir. The termination payment is then as shown in Figure 4.8. The portfolio manager either can purchase default protection separately on the remaining assets or can reform a new basket, possibly adding more uncorrelated credits.

Because of this contingency, in which a portfolio manager is left with unhedged assets, the strategy of the composition of the basket is very important. Basket structures are generally best suited for investment-grade credits with low correlations and low covariance. It is generally best to use credit risks with similar credit ratings as well. Otherwise, a very weak credit risk

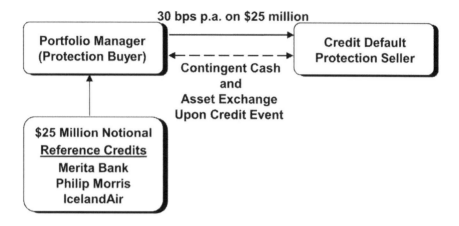

An Institution receives a 30 basis point p.a. fee in return for making a Contingent Payment if a predefined Credit Event occurs to one of the credits.

FIGURE 4.7   Basket Credit Default Swap

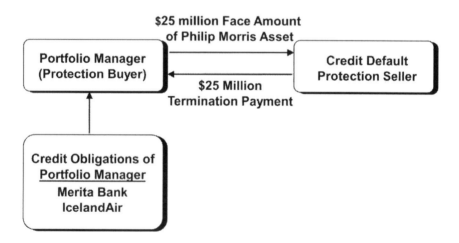

If the Notional Amount has not been reduced and Philip Morris defaults on any of its obligations, the Credit Default Protection Seller accepts delivery of the Philip Morris Reference Credit vs delivery of $25 million to the Portfolio Manager. The Basket Swap terminates with no further obligation by either party.

FIGURE 4.8   Basket CDS Termination if Philip Morris Defaults

would dominate the basket pricing, and one would have to question the value of the hedge on the stronger credits. Low correlation between the basket credits and the default protection seller is obviously another important constraint. If the default protection seller were highly correlated with the credits in the basket, the value of the "protection" would be open to question. If the creator of the basket follows these guidelines, the likelihood of multiple defaults declines.

Why not use uncorrelated high-yield, or "junk," bonds? There is nothing wrong with this strategy, if one can tolerate potential problems. If a portfolio manager uses high-yield debt, even uncorrelated names might result in a basket in which two names default within a short time of each other. This is because the probability of default matters. The probability of default of high-yield bonds is generally higher than that for investment-grade debt, and two uncorrelated credits may experience a coincident (or nearby time frame) default. Even if high-yield bonds do not experience actual coincident default, a couple of credits may have deteriorated to the point where they are unsuitable for another basket and the individual cost of a hedge is prohibitive.

The probability of default of investment-grade credits is generally much lower than for high-yield bonds, as we saw earlier. If one investment-grade credit defaults, it is very likely a portfolio manager can repurchase protection on the remaining viable names at a cost-effective level. The remaining credits are very likely to be suitable as components of a new basket or as an individual credit default swap.

The credit event on a basket of loans can be defined as bankruptcy, restructuring, default on an obligation in excess of a threshold level, failure to meet financial covenants, adverse change in a credit spread greater than a pre-agreed amount, or a ratings downgrade below a prespecified rating. These events are included in the criteria discussed earlier.

Default payments are generally structured as payment versus delivery of the defaulted credit asset (as we saw earlier) or as cash settlement. Cash settlement is usually the notional amount (or original price minus default price times the notional amount) minus the market value of the asset whose credit is in default as determined by a dealer poll, or cash settlement based on a pre-agreed fixed percentage of the notional amount.

PRICING BASKET CREDIT DEFAULT SWAPS

How does one price a basket credit default swap? Basket credit default pricing is subject to the same challenges we discussed earlier. We can, however, get an intuitive feel of the boundary conditions that occur in a public well-traded market.

Let's take a cash settlement example of three uncorrelated investment-grade credits, W, X, and Y, each with a $25 million notional amount. If one of the credits defaults, the protection seller's cash payment is $25 million × (Original Price − Recovery Value) on the defaulted credit. After that, the protection seller has no obligation whatsoever.

Let's assume that for the three credits, W, X, and Y, we know that the upper bound is the sum of the premiums of credit default protection on W, X, and Y. We also know this is too much. The protection buyer is not getting default protection on all three credits, only on the first one to default.

Suppose we also know that W is the weakest among "equals" and most likely to default. The price of the basket protection at the lower bound should be the price of credit default protection on W's $25 million notional amount. Intuitively, we know this is not enough. The credit default protection seller must be compensated something beyond this. The probability of exercise of the option is greater than just the probability of W's default. The probability of exercise is equal to the probability of W or X or Y defaulting.

It is a common misunderstanding of probability theory to say that the probability of W or X *or* Y is the product of each of the individual probabilities. That is simply incorrect. Assume for a moment that the transaction is a two-year transaction and that the marginal default rates for W, X, and Y are as follows:

Marginal and Cumulative Default Rates for W, X, and Y

Default Rates for W, X, and Y	Year 1 Marginal Default Rate	Year 2 Marginal Default Rate	Cumulative Default Rate in Year 2
W's Rates	0.28%	0.42%	0.70%
X's Rates	0.20%	0.30%	0.50%
Y's Rates	0.24%	0.36%	0.60%

Given these default rates, what is the likelihood of W or X or Y defaulting in either year one or year two? It is easier to consider the probability of no default for the three credits, W, X, and Y, that is, to find the probability of none of the credits defaulting. First, look at the probability of W and X and Y not defaulting in year one and then the cumulative rate in year two. The probability that a default has not occurred for each of the individual credits is as follows:

Default Rates	No Default Year 1	No Default for 2 Years
W's Probability	99.72%	99.30%
X's Probability	99.80%	99.50%
Y's Probability	99.76%	99.40%

Notice that the probability of no default is very high. This is because we are using investment-grade credits. I made the assumption that these are all BBB credits as rated by Standard & Poor's (S&P) and at least investment grade as rated by Moody's. The probability that none of the credits will default in year one is the product of the probability of no default. The probability of no default for the entire two-year period is the product of the cumulative probabilities of no default for two years.

For year 1, the probability of no default is $(0.9972 \times 0.9980 \times 0.9976) = 0.9928$, or 99.28 percent. The probability of at least one default during this period is simply $(1 - 0.9928) = 0.007182$, or 0.7182 percent. For a trade lasting two years, the probability of no default is $(0.993 \times 0.995 \times 0.994) = 0.9821$, or 98.21 percent. The probability of at least one default during this period is simply $(1 - 0.9821) = 0.0179$, or 1.79 percent. Notice that this is 2.55 times as likely as the cumulative probability of default of the three credits in year one.

We can see, however, that the probability of default of any one of the credits is very low individually, or as an agglomeration of credits, or as a first-to-default basket structure. Default rates for the individual credits and the basket first-to-default structure for W, X, and Y are shown in the next table.: The default rate of the basket is higher than any individual default rate. In year one, the basket default rate is 257 percent higher than W's default rate, the highest in the group, and almost exactly the same as the

Comparison of Individual and Basket Default Rates

Default Rates	Individual Year 1	Basket Year 1	Cumulative Individual Year 2	Basket Year 2 Cumulative
W's Rate	0.28%	0.72%	0.70%	1.79%
X's Rate	0.20%	0.72%	0.50%	1.79%
Y's Rate	0.24%	0.72%	0.60%	1.79%

sum of the individual default rates. However, on an absolute level, the basket default rate is still a very low rate—less than 1.00 percent. The basket cumulative rate for year two is 1.79 percent, 255 percent higher than W's rate of 0.70 percent and just slightly below the sum of the individual default rates.

How much, then, do we add on to the fee over and above what one would pay for credit default protection on W alone? One reasonable method is to add the sum of the commitment fees for unfunded loans on the remaining credits, X and Y. This theoretically compensates the protection seller for the increased probability of default. This method also implies that differences in recovery value have been factored in via different commitment fee levels.

Often a market professional might say that the protection buyer should pay the sum of the credit default protection fees because the basket probability of default is almost the same as the sum of the individual credits. This is an error in logic. The default protection seller will make a payment on only one of the credits, not on all three; so the protection seller is compensated for only one default plus the increased likelihood of a default occurring. When that increased likelihood is still low, the probability of payout is still low.

Of course, one could also look at the individual credit default price of each of W, X, and Y and the relative likelihood of default. In this way, a proportional amount of each individual fee could be used. The weakness of this method is that it requires a fudge number to compensate the seller of protection for the increased likelihood of exercise. This pricing methodology is more difficult to defend, and the results are not reproducible across baskets. Consistency in methodology breaks down. The pricing ultimately comes down to what the buyer and the seller of the basket credit default protection agree is fair.

A note at this point on the importance of using investment-grade credits might be helpful. If I use, instead, noninvestment-grade credits with a higher probability of default, how much does this affect the increased likelihood of default? The answer is quite a bit. A look at the following table for default rates on assets rated single B by S&P illustrates this point. The lower-rated credits here are W*, X*, and Y*.

Marginal and Cumulative Default Rates for W*, X*, and Y*

Default Rates for W*, X*, and Y*	Year 1 Marginal Default Rate	Year 2 Marginal Default Rate	Cumulative Default Rate In Year 2
W*'s Rates	5.70%	6.01%	11.71%
X*'s Rates	7.90%	6.30%	14.20%
Y*'s Rates	6.50%	7.00%	13.50%

Notice the dramatically higher default rates for each of the credits compared to W, X, and Y. Let us look at the reduction relative to the investment-grade credits in the probability of no default for each of the credits.

	No Default Year 1	No Default for 2 Years
W*'s Probability	94.30%	88.29%
X*'s Probability	92.10%	85.80%
Y*'s Probability	93.50%	86.50%

Performing the same analysis as we did for the investment-grade credits, we can examine the probability of at least one default in year one and also for the entire two-year period. For year one, the probability of no default is $(0.9430 \times 0.9210 \times 0.9350) = 0.8121$, or 81.21 percent. The probability of at least one default during this period is simply $(1 - 0.8121) = 0.1879$, or 18.79 percent. For a trade lasting two years, the probability of no default is $(0.8829 \times 0.8580 \times 0.8650) = 0.6553$, or 65.53 percent. The probability of at least one default during this period is simply $(1 - 0.6553) = 0.3447$, or 34.47 percent.

Comparison of Individual and Basket Default Rates

Rates	Individual Year 1	Basket Year 1	Cumulative Individual Year 2	Basket Year 2 Cumulative
W*'s Rate	5.70%	18.79%	11.71%	34.47%
X*'s Rate	7.90%	18.79%	14.20%	34.47%
Y*'s Rate	6.50%	18.79%	13.50%	34.47%

The default rate for the first-to-default basket in year one is 18.79 percent versus 20.1 percent for the sum of the three credits in the basket. In year two, the first-to-default basket probability is 34.47 percent versus 39.41 percent for the sum of the individual credits. The difficulty here is that although there should be some theoretical savings for the difference in the default rates, the probability that at least one of the credits in the basket will default is very high. It is 242 percent higher than in the case of X*'s rate of 14.2 percent for the two-year cumulative rate. Unlike the investment-grade case, however, the absolute probability of default is high. The protection seller should demand a much higher premium for this protection because of the dramatically increased likelihood of exercise.

The first-to-default basket default rate is 34.47 percent for only three credits, and that is assuming zero correlation among the three credits. If I add another credit with a two-year cumulative default rate of 13 percent, the probability of at least one default during the two-year period jumps to 43 percent! This, again, assumes no correlation between the credits in the basket. The probability of no default increases with increasing correlation between the credits in the basket. Stated more simply: The probability of at least one default decreases with increasing correlation between the credits in the basket.

The problem with correlation between assets has to do with concentration risk. The following example illustrates this concept. Let us use a simple two-asset basket, and let us assume that the correlation between the assets in the basket and the counterparty is equal to zero. Let us assume that the probability of default for asset i is 0.2 and the probability of default for asset j is 0.3. The basket is comprised 50 percent of asset i and 50 percent of asset j. The correlation between the assets is 0.4. The equation for credit exposure due to event risk is as follows:

$$UL_{(u,\ c)} = \sqrt{\sum \rho_{ij} n_i n_j \sqrt{\frac{(P_{(ui|c)})(1 - P_{(ui,\ c)})(P_{(uj|c)})(1 - P_{(uj,\ c)})}{(1 - P_{(c)})}}}$$

where UL = Unexpected Loss due to credit event risk

$P_{(ui|c)}$ = 0.2 = Probability of default of asset i

$P_{(uj|c)}$ = 0.3 = Probability of default of asset j = 0.3

$P_{(ui,\ c)}$ = 0 = Joint probability default of asset i and counterparty

$P_{(uj,c)}$ = 0 = Joint probability default of asset j and counterparty

$P_{(c)}$ = 0.05 = Probability of counterparty default

$\rho_{(i,j)}$ = 0.4 = (Correlation of default between asset i and asset j

n_i = 0.5 = Asset i's weight in the portfolio

n_j = 0.5 = Asset j's weight in the portfolio

where UL = Unexpected Loss due to credit event risk

$P_{(ui|c)}$ = 0.2 = Probability of default of asset i

$P_{(uj|c)}$ = 0.3 = Probability of default of asset j

Plugging into the formula, the credit exposure due to event risk is 0.15852. If the assumed correlation between the assets is 0.6, the credit exposure due to event risk increases to 0.19415.

Because we are not protecting market risk or the risk of credit downgrade but only the risk of the probability of default, we can multiply the notional amount of the transaction by our result to get the credit exposure.

As long as investors stick to investment-grade credits with very low default rates, the basket trade does not pose much of a problem. Investors and structurers alike should avoid using this structure for noninvestment-grade-rated securities.

The reasons for doing this transaction include the fact that the buyer of the credit default protection gets default protection at a lower cost than hedging each of the credits in the basket individually. Basket default structures can aid management of concentration risk within a credit portfolio, where the portfolio is overconcentrated in certain investment-grade credits but does not want to sell holdings to reduce concentration.

REGULATORY VIEWPOINTS

The challenge for the buyer and the seller of basket protection is in viewing the results of the trade. The Bank of England suggests that in the banking community the protection seller adopt a "worst-case" approach. The seller should consider the exposure of the highest possible payoff amount under the contract. This highest possible payoff amount is applied to the issuer in the basket with the highest risk weighting. The buyer of protection would have protection against the issuer in the basket, which attracts the lowest risk weighting. The protection amount is limited to the lowest possible payoff amount under the contract.

Let us see how this would work in practice using three hypothetical credits, two corporates and one bank, each with a notional of $100 million.

Payoff Profiles for Credits with $100 Million Notional

Credit Type	BIS Capital Ratio	Recovery Value	Payoff
Bank	20%	75%	$25,000,000
Corporate 1	100%	80%	$20,000,000
Corporate 2	100%	65%	$35,000,000

The seller of protection must apply the $35 million payoff amount against one of the 100 percent risk-weighted corporate credit risks for purposes of calculating its return on capital for this transaction. Its risk capital is 8% × 100% × $35,000,000, or $2,800,000.

The buyer of protection can reduce its risk capital by only $20 million applied to the lowest risk-weighted asset, in this case, the bank at 20 percent. The buyer of protection can reduce risk capital by 8% × 20% × $20,000,000, or $320,000.

No one ever said life is fair in the land of bank regulations. The adoption of this worst-case approach from the perspective of both the buyer and the seller of the credit default protection is meant to protect banks from overstating protection (when buying protection) or understating risk (when selling protection). This seemingly arbitrary approach is the best the Bank of England could come up with in the absence of defensible models. This does not mean regulators will not entertain a different treatment if they see a thoroughly reasoned approach. The burden is on the market to provide the approach.

The U.S. Federal Reserve had yet a different view on basket first-to-default swaps when I checked with them in the fall of 2000. The protection buyer gets a break on one of the exposures, but not on all four. For instance, if there are four reference obligors each with a notional exposure of $20 million and each rated A, the protection buyer can assign protection to only one of the obligors. In this instance, the Fed does not care which of the obligors gets the capital relief.

But the Fed stance becomes really interesting when the basket *is not* homogenous. If the basket is composed of three single-A rated obligors and one BBB rated obligor and if the notional amounts are each $20 million, the Fed does not address the credit quality at all. The Fed does not care which of the obligors gets the capital relief. If the notional amounts are asymmetrical—the notional amounts for the four obligors are $5 million, $10 million, $15 million, and $20 million—only the smallest exposure will get capital relief.

Of course, the "worst-case" approach affects only banks. But the bulk of loans used in basket default swaps are on the balance sheet of banks, so what affects banks is likely to affect the rest of the market.

Booking of fees and reduction of credit exposure might follow the example of regulatory capital, but not necessarily. Although the banking authorities can dictate regulatory capital, they do not dictate how banks view their risk-adjusted rate of return on capital (RAROC). They also do not dictate how banks should reduce their line exposure.

Banks and nonbanks could just model the above approach and take a worst-case approach for determining credit exposure and fee booking. The seller could view that they have sold protection on the worst credit (not necessarily the highest BIS risk weighting). Fees could be booked against this credit only and switched if this is not the first credit to actually default. The buyer could reduce the credit exposure to the best credit in the basket and view the cost of protection as being paid out against this protection. But we have already said this is arbitrary, and the recognition of the fee in this manner goes against our intuitive boundary conditions set out earlier.

Unfortunately, there are no completely satisfactory alternatives. One alternative has the virtue of being fairly straightforward and consistent for both the buyer and the seller of protection. Both the buyer and the seller estimate the likelihood of being the first to default for each of the names in the basket and for the protection seller. They then take into account any correlation of the basket names and the protection seller and then allocate the fees and line usage to each name proportionally.

There is as yet no set guidance for banks on the regulatory capital issues, although the Federal Reserve and the Bank of England are leaning in the direction mentioned earlier. For internal accounting and exposure management and for rate of return on economic capital, banks have a great deal of discretion in how to handle basket credit default swaps. Insurance companies closely watch what the banking community is doing to determine how they are going to view credit derivatives. Corporations and fund managers are subject to fewer regulatory constraints in these matters and have yet to come to a consensus on how to handle these issues.

KNOCK-IN BASKET OPTIONS

The cost of credit default basket options and of stand-alone credit default options cannot be significantly reduced using a knock-in structure. Knock-in default swaps are more accurately called credit event trigger swaps, or options. The reference asset does not have to default; in fact, the reference asset may be a performing asset. Nonetheless, the protection buyer has the right to put the asset to the credit event protection seller at a pre-agreed price or at a pre-agreed spread, which corresponds to a market price. Knock-in credit default options are usually priced deeply out of the money. They are, in fact, deep out-of-the-money puts.

The protection seller feels that the likelihood of default is low and is happy to own the asset at a wider level. The protection buyer feels that if credit spreads widen, the reference asset is either headed to default or to a credit rating and credit risk that is no longer acceptable to the protection buyer. The protection buyer may have another motive, however. The protection buyer may be looking for a cheap source of credit default protection. This is the same as buying an out-of-the-money put. The protection buyer will tolerate a credit spread widening. The market does not as yet efficiently price the difference in these products.

For the most part, the market does not see a real difference between these products reflected in price. One German bank offers this product in the two-to-five-year maturity range for corporate names. The German bank gets favorable capital treatment for selling a deep out-of-the-money put. Credit default options, however, attract a 100 percent BIS regulatory capital charge. Because of this favorable capital treatment, there may be a regulatory capital charge arbitrage. It may be more advantageous to buy credit default protection in this form from a bank that gets favorable capital treatment than from a bank that does not get favorable capital treatment. We will look at economic and regulatory capital treatment in more detail in Chapter 8.

REDUCED LOSS CREDIT DEFAULT OPTIONS

One way to reduce the cost of credit default protection is for the default protection buyer to offer to take a fixed percentage of the loss in the event of default. One large European export finance company approached me about reducing the credit risk in their portfolio to corporate names in their home country. Their lines were full to corporates, including a gas company, an auto manufacturer, an engineering construction company, and a telecommunications company. All of the corporations were investment grade and theoretically should have had low correlation credit risks with each other.

The export finance company wanted to know how much they could reduce the cost of credit default protection on a first-to-default structure if they agreed to absorb the first 30 percent of the decline in market value. There is no absolute model for determining this.

One way to evaluate this is to look at the weakest credit in the portfolio. This means that the expected recovery rate for the weakest credit in the portfolio would be 30 percent higher than expected. This is as if there were a senior or a subordinated structure created from this credit. The subordinated piece would absorb the first 30 percent of loss in the event of default (LIED), and the senior piece would not lose any principal until this buffer had been exhausted.

In earlier discussions, we saw that the expected loss and LIED are related according to the following formula:

Expected Loss = Probability of Default × Loss in the Event of Default

The structure is different from the usual senior/subordinated structure, however. In a typical senior/subordinated structure, we examine a pool of assets. The lower-credit-quality assets in the pool have a higher probability of default than the higher-credit-quality assets in the pool. This lower probability of default is assigned to calculations for the subordinated piece. For a single reference asset, however, the probability of default for the senior and the subordinated tranches is exactly the same. We can rewrite the equation as follows:

Expected Loss Senior Piece = Constant × LIED of Senior Tranche

Expected Loss Subordinated Piece = Constant × LIED Subordinated Tranche

We can ignore the probability of default and concentrate on the LIED or on the recovery rate, which is simply equal to 1 − LIED. One very quick method to determine how much the credit default swap price can be reduced for a company that will absorb the first 30 percent of the expected loss is to look at the Moody's table for recovery rates. Senior unsecured debt has a mean recovery rate of 51.13 percent, with a standard deviation of 25.45 percent. Subordinated debt has a mean recovery rate of 32.74 percent, with a standard deviation of 20.18 percent. Junior subordinated debt has a mean recovery rate of 17.09 percent, with a standard deviation of 10.9 percent. If the first 30 percent of the loss is absorbed by the export finance company, that is similar to upgrading junior subordinated debt to a recovery rate of 47.09 percent or upgrading subordinated debt to a recovery rate of 62.74 percent. Notice that the standard deviations still indicate a lot of overlap across debt classes in recovery rate. The point is, however, that the absorption of 30 percent of the LIED upgrades the implied debt rating by a full notch and possibly by two notches for single-A reference assets. This single-notch upgrade in credit quality is worth something.

In a basket credit default structure, the cost of the basket option can be reduced by the credit spread differential between a strong AA asset and a single-A asset. If that credit spread differential is 10 basis points, the basket option cost is reduced by at least that amount. The add-on for the remaining assets in the basket can also be slightly reduced, by approximately 2 basis points each for the difference in unfunded commitment fees between a strong AA and single-A asset. The total cost reduction would be approximately 16 basis points.

This is a quick estimate, but as we discussed earlier, there is general market dissatisfaction with basket option pricing models. Rule-of-thumb pricing as a supplement to unsatisfactory models is an essential part of any toolkit. In most cases, the market will negotiate around these rules of thumb as opposed to having "dueling models" when credit derivatives specialists negotiate prices.

PRO RATA DEFAULT STRUCTURES

Pro rata default structures are often incorrectly called basket structures. This is a mistake and can lead to pricing confusion. The market standard currently understands a basket structure to mean a first-to-default basket *structure,* as discussed earlier. The pro rata structure is commonly called a pooled structure.

The purpose of the pro rata default structure is simply documentation convenience. Several separate credit default swap transactions are documented under the same letter confirmation. Each transaction relates to one reference obligation issued by one reference credit.

Transactions may have different maturity dates. The credit default protection seller offers performance protection on each specified reference obligation. The credit default protection buyer pays a pro rata premium representing the sum of the protection premiums on each of the individual reference credits.

If a reference credit experiences a defined credit event during the term of the transaction, the default protection seller pays the default protection buyer the calculation amount. In exchange, the default protection seller receives delivery of the relevant reference obligation with a face value subject to the transaction. Neither the default protection seller nor the default protection buyer has any further obligations with respect to this particular reference credit. The pro rata premium paid on the remainder of the transaction is reduced by the premium on the reference credit that experienced the credit event.

A credit event with respect to one reference credit does not constitute a credit event with respect to any other reference credit. If the other reference credits do not experience a credit event during the term of the transaction, the credit default protection seller will make no payment on any other reference obligation. If any of the other reference credits experiences a credit event, the credit default protection seller will make a payment versus delivery only on the occurrence of one or more additional credit events. Obligations for both the credit default protection seller and the buyer terminate for each individual reference credit upon a credit event and satisfaction of required payments or upon maturity of each individual reference credit.

THE MAYA: DRAGONGLASS DERIVATIVES

During the 1562 *auto da fé*, Franciscan missionary Diego de Landa burned the Maya codices. But Maya math endured, and it seems it was a system invented for early trade. The Maya dominated commerce in a pre-Columbian, multi-lingual, multi-country region. The Maya used glyph writing, but not all the languages spoken in the region used writing. These logistics posed daunting problems, yet the Maya developed a method so efficient that they dominated Central America's trade in cotton, copper tools, slaves, salt, feathers, gold, copper, guanine (a gold-copper alloy), stone beads, jadeite, honey, and obsidian—*Game of Thrones* fans prefer to call obsidian "dragonglass." Crucially, the Maya also traded cacao nuts. Cacao beans were used for money.

The Maya traded with tribes at distances up to 300 km. Yet many tribes did not speak Mayan. Mining required manual labor, storage, expensive transportation, and a long lead time. Given the investment, one needed to plan how much to mine, and how to divide and allocate shipments. Similar issues applied to crops such as cotton and cacao. It was extremely useful to strike a deal with a distant customer to buy and sell, say, Guatemalan Dragonglass, at a specific price on a specific future date. This customized forward contract is a financial derivative. Derivatives contracts have existed for as long as men have traded goods.

Derivatives: Accurate Calendar and Maya Math

Ancient Romans used forward agreements. The Roman calendar was not as precise as the Maya calendar, but it was accurate enough for trade purposes. Their math system used Base-10, but Roman numerals made calculations needlessly cumbersome, and there was no concept of zero either as a position marker or as the null value.

The Maya had everything they needed to strike a bargain for future execution. Like the Romans, the Maya had an accurate calendar. The Maya created a 260-day calendar. But every day in the Gregorian calendar corresponds to a day in the Mayan calendar. It accurately represents the length of the year within 45 seconds.

The Maya also had a math system that could have been devised for pre-Columbian commerce. It used only three symbols and could be learned quickly. Teaching the mechanics of the system required few language skills. No writing was necessary to perform large-number calculations. The Maya could easily visualize and remember the results. Calculations were both fast and accurate.

The Mayans used stones, cacao beans, or other convenient objects to represent units which were multiples of powers of 20. A stick or bar represented units of five, and a shell or other object represented zero. Any three types of handy objects could be used to aid calculations.

Maya calendar calculations use a modified base 20. It is a 260-day calendar. Yet every day in the Gregorian calendar corresponds to a day in the Mayan calendar. It accurately represents the length of an actual year within 45 seconds.

But the Maya used regular base 20 for commerce. Figure 4.9 illustrates an example of division. I have not seen an example anywhere else, so I created one myself. Notice how easy it is to calculate, visualize, and remember numbers.

Each cell position, in order, stands for a different power of 20. Every time you move a one unit to a lower cell (a lower power of 20), it is equal to 4 bars (or 20 since each bar is worth 5 units).

Likewise, when you move a unit of 20 to a lower cell, you can instead use 3 bars and 5 (lower power of 20) units. You can see how easy this is do manually on a flat surface with say, sticks for bars, cacao beans for units, and shells to represent zeros.

Division rules: subtract the same number of units and bars from each cell as are in the divisor (the number by which you are dividing). Do this until you do not have enough, move a unit/s to a lower power cell below, until you cannot do it anymore. Anything left over at the end is a fraction of 20.

Scholars have argued that the Maya only used zero as a placeholder, but having used the calculations, I believe that is untrue. Zero was understood as both as a place marker and as a representation of null value.

One understands it as the additive identity in performing the mental math. Likewise, one understands that in the zero-power place, multiplying anything in that place by 20 to the zero power is to multiply it by one. I do not understand how anyone who has performed calculations using Maya math concluded that the Maya were clueless on this issue. I believe that is a false conclusion, and the Maya designers of the system understood the concept completely.

Unlike math used in the ancient Roman Empire, Maya math used zero both as a placeholder and to represent the null value. Maya math included addition, subtraction, multiplication, division, fractions, exponentiation, and square roots. It is possible that any mathematical function in the Hindu-Arabic system can be solved using Maya math.

The original designers of Maya math wisely chose Base-20. The three-symbol system also works perfectly in Base-10, but for large numbers, it takes one longer to arrive at the answer. The Base-10 answer is harder to visualize and remember without writing it down.

Another advantage is that after choosing Base-20, the Maya used sticks or bars to represent five units, and each unit was a multiple of a power of 20. Why didn't the Maya have each bar represent ten units? After all, it would require fewer sticks or bars. The counterintuitive answer is that when each bar represents five units, instead of ten units, the computations are faster, and it is harder to make a mistake. (I tried it myself both ways.)

FIGURE 4.9 Maya Math: Divide 487 by 23

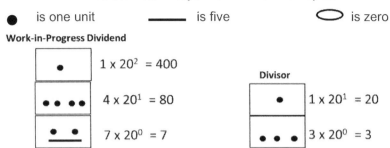

● is one unit   ───── is five   ⬭ is zero

Work-in-Progress Dividend

$1 \times 20^2 = 400$

$4 \times 20^1 = 80$

$7 \times 20^0 = 7$

Divisor

$1 \times 20^1 = 20$

$3 \times 20^0 = 3$

Use the rules to rewrite the numbers to make division easier.

23 Rewritten
Divisor

Divide the top unit by 23 and rewrite dividend as below. This division is even easier if you're removing sticks & stones.

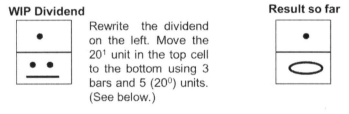

WIP Dividend

Rewrite the dividend on the left. Move the 20^1 unit in the top cell to the bottom using 3 bars and 5 (20^0) units. (See below.)

Result so far

Divide again. Result includes a remainder of 4/23.

Result

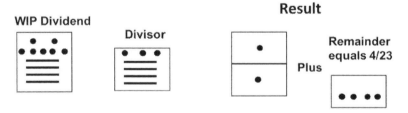

WIP Dividend

Divisor

Plus

Remainder equals 4/23

If you were a Maya dry goods merchant, you might stop there, and throw in an extra item to keep your customer happy. But if you were trading a valuable commodity such as gold, you would probably continue dividing to calculate fractional ounces by adding boxes for 20^{-1}, 20^2, 20^{-3}, and so on. Use the same methods as before.

Humans can easily glance at a group of five objects and instantaneously process an accurate count. It is harder to do this with eight or more units. Moreover, five stones (or marbles) fit easily in one hand, which also makes the physical computation easier.

Maya Forwards

There are no written records of Maya forward trade agreements, but the absence of evidence is not the evidence of absence. The Maya needed forward agreements. Without them, it is unlikely the Maya would have become the most active traders in the Central American region.

According to the Tarlton Law Library's online article, "Maya Property and Commercial Law":

The Maya used contracts, which were formalized when the parties drank balché [a mild alcoholic drink] in front of witnesses.

Tarlton Law Library claims the Maya did not charge interest, and that may be true. But a risk premium, and perhaps an estimate of future costs of transportation, storage, and other normal charges of commerce result in a higher forward price.

I believe that given the ease of use of Maya math, no written record was required, and a written contract would not have been possible with trading partners who could not read Maya glyphs. London cabdrivers recall complicated routes through a twisting labyrinth of irregular streets. Maya depictions of large numbers are a snap to remember compared to that.

Counterparty Risk

Even more interesting is how the Maya managed counterparty risk. Whether an agreement is oral or written, one has to rely on one's counterparty to honor the terms of the contract. The Maya did not charge interest or have criminal penalties. But those who could not pay debts became the slaves of their creditors. If the debtor died before the debt was paid, the deceased's family became responsible for the debt.

CHAPTER 5

Sovereign Risk and Emerging Markets

The emerging-markets credit derivatives market is much more driven by supply and demand than is publicly traded investment-grade European or U.S. debt. Although it is true that these markets are supply-and-demand driven, spreads commanded for credit default protection tend not to get seriously out of line with asset swap spread levels. This is because the market is well known, management at financial institutions is more familiar with the history of the market, and more institutions have an appetite for these risks.

The emerging markets are a different matter, however, for the following reasons:

- The emerging markets experience more price volatility.
- There are fewer traders and fewer reliable pricing sources for these assets.
- Fewer institutions have the authority to invest in these securities.
- Size constraints tend to be more stringent for the institutions, which have investment authorities.
- These markets have fewer instruments and less trading history.
- Fewer pricing sources, such as Telerate, Bloomberg, and Reuters, offer reliable prices on the spectrum of countries. Some prices exist only in the off-screen markets.
- These markets are more subject to event risk.

- When a severe credit event occurs in one emerging market region, spreads tend to widen globally. Credit spreads exhibit correlation

Emerging markets is the term usually reserved for developing economies. The liquidity and depth of the debt markets is relatively undeveloped. The emerging markets are often classified as Latin America, including Mexico, Eastern Europe, and most Asian countries. There is debate about this definition. Several market professionals claim that Latin American countries such as Brazil, Argentina, and Mexico should not be included in the list. Further, Korea and Thailand are often excluded, although most professionals agree the Philippines and Vietnam are emerging markets.

For the purposes of this book, all of the above markets are included. One of the reasons for this is that Asian event risks and Latin American event risks tend to affect spreads across the board. In the late 1990s, currency events in Indonesia and Thailand suggested the classically defined emerging markets rather than developed debt and currency markets. Further, these instruments are usually traded in the emerging-markets groups of most financial institutions. Therefore, I classify them as emerging markets for credit derivatives as well.

In the fall of 1997, the correlation between emerging markets in Asia, Latin America, and Eastern Europe was clear, at least in terms of credit spreads and, in some instances, perception of ability to repay debt. Even the superpower economies felt repercussions. On July 2, 1997, Thailand's decisions to allow the baht to float sparked a series of currency devaluations in Asia. The Malaysian ringgit, Philippine peso, Indonesian rupiah, and South Korean won plunged in value versus the U.S. dollar. This in turn sparked an Asian debt and stock market crisis. The effects were felt globally as spreads dramatically widened in Latin America and Eastern Europe in sympathy with Asia. By the end of 1997, the South Korean banking and corporate debt system was in severe crisis, and the International Monetary Fund (IMF) constructed a $57 billion bailout for the South Korean economy. Other measures were under consideration for Malaysia, Indonesia, and Thailand. Russia was in the process of refinancing its debt. Japan's economy and banking system suffered partly because of the Asian crisis and partly because of internal tax increases. Japan's fourth-largest securities firm and Japan's tenth-largest bank declared bankruptcy. Although Japan is the world's second-largest economy with enormous foreign currency reserves and huge

trade surpluses, funding costs for all Japanese banks soared. Spreads of Latin American debt widened several hundred basis points in the fall of 1997, recovering steadily
toward the end of 1997. Even the United States felt the effects. By the end of 1997, economists were predicting slower growth for the U.S. economy, partly due to turmoil in the Asian markets.

THE GUESSTIMATERS' MARKET

The debt markets of emerging-markets countries are complicated by past debt restructuring, particularly in Latin America. Brady bonds were named after former U.S. Secretary of the Treasury Nicholas Brady. They were created in 1989 in response to the Latin American debt crisis in the early 1980s. The program ended in the 1990s, but some of the features have been used in other sovereign restructurings since then.

In the 1970s, U.S. banks took massive deposits from oil producing countries and lent the money to Latin American countries. The U.S. banks were eager to act as middleman, since they wanted to earn *fees*. They persuaded oil producing countries that they were liquid and safe. The reality is they were reckless and greedy. According the Federal Reserve, in 1970, total Latin American debt to the U.S. was $29 billion. By 1982, the debt ballooned to $327 billion. The result was that many Latin American countries amassed foreign debt that they couldn't service.

U.S. banks were stuck with an overconcentration of failing Latin American loans. The Latin American economies produced commodities whose prices were declining. Interest rates were on the rise to stem inflation. Latin American countries were unable to buy raw materials as U.S. banks began refusing additional loans due to tightening.

In August 1982, Mexico's finance minister told the U.S. Treasury Secretary and the Fed that Mexico could not handle the payments on its foreign debt. Mexico's debt was then $80 billion. Sixteen Latin American countries restructured their debt. The U.S. was the international lender of last resort. Banks, the IMF and the World Bank encouraged austerity in Latin America. Banks were pressured to restructure debt and loans were given to Latin American countries to pay interest.

An episode during this period struck me as poignant. The late Alan Garcia won Peru's presidential election in 1985. He announced his Peru-first policy to the world. Peru could not pay back its debt. Peru had not made principal payments on its commercial debt in more than a year. It was $475 million in arrears on interest payments. The banks knew this, but Garcia committed the mortal sin of saying it out loud. Garcia said Peru was honest and would repay. Peru's $14 billion in foreign debt was equivalent to Peru's entire annual national income. Peru's projected exports would not cover principal and interest payments of $3.7 billion due in 1985.

Six months after Garcia took office and despite his announcement, U.S. bank regulators decided *not* to declare Peru's debts as impaired. They stalled. since Garcia had not yet clarified his new policies. If the banks admitted Peru's loans were "value impaired," U.S. banks would have to build up reserves and report lower earnings. This sort of blatant dishonesty is a hard habit to break. Banks did the same thing with impaired mortgage loans and the toxic financial products that used the loans as collateral prior to the financial crisis.

Garcia proposed to pay only 10 percent of Peru's export earnings each year to service Peru's foreign debt. At that rate, Peru wouldn't *ever* pay back all of its interest much less its principal. In March 1986, the week after Peru's central bank announced it withdrew all of Peru's deposits of gold and silver from European and U.S. banks. Garcia said all successful revolutions require a foreign enemy, and the IMF was his enemy. the IMF a foreign enemy.

U.S. banks reserveed 15% against their exposure to Peru. It was chump change, but it drove U.S. banks nuts. Tiny Peru wasn't close to being the U.S.'s largest Latin American debtor, and it wasn't even the worst. But Alan Garcia had decided to restructure Peru's debt without so much as genuflecting at the Fed's doorstep.

Moreover, Garcia repatriated his gold, and the U.S. had kicked the gold standard to the curb in August 1971. The U.S. dollar was the world's reserve currency and king of the petrodollar. Peru revealed chinks in its armor. They had to teach this guy a lesson.

The IMF warned Peru that if it did not accept IMF-style austerity and debt, it would cut off assistance. The World Bank would cut Peru off, too.

Banks cut credit to Peru, even short-term credit needed to finance foreign trade. A year later, Peru was in economic chaos. Peru relented. It *still* didn't have the means to pay all of the interest owed on foreign debt. But now, just like the other Latin American debtors, Peru shut up about it. Banks restored Peru's credit. By the 1990's Peru struggled with hyperinflation.

Alan Garcia wasn't wrong. But Peru was too small to defy U.S. banks and win. Peru didn't owe the U.S. enough money. The U.S. banks and their allies at the IMF and World Bank ganged up on him. He needed a gang of his own. If he had negotiated a joint strategy with Mexico, Brazil, and Venezuela, their combined debt would have given them real clout.

By the late 1980's U.S. banks could no longer "extend and pretend." Banks needed money they didn't have to add to reserves. That would mean revealing banks' problems, unseating CEOs, and cutting bonuses. Most of Citibank's equity would have been wiped out. Losses at Bank of America and Manufacturers Hanover (now part of JPMorgan Chase) would have wiped out all their equity and then some.

TAVAKOLI'S LAW OF SOVEREIGN BAILOUTS

Secretary Brady averted a banking crisis in the United States by restructuring the bank loans and coaxing U.S. banks to forgive part of the debt. The U.S. banks had little choice. U.S. bank does not have as much clout over a Latin sovereign nation as it does over a U.S. consumer behind in his or her home mortgage or automobile payments. The U.S. banks eventually realized that if a sovereign debtor does not pay its bills, an overexposed lender has much more to worry about than the borrower.

Brady bonds mitigated what otherwise would have been a horrific write-down for U.S. banks. Here is a simplified example. A bank forgave half of a Latin American country's $20 billion debt to the bank. A zero-coupon U.S. Treasury bond trading at $2 billion secured a Brady bond's $10 billion face value. The Latin American debtor agreed to service the interest payments.

None of this required banks to get any smarter or better disciplined. Ongoing taxpayer subsidies and fantasy accounting keep the U.S. banking system alive. Instead, banks embraced a template for the future:

Tavakoli's Law of Sovereign Bailouts

Never call bad debt bad debt. "Restructure" bad debt to "good" debt by lending bad debtors more money to pay interest on the bad debt. Done properly, you will transfer wealth from lower classes to the upper classes, preferably to executives in the global banking industry.

With this method, the status, and bonuses of banking executives and their cronies are preserved. If you are a sovereign debtor, you might be an idealist who thinks the truth matters. But remember. If you break this law, banks and their water-carriers at the IMF and World Bank will cut your credit lines. They will cut you until you stop screaming. All bailouts will be done on their schedule and in their own way to minimize the impact on banks in countries with the most clout.

The structures used in the Brady bond program can be adapted to future sovereign restructurings. Here are some structures to consider. The principal of Brady bonds were backed by long-dated U.S. Treasury zero-coupon bonds. Interest-due-and-unpaid bonds (IDUs) had no collateral except in the case of Costa Rica. Debt conversion bonds (DCBs) also had no collateral for principal or interest. Front-loaded interest-reduction bonds (FLIRBs) had no principal collateral, but they did have a rolling interest guarantee (RIG), which with AA rated backing, covered 12 months of interest payments for the first five years of the life of the bond. Zero-coupon U.S. Treasury bonds collateralized the principal of collateralized floating-rate discount bonds . They also had a rolling interest guarantee, which covered 12 to 18 months of interest payments. Collateralized fixed-rate par bonds (par bonds) had principal collateralized by U.S. Treasury bonds and a rolling interest guarantee covering 12 to 18 months of interest payments.

Brays were usually quoted in terms of the *stripped yield*—the yield on the non-U.S. dollar exposure of the bond. The sovereign spread was quoted after normalizing for the U.S. Treasury collateral. There was no standard method, and the various methods often resulted in different values of sovereign spread.

Credit spread options allowed investors to buy options of the credit spread of Brady bonds over U.S. Treasuries. Call options on the Brady spread over U.S. Treasuries increased in value when credit spreads tightened, and puts increased in value when the credit spreads widened (when the market for Bradys weakened). The ambiguity in the method for calculating residual sovereign spread from Bradys meant that hedges were imperfect. Some banks were unwilling to manage this risk.

But most banks were and are willing to sell credit default protection, even on esoterica. Reference pricing is based on the prices of liquid and semiliquid bonds and hedge instruments. Table 5.1 shows prices for selected hard currency—denominated Eurobonds for emerging market countries on July 14, 1997. Table 5.2 shows broker prices for emerging-market debt credit default swaps on the same day. The prices for long-dated credit default protection represent what I usually refer to as a "Guesstimaters" market. As one moves farther along the maturity curve, credit default premiums decouple from asset swap spreads.

One cannot purchase a long-dated emerging-markets asset and purchase credit default protection and still earn a positive spread. Five-year Mexico trades at the London interbank offering rate (LIBOR) plus 126 basis points (bps), whereas the credit protection trades at Treasuries plus 195 (midmarket), or around LIBOR+165 bps. Purchasers of long-dated credit default protection are often hedging lucrative transactions, freeing up credit lines for very profitable transactions, or are the beneficiaries of a tax advantage.

Most offers for credit default protection are for smaller sizes, blocks of $5 million to $10 million. There are no offers for blocks of $50 million. The broker market indications are often thrown up on a screen without a real counterparty behind them, merely an indication of where someone might do a transaction if a deal is brought to them. Often brokers have no details on exact structure or language requirements. Early in the credit derivatives business, many brokers had no idea which reference asset was used. Large transactions are almost exclusively private, nonbroker-negotiated transactions between financial institutions. As size and maturity of a credit default swap increase, so does the ability to negotiate a price between counterparties.

*****

TABLE 5.1 Eurobond Prices for Selected Emerging-Market Countries

Country	Coupon	Currency	Final Maturity	Issue Spread	Issue Size	Bid Price	Offer Price	Bid Yield	Offer Yield	Rating Moody's	Rating S&P
Argentina											
Argentina	10.950	USD	1-Nov-99	350	500 thou.	108.70	108.88	T + 82	74	B1	BB
Argentina	9.250	USD	23-Feb-01	410	1 bil.	105.20	105.38	T + 151	147	B1	BB
Argentina	8.375	USD	20-Dec-03	280	1 bil.	102.90	103.00	T + 157	156	B1	BB
Argentina	11.000	USD	9-Oct-06	445	1 bil.	114.50	115.00	T + 246	239	B1	BB
Argentina	11.375	USD	10-Jan-17	462.5	2 bil.	114.90	115.00	T + 307	306	B1	BB
Brazil											
Brazil Republic	8.875	USD	5-Nov-01	265	750 thou.	104.125	104.38	T + 161	154	B1	BB–
Brazil Republic	10.125	USD	15-Mar-27	395	3 bil.	99.00	99.15	T + 366	365	B1	BB–
Mexico											
BNCE	7.250	USD	2-Feb-04	163	1 bil.	94.50	94.55	T + 214	213		
UMS	9.750	USD	6-Feb-01	445	1 bil.	106.50	107.00	T + 158	143	Ba2	NA
UMS	3 mn L + 125	USD	27-Jun-02	138	1 bil.	99.98	100.08	L + 126	123	Baa3	BBB–
UMS	9.875	USD	15-Jan-07	335	1 bil.	107.2	107.40	T + 252	249	Ba2	BB
UMS	11.375	USD	15-Sep-16	445	1 bil.	115.90	116.00	T + 298	296	Ba2	BB
UMS	11.500	USD	15-May-26	552	1.75 bil.	118.10	118.25	T + 305	304	Ba2	BB
Russia											
Russian Republic	9.250	USD	27-Nov-01	345	1bil.	101.85	102.15	T + 260	252	Ba2	BB–
Russian Republic	9.000	DEM	25-Mar-04	370	2 bil.	103.75	104.00	T + 317	312	NA	BB–
Russian Republic	10.000	USD	26-Jun-07	375	2 bil.	101.52	101.72	T + 352	349	Ba2	BB–

TABLE 5.1 *(continued)*

Country	Coupon	Currency	Final Maturity	Issue Spread	Issue Size	Bid Price	Offer Price	Bid Yield	Offer Yield	Rating Moody's	Rating S&P
Turkey											
Republic of Turkey	8.250	USD	11-Jun-99	222	250 mil.	100.35	100.70	T + 215	195	B1	B
Republic of Turkey	10.0	USD	23-May-02	348	500 mil.	104.45	104.85	T + 272	262	B1	B
Specials											
Russia											
City of Moscow	9.5	USD	31-May-00				102.375		L + 222	Ba2	BB–
City of St. Petersburg	9.5	USD	18-Jun-02		300 mil.		101.60		L + 260		BB–
SBS-Agro Bank	10.25	USD	21-Jul-00		200 mil.		99.65		L + 382		B+
Turkey											
City of Ankara	6.8	yen	10-Nov-97		50 bil.				L + 280		
Republic of Turkey	6.0	yen	10-Jun-98		100 bil.				L + 235	B1	B
Republic of Turkey	4.0	yen	14-Dec-98						L + 260	B1	B
Republic of Turkey	6.8	yen	24-Sep-99		50 bil.				L + 320	B1	B

Notes: "3mn L": 3-month LIBOR; "T": Treasuries; "L": LIBOR; "B": rating grade; "USD": U.S. dollars; "DEM": Deutsche marks; S&P: Standard & Poor's.

Source: Marc Phillips, Bank of America London Branch, July 14, 1997.

TABLE 5.2 Sovereign Default Protection for Selected Emerging-Market Countries, Bid/Ask Broker Indications (basis points per annum)

	6 months	1 year	2 years	3 years	4 years	4.4 years	5 years	5.5 years
Argentina								
Cantor								
Prebon		74/90	115/145	140/175	165/195		175/210	
Tullett		70/NA						
Brazil								
Prebon	65/85	NA/90	115/145	130/NA	150/NA		215/240	
Tullett		70/95						
Bulgaria								
Cantor								
EXCO	NA/350	NA/600						
Intercapital		250/NA						
Prebon	215/NA						400/NA	
Tullett	270/350							
Mexico								
Cantor		NA/65						
Prebon	NA/95	65/75	100/125	140/175	165/195		180/210	
Tullett		70/105						
Russia								
Cantor		195/215						
EXCO	NA/195	190/210				240/350		
Intercapital		NA/210						
Prebon	170/NA	190/NA				210/NA		
Tullett		190/215						NA/460
Turkey								
Cantor		250/NA	275/NA	300/NA				
EXCO		245/NA	275/NA	295/NA				
Intercapital				330/NA				
Prebon		250/NA	275/NA	300/NA			320/390	
Tullett		245/315	270/NA	295/NA				

Note: NA indicates bid or offer was not available.
Sources: Cantor Fitzgerald; EXCO; Intercapital Credit Derivatives, Inc.; Prebon Yanmane; Tullett Capital Markets.

TAX ARBITRAGE

Many emerging-markets transactions are dominated by tax considerations. For instance, many European countries have double tax treaties with emerging-market countries, which they would like to exploit. In most instances, although European investors are ready to take on tax-law-interpretation risk, they are not as keen to take sovereign credit risk of emerging-market countries. Often these European investors will pay an off-market price for credit default protection because the number of credit default protection sellers is limited and the rewards of the tax advantage allow the investor to earn an above-market spread on the securities.

Austrian investors, for instance, took advantage of a double tax treaty with Brazil to purchase Brazilian Brady bonds with a put back to the bank that sold them the securities. The following term sheet shows the transaction.

BRAZILIAN BRADY BONDS WITH PUT/CALL
INDICATIONS AS OF AUGUST 4, 1995
TERM SHEET

Underlying Bond:

Issuer:	Federative Republic of Brazil, DCB.
Notional Amount:	USD 50 million.
Maturity Date:	April 15, 2012.
Coupon:	7.3125% (six-month USD LIBOR + 87.5 bps) (on a semiannual A/360-day basis, where A is the actual number of days in the period). (Next coupon date: October 16, 1995).
Sale Price:	51.692% (50.25% + Accrual of 1.442%).
Settlement Date:	June 28, 1995.
Put/Call Expiry Date:	October 11, 1995.
Put/Call Settlement Date:	October 13, 1995.
Strike Price of Put:	51.862% (48.246% + Accrual of 3.616%).
Strike Price of Call:	51.862% (48.246% + Accrual of 3.616%).

Credit Protection:

While the client is the owner of Brazilian Brady bonds for the length of the trans-action, a bank provides credit protection on the principal amount in the form of a put option. Bank protection provider is rated AA3/AA—.

Put/Call:

The investor has the right to put the bond at the strike price of the put option to the bank. The investor agrees to sell a call to the bank on the trade date through a side letter agreement. Under the terms of the side letter agreement, the bank is obligated to enter into the call option agreement three weeks from the trade date. The strike and the exercise date of the call option are the same as that of the put option.

Assumed Relevant Customer Tax Rate:	34.00%.
Net Interest Income (Coupon Interest — Accrued):	USD 1,086,718.
Call Option Premium (Income):	0.
Put Option Premium (Payment):	0.
Tax Deductible Capital Loss:	USD −1,001,762.
Tax Offset (Tax Rate x Capital Loss):	USD 340,599.
Cash Benefit to Investor:	USD 425,555.
Yield on Tax-Adjusted Cash Flow (A/360):	5.54%.
Equivalent Pretax Yield (A/360):	8.39%.

The equivalent pretax yield at the time was equal to LIBOR+200 bps for the investor in a transaction, which lasted three and one-half months. The tax benefit in Austrian schilling (ATS) terms was even greater. The yield curve in Austria had lower interest rates than in the United States, and the investor was able to take advantage of a tax benefit for loss on forward sale of foreign currency in converting USD to ATS.

The investor had the right to put the securities to the bank. In a side letter agreement, the investor gives the right to the bank to call the securities at the end of the transaction. Either way, the bank got the securities back at the end of the transaction.

This is like a buy/sell back or to a repurchase agreement. The structure has some subtle differences, however. In the event of default of the Brazilian reference securities, the investor can put the bonds back to the bank at the end of the transaction period at the original agreed-on price. If the securities default, there is no margin call as there might be in the case of a repurchase agreement. The investor has what appears to be a credit put to the bank. The investor's credit risk is no longer the Republic of Brazil but the bank.

This transaction worked only because the investor had capital gains against which to deduct the capital loss generated in this transaction to get an effective pretax equivalent yield of LIBOR+200 bps on an essentially AA rated transaction.

Another key element of the transaction was the double tax treaty between Brazil and Austria. Austrian corporations paid no tax on the coupon interest income from Brazil. For a period of two years, Austrian investors purchased Brazilian government bonds via this method at levels where the pretax cash flow was *negative*. The premium paid to get the credit protection was worth it to Austrian investors. After tax, the returns were well above market levels. As more competitors figured out the driving forces of these transactions, Austrian investors were able to earn a slightly positive pretax cash flow and even higher pretax equivalent yields.

CREDIT PLAYS—THE HOME CURRENCY ADVANTAGE

Standard & Poor's (S&P) often rates sovereign debt higher in the home currency than in a foreign currency. It is more likely for a sovereign to increase revenues via taxes and duties in their home country and thus meet debt obligations. Often market professionals will claim that the government can always "print more money" to meet debt obligations. Although this is theoretically true in the short run, it leads to economic chaos, which could overthrow even the strongest dictatorship. Therefore, the S&P ratings are based on claims paying ability through conventional governmental revenue sources.

The local currency debt ratings are stronger than those for foreign currencies, although the ability to pay is not viewed as unlimited. Table 5.3 shows the ratings in foreign and local currency for most emerging-

TABLE 5.3 Comparison of Emerging-Markets Sovereign Foreign and Local Currency Debt Ratings in 1998

Obligor	Foreign Currency Debt Ratings			Local Currency Debt Ratings		
	Moody's	S&P	IBCA	Moody's	S&P	IBCA
Argentina	B1	BB	BB	B1	BBB–	NR
Barbados	Ba1	NR	NR	NR	NR	NR
Bermuda	Aa1	AA	AA	NR	NR	AAA
Brazil	B1	BB–	B+	NR	BB+	NR
Bulgaria	B3	NR	NR	NR	NR	NR
Chile	Baa1	A–	A–	NR	AA	AAA
China	A3	BBB+	NR	NR	NR	NR
Colombia	Baa3	BBB–	NR	NR	A+	NR
Costa Rica	Ba1	NR	NR	NR	NR	NR
Cyprus	A2	AA–	NR	NR	AA+	NR
Czech Republic	Baa1	A	A–	NR	NR	NR
El Salvador	Baa3	BB	NR	NR	BBB+	NR
Hungary	Baa3	BBB–	BBB	NR	A–	A–
India	Baa3	BB+	NR	NR	BBB+	NR
Indonesia	Baa3	BBB	BBB–	NR	A+	NR
Korea	A1	AA–	AA–	NR	NR	AAA
Latvia	NR	BBB	NR	NR	A–	NR
Lithuania	B1	BB–	BB	NR	BBB+	BBB+
Lebanon	Ba2	BBB–	BB+	NR	BB	BBB–
Malaysia	A1	A+	NR	NR	AA+	NR
Malta	A2	A+	A	NR	AA+	NR
Mexico	Ba2	BB	BB	Baa3	BBB+	NR
Moldova	Ba2	NR	NR	NR	NR	NR
Pakistan	B2	B+	NR	NR	NR	NR
Paraguay	NR	BB–	NR	NR	BBB–	NR
Philippines	Ba1	BB+	NR	NR	A–	NR
Poland	Baa3	BBB–	BBB	NR	A–	A–
Romania	BA3	BB–	BB–	NR	BBB–	NR
Russia	BA2	BB–	BB+	NR	NR	NR
Singapore	AA1	AAA	NR	Aa1	AAA	NR
Slovakia	Baa3	BBB–	BBB–	NR	A	A–
South Africa	Baa3	BB+	BB	Baa1	BBB+	BBB
Taiwan	Aa3	AA+	NR	NR	NR	NE
Thailand	A3	A	NR	NR	AA	NR
Trinidad & Tobago	Ba1	BB+	NR	NR	BBB+	NR
Tunisia	Baa3	BBB–	BBB–	NR	A	NR
Turkey	B1	B	B+	NR	NR	NR
Uruguay	Baa3	BBB–	BBB–	NR	BBB+	NR
Venezuela	BA2	B+	NR	NR	NR	NR

Note: NR means not rated.
Sources: Moody's Investor Service, Standard & Poor's, Fitch IBCA.

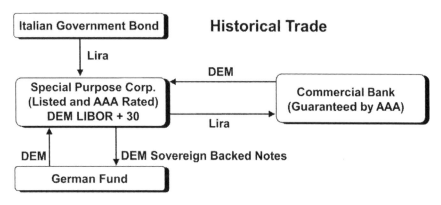

Italy lost its home currency advantage when it gave up the Lira. The AAA rating Is no longer possible denominated in Euros.

FIGURE 5.1 Historical Home Currency Advantage: SPC with pre-Euro Italian Lira Government Collateral and German Fund Investing in DEM

market countries. S&P rates Indonesia's foreign currency obligations as BBB but its local currency obligations A+. Lithuania's foreign debt gets a below-investment-grade rating of BB—, whereas its local debt gets an investment-grade rating of BBB+. This difference in foreign currency and local currency debt rating suggests some market opportunities.

Commercial banks and investment banks created special purpose corporations (SPCs) incorporated in Luxembourg or the Netherlands. Both countries had tax treaties with Italy. The SPCs claimed back the withholding tax on the coupons of Italian government bonds. This transaction was created for funds in countries that did not have a double tax treaty with Italy. At the time when these transactions were most popular, Italy's foreign currency rating was single A (Italy is now rated AA). The SPCs, however, were rated AAA. The actual transaction is diagrammed in Figure 5.1 for the then Deutsche mark denominated investment.

The SPC got a AAA rating because the Italian government debt was denominated in lira, Italy's then home currency. Because there is a swap from Italian lira to Deutsche marks, the swap counterparty had to either have a AAA rating or be guaranteed by a AAA guarantor.

Many of these structures were sold as "black box" structures: Investors were told they were buying AAA Organization for Economic Cooperation and Development (OECD) sovereign collateral. A list of OECD countries was provided in the offering circulars. What investors purchased, however, was Italian government debt via the structure shown in Figure 5.1. Dresdner Bank (later acquired by Commerzbank) was then AAA rated and guaranteed one of these swaps for the now-defunct Kidder Peabody. Dresdner asked whether the lira was domestic lira or euro lira. Would the lira be delivered to Dresdner Bank inside of Italy, or would the lira be available to Dresdner Bank in a European bank account? This mattered to Dresdner. Although Dresdner Bank was willing to guarantee the lira payment Italy would make, but it was not willing to risk owing a lira payment in Europe if Dresdner Bank's only access to lira was within Italy itself.

Today, in most markets S&P rates local currency debt for many countries higher than the foreign currency debt. The credit derivatives market has not yet exploited these opportunities, but I anticipate we will see various structures using this theme.

THE CURRENCY QUESTION IN SOVEREIGN DEFAULT PROTECTION

Inconvertibility and Nontransferability

The issue of currency, unrelated to the actual exchange rate for the currency itself, has fallen into the category of credit derivatives. The currency question is different from the credit derivative question, however, and in many ways more complicated. The sovereignty of a government itself is closely tied up with the issue of currency.

It does not matter whether we are talking about gold, salt, cowry shells, silver, cacao, or tulip bulbs; currency is nothing more than a store of value. It helps if the standard store of value is measurable in a reliable manner and abundant. It was not until nation states arose that "money" in the form of coins and paper replaced commodities. Central banks still use gold as a store of value and go to great lengths to stockpile physical gold. The gold standard in an official or unofficial form existed in Europe for approximately nine hundred years prior to the dissolution of the gold standard in 1971. Nonetheless, gold is still viewed as a benchmark, although the "hard currencies," such as the dollar, Euro, and yen, are used as world standards, with the dollar still in the forefront as the world's reserve currency.

There are three basic kinds of money. Any child who has swapped toys with another child understands the first kind of *money—commodity money,* now represented by gold, silver, or oil, and formerly represented by cowry shells, beads to purchase Manhattan, wheat, salt, or any other usable commodities humans valued.

The second kind of money is *credit.* Most of us understand this in the form of checking accounts. Earlier, money flows were understood in the form of trade receivables, credit against a shipment of salable goods. In fact, international banking arose around the need to trade goods between various countries.

The international Jewish community was instrumental in the formation of early banking practices such as banker's acceptances, trade receivables, and letters of credit. The Jewish community was educated; they could read and write and cipher. More than that, they could read, write, cipher, and communicate in a common language. Even more important than the former, they had a close-knit community, a common code of ethics bound in religious law. The Jewish people had a means of censuring members of their community who broke the law through social and commercial ostracism. These were the reasons that the first world bankers were Jewish. A merchant in one country could rely on the standards of banking in his home country to agree with the standards of banking in another country, whose common thread was not a fickle sovereign edict but the standards of a community of people with common goals. Indeed, that is the definition of a sovereign state, and the Jewish people had their first international "sovereign" state visible outside of their community in the form of the first standards for international banking.

The third kind of money is *fiat money.* (This is not money used to buy Fiats, a commodity, as one investment banker once tried to explain.) Fiat money is a government-issued currency note. Fiat money is not backed by a commodity, as is commodity money. Fiat money is not backed by an asset, as is a checking deposit or trade receivable. Fiat money is backed by the faith and the credit of a government.

We use sovereign debt as money, as collateral, and as an exchange for goods and services. This works only because we agree that it has value and that the government would pay us back. We have a common hallucination of what this "money" is worth.

This seems arbitrary, but the other two forms of money are also arbitrary. Commodity money is less arbitrary than the other two, especially when the commodity has a use. In times of war, I can eat wheat, but I cannot eat gold. When I am hungry with no hope for quick replenishment of supplies, I would prefer to stockpile wheat rather than gold. This is how the concept of money began—as a practical means of enhancing the conditions of survival for a community. Nonetheless, gold would have more value to me than credit in these circumstances. The reason is that I would have a strong demand for a reliable means of exchange. The physical commodity seems less arbitrary in a distress situation.

Credit money has assets to back it and a definable benchmark for value. Although inflation can cause fluctuations in the value, there is a common standard of value. Fiat money is backed not by bank assets or commodities but by the wealth and production of a country.

Special Event Risks

A variety of events can happen to a sovereign currency. A government that does not choose to participate in a currency area, such as the European Monetary Union (EMU), values monetary policy autonomy and tries to control capital mobility and exchange-rate stability. The harder a government, such as a dictatorship, tries to maintain monetary policy autonomy, the more it must either limit the movement of capital into and outside of the country or compromise exchange-rate stability.

I lived in Iran when the shah was overthrown in 1978; shortly after, Khomeini returned in 1979. The new government wanted to prevent flight capital from leaving the country. It also wanted to prevent sympathizers to the shah's regime from getting out of the country alive. It further wanted to preserve a sense of economic normalcy to the outside world.

There was nothing normal about it. Citizens thought to be beneficiaries of the shah's largess were dragged out of their homes in the middle of the night. Often their accuser was a jealous neighbor. Kangaroo courts called "komites" condemned citizens to death. Their assets were confiscated.

In the panic to leave the country with some of their wealth, citizens found that although there was an official exchange rate of 7 toman (10 rials) to the U.S. dollar, there was no means to convert money. Banks were closed much of the time. The government put a further restriction on conversion of currency: Citizens could take only $1,000 in U.S. currency out of the country and could take only a suitcase of clothing. The idea was to prevent citizens from taking valuable carpets, now labeled "national protected works of art," out of the country.

Individuals found ways around these restrictions, proving once again that "governments rise and fall, but the economy goes on." A black market for hard currency quickly sprouted up. There were severe penalties if one were caught exchanging money. Nonetheless, people just became cleverer about the exchange.

Merchants were given dispensations to do business. Importers would fake invoices to reflect that they had increased orders by 100 percent. They hadn't doubled their orders with merchants in Europe. They created this fiction so that they could exchange currency for Deutsche marks or dollars. In this way, they accumulated hard currency deposits in Europe. Land and housing values went to almost zero in the wake of the upheaval. This was the time to pick up bargains on the back of someone else's crisis. If you wanted land or a nice house and you had hard currency deposits, you could strike a hard bargain. People purchased diamonds and gemstones, which were portable currency when they were fleeing the country. People bartered land, Persian carpets, and homes for portable, concealable wealth.

Importers did not have a problem faking their invoices. This raised no suspicion. The population eagerly purchased freezer chests to keep their meat frozen during the frequent electrical "brownouts" with the new inefficient government. They purchased televisions, stereos, and refrigerators as the only hard goods of value. Money was almost meaningless, so why not have conveniences? Sales skyrocketed.

In a situation like this, the ability to convert currency, either legally or in a way that was not transparent to a punitive government, would have been very valuable. Unfortunately, an easy way did not exist. This is one of the reasons for the growth of currency convertibility protection in the credit derivatives market.

Russian Civil War

Revolutions upset currency flows. During the Russian civil war in 1919, most Russian currencies devalued, except for the North Russia ruble. The National Emmission Caisse, formed in November 1918, issued notes denominated in rubles pegged at a fixed rate of 40 rubles per pound British sterling. The notes were backed by a reserve equal to 75 percent of the issue, an interest-bearing deposit in the Bank of England. North Russian government bonds backed the remainder. When North Russia fell in February 1920, the North Russian bonds were worthless. This scheme to keep convertibility at a fixed exchange rate in this currency nearly worked. If the Caisse bonds had not been partially backed by bonds, which became worthless after the Bolshevik Revolution, it would have worked. As it was, this currency was convertible until April 1920, when the Caisse stopped redeeming its notes.

That is the key to evaluating currency risks: What backs the currency? In times of political upheaval, having additional backing by a bank willing to convert currency is an alternative.

TRADE FINANCE: VENEZUELA EXAMPLE

In this decade, trade finance has become a key area of focus for convertibility. Trading companies cite Venezuela as typical of the problems they encounter. In the early 1990s, foreign exporters received payment in Venezuelan currency that they could not easily convert to their home currency or another hard currency. The government never declared an inconvertibility event or a change in exchange rates. Instead, the government forced foreign exporters to get permits to exchange currency. Once and if the permits were obtained, the window of opportunity for conversion was only a few hours every week. It was physically impossible for conversion demand to be met. There was not enough banking time allocated to fulfill the business demand.

One large, Japanese, London-based securities firm, a subsidiary of a large Japanese bank, routinely takes on enormous amounts of convertibility risk. So far, this convertibility risk has not caused any major problems. Nonetheless, the risks are considerable. Recently, the Japanese securities firm provided Mexican-government default protection to investors in Mexican-government foreign currency debt. The Japanese securities firm then bought default protection from a Mexican local entity That protection was denominated in pesos. The first potential problem is the correlation of the local guarantor with the government of Mexico. A second potential problem is that in the event of a default by the government of Mexico, there may be a convertibility event, which makes it impossible to convert a large amount of pesos to a hard currency. How valuable is the protection? The Japanese security firm's auditors did not think it was very valuable. They refused to sign off on the strategy after the fact.

From the foregoing discussion, it is easy to see that different events can trigger an inability to exchange money. The event could be a revolution and a change in limits of convertibility, it could be the inability to transfer local currency out of the country, it could be lack of reserves, or it could be a new type of government barrier to conversion.

Solutions to Currency Risk

Convertibility protection language is often very broad. Trigger events are often defined as war, hostilities, confiscation of nonlocal bank assets, a moratorium, and a broad definition of any event that restricts conversion.

The following is typical of language for the definition of a credit event found in a term sheet or confirmation.

Sovereign risk means:

1. Failure by the Central Bank generally to approve or permit the exchange of Brazilian reals for USD, or any other action by the Central Bank party of the government that has the effect of prohibiting such exchange, or the transfer of any funds outside the Republic of Brazil, or the transfer of Brazilian reals within the Republic of

Brazil, or USD are unavailable in any legal exchange market in the Republic of Brazil in accordance with normal commercial practice;

2. The existence of any prohibition on the receipt within the Republic of Brazil or the repatriation outside the Republic of Brazil of all or any portion of the principal, interest, capital gains, or other proceeds of assets owned by foreign persons or entities in the Republic of Brazil, including but not limited to any prohibitions imposed by the government;

3. A declaration of a general banking moratorium or any general suspension of payments by banks in the Republic of Brazil;

4. Any war (whether declared or not declared), revolution, insurrection, or hostile act that prevents the convertibility of Brazilian reals into USD; or

5. A general expropriation, confiscation, requisition, nationalization, or other action by the government that deprives OECD-domiciled banks of all or substantially all their assets in the Republic of Brazil.

The last clause is usually inserted only when dealing with non-OECD countries.

Contrast the preceding definition of credit event with the following language:

"Convertibility event" means, in the determination of the calculation agent, the enactment, promulgation, execution, or ratification of, or any change in or amendment to, any law, rule, or regulation (or in the application or official interpretation of any law, rule, or regulation), or any other act, by any governmental authority that (other than due to the failure by the counterparty to comply with such law, rule, regulation, or act) in a transaction conducted through any customary legal channels, (1) makes the conversion in all legal methods of Brazilian reals into United States dollars impossible, (2) makes the payment in all legal methods of Brazilian reals from accounts inside the Republic of Brazil to accounts outside the Republic of Brazil impossible, and/or (3) makes United States dollars unavailable in all legal methods at a spot rate of exchange from Brazilian reals. As used herein, "governmental authority" means any de facto or de jure government (or any agency or subdivision thereof), court, tribunal, administrative or other governmental authority, or any other entity (private or public) charged with the regulation of the financial markets (including the Central Bank) of the Republic of Brazil.

This definition is an attempt to cover every contingency. The language does not matter so long as both parties agree and are aware of what the protection will and will not do for them if a convertibility event occurs.

Settlement must be physical settlement. All payments are on a payment-versus-payment basis. But where does settlement take place? What if you cannot get local currency out of the country?

Provisions are usually made for this. Physical settlement can be made to an escrow agent. This means that the protection buyer can deliver local currency to a local bank and receive U.S. dollars in an account in the United States. This satisfies the requirement that in the event of local restrictions on transferability and convertibility, the protection buyer can deposit currency locally and receive hard currency outside of the country. Exchange rates are decided by an average of a dealer poll.

Let's look at a typical term sheet for Argentine peso convertibility risk.

REPUBLIC OF ARGENTINA CONVERTIBILITY RISK PROTECTION
Indicative Term Sheet

Protection Buyer:	Protection buyer.
Protection Seller:	Commercial bank.
Protection Type:	Currency convertibility.
Notional:	USD 50 million.
Trade Date:	As soon as practical.
Effective Date:	One week from trade date.
Termination Date:	One year from effective date.

Protection Premium:	140 basis points per annum on the notional amount payable on an actual/360 basis paid semiannually at the beginning of the period.
Payment Terms:	On the occurrence of the defined convertibility event, the protection buyer has the right to exercise the option. Two business days after the exercise of the option (the settlement date), the seller of protection will pay the protection buyer the notional amount by wire transfer of funds immediately available in New York City. The protection buyer will pay to the protection seller the convertibility amount.
Convertibility Event:	As determined by the calculation agent, the occurrence of any of the following:

1. failure of the government of the Republic of Argentina to exchange or to approve or to permit the exchange of Argentine pesos (ARP) for U.S. dollars (USD); *or*

2. the general unavailability of USD at a spot rate of exchange (applicable to the purchase of USD for ARP) in any legal exchange market transfer officially recognized as such by the government of the Republic of Argentina and in accordance with the normal commercial practice; *or*

3. the issuance of any order or decree by any regulatory authority in the Republic of Argentina, which has the effect of imposing any material exchange controls, limitations, or restrictions on the convertibility of ARP to USD or limiting or restricting the transfer of ARP or USD in any fashion outside the Republic of Argentina; *or*

4. the general unavailability of USD at a spot rate of exchange (applicable to the purchase of USD for ARP) in any legal exchange market transfer officially recognized as such by the government of the Republic of Argentina and in accordance with the normal commercial practice; *or*

5. any suspension of payments by banks in Argentina due to imposition by the government of the Republic of Argentina of any moratorium on the payment of indebtedness; *or*

6.war (declared or undeclared), civil strife, hostilities, or similar events in which Argentina is involved; *or*

7.the expropriation, confiscation, requisition, nationalization, or any action by the government of the Republic of Argentina that deprives Argentine or foreign entities of all or a significant portion of their assets without the assumption of liabilities of these assets in connection with the aforementioned government actions, having the effect of prohibiting these entities from paying amounts owed in USD; *or*

8, any action taken by the Central Bank (or any successor thereto) that has the effect described in (1) or (2) in this paragraph.

Convertibility:

The convertibility amount is the notional amount multiplied by the Argentine peso exchange rate. The protection buyer will pay this amount to the protection seller either in ARP in immediately available or same-day funds by wire transfer to the account maintained by the protection seller with a bank or other financial institution in the Republic of Argentina, or in any other form then legal and continuing for settlement of ARP obligations.

Argentine Peso Exchange Rate:

The Argentine peso exchange rate will be computed based on the exchange rate determined by the calculation agent equal to the spot ARP/ USD foreign exchange rate fixed by the Central Bank of the Republic of Argentina or any entity succeeding to its functions as the Central Bank and monetary authority of the Republic of Argentina (the "Central Bank of the Republic of Argentina") two business days prior to the settlement date, as such exchange rate is published. If no such quote is available on that date, the calculation agent will determine the Argentine peso exchange rate based on the foreign exchange rate then quoted by a major ARP/USD dealer in the Republic of Argentina for buying pesos for U.S. dollars in commercial or financial transactions or, if no such quote is available, the Argentine peso exchange rate will be based on the foreign exchange rate then quoted by a major ARP/USD dealer in New York for

	buying pesos for U.S. dollars in commercial or financial transactions. In the event that no such rate can be obtained, the calculation agent will determine the ARP/USD exchange rate in a commercially reasonable manner.
Calculation Agent:	Protection seller.
Business Days:	Days on which commercial banks and foreign exchange markets settle payments in New York, London, and Buenos Aires.
Law:	New York law shall govern this note.
Documentation:	The issuance of the protection will be documented under an International Swaps and Derivatives Association, Inc. (ISDA) master agreement.

This document simply says that the protection buyer must deliver Argentine pesos to an account in Argentina equal to the U.S. dollar notional amount at the exchange rate at the time of the convertibility event. The protection buyer has two business days to get the money to the account. If the protection buyer does this, the protection buyer will get the notional amount in U.S. dollars delivered to a New York City bank account.

The foreign exchange (FX) spot rate is the rate prior to the day of the event announcement. Most agreements allow for first looking for the Central Bank published rate for that day for the previous day. If the Central Bank has not published a rate, the counterparties look to four leading Brazilian banks for an average rate. If that is not possible, the counterparties look for an average offshore rate from credible offshore dealers.

As we saw before, most of the details are negotiable, but the basic transaction is as outlined in the previous paragraph. Dealer polls, adjustments to business days, and other terms are negotiable.

Physical settlement days are often adjusted so that in the event that a payment cannot be made, a grace period to make the remainder of the payments may be allowed. The period is usually three days. This is a negotiable feature between counterparties in this transaction.

The convertibility option is a solution to the currency issue. Export credit agencies and trade finance contracts can also provide protection for currency convertibility in the form of insurance guarantees. These can be expensive, however, and are not accessible in all cases to people wishing to do business in a particular country.

It is possible to purchase risk protection from a variety of sources, such as some export credit agencies, private insurers, and the trade finance market. Private insurers are rare and tend to be expensive. The trade finance market is currently looking for more convertibility protection. The market viewed recent conventional protection as inadequate (as in the case of Venezuela, mentioned previously).

Export credit agencies include, but are not limited to, the Overseas Private Investment Corporation (OPIC) in the United States or the Multilateral Investment Guarantee Agency (MIGA). OPIC will cover political risks, such as currency inconvertibility, expropriation, and political violence, with up to 20 years of protection. OPIC will insure 90 percent of the investment, but investors must bear the remaining 10 percent of risk. MIGA will cover up to 15 or even 20 years of protection, which is noncancelable by MIGA but cancelable by the insured on any anniversary date.

Although insurance from export agencies is usually cheaper than convertibility protection, it is not always available. Japan's Ministry of International Trade and Industry (MITI) recently suspended its foreign exchange risk insurance. Further, export agencies may not cover the full amount of the risk. OPIC leaves an investor with a need to hedge a residual risk of 10 percent. MIGA used to insure only the first $50 million of exposure; this amount may have increased. If the project creates more exposure than that, the investor must look elsewhere for protection. Many project finance groups are up to their limit on certain country risks and require more sources of longer-dated protection for both sovereign default and convertibility events.

A further difficulty arises with export agency protection. Investors often encounter delays in realizing the value of their protection. Investors are often instructed to "see what you can negotiate, then come back." The delay can be intolerable to an investor who is temporarily short of liquidity. An investor caught in a situation like this finds that the "cheaper" protection offered by an export agency can end up costing him more in business problems.

PRICING CONVERTIBILITY PROTECTION

Most investment banks and corporations are looking to the banking community for convertibility protection. Given the ambiguities surrounding this protection, should banks be involved in providing convertibility protection? Banks already have this risk. That is what international commercial banks do, whether that is their intention or not. Having local currency deposits forces them into the position of having convertibility risk.

It seems a natural fit for banks to offer convertibility protection, provided they can put a price on the cost of this protection and mark it to market on their books. Another consideration is regulatory risk capital. How should banks account for it?

I called the Federal Reserve Bank of New York in July 1997 to ask them what the board of governors of the Federal Reserve System says about accounting for risk capital when a bank buys and sells currency convertibility protection. They had not examined this issue. They had to ask me for whatever materials I had on the subject because they were unfamiliar with the product. In the end, they decided to lump convertibility protection in with several foreign exchange issues and said they would get back to me on the capital treatment.

Although banks have always had this risk, it is only recently that banks have looked at buying and selling this protection. With this focus comes a need to agree on a pricing methodology for this difficult-to-define risk.

Table 5.4 shows a comparison of convertibility option premiums with credit default risk premiums in the broker market. Notice that convertibility premiums trade wider than the premiums for credit default protection.

Disinformation and misinformation plague the credit derivatives market. When asked, the broker showing indications for one-year Argentine peso convertibility protection said that although he shows a bid of 100 basis points and an offer of 140 basis points, there is no actual bid or offer. This broker thinks that convertibility protection would "trade" at 120 basis points, the midmarket of the indications.

In other words, levels are thrown up on broker screens without substance behind them. This market trades between real counterparties. These are negotiated transactions. Price, terms and conditions, and size are all

TABLE 5.4 Sovereign Credit Default Protection versus Convertibility Protection Prices, Bid/Ask Broker Indications (basis points per annum)

	6-Month Default	6-Month Convertibility	1-Year Default	1-Year Convertibility
Argentina			70/NA	NA/140
Brazil	60/80	110/NA	70/95	120/170
Mexico			65/75	NA/110
Russia	NA/19.5	150/185		

Note: NA indicates bid or offer was not available.

Sources: Prebon Yanmane, Tullett Capital Markets, July 14, 1997.

negotiated directly between counterparties. As there are so few real counterparties for this type of protection, the broker market is useless. It is much better to call the well-known names in the credit derivatives market and negotiate and get market levels directly. This market is driven by supply and demand, and prices vary from counterparty to counterparty.

One emerging-markets credit derivatives head trader describes this protection as a knock-in spot trade in which the knock-in is independent of currency levels but dependent on the whims of sovereigns. He feels one must look for the "pocket" in the market, the "pocket" of opportunity. This is not a dealers' market. One cannot go into the market to find a "fair market." When he goes to the broker market, he finds the levels are not there; the screen prices are fiction. In his view, one must find out where one can trade. Credit spreads do not matter; models do not matter; intuition does not count. The market tells you where the spread is.

There is no exact mathematical model for convertibility protection. Most banks have not sold any convertibility protection on a stand-alone basis. They have only traded this combined with default risk. When convertibility is lumped with default protection language, a bank can purchase the hedge imbedded in macro country default protection risk. It is difficult to determine whether the buyer or the seller got a fair price for convertibility protection if there was indeed a premium at all over the regular default protection market. This is especially confusing when a convertibility event is used as a credit default trigger event. We discuss this in more detail in the section on hidden costs in default language in Chapter 8.

Dr. Hei Wai Chan then of J.P. Morgan's New York office researched the issue of convertibility pricing. Chan feels the likelihood of convertibility default is greater than default of a sovereign on its debt obligations. The fact that most convertibility premiums trade above default options is intuitively correct. But Chan also says: "There is not an easy way to model the convertibility risk. It is quite a challenge. In principle, I can create a balance sheet for a country, with data limitations, and produce a default price. With convertibility, there are other issues involved. It's almost like trying to build an economic model and come up with a forecast."

One of my colleagues once said that convertibility protection should be priced like a foreign exchange knock-in option. It is nothing like a foreign exchange knock-in option. Knock-in options have an exchange rate trigger. That is not the case for convertibility options. The convertibility option gives the protection buyer only the right to convert at the then-current exchange spot rate. It is like a contingent option to exchange at the spot rate in which the trigger is a government or Central Bank action.

Other market professionals sometimes describe convertibility options as a "sovereign-linked currency `\'swaption.'" Chan maintains that this doesn't describe the risk at all; this false analogy actually confuses people. This is not a swaption—it is more like, but different from, a default option.

There are important differences between default options and convertibility options. These differences are currently reflected in the fact that convertibility options trade at a premium to default options. But that need not always be the case. The spread between a default option and a convertibility option may contract as a default event approaches, if there is certainty that both events will occur simultaneously. If a default on sovereign debt seems imminent, but convertibility of currency exists and seems continuing—albeit at a probable depreciated value—the convertibility option will trade well below the default option.

A further complication is the lack of understanding of convertibility issues, which keeps many potential market makers out of this market. Supply-and-demand factors dominate the pricing of convertibility protection. Some banks are booking convertibility premiums in the banking book. They do not mark it to market. They view the sale of convertibility protection as the functional equivalent of a loan.

Other banks are not prepared to do this and must grapple with a difficult mark-to-market decision. There is no economic measure other than what the dealers quote, and it is usually a one-way market. One can poll dealers for a mark-to-market. One can also develop a model. As of this writing, I am not aware of anyone who has developed a model for marking convertibility protection to market, a model that reflects market levels.

Nonetheless, there are some methods to find out what the market might be. For instance, one might look at local-currency, domestically traded sovereign debt swapped to U.S. dollars and compare it with euro dollar debt for the same sovereign. For Mexico, one might look at Cetes, Federal Treasury Certificates denominated in pesos with maturities under two years. At the start of 2022, Cetes were rated Baa1. Swap the Cetes to U.S. dollars and compare the differential between this Baa1 and an actual dollar-denominated Baa1; the differential in spread should be the convertibility risk. That sounds easy, but there may not be a well-developed swap market in the currency in which one is most interested. A further difficulty is that many countries do not have depth and breadth to their debt markets to enable such a comparison.

In the late 1990s, the Bank of Boston was a buyer of Brazilian convertibility protection. The bank was comfortable with Brazilian risk, but on their overall balance sheet, Brazilian risk was a high percentage relative to other banks. Their Brazilian risk rivaled that of Citibank. Bank of Boston attempted to reduce this risk. One professional bemoans the premiums he paid for convertibility protection: "To be honest with you, if you ask me, it's free money."

In 1998, Bank of Boston issued U.S. dollar—denominated one-year maturity certificates of deposit (CDs) in Brazil, which traded at LIBOR+80 basis points to LIBOR+100 basis points. The CDs had convertibility risk. If Bank of Boston were unable to pay in dollars because of convertibility restrictions, the CDs would pay off in Brazilian reals. Meanwhile, Bank of Boston's U.S.-issued dollar-denominated CDs trade at LIBOR flat. This would imply that convertibility should trade at 80 to 100 basis points. But Bank of Boston paid 115 basis points for this protection. The price reflected the fact that it was difficult for Bank of Boston to find counterparties.

Most countries do not have convenient issues available, as does Brazil, for short-term exposures. It is even difficult to find references in the Brazilian market as one goes longer than one year in maturity. For Russia, it is possible to try to come up with approximate pricing. One can look to the dollar-hedged Gosudarstvenii Kratkrasochnli Obligatsii (GKOs), Russian Ministry of Finance zero-coupon bills. Some period before the maturity date, the investor is required to hedge the currency risk with a Russian bank with an FX forward. If one can assess the credit risk, this can be accounted for and the rest is convertibility. But the Russian banks are state owned. The spread contains elements of convertibility and default combined. One could also account for Russian state default risk for GKOs, because if there is a default, there is default risk on the FX contract. Another alternative is to find non-Russian GKO dealers who will quote the FX market. Ideally an FX hedge with a non-Russian counterparty would make it easier to back out the convertibility premium.

There are other ways to find out where the market clears for convertibility, and these involve convertibility-linked notes. Even AAA rated banks offer notes with their own issue with a convertibility event tied to principal redemption. That is one way of creating the hedge and determining where the market prices this risk. The market prices the risk where it will purchase the note linked to a convertibility event.

CLASSIC BIFURCATION OF SOVEREIGN RISK AND CONVERTIBILITY RISK

A classic historical example of how this works, which incorporates stripping the convertibility risk out of a sovereign issue, was the Tesobono trade. Tesobonos were one-year instruments issued by the Republic of Mexico. They had an unusual feature. When an investor purchased a Tesobono, the investor paid the principal amount in U.S. dollars and immediately converted the dollars to pesos. The coupon on the Tesobonos was paid in U.S. dollars. At maturity, the investor received pesos at the then-current exchange rate and had to convert the pesos to dollars.

Although many Japanese investors were willing to accept Mexican sovereign risk, they were unwilling to accept the convertibility risk. Many Japanese investors remembered the early 1980s when Mexico declared a convertibility event and it was impossible to convert pesos to dollars. Investors felt that if this happened, the exchange rate would deteriorate while they held onto pesos waiting for the next opportunity to convert.

One bank-owned Japanese securities firm developed a clever solution. They put the Tesobonos into a special purpose vehicle (SPV). Japanese investors purchased the notes backed by Tesobonos because the notes had high yields relative to other fixed income investments. The investors paid dollars for the notes, received dollar coupons, and received dollars at maturity. Although the Tesobonos backed the notes, investors were guaranteed dollars. The guarantor was a AAA rated Japanese insurance company affiliated with the Japanese bank.

The Japanese securities firm then created a hedge. They persuaded the

Japanese bank to issue dollar-denominated CDs in the United States with the payoff at maturity linked to Mexican peso/U.S. dollar convertibility. If there were an inconvertibility event, the investors received pesos instead of dollars.

At the time of the transaction, before the "tequila effect" of December 1994, the Tesobonos were trading at about LIBOR+120 bps. The Japanese investors purchased the SPV notes at LIBOR+25 bps. The U.S. investors purchased the Mexican peso/U.S. dollar convertibility-linked notes at LIBOR+40 bps, about 50 basis points higher than the Japanese bank's funding cost in the United States at that time. U.S. investors purchased the CDs at a level around 40 basis points cheaper than where they could have purchased secondary market paper for this Japanese bank. This meant that the price the U.S. investor put on this convertibility risk was 40 basis points. The net profit to the Japanese securities firm in the transaction was 45 basis points (120 basis points on the original Tesobono minus 50 basis points on the bank new-issue CD minus 25 basis points to the SPC for the Japanese investors). The transaction was as shown in Figure 5.2 for the sovereign risk and in Figure 5.3 for the convertibility risk.

Although Mexican bonds widened dramatically after December 1994 all the investors who held their positions in a transaction that had less than a year to maturity got their money back in dollars. The inconvertibility event never occurred, and Mexico did not default on its obligations within, that time frame. Depending on the country, your mileage may vary. There is some brinkmanship involved in taking this sort or risk.

Classic Bifurcation of Sovereign Risk and Convertibility Risk

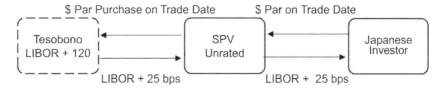

At maturity, the Tesobonos paid a Peso amount equal to the Dollar Par amount reflected at the then-current exchange rate.

The Japanese investor took Mexico default risk but was assured a USD Payment if there were an inconvertibility event.

FIGURE 5.2 Classic Bifurcated Sovereign Risk: Tesobonos

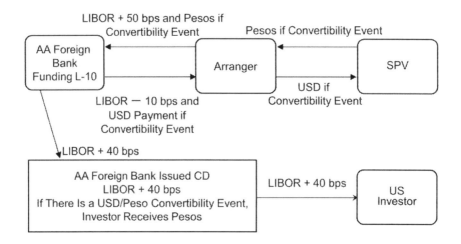

FIGURE 5.3 Classic Bifurcated Convertibility Risk: Tesobonos

The method just described for finding a market clearing price for convertibility protection works and is defensible because it relies on true market levels. It is extremely difficult, however. We have now examined several different methods to try to get a feel for convertibility option market levels. Each has its strengths, weaknesses, and challenges. The following summary lists ways one might mark-to-market convertibility options.

- Observe market levels—the market defines the price, of course. The difficulty is that this is a one-sided market, and you may not be able to get accurate marks at all times. Broker levels are unreliable for this product.
- Arbitrarily say that convertibility trades at some percentage spread above credit default protection, say 150 percent. This has the appeal of being easy as well as being currently observable for some currencies. Greater illiquidity, supply-and-demand factors, and higher probability of event risk dictate that convertibility will trade wider; but there are scenarios in which it can trade inside the credit default spread. This would be when a default exists, but deeply devalued currency can still be converted. Even currently, this formula method is not true across maturities.
- Access domestically traded securities in the local currency and look

at a Eurodollar sovereign issue in U.S. dollars. Swap the domestically traded security to dollars and compare the spread difference between the two. This spread difference should reflect the convertibility premium for the currency. This also means that there must be priceable local instruments as well as a Eurodollar issue that can be priced and referenced in the maturity of interest. At the very least, one must be able to build a convertibility curve. For many countries, there is a dearth of local currency and Eurodollar debt, which makes this method virtually impossible to implement.

- Find a USD issue of a foreign bank that collects local deposits. This bank must convert local currency to USD. Compare that with where they issue in the U.S. market. The difference is convertibility risk premium. For example, a USD-denominated CD issued by a U.S. Brazilian bank branch that collects local deposits is Bank of Boston (A2/A). If this trades at LIBOR+125 bps and Bank of Boston trades at about LIBOR+20 bps for one year, the implied convertibility premium is about 105 basis points.
- Find a convertibility-linked note and back out the convertibility premium. This method works, but you may not be able to find such a convenient issue in the market.
- Find a sovereign with convertibility risk and strip out the convertibility risk (as shown earlier with the Tesobono transaction). The hard-dollar sovereign level in the market reflects the sovereign risk premium. The remaining spread is what the market implies is the convertibility premium. For instance, Tesobonos were trading at
- LIBOR+120 bps. The Mexico dollar SPV traded at LIBOR+25 bps, and the convertibility-linked CD traded 65 basis points above the funding cost of the issuing bank. Therefore, the convertibility premium was 65 basis points at that time. The remaining difference was $120 - 65 - 25$, or 30, basis points profit, and expenses. The challenge with this method is the unavailability of suitable debt instruments for many emerging-market countries.

*****

If one must mark convertibility options to market, the best solution may be to adopt a policy based on a pragmatic combination of a few of the preceding reasonable methodologies. The key is to continue to observe market levels, however, because supply-and-demand factors dominate this market. "Reality checks" are essential.

I would rather be a seller of this protection than a buyer in almost all cases, with a few exceptions as noted in the next section. Banks, trading companies, leasing companies, and multinational corporations already take oh convertibility risk, even if they do not currently attempt to quantify the risk on their balance sheets. At the high premiums achievable in many of these markets, banks should sell this protection.

CROSS-BORDER ISSUES

Convertibility issues vary by country. There is no substitute for economic research on specific country risk. For instance, when one is trying to evaluate risks in an Asian country, one would not view all Asian countries as the same. In the late 1990s, short-term interest rates in Thailand reached quadruple-digit levels, as high as 1,500 percent. There is a two-tiered foreign exchange system in Thailand, however, which means that there will not be an obstacle to delivery of the Thai baht currency, and convertibility risk was diminished. Further, Thailand country cash flow was robust. Contrast that situation with Indonesia: There was a high degree of political risk in Indonesia. The largest currency issue in Indonesia was a *yen* issue. A bigger slice of Indonesia's foreign debt obligation was yen-denominated than anywhere else. This was due to Japanese investment in the Indonesian local manufacturing markets and investment in debt markets.

Economists look at foreign exchange reserves as a cover against imports. Vietnam's foreign exchange reserves, for instance, were low, and trade increased. The import cover as of summer 1997 was only six to seven weeks. Vietnam was watched carefully for a possible default in ability to convert the local currency to hard global currencies. One of the key issues is the country cash flow with respect to foreign exchange reserves. *Country cash flow is measured as the change in foreign exchange reserves minus the change in the trading account.*

In March 1995, Argentina looked close to default. In February 1997, Bulgaria looked close to default. The Czech Republic ratio looked sick in summer 1997. Cash flow was rapidly draining out of the Czech Republic. Most of this money was flight capital. This looked like a situation ripe for convertibility restrictions. South Africa had five weeks of foreign exchange reserves. Nonetheless, South Africa relaxed convertibility laws. Despite the low reserves, lack of convertibility was strangling foreign trade. South Africa realized there was a trade-off and made the decision that trade was more important.

Brazil put a transaction tax on financial import and export of capital. There was a 7 percent transaction tax to repatriate capital. Once capital was out, it was costly to get it back in. In 1997, Brazil eliminated the tax or in some cases cut the tax to 1 percent, depending on the instrument. This means that Brazil may see more volatility in its country cash flows, although in general Brazil is a good short-term bet for sellers of convertibility protection.

Not every bank would agree with me that selling convertibility protection is a good idea. The head of credit derivatives in New York for a Japanese bank capital-markets subsidiary felt that the ability to transfer local currency can be a problem. Even if the convertibility agreement calls for a local currency deposit in the home country and a U.S. dollar deposit outside the home country, there may be a problem. Central banks may try to buttress the spirit of the regulatory environment. They could limit the ability to increase local currency deposits so that the buyer of the convertibility protection cannot meet the requirements of the convertibility contract because the buyer will not be able to deliver local currency to a domestic account. He may be right. Government intervention is a wild card. Yet I would risk this and sell the convertibility protection.

SOVEREIGN CDS LANGUAGE "ARBITRAGE"

Hedge funds Eternity Global Master Fund Ltd. (Eternity) and HBK Master Fund LP thought they purchased protection against an Argentina default. They sued J.P. Morgan when the bank refused to pay off on Argentina credit protection contracts that the hedge funds had purchased.

At issue was the definition of restructuring, a credit event defined in the trade's documentation. Did Argentina's "voluntary debt exchange" in November of 2001, meet the definition of a restructuring under ISDA's "standard" 1999 language which had been used in the contract? Was it a triggering credit event?

The Republic of Argentina gave bondholders the option to turn in their bonds in exchange for secured loans backed by certain Argentine federal tax revenues. J.P. Morgan claimed this did not meet the definition of restructuring, at least for the protection it sold to Eternity. The courts agreed with Morgan Guaranty Trust Co., the J.P. Morgan entity named as defendant. Even though the exchange option was revolting to Eternity, it was not mandatory.

Do you know what else isn't mandatory in over-the-counter contracts? ISDA language. J.P. Morgan's language. Contracts are negotiable. ISDA is not a "standard" unless you want it to be. ISDA's "standard" language is a suggestion from ISDA.

J.P. Morgan's story was different when it wanted to collect on the protection it bought from Daehan Investment Trust Management. J.P. Morgan claimed its slightly different contract language met the definition of restructuring under the credit default protection contract it had with Daehan. The credit default protection was embedded in a complex note. JPMorgan said the note predated the "standard" narrower language for restructuring released by ISDA in 1999.

CDS on Greece: ISDA's Trojan Horse

In October 2011, financial professionals familiar with the International Swaps and Derivatives Association, Inc.'s hollow reassurances about its "standards" were not surprised when ISDA's Determinations Committee stonewalled the global credit derivatives market. It refused to recognize a credit event for credit default swaps on Greek sovereign debt.

"Customers" who accepted ISDA documentation when buying credit default protection on Greece discovered that ISDA defended the position that a 50% discount on Greek debt was "voluntary." ISDA claimed this was the correct interpretation of its "standard" language.

ISDA's "standard" credit default swap (CDS) was an ineffective as a hedge for the widened spreads (reduced price) of Greek debt. It was also useless as credit default protection. Protection buyers could not settle their credit default contracts. But if one used reasonable standards of impairment to define default, a protection buyer would trigger a credit event and the protection seller would pay the buyer the determined settlement amount. ISDA was not reasonable. Intentionally or otherwise, ISDA disserved the global credit derivatives market. I will let you decide whether you believe it was intentional.

Banks that play this game call it "language arbitrage." Anyone that bought sovereign credit protection on Greece after accepting ISDA "standard" documentation without modifying the language found that they are on the wrong side of an "arbitrage." An arbitrage is a riskless money pump. In this case, it means that money has been pumped out of credit default protection buyers with no risk to their counterparties, the financial institutions that ostensibly sold them credit default protection on Greece.

But some investors were savvy enough to rewrite their contracts and were immediately paid. Those who took "standard" contracts had to wait. Four months later, under enormous pressure from outraged default protection buyers, ISDA ruled the restructuring was a credit event, after all.

Who benefitted from ISDA's delay? Four months is a long time to hedge a losing position if you were a seller of credit default protection on Greece. In four months, a seller of credit default protection might even find a sucker—eager for the premium income and who thought ISDA would never deem the restructuring a credit event—to take the risk off his hands.

ISDA tried spin, claiming the Greek CDS debacle showed the market worked. That is like Doctor Frankenstein conceding that pitchforks work.

How did waves of debt restructuring work out for Greece? Did the high debt load mean huge investment in the Greek economy with a surge in productivity? Panagiotis Kouroumplis, a member of the Greek Parliament who supported the first bailout, explained, "every single euro we got went for debt. We haven't spent a single euro on development." (Charles Forelle, "For Ordinary Greeks, Big Bailout Adds Up to Years of Hardship," *The Wall Street Journal*, October 29, 2011.

*****

Protect Yourself with Customized Language

Sovereign credit default disputes demonstrate that credit protection buyers and sellers should rewrite ISDA "standard" language and agree to sensible terms, before concluding the initial trade. One must first protect oneself from the ISDA "standard" documentation. There is reason to accept "standard" documentation in the credit derivatives market if it doesn't suit you, particularly the sovereign credit derivatives market.

CHAPTER 6

Credit-Linked Notes

Credit default swaps can be imbedded in notes, which are referred to as credit-linked notes (CLNs). Earlier, we saw some examples of credit-linked notes. All the types of credit derivatives we have reviewed up to now can be imbedded in note form. If credit derivatives and their off-balance sheet nature have so many benefits, why would anyone ever want to buy credit derivatives in note form?

There are five reasons to do so. The first two reasons apply to transactions in which an investor is buying either a credit-enhanced note or a note that has additional imbedded credit risk. The last three reasons apply to transactions in which an investor buys a note with additional imbedded credit risk.

1. There is no need for an International Swaps and Derivatives Association, Inc. (ISDA) master agreement or confirmation. Documentation is as simple as that for a medium-term note.
2. Investors who are not authorized to do derivatives or off—balance sheet transactions can participate in the credit derivative market through credit-linked notes.
3. Credit lines to the investor, the hedge provider, are not used. This is particularly valuable for very long dated or leveraged transactions. Unused credit lines remain open for future business.
4. If the investor is providing a hedge and is highly correlated with the reference credit, it does not matter. If an investor buys a note with principal risk linked to a default by the Mexican government,

this creates a hedge on the Mexican government for the issuer. The issuer gets par up front. If Mexico defaults, either the issuer pays par minus the defaulted bond value, or the issuer delivers the defaulted bonds to the investor. The issuer therefore has the hedge money up front. The issuer has no credit risk to the investor. The issuer therefore does not care if the investor is another Mexican counterparty, for instance, because credit correlation between the reference credit and the investor is irrelevant.

5. For the same reason that correlation between the investor providing a hedge and the reference credit is irrelevant, the credit quality of the investor is irrelevant. A credit-linked note issuer can create a long-dated hedge with a massive payoff in the event of default with absolutely no concern about the credit quality of the investor.

The following sections discuss some typical examples that can serve as prototypes for imbedding other credit derivatives or credit risks in notes. Structured product often includes credit derivatives as a method of providing off-balance sheet transactions with trust vehicles or as means of providing credit enhancement or credit risk in structured products.

CREDIT DEFAULT-LINKED NOTES

As we saw in Chapters 3 and 5, credit default language can include many events, including convertibility events, but the events included are negotiable. There are as many variations in the definition of credit event for CLNs as there are for credit default swaps and options. Credit default—linked notes (limited recourse notes) are of four major structure types:

1. Principal-protected notes, which receive the credit rating of the issuer, but the investor risks loss of coupon income in the event of default of a different reference credit.

2. Boosted coupon notes, which receive the credit rating of the issuer, but the principal payment is linked to the default event and default value of a different reference credit, with underlying credit risk of a lower-rated credit.

3. Boosted coupon notes, which receive the credit rating of the issuer, in which the principal payment is linked to a default event of a different reference credit or credits and the principal payment may have levered risk or even risk of loss of the entire principal amount in the event of a default of the reference credit or reference credits.

4. Reduced coupon notes, which receive the credit rating of the issuer, in which the principal repayment is the face amount, and if there is a reference credit event, the termination payment is enhanced by the loss in the event of default of a reference asset.

Principal-protected notes are very popular with European investors. The investor receives a boosted coupon if there is no default on the part of a reference credit. If there is a default, however, the investor receives no further coupons and may not receive the original investment until the maturity of the note. The forgone interest income on the note mitigates the loss in the event of default for the issuer of the principal-protected note, but it may not cover all of the loss in the event of default.

The value of this note is that the implied recovery value of the reference credit can be enhanced by the present value of the forgone interest on the note. This enhancement to the recovery value, particularly in the early years, can provide credit enhancement for a risky credit in a portfolio. Although this does not provide complete default protection, the asset quality of a portfolio, which benefits from this partial protection, can be enhanced. This partial protection may be enough to increase the implied rating of the reference credit from noninvestment grade to investment grade in certain instances.

The following term sheet gives an example of a boosted coupon note that receives the credit rating of a European bank, but the principal payment is linked to a default event for the Hellenic Republic. The principal repayment is also linked to the default value of a specific Hellenic Republic reference bond. These notes are also called limited recourse notes because the noteholder has no right to the issuer's general assets.

CREDIT-LINKED NOTE—LINKED TO DEFAULT BY THE HELLENIC REPUBLIC
Indicative Term Sheet

Issuer:	AA rated European bank.
Face Amount:	USD 100 million.
Currency Denomination:	USD.
Trade Date:	Today,
Settlement Date:	Five business days after trade date.
Maturity Date:	The earlier of:
	1, the early termination date, if any, *or*
	2. seven years from the settlement date.
Issue Price:	Par.
Coupon:	Six-month USD LIBOR + 125 basis points (Act/ 360, semiannual).
Redemption Amount:	If there is no credit event, par in U.S. dollars.
	If a credit event on the part of the reference credit has occurred prior to the maturity of the note, the obligation of the issuer to pay the USD redemption amount shall be discharged, and the note shall be redeemed with the early termination amount on the early termination date.
Early Termination Payment:	If a reference credit event has occurred, the issuer shall take a dealer poll of five dealers acting in good faith to obtain a market value for the reference asset. This value shall be converted to USD at the then-prevailing spot exchange rate. This amount shall be distributed to the noteholders on a pro rata basis, subject to a maximum of 100 percent.
	If the issuer is unable to obtain a market value for the securities prior to the termination date, the issuer shall deliver the reference asset to the noteholders on a pro rata basis.
Early Termination Date:	The 15th business day after a credit event.

Credit Event	Occurs when the calculation agent is aware of publicly available information as to the existence of a credit condition.
	Credit condition means either a payment default or a bankruptcy event in respect of the issuer.
	Payment default means, subject to a dispute in good faith by the issuer, either the issuer fails to pay any amount due of the reference asset, or any other present or future indebtedness of the issuer for or in respect of moneys borrowed or raised or guaranteed.
	Bankruptcy event means the declaration by the issuer of a general moratorium in or rescheduling of payments on any external indebtedness.
	Publicly available information means information that has been published in any two or more internationally recognized published or electronically displayed financial news sources.
Reference Credit:	Hellenic Republic.
Reference Asset:	Hellenic Republic bonds.
Currency:	Greek drachma (GDR).
Amount:	To be determined (based on the USD/GDR exchange rate at settlement).
Coupon:	11.75%.
Maturity:	Seven years.
Nonrecourse Clause:	The noteholders have no right to the issuer's general assets. The principal of the note is repayable based only on the performance of the reference asset at the early termination date or at maturity, whichever is sooner.
Noncollateral Clause:	The reference asset does not serve as collateral for the noteholders. If a credit event occurs, the noteholders have no priority claim to the reference asset.
Denomination:	USD 1 million.

Business Days:	Days on which commercial banks and foreign exchange markets settle payments in London, New York, and Athens.
Listing:	London Stock Exchange.
Lead Manager:	Issuer.

Although the note is USD denominated, in the event of default, the noteholder may take delivery of Greek drachma-denominated bonds. The investor then has not only the risk of default on the part of the government of Greece, the Hellenic Republic, but also the potential risk of convertibility from Greek drachma to USD.

The preceding is a term sheet and is not meant to be a legal document on which clients can rely in the event of a dispute. As such, the default events are loosely defined, and investors must examine final documentation drafts as well as final documentation for actual default language. For examples of possibilities of events that may be included in default language, refer to the section in Chapter 8 on hidden costs in default language.

Although it is not the final document and is not meant to be as complete in language, this term sheet includes important caveats as to the nonrecourse status of the note and clarifies that the reference asset is not deemed to serve in any way as collateral for the noteholder. Although term sheets are not necessarily meant to be drafted by lawyers, they should not be misleading and are often held in deal files. It is good practice that if key conditions of a term sheet are renegotiated, a final term sheet should complement the final legal documentation so that all parties to the transaction have up-to-date representations of the trade that replace outdated material.

Credit default notes referencing emerging-market debt and pools of emerging-market debt are becoming more popular. In June 1997, Dresdner Kleinwort Benson and J.P. Morgan brought a deal to market. The DEM 100 million note had a seven-year maturity. The credit event is based on a credit default event of any one of a pool of reference credits: Brazil, Argentina, Venezuela, Ecuador, Mexico, Turkey, or Russia. If a credit event occurs, the investor gets a reduced principal amount.

In Chapter 4, we saw an example of a geared default option imbedded in a credit-linked note, linked to a default by the government of Mexico.

The principal payment had levered downside risk in the event of a default of the reference credit. These notes are even riskier than the notes with one-for-one payoff amounts linked to potential credit events of a reference asset.

A rarer form of credit default note gives the investor an *enhanced* payoff in the event of a default of a reference credit. In this instance, the coupon on the note can be thought of as an option premium payment. Part or all of the coupon is reduced by the per annum option premium that would be paid for the credit protection purchased by the note investor. The investor receives a minimum of par or par plus the loss in the event of default of a reference asset.

The following term sheet shows an example of a credit default—linked note in which the investor receives an enhanced payment in the event of default by the United Mexican States (UMS). The principal payment is enhanced by the decline in the value of the reference asset.

CREDIT-LINKED NOTE—LINKED TO UMS CREDIT EVENT
Indicative Term Sheet

Issuer:	AA rated European bank.
Face Amount:	USD 10 million.
Currency Denomination:	USD.
Trade Date:	Today.
Settlement Date:	Five business days after trade date.
	The earlier of:
	1. the nonscheduled termination date, if any, *or*
	2. February 1, 2001.
Issue Price:	Par.
Coupon:	3.00% payable semiannually on a 30/360 basis.
Redemption Amount:	If there is no credit event, par in U.S. dollars.
	If there is a credit event, the investor shall receive the termination payment on the nonscheduled

	termination date, and all obligations of the issuer shall be discharged.
Nonscheduled Termination Date:	With five business days' notice (even if this date is after the maturity date) following a credit event with a termination payment being made.
Termination Payment:	Investor receives the U.S. dollar amount calculated as follows *only* upon a credit event:

[(Face Amount Par) + (Face Amount × Par − Market Value)] + Accrued Coupon Interest, if any

where Market Value means the USD-denominated market value of the reference security on the notification date determined by the calculation agent with reference to a dealer panel.

Note: The issuer pays accrued coupon interest up to the earlier of the nonscheduled termination date *or* the maturity date.

Dispute:	If there is a dispute between the parties as to the occurrence of a credit event unresolved on the maturity date, a credit event will be deemed to occur on that date.
Notification Date:	If a credit event occurs during the term of the transaction, the investor shall have the right to designate a nonscheduled termination date by delivering notice (on the notification date) to the issuer of the occurrence of such credit event. Such notice must contain a description in reasonable detail of the facts giving rise to the credit event.
Credit Event:	Occurs when the issuer is aware of publicly available information as to the existence of a credit condition and at the same time materiality exists.

Credit condition means either a payment default or a bankruptcy event in respect of the issuer; any war, revolution, insurrection, or hostile act that interferes with foreign exchange transactions; or the expropriation, confiscation, requisition, or nationalization of nonlocal banks, the declaration of a banking moratorium, or suspension of payments by local banks.

Payment default means, subject to a dispute in good faith by the issuer, either the issuer fails to pay any amount due of the reference asset, or any other present or future indebtedness of the issuer for or in respect of moneys borrowed or raised or guaranteed, in an amount in aggregate of not less than USD 100 million (or its equivalent in other currencies) becomes due and payable prior to its stated maturity otherwise than at the option of the issuer or any such amount of indebtedness is not paid when due or, as the case may be, within any applicable grace period.

Bankruptcy event means the declaration by the issuer of a moratorium in or rescheduling of payments on any external indebtedness.

Materiality means that the price of the reference asset less price adjustment is 90 percent or less relative to the initial price as reasonably determined by the calculation agent.

Publicly available information means information that has been published in any two or more internationally recognized published or electronically displayed financial news sources.

Nonetheless, if either of the parties or any of their respective affiliates is cited as the sole source for such information, then such information will be deemed not to be public information.

Price adjustment means the price of a reference U.S. Treasury security on the valuation date less the price on the effective date. The reference U.S. Treasury security will be selected by the calculation agent to match, as far as possible, the maturity and other features of the reference asset.

Market value means on any day, with respect to the relevant reference security, the percentage equal to the unweighted arithmetic mean of the firm USD-denominated bid prices (exclusive of any accrued but unpaid interest and expressed as a percentage of principal amount) for such reference security provided to the calculation agent on such day by at least two but not more than five referenced dealers.

Reference Credit:	United Mexican States (Ba2).
Reference Security:	United Mexican States, global bond.
	Maturity: February 2001.
	Currency Denomination: USD.
	Coupon: 9.75%.
Business Days:	Days on which commercial banks and foreign exchange markets settle payments in London and New York.
Calculation Agent:	Issuer.
Denomination:	USD 1 million.
Listing:	London Stock Exchange.
Lead Manager:	Issuer.

*****

CREDIT-SENSITIVE NOTES

Credit-sensitive notes provide for an increase in the coupon paid to an investor in the event of a downgrade. If the credit downgrade is severe enough, the investor may have the right to put the note back to the issuer.

EEC Thailand (IFCT) issued a credit-sensitive note in August 1997. The maturity of the note is 10 years, and the investor has the right to put the note to the issuer for any reason at the end of five years (European-style put). At the time of issue, IFCT rating was A3/A−. The coupon adjusts if the note is downgraded. If the note rating slips two notches to BBB, the coupon increases by 50 basis points (bps). If the note slips to BBB−, the coupon increases 75 basis points. If the note slips below BBB−, the investor can put the bond to the issuer any time over the life of the bond. This credit put is unrelated to the European put at the end of year five. Shortly after this bond came to market, five-year credit default put for IFCT traded at 50 basis points per annum.

INDEX-LINKED NOTES

Index-linked notes have been in the market for several years. The payoff at maturity, or sometimes the coupon of the securities, is subject to the performance of a basket of reference credits. This is very similar to the concept of an index-linked bond. Notes can be structured to give an enhanced payment if a basket of securities increases in value. Similarly, the note may give an enhanced payment if the basket of securities declines in value. This allows investors to take either a bullish or a bearish view on a basket of emerging-market countries or on a selected set of countries. The investor may earn a reduced coupon. The coupon is reduced by the amount of premium necessary to purchase an option on the upside or downside of the selected reference credits. These notes can also be structured as discount notes. If investors are willing to take principal risk, highly leveraged structures can be created.

For instance, an investor may accept a zero-coupon for the upside of a basket weighted with a pro rata payout of a basket of selected reference assets. The investor might choose one-third of the price upside of an

Argentine government bond, one-third of the upside of a Brazilian government bond, and one-third of the upside of a Russian government bond.

This concept can be extended to commodity price performance, first-to-default basket structures, or indexes of any kind. The following term sheet shows an example of a Standard & Poor's (S&P) bear note. The investor receives a payoff at maturity linked to the downside of the S&P 500 index. For every percentage point decline in the S&P, the investor receives one percent over par at maturity. This is a one-for-one payout on the downside of the S&P. If the investor were willing to take some principal risk and risk receiving 98 instead of 100 at maturity, the leverage on the payout could be increased. This type of structure, either a bear structure as shown in the term sheet or a bullish structure, is typical of index-linked notes.

The S&P bear note provides an enhanced return in the event of a sustained weakness in the U.S. equity market while protecting the investors' initial capital outlay. The S&P bear note could also be useful to partially hedge an underlying equity portfolio that the investor may wish to continue to hold for strategic reasons.

S&P BEAR NOTE
Term Sheet

Indicative Terms & Conditions:

Issuer:	AA rated financial institution.
Instrument:	Euro medium-term note.
Size:	Minimum USD 10 million.
Issue Date:	As soon as practical.
Maturity:	One year from issue date.
Issue Price:	100% of size.
Coupon:	Zero.
Redemption:	$100\% \times \{1 + [(\text{S\&P } 500_{\text{trade date}} - \text{S\&P } 500_{\text{maturity}})/ \text{S\&P } 500_{\text{Trade}}]\}$

expressed as a percent of par.

Minimum redemption 100% of par, where:

$S\&P\ 500_{trade\ date}$ = S&P 500 index at trade date as determined by calculation agent.

$S\&P\ 500_{maturity}$ = S&P 500 index closing level two days prior to maturity date as determined by the calculation agent.

Listing: None.

Arranger: Investment bank.

Calculation Agent: Arranger.

Note Seller: Investment bank.

Suitability: The bonds will be sold to an investor with such knowledge and experience in financial and business matters to be capable of evaluating the merits and risks of the prospective investment.

Updates: Calculation agent will provide updated pricing and payoff profile information for this note, upon request.

CHAPTER 7

Synthetic Collateralized Loan Obligations

Balance sheet management requires many tools. While single-name credit derivatives are gaining in popularity, they are an inefficient tool for laying off credit risk for a balance sheet of loans. In many ways, total return swaps (TRS) and credit default swaps are condiments to be used in conjunction with a broader strategy. We will talk more about bank best practices and credit management strategies later in this book. Key to the strategy of banks keen to lay off credit risk are synthetic collateralized loan obligations (CLOs).

This book is not meant to be a guide to securitization. The following discussion gives a brief refresher on some of the key features of securitization, but I will not delve into detail about the difference between term securitizations and conduits. Later, when I introduce some of the structures, I may leave out features that are not germane to the focus of the discussion, which will center around the imbedded credit derivatives and structural risks. For practitioners interested in more detail, I list some of my favorite resources in the bibliography.

COMMENTS ON SECURITIZATION

Most of the following comments apply to U.S. law and tax and accounting treatment, but the issues raised apply to any securitization. Securitizations must address issues of bankruptcy, accounting issues, tax and credit enhancement. For investors to have the highest priority claim against the assets in a securitization, they must have protection from bankruptcy of the original owner of the assets (the "seller") or any creditor lien including a government lien involving taxes. If a bank is the seller of the assets, then protection from bankruptcy of the original owner is not an issue. This protection is usually accomplished via a "true sale at law" of the assets to a special purpose entity (SPE). The SPE is a specially created corporation or trust that is "bankruptcy remote" from the original seller of the assets.

Accountants will want to ensure that the financing gets off—balance sheet treatment. Usually this means that the SPE must be legally independent of the seller. For instance, the SPE cannot be a wholly owned subsidiary of the seller, or the assets of the SPE would have to be consolidated on the seller's balance sheet under U.S. general accepted accounting procedures (GAAP).

Sellers want to avoid creating a taxable event by the sale of assets. For tax purposes, the seller wants to characterize this transaction as a financing. Tax laws are independent of bankruptcy treatment and accounting treatment. The securitization is usually structured as seller debt for tax purposes but as a sale for bankruptcy purposes.

Credit enhancement is another key feature of securitizations. Often several strategies for credit enhancement are employed in a single securitization. One method is to purchase a credit wrap purchased from a guarantor. This can be in the form of a surety bond guaranteeing principal and interest, although sometimes just principal is guaranteed. In this instance, the highest rating possible will be that of the credit wrap provider. The amount of credit enhancement depends on the deal structure and is usually expressed as a multiple of the expected loss level. For instance, to get an AAA rating, a general rule is that the credit enhancement must equal five times the expected loss level. The amount of enhancement required declines for lower rating requirements.

Overcollateralization is another form of credit enhancement. This may mean that more assets are placed in the SPE than are required to meet the deal's cash flow needs in a static environment. It may also mean that exogenous collateral, such as U.S. Treasury bills (T-bills) or bank certificates of deposit (CDs), is introduced to provide additional cash flow certainty.

Another credit enhancement method is using tranching to create more than one class of debt within a given structure. The holders of the lower or subordinated classes get a higher return along with higher risk. The subordinated debt holders agree to absorb losses before the senior debt holders. Several tranches may exist in one deal, and the payments due to each tranche holder are defined in the prospectus according to the tranche payment priority. Obviously, the more certain the payment, the higher the credit rating and the lower the return.

Two other methods are cousins and are often confused. The first is use of a reserve fund. The issuer will deposit cash or excess spread in a trust account, and these funds can be used to meet principal and interest payments as needed. The second method also involves excess spread and collateral interest remaining after payment of investor coupons, and fees can be used to offset nonperforming assets.

"Cash flow" transactions focus on the sufficiency of cash flow generated by the collateral pool to meet the interest and principal obligations arising from the notes issued by the CLO. The rating of the notes depends on this cash flow sufficiency. The notes issued in the Secured Loan Trust structure discussed later in this chapter get their ratings based on an estimate of sufficiency of cash flow to be roughly equivalent to those generated by an investment-grade-rated note. If the cash flow deal is properly structured, investors only experience a loss if there are defaults in the collateral pool. Cash flow CLO transactions have a two-to-four-year revolving period. Principal is reinvested, and there is no amortization during this "lock-out" period. The coupon is paid out of interest on the underlying collateral, and fees are also paid from this cash flow stream. During the lockout period, the excess spread in the deal usually generates cash flows to build cash reserves. Cash flow deals usually restrict trading. The lock-out period is followed by an amortization period in which both principal and interest are repaid usually according to a predetermined amortization schedule. These CLOs may amortize early if one of several unwind triggers is breached. In that case, investors will receive sequential payments of principal and interest. Their payment priority will depend on the tranche in which they invested.

"Market value" CLOs generally do not restrict trading and derive income both from trading and from interest on invested assets. The portfolio of assets is actively managed, and market as well as credit considerations are important to the asset manager. Investors who require a mark-to-market on their investments might prefer these structures. The ratio of the market value of assets to the face value of liabilities is the focus of a market value CLO. The "haircut" (required overcollateralization) of the assets protects investors from the price volatility, or volatility of the market value of the assets. These deals have built-in triggers so that the minimum haircut level must always be maintained or else the assets must be sold to pay down liabilities or the assets must be sold and exchanged for very highly liquid instruments. Market value deals are rarely used in synthetic securitizations because the trigger usually kicks in at the worst possible time. In the trigger scenario, the assets are likely to be at their most illiquid. Nonetheless, we may see more of these deals in a deteriorating economic environment when defaults increase. When the collateral pool includes defaulted bonds or loans, the market value approach may be more appealing because these assets do not generate predictable cash flow streams.

UNWIND TRIGGERS

There are several types of possible unwind triggers that can cause the early termination of a fixed-level structure or that can cause early amortization of an amortizing structure. These triggers will vary by structure and include insolvency of the issuer if applicable, breaching a boundary condition for collateral maintenance, or reaching a certain level of defaults on the underlying reference obligors or assets, among others.

Triggers are usually labeled as dynamic or static. The following is a description of a *dynamic trigger:* When a structure is linked to the issuer, if the mark-to-market of the swap reaches a prespecified percent of the market price of the asset, the issuer as swap counterparty may have the right to trigger an unwind. This prespecified trigger, known as the "gap margin," is usually set to 85 percent of the market price of the asset for liquid investment-grade assets, as this is the usual worst-case overnight move in underlying assets. This trigger will be set based on several factors: credit quality of the underlying assets, maturity of the transaction, size of the transaction, price volatility of the assets and derivatives transaction, and available endogenous and exogenous factors related to the quality of the underlying *asset* and swap. As an added fail-safe feature, this dynamic trigger can be scaled to decline as the public credit rating of the underlying assets declines.

A key factor in determining unwind triggers is the degree of liquidity of the underlying assets. The deal structurer usually conservatively sets unwind triggers to liquidate the underlying assets to cover the expected potential market-risk exposure on an imbedded swap. The potential market-risk exposure is the sum of the mark-to-market exposure on the swap plus the potential move of the underlying asset price and the swap mark-to-market between notice of liquidation and closeout.

Interest rate swaps imbedded in credit-linked structures are problematic. When they are employed at all, the issues that swaps pose depend on the seniority of the swap counterparty in the event of an unwind. Sometimes credit wraps are applied either to the swap or to the underlying assets themselves. Credit wraps enhance the overall rating of a structure.

A *static trigger* usually comes into play when a certain boundary condition is met. A predetermined level of defaults of the underlying assets, regardless of price, is an unwind trigger. In the event of default of the underlying asset, the Security Trustee liquidates the underlying assets by soliciting dealer bids. In the case of loans, there must be some pre-agreed pricing mechanism. If there is an interest rate swap involved, a deal poll will usually provide the mark-to-market on the derivatives transaction. The Security Trustee pays the swap counterparty the positive mark-to-market on the swap (if any) and remits any remaining value to the investors.

Another static trigger takes into account hypothetical worst-case assumptions about absolute price levels as a percentage of par value of the assets. An unwind trigger will be set for the asset prices reaching the estimated recovery value of the underlying assets in the event of default. Additional triggers may be set on a case-by-case basis.

SYNTHETIC CLOS

Investors have become familiar with the concept of tranching risks through products that have been in the market for years: collateralized mortgage *obligations* (CMOs), collateralized debt obligations (CDOs), and other tranched asset-backed securities. Synthetic CLOs create tranched exposure to a portfolio of reference credits. The difference between a synthetic CLO and another CLO is simply that we employ credit derivatives in the structure of the synthetic CLO. In fact, it is possible to create a synthetic CLO using only credit derivatives.

The terminology applied to synthetic CLOs is often confusing, and the only defense for this problem is to have a clear understanding of the structural features rather than to rely on arbitrary labels to guide understanding. The benefits of synthetic CLOs vary depending on the structure. In general, they are used to synthetically take assets off the balance sheet, in whole or in part; to reduce the required regulatory capital held against assets; to create a new source or sources of funding; to increase return on equity (ROE); and to increase return on assets (ROA). The effectiveness of various types of synthetic CLOs at accomplishing these goals is arguable. As we shall see later, reduction in asset risk is mixed, reduction in required regulatory capital varies by structure, and internal calculations of ROE or return on economic capital and ROA vary by financial institution.

Synthetic CLOs are sometimes called "balance sheet CLOs" to indicate that the issuer retains risk in the form of a first-loss piece. This first-loss piece is also called the equity piece and provides credit enhancement to the other tranches in the deal. If there is a default, the equity piece will absorb losses first, up to the cap amount indicated for this tranche. The J.P. Morgan structure discussed in a later section is a balance sheet CLO.

Arbitrage CLOs are created to sell the equity piece to outside investors who want the benefits of high yields and leverage at the cost of high risk. The investor requirements are an important deal driver for these structures. The "securitized loan trust" transaction discussed later is an arbitrage CLO.

One type of synthetic CLO works best for highly rated banks, and it is usually termed a hybrid structure. Credit risk is first imbedded in unrated or rated medium-term notes, and the medium-term notes are then securitized. There are several types of hybrid structures, but the two common major types illustrate the key concepts. First, if the medium-term notes were each linked to a specific balance sheet asset and if the entire credit risk of the asset were imbedded in the medium-term note, the structure would have all the elements of both a balance sheet CLO and an arbitrage CLO. In the event of default of the reference obligation, either the reference obligation would be delivered to the investor in lieu of par at maturity, or the investor would receive an early payout on the medium-term note equal only to the recovery value of the reference obligation. This is the case with some dedicated structures issued by SPEs. This structure is a pro rata basket credit-linked note, which has been dubbed a securitization. The second major type of hybrid synthetic CLO is a balance sheet CLO. Credit-linked notes are linked to the credit risk of a reference obligor but may not specify the exact reference obligation, although the seniority in bankruptcy will be specified. This is usually specified as a senior unsecured debt obligation that would have a recovery value of 51 percent, the average recovery value according to Moody's. This structure may or may not cover all the risk of the original owner of the asset. If the amount recovered is greater than 51 percent, this is a windfall for the original owner. If the amount recovered is less than 51 percent, the original owner may have residual unhedged risk to the reference obligor's senior unsecured debt. The credit-linked notes are then packaged in an SPE. The resulting pool of credit risks is then tranched and sold to investors. The junior notes are equivalent to the equity, and the original owner of the credit risks retains the junior notes. Because the original credit-linked notes used to create the pool of risks have the credit rating of the original seller of the credit risk, this structure works only for highly rated banks. To get the tightest offering spread possible for the senior tranche sold to public investors, an explicit credit rating is required.

Synthetic CLOs can be linked or delinked transactions. If the bank selling the assets is issuing medium-term notes in its own name with imbedded credit risk of another senior secured reference obligor, the CLO is said to be *linked.* This means that the medium-term-note rating is linked to the bank selling the assets, since the medium-term note can have a rating no higher than the credit rating of the bank selling the assets. If the selling bank's credit rating is not a factor in the structure of the synthetic CLO, the transaction is said to be *delinked.* This is the case for assets that have the status of "true sale under law."

The quality of the portfolio of reference credits is usually strictly controlled with an optimization program, which constrains credit quality, credit enhancement based on historical default levels, maturity, portfolio diversification, asset-to-liability maturity gap, and liquidity eligibility, among other potential criteria. The program uses many data inputs and takes into account recovery rates based on the debt position in the capital structure and collateral type. It is impossible to list all the possible model inputs and protective covenants. In fact, these may change depending on the collateral and deal structure. Future sections in this chapter will give the reader a better idea of the more common types of synthetic CLOs, and these descriptions should provide some intuition of the types of criteria required for individual synthetic CLOs.

The key to bringing a synthetic CLO to market is understanding how to structure and to sell the synthetic CLO. The structurer must understand the investors' needs, including regulatory, tax, and accounting issues. What investors have in common is that they value diversification as a good. As we mentioned before, the CLO should be structured so that the underlying reference obligations represent a well-diversified portfolio of credits. What constitutes a well-diversified portfolio of credits? One way to determine this is to calculate a Moody's diversity score. For instance, one could map each reference obligor to the appropriate industry classification. Standard & Poor's (S&P) has 39 industry classifications originally developed for collateralized bond obligations (CBOs), but the diversity score concept was first introduced by Moody's. Moody's has classifications for 32 distinct industries. Let's use Moody's for the following example. The mapping may require judgment calls, but one can get advice from Moody's while doing this. Once the reference obligors have been mapped, the structurer can use Table 7.1.

Usually for up to 20 firms in the same industry, the Moody's diversity score is 5.00, but this may be different depending on the names and the overall structure. For instance, if you have three reference obligors that fall into the industry classification "oil and gas," the diversity score is 2.00. Once you have done this for all your reference obligors and industry classifications, you sum the diversity scores to get the total diversity score for the portfolio. If you have only 32 reference obligors in a given portfolio, the best diversity score you could achieve is 32. This means that you have only one reference obligor in each industry classification. In terms of industry concentration, this is the most diversified portfolio, comprised of 32 reference obligations. Once the diversity score for a given deal is decided, this level must be maintained or bettered throughout the life of the deal, and the diversity score is stated in the deal prospectus.

The diversity score is not the entire story, however. The concentration by individual reference obligor is important. The concentration by country and sometimes by region in a country is also important. Synthetic CLOs will have limits on the maximum percentage in any given reference obligor, as well as on the maximum percentage in any given industry classification.

If we had only 32 reference obligors, the most diversified portfolio would invest only 1/32 in each name, or 3.125 percent in each reference

TABLE 7.1 Diversity Score of Firms in Same Industry

Number of Firms in Same Industry	Diversity Score
1	1.00
2	1.50
3	2.00
4	2.33
5	2.67
6	3.00
7	3.25
8	3.50
9	3.75
10	4.00
>10	Individually determined

Source: Moody's.

obligor. Of course, this is a simplified view because synthetic CLOs have many more reference obligations. For multinational deals, there may be limits for country risk concentration and for maturity for any given country. The key is to diversify and to limit concentration risk. For this purpose, an optimization program can be employed to help establish the reference portfolio. As with other models, the optimization program is a helpful guide, not a substitute for some manual labor and management judgment.

RATING CRITERIA

Moody's and S&P designed minimum rating-level criteria for the CEO market that can be adapted to the CLO market. Each rating agency is slightly different. I will once again focus on Moody's criteria. Moody's provides a table of rating factors to assign to each rating category. The principal amount of the loan is then multiplied by the rating factor for its assigned rating. The sum of these values is the cumulative rating. This cumulative rating must remain at a prespecified minimum level. Table 7.2 gives an example of how this would work for a portfolio comprised of equal amounts of four loans that have their internal credit categories already mapped to Moody's ratings. The weighted average sum of the rating factors is 282.5. On the Moody's

TABLE 7.2 Summary of Asset Rating Factors

Obligor	Amount ($M)	Moody's	Rating Factor
Loan 1	25	Aa3	40
Loan 2	25	A2	120
Loan 3	25	Baa3	610
Loan 4	25	Baa2	360

look-up table, a Baa1 rating has a rating factor of 260, and a Baa2 rating has a rating factor of 360. Therefore, we would assign a rating of Baa2 to this portfolio.

Of course, as we saw before, other considerations such as collateral could affect the portfolio rating. In an actual synthetic CLO, other considerations such as cash flow priority will affect tranche ratings.

In the preceding discussion, I avoided the issue of credit mapping. One of the key challenges for banks and other institutions hoping to securitize loans in the form of a synthetic CLO is mapping internal credit ratings for loans to Moody's and S&P credit ratings. Sometimes banks find that they are not internally consistent in the way they classify loans. This is an especially poignant problem when large banks merge. The merged bank may find they have dueling credit standards and incompatible loan systems. First, the merged bank must overcome these challenges and vet the new loan portfolio. Second, the merged bank must tackle the internal systems issues to be able to organize what is now a massive loan portfolio. The bank must set standards on economic capital to be reserved against the loan portfolio. This should lead to a consistent method for calculating the ROA and the ROE for the loan portfolio. When the bank is finally ready to securitize these assets with a synthetic CLO, it must map its internal credit ratings to the rating agency credit ratings. Now the bank is ready to evaluate the menu of structures available to determine the optimal benefits to reduction of regulatory and economic capital that affect returns. The various structures pose trade-offs in the available benefits, and newly merged banks typically spend more time wrangling with internal politburos than in the actual structuring of the first synthetic CLO.

BLACK BOX STRUCTURES

Many structures in the market present investors with a "black box." This refers to the fact that the collateral in the black box is not disclosed. Figure 7.1 shows one example of this type of structure in which a trust receives the total rate of return (TROR) of a pool of undisclosed assets. The investors receive the total rate of return on the pool of securities less a "funding cost," or fee paid to a bank arranger. The total rate of return to the investor is further enhanced because the investor receives an added premium for assuming the credit default risk in the event of the default of a defined reference credit. The diversified securities in the black box may receive a rating, and the reference asset rating is as high as or higher than the black box.

SECURED LOAN TRUSTS: SYNTHETIC CLOS AND TOTAL RETURN SWAPS

Collateralized bond obligations and collateralized loan obligations have been used in the mortgage market for more than 10 years. Just as in the "black box" structure, credit derivatives are used to create slight differences

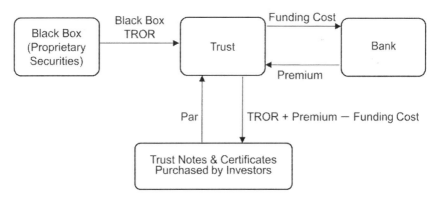

The Note Holders receive the TROR of the Black Box minus a fee (funding cost) except if a Reference Credit Event occurs. In that case, the Note Holders receive the recovery value of a Reference Credit Asset.

FIGURE 7.1 Credit-Linked Note: Total Return Swap and a Credit Default Swap

to well-known structures. Insurance companies in particular because very interested in these structures, particularly for CLOs backed by noninvestment-grade collateral. Whereas securitized loan trusts are created that result in AA rated floaters, the more interesting side of the transaction is the residual piece, also known as the equity piece. Figure 7.2 shows this side of the transaction.

Three major challenges in bringing a successful CLO deal backed by noninvestment-grade collateral to market revolve around the following three issues:

1. Finding appropriate collateral, whether highly leveraged transactions (HLTs), total return swaps on HLTs, marginal investment-grade collateral, or a small component of acceptable high-yield bonds.

2. Finding the fund manager.

3. Finding the equity piece buyer compatible with the fund manager choice.

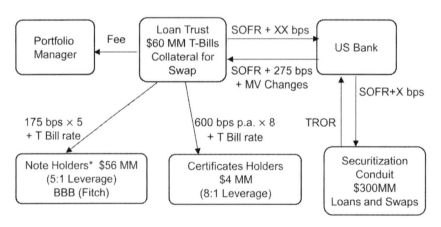

* Note Holders and Certificate Holders have pari passu cash flow priority. Profit and loss are magnified by leverage.

FIGURE 7.2   Secured Loan Trust

For CLOs with insurance company investors, the equity piece is tranched into two categories: a note and a certificate. The note is often investment-grade rated and held by an insurance company. Reclassified as a note, these cash flows now receive favorable balance sheet treatment for insurance companies. The certificate is now technically the equity piece. It is pari passu with the note, however. There are structures in which the certificate is subordinated, but it need not be, as in the example shown in Figure 7.2.

The only difference in cash flows is that the certificate has 8:1 leverage whereas the note has 5:1 leverage. The leverage will depend on the collateral and the structure. Rating agencies have strict criteria on how the collateral must be diversified for the note piece to achieve an investment-grade rating.

Diversification is key because it is related to correlation. As we saw earlier with first-to-default basket structures, concentration risk increases with increasing correlation. This is to say that the credit exposure due to event risk increases with increasing correlation. Furthermore, the point of the CLO is to diversify credit risk. Therefore, minimizing correlation among assets is key.

Both the note holders and the certificate buyers put up cash. This is used to purchase T-bills or other highly rated assets, which serve as collateral enhancement for the trust. If loans in the trust default, and if there is insufficient cash flow, the note holders and certificate holders suffer first. The note holder investment-grade rating is not on the entire cash flow amount of the base case scenario. In the case of the example shown in Figure 7.2, that would imply that the note holders receive an investment-grade rating on a note that has a coupon of around 14.75 percent $[(5 \times 1.75\%) + 6\%]$. The investment-grade rating may actually be on return of initial cash investment plus a nominal return. The note is technically investment-grade rated, but only for a low coupon. The potential excess above this low coupon would not receive an investment-grade rating due to the lower probability of receipt of a high, above-market return for a BBB asset.

In this way securitization conduits can obtain additional collateral to enhance a portfolio of assets and create salable equity or residual cash flows.

EQUITY PIECE BUYERS

The buyers of the certificate, or nominal equity piece, have typically been high-yield investors reaching for yield. In the example shown in Figure 7.2, the equity investor has the opportunity to earn interest on the posted Treasury collateral and a net of 600 basis points (bps) per annum (p.a.) with 8 times leverage. If we assume 6 percent for the Treasury collateral, plus 6 percent × 8 for the equity piece, the hedge fund has the opportunity to earn 54 percent. But these "opportunities" come with a great risk. Any losses on the reference obligations will hit the equity holder pari passu with the note holders, but with the impact of greater leverage. A rating is irrelevant to the certificate investors, but the quality and the diversification of the reference obligors are of keen interest to them due to the great risk involved. Certificate holders often demand full disclosure of the composition of the underlying portfolio and perform their own stress tests to satisfy themselves that the potential net reward is worth the risk.

Hedge funds will often ask to receive the equity cash flows in the form of a TRS, if this is possible. The hedge fund assumes the market risk and the credit risk of the equity piece, but this is a synthetic purchase in the form of a TRS and has the added advantage of providing additional leverage to the hedge fund as well as a potential tax advantage in some venues.

In the U.S. there are distinct tax advantages to doing a TRS on an equity piece, as opposed to purchasing the equity piece outright. Netting of interest income and expense can be difficult, and using a swap gets around a possible disallowance for Federal tax purposes. Swaps maintain the character of the income. All swap income is ordinary income. For an outright purchase, equity income can fall into the interest income and capital loss categories. Furthermore, for Federal income taxes, 3 percent of itemized deductions may be disallowed for highly leveraged assets. For state tax purposes, especially in New York where many investors are located, the investor may lose additional deductions. This treatment may change by the time you read this. The idea is to check the current tax and accounting treatment of structures. There may be hidden disadvantages or advantages.

CASH FLOW OVERVIEW

Earlier we mentioned that the note holders and the certificate holders could receive highly leveraged returns. What is the source of these cash flows? In the example shown in Figure 7.2, $300 million of reference obligations are paying an average coupon of the London interbank offering rate (LIBOR) plus 275 basis points. The loan trust receives these cash flows and pays LIBOR+XX bps to the bank sponsor. The net cash flow available to pay the note holders and the certificate holders is then 275 basis points per annum on $300 million minus the following: fees to the portfolio manager; XX, representing compensation to the bank sponsor in the form of the funding cost of the loan trust; and any retained spread to enhance the collateral of the loan trust.

Because we stated the returns in the static case environment for the note holders and the certificate holders, we can back out the remaining cash flows. We can ignore the interest rate return on the collateral because that cash flow stream is not involved in netting out the cash flow stream derived from the reference obligations. For the note holders, the net cash flows in the static case are $56,000,000 × 5 × 0.0175, or $4,900,000. For the certificate holders, the net cash flows in the static case are $4,000,000 × 8 × 0.06, or $1,920,000. The sum is $6,820,000 and represents approximately 227 bps per annum on $300,000,000. The underlying assets throw off 275 bps per annum. The bank sponsor, the portfolio manager, and the loan trust *have* more than 47 bps per annum to divide among themselves. On a deal $300,000,000 in size, this represents more than $1,410,000 per annum. There are obvious economies of scale in doing these deals, and that is why these deals are usually done with several hundred million dollars in underlying assets.

How much does the bank sponsor require? This figure is negotiable, but it is compared with opportunity costs for the bank sponsor. The bank sponsor is receiving the cash flows of a synthetic floating rate note (FRN). The implied rating of the floating rate note is usually approximately A or at worst BBB. The bank sponsor evaluates the degree of protection provided by the Treasury collateral, the diversification of the portfolio of HLTs, and the structural considerations of the secured loan trust (SLT).

Notice that I started from the point of view of the investor rather than from the point of view of the bank sponsor when I calculated the economics. In practice, this is usually the other way around—the bank sponsor chooses the collateral to create a structure appealing to investors while ensuring that payments to the bank sponsor represent adequate compensation.

RISKS TO THE BANK SPONSOR

Let's take a look at the other risks in this transaction. The TRS imbedded in this transaction is usually booked in the trading book of the bank sponsor. The bank sponsor engages in a "matched position" TRS. The TRS is a "back-to-back" transaction, and the bank sponsor's counter parties for both sides of the TRS are SPEs. The transaction structure is key to how the bank sponsor views the risk of the TRS.

The bank sponsor sells HLTs to the securitization conduit, or SPE. Alternatively, the HLTs may be owned by another entity. The securitization conduit pays the TROR of the HLTs to the bank sponsor, and the bank sponsor pays a funding cost. The bank sponsor then pays the TROR to the loan trust, which is a collateral enhanced SPE, thus hedging its position. The bank sponsor receives a "funding cost" from the loan trust. The bank sponsor is laying off the TROR risk with the loan trust, so the diversification of the loans in the securitization conduit and the degree of collateral enhancement are important structural considerations to the bank sponsor.

THE BANK SPONSOR AND COUNTERPARTY RISK

There are two counterparty risk scenarios from the point of view of the bank sponsor: (1) appreciation of the HLTs, and (2) depreciation of the HLTs. The scenarios are depicted in Figure 7.3. If the assets appreciate in value, the bank sponsor has risk to the securitization conduit. This risk can be miti-gated by frequently marking the TRS to market and settling value. U.S. regulatory capital guidelines provide a way to assess this risk. The first step is to mark-to-market on assets used as the underlying reference obligations in the TRS. The second step is to look up the add-on factor for the reference

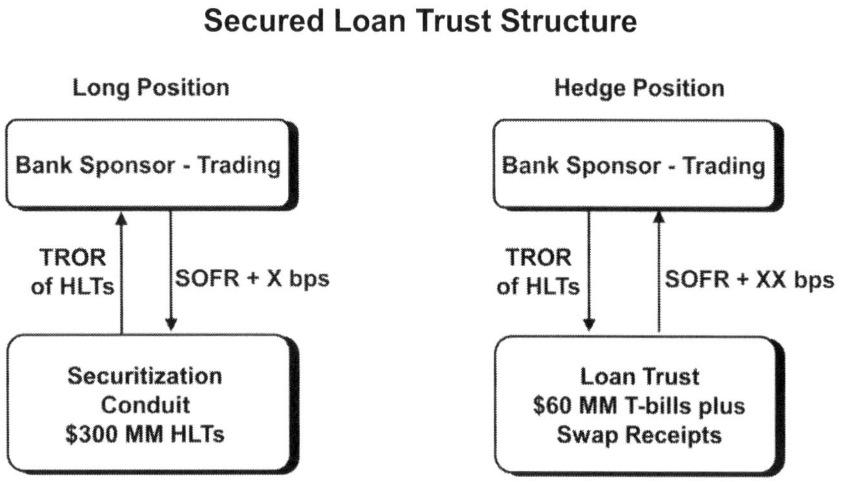

Secured Loan Trust Structure

Long Position   **Hedge Position**

Bank Sponsor - Trading   Bank Sponsor - Trading

TROR   SOFR + X bps   TROR   SOFR + XX bps
of HLTs   of HLTs

Securitization   Loan Trust
Conduit $60 MM T-bills plus
$300 MM HLTs   Swap Receipts

Long Position: Counterparty risk to bank if assets *appreciate* in value. Bank receives the appreciated value minus the original value (or the value at the start of the mark-to-market period) from the Securitization Conduit.

Hedge Position: Counterparty risk to the bank if the assets *depreciate* in value. Bank receives the original value (or the value at the start of the mark-to-market period) minus the depreciated value. The "depreciated value" is the recovery value in the event of defaults.

FIGURE 7.3 TRS: Bank Sponsor's Risk Perspective

asset specific risk. Unless one has modeled this risk in a way acceptable to U.S. regulators, one must use the former method for calculating regulatory capital. This method should be checked by venue, as regulations vary. For economic capital purposes, the bank sponsor evaluates the credit exposure to the securitization conduit, using a method similar to that outlined in the credit exposure section in Chapter 2.

The bank sponsor has risk to the loan trust, which as we mentioned before is an overcollateralized SPE. The bank sponsor in effect purchases market risk and credit default protection on its long position from the loan trust. If assets *depreciate* in value, the bank sponsor must receive a payment from the overcollateralized SPE. This should be mitigated by frequent mark-to-market and structural protection. For regulatory capital purposes, evaluating the counterparty risk captures this risk assessment. As we saw before, looking at the risk weight of the counterparty currently captures counterparty risk. In this case, the risk weight can be reduced initially by the amount of overcollateralization, but only because the collateral consists of T-bills, a cash equivalent. Under U.S. market risk guidelines, there is a provision for calculating the regulatory capital requirements. Adding the mark-to-market to the counterparty risk factor captures counterparty risk. The counterparty risk factor is available in a Federal "look-up" table. The economic capital required for the "long" position (receiving the TROR from the securitization conduit) is reduced by the amount of capital relief from the "short" position (paying the TROR to the loan trust).

STRUCTURAL CONSIDERATIONS

If the bank sponsor participates in these transactions, the TRS payment stream to the bank sponsor from the loan trust must be evaluated in the context of the CLO structure. The key consideration is the ability of the overcollateralized SPE to provide protection in the event of deterioration in the value of the HLTs.

The risk is analogous to a convertible bond. The TRS sometimes behaves like debt. When there is a rapid deterioration in the value of the HLTs, the TRS behaves like equity. The main risk to the bank sponsor is a big discontinuous drop in the value of the HLTs.

Without examining the key structural elements related to the TRS, it is impossible to assess counterparty risk. Key items to consider are shown in the following list, which is not intended to be all-inclusive because new structures raise new issues:

- What is the nature of the early wind-down trigger in the event of deterioration in value of the HLTs?
- What is the nature of the HLT collateral—credit quality, diversification?
- How much protection is provided by the degree of over-collateralization of the loan trust? What do the stress tests show?
- What is the priority of the bank sponsor in the event of an unwind?
- What is the nature of the collateral pledge in favor of the swap (in favor of the bank sponsor)?

Before attempting to view economic capital considerations, these key issues must be addressed.

Some bank sponsors view collateralization as a way for a counterparty to move up in credit class, in the internal implied rating system. Credit exposure, however, is unaffected for the purposes of managing internal credit lines. In the case of the Secured Laon Trust, there is no margin call on collateral. The equity investors and the certificate investors do not post additional collateral. The investors can lose no more than their initial investment. The structure must be evaluated in the context of the initial collateral and potential future risks.

SYNTHETIC SECURITIZATIONS
FOR HIGHLY RATED BANKS

On September 10, 1997, SBC Warburg (now UBS) launched a watershed deal in the credit derivatives securitization market. At an original initial offering size of U.S. $1.5 billion, it was the largest credit derivative transaction to date. The deal proved so popular that SBC upsized the deal to $1.75 billion at its launch. Motivated by the need to free up regulatory capital, return on capital considerations, dynamic credit risk management, and client confidentiality, SBC launched a credit-linked vehicle transaction, CLiVe.

Glacier Finance is the name of the special purpose vehicle (SPV) domiciled in the Cayman Islands that issues the senior/subordinated notes that are a part of the CLiVe. The senior notes are rated AA+/Aa1, and the amount of subordination is 8.25 percent. Unlike the CLOs issued previous to this deal, the SBC senior notes are bullet tranches with bullet maturities of five years and seven years. The five-year tranche was priced at LIBOR+16 bps, and the seven-year tranche was priced at LIBOR+19 bps.

An especially high degree of importance of client confidentiality is peculiar to Swiss banks because Swiss banking laws are very stringent and call for a 15-year prison penalty for violation of client confidentiality. To pre-serve this confidentiality, SBC imbeds the client credit risk in credit-linked notes (CLNs)—medium-term notes (MTNs) issued by Swiss Bank's New York branch. SBC chose the New York branch because funding is an expense item for tax purposes in New York. The credit risks arise from investment and commercial banking business: loans, derivatives, securities, and project loans. The MTNs are rated Aa1/AA+, the same as Swiss Bank's rating. The CLNs, the Swiss Bank MTNs, are used as collateral for the Glacier Finance SPV. The CLNs with the imbedded client risks are used in the place of loans. The maturity of the underlying credit risks and of the CLN collateral does not need to match the maturity of the notes issued by the SPV. The CLNs are callable by SBC on any interest-payment date, and SBC can therefore revolve credits imbedded in the CLNs into and out of the SPV. As CLNs in the SPIT mature, the SPV can use the cash to purchase other CLNs.

The MTNs collectively imbed the credit risk of a diversified pool of investment-grade borrowers. These credit exposures are referenced through a trust (see Figure 7.4). These credit risks are then tranched into a five-tranche structure. The mezzanine notes and the junior notes issued by the SBC Glacier Finance Ltd. SPV would merit lower credit ratings than the Aa1/AA+ rated senior notes. Therefore, this structure works best for highly rated banks.

The relationship managers and the line credit officers of the bank do not manage the credit exposures and do not know whether their client's credit is imbedded in CLNs used as collateral for the SPV. Only a few key credit officers have this information. In this way, client confidentiality is preserved because the assets in the SPV are Swiss Bank—issued medium-term notes, the CLNs.

SBC worked for months with Moody's and S&P to meet the diversity score tests for Moody's and the industry and issuer concentration tests for S&P. SBC also mapped their internal bank rating system to the ratings of Moody's and S&P. This allows SBC to continually revolve collateral in the SPV. SBC can call its CLNs and substitute others. This vehicle allows SBC's trading department to manage credit exposures. The rating agencies do not see the individual obligors. This is a blind pool, or a black box.

SBC defines the credit events for the MTNs it issues. The underlying reference credits are never revealed. The underlying credit risk is black box structure. The investors have recourse to the CLN, not to the underlying credit risks. If there is no credit event, SBC pays par at the maturity of the CLN. If there is a credit event, SBC calls the CLN and redeems the CLN at

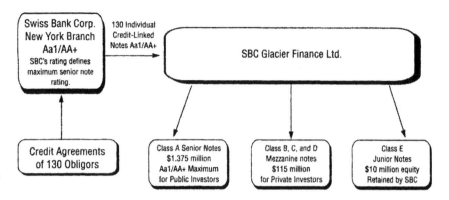

FIGURE 7.4 Historic Securitization: Glacier Finance Ltd.

the recovery value. The recovery value is determined by the senior unsecured debt obligation of the underlying reference credit. The SPV would receive a payment after 18 days of the determined recovery value. If there is no reference security, the payout is preset at 51 percent. As we saw in our discussion in Chapter 4 on pricing credit default swaps, 51 percent is the average recovery value for senior unsecured obligations according to the Moody's standard.

This structure sold well globally to banks, insurance companies, funds, and money managers. Although the investors bought a black box, the key to investor comfort was the stringent requirements for diversification that SBC had to meet to achieve its target ratings. Unlike first-to-default baskets, senior/subordinated SPVs must meet specific tests to maintain their ratings. For example, there is a concentration limit of 2 percent per obligor, although the individual obligors are not revealed. Diversification tests must also be met to minimize correlation. SBC achieved its goal of regulatory capital relief because the regulators look at the resulting credit protection as cash collateralized exposure.

The credit derivatives imbedded in the MTNs transfer the economic risk but not the legal ownership of the underlying reference assets. There is no sale of assets. In fact, there does not need to be an actual reference asset. The credit exposure can be any notional exposure wherever it occurs. The first loss is covered up to 49 percent if there is no defined reference asset because the assumed recovery rate is 51 percent. The structure provides regulatory capital relief and internal economic capital relief, but there is no accounting benefit under GAAP.

BISTROS

J.P. Morgan's signature product is the Broad Index Secured Trust Offering (BISTRO). Irreverent practitioners claim that the acronym's true meaning is BIS Total Rip-Off because the regulatory capital relief on this structure was not as great as originally anticipated. This is not entirely fair because limited regulatory capital relief is usually a feature of any structure in which the seller bank retains an equity piece. This synthetic securitization is a balance sheet CLO. The overall credit quality of assets referenced in a BISTRO is usually very high—single A and higher. Furthermore, these structures usually have very well diversified reference credits.

J.P. Morgan brought a five-year maturity private placement structure to market in December 1997, which appeared very similar to a reinsurance structure. J.P. Morgan referenced $10 billion of a variety of investment-grade exposures while issuing a deal of only $700 million in size.

J.P. Morgan created an SPV, which took in $700 million in proceeds and invested in U.S. Treasuries. The SPV then sold credit default protection to J.P. Morgan in the form of a $10 billion notional credit default swap, earning fee income in the process. The credit default swap referenced approximately 300 reference credits, each with a notional size of approximately $35 million and with an average credit rating of A3.

J.P. Morgan took the first loss piece, which comprised approximately 3 percent of the deal. Approximately 70 percent was an AA rated tranche priced at around LIBOR+30 bps. The remaining tranche was rated BB. Investors in the SPV's tranches received cash flows derived from the U.S. Treasuries plus the fees from the credit default swap with J.P. Morgan.

By June 2000, J.P. Morgan had closed 20 BISTRO transactions. The underlying exposures of the deals totaled more than $90 billion. By the time J.P. Morgan finished with its own balance sheet, it had developed a marketable technology. J.P. Morgan now structures BISTROs for other banks for millions of dollars in fees for each deal closed. The only thing inhibiting faster growth in the number of deals done is education in the banking community. The cost of funding BISTROs versus traditional CLOs is lower. Because legal ownership of the underlying assets is not transferred, the deals seem simpler legally. BISTROs also seem structurally simpler than traditional CLOs yet solve many of the economic and regulatory problems facing banks_

BISTROs employ credit default swaps using Morgan Guarantee Trust (MGT) as the credit protection purchaser, which pays a fee to the investors in exchange for the investors making a contingent payment to MGT under the conditions outlined for the investor-purchased tranche of the structure. These structures may also employ credit-linked notes in a fashion like the Glacier deal to transfer the risks of the portfolio of reference entities. The notes can be issued by either an SPE or by a bank. As with the Glacier deal, the exposures can derive from any number of sources, including loans, bonds, structured securities, or derivative transaction counterparties. BISTROs allow synthetic securitization of the risks of both funded and unfunded commitments.

The bank seller of the credit risks usually retains the first loss piece, or the equity piece. This first loss piece is also referred to as the "junior piece." It is sometimes misleading to say junior piece because many long-time structurers refer to subordinated tranches, which are lower-rated nonequity tranches, as junior pieces. When professionals discuss junior pieces, it is a good idea to ask for clarification to be sure which tranche is being referenced. Investors usually do not invest in the first loss (equity) piece.

The credit events are based on International Swaps and Derivatives Association, Inc. (ISDA) credit swap definitions. J.P. Morgan usually calculates the loss by soliciting bids from the market on senior unsecured obligations or even for specific bank credit facilities. As we shall see in Chapter 9's section on basis risk, we can no longer confidently refer to the documentation used in BISTROs as the industry standard. Practitioners are questioning ISDA credit swap definitions for credit events, especially where "restructuring" is used as a credit-event trigger. The market is now sensitive to the fact that different senior unsecured obligations may have very different price levels after the breach of a credit-event trigger. This may lead to scrutiny of documentation used in the creation of synthetic CLOs.

Investors may still take comfort in the overall high-credit quality of the underlying exposures, albeit the pool is usually on the order of 10 times the principal amount of the notes. Traditional CLOs are on the order of one-to-one, although this is a generalization. Overcollateralization may change that ratio. The key is the investor's loss exposure and the amount of credit enhancement. The rating is based on the former.

The motive of the bank credit-risk seller is regulatory and GAAP, if possible, capital relief. Notice that the original bank seller of the credit risks usually retains the equity piece. This means that the bank seller keeps the underlying credit risks on the balance sheet up to the threshold of the equity piece. This threshold provides credit enhancement for the buyers of the more senior tiers of the CLO.

The retention of this risk may be problematic for banks. The original sellers of the risks have not really rid themselves of all the credit exposures. Rather than generalize about the treatment of equity pieces, one should check the regulations appropriate for the venue. This may be as much as 100 percent capital to a lesser amount, depending on the venue and on the structure. If one requires further capital relief, it may be possible to securitize all or a portion of the first loss piece using technology for principal protected notes as discussed later in this chapter.

SECURITIZING FIRST LOSS RISK WITH PRINCIPAL PROTECTED NOTES

Virtually anything can be securitized. Even the first loss pieces of CLOs can be securitized. Hedge fund purchasers of the certificates in Secured Loan Trust (SLT) structures sometimes seek to perform just this type of securitization. The first loss equity piece is combined with either a Treasury zero-coupon bond or a corporate zero-coupon bond. The zero-coupon bond provides enhanced protection to the potential return of the original principal investment. Figure 7.5 shows an example of a principal protected structure.

I will simplify the economics of this transaction to illustrate the basic concept (see Figure 7.5). The investor pays par for the note. The proceeds are used to buy a zero-coupon bond trading at a discount to pat Suppose the investor pays $10 million for a five-year maturity note. The investment bank

Note: Fees are usually deducted from the note proceeds.

FIGURE 7.5 Securitizing First Loss Risk with Principal Protected Notes

takes out $250,000 in fees for structuring the note. If the five-year U.S. Treasury (UST) zero rate is 6 percent, the note will trade at a price of about 74.4. The remaining $2,310,000 can be used to invest in a pro rata portion of a basket of first loss pieces or even in a single equity tranche. At the end of the five years, the zero will accrete to par, and the investor will receive that amount at maturity with the credit assurance of the Treasury. Typically, a Treasury zero or a zero-coupon investment-grade-rated corporate bond is used for these structures.

The coupon on this security is another matter. Suppose the investor purchased the certificate for the SLT structure we mentioned earlier. The static case coupon was 54 percent, so the static case coupon on this note would be 23.1 percent of that (remember the fees), or 12.4 percent. This seems great! The investor has principal protection and a very high static case coupon. But what is the certainty that the investor will realize this coupon? That depends on the defaults in the original SLT structure. In other words, the investor should not be indifferent to the type of equity piece and the quality of the underlying SLT structure.

The expected loss to the equity tranche-based interest component of a principal-protected structure will be significantly greater than the expected loss to the principal component of the transaction. The effect of the greater expected loss on the expected loss to a transaction as a whole depends, in turn, on the relative current values of the interest and the principal components. Thus, the longer the life of the transaction and the higher the promised interest rate, the greater the effect that the credit risk associated with the interest component of the transaction will have on the expected loss.

To determine the expected loss to the principal-protected investor, the current values of the principal and the interest components of the certificates and the expected loss to each are combined. The expected loss to the entire instrument is the sum of the expected loss to the principal piece and the expected loss to the interest piece, each weighted by its respective present value.

The rating of a principal-protected note depends on how the "promise" of the note is structured. The rating is usually dependent on one of three scenarios:

1. The rating is based on potential return of principal only.
2. The rating is based on return of principal plus a "minimum" coupon. Or
3. The rating is based on return of principal plus all cash flow from the collateral.

Usually, Moody's is the rating agency of choice for principal-protected notes. In each case the rating is based on the expected loss to the investor from the benchmark of the promise. It is very important to refer to the benchmark on which Moody's is basing its rating.

Note that if the principal-protected note is rated AAA, the rating is based on return of principal only. The cash flows thrown off by the SLT certificate investment, which contributes the coupon cash flows, would not merit an investment-grade rating. The combined principal and "minimum" coupon-based rating might be investment grade. This would depend on the stated level of the minimum coupon and on the certainty of the cash flows. The third scenario is even more problematic. This rating will depend on the ratio of the principal to the more uncertain coupon cash flow stream and on the overall probability of receipt of the combined cash flows.

CREDIT ARBITRAGE FUNDS

Citibank was successful for more than twenty years prior to the 2008 financial crisis with credit arbitrage funds that it set up in its subsidiary. This was chiefly due to the expertise of the people Citibank had working for it.

Former staff from Citibank started their own funds or joined other banks to form new funds. The critical mass of people, talent, effort, and long lead time is usually the sticking point for banks. An additional stumbling block is that many bank boards have difficulty understanding the structure.

Most of these funds imploded during the 2008 financial crisis. If they did not have leveraged exposure to CDOs, they had exposure to Lehman or other entities that imploded. Just before the financial crisis, poorly managed funds proliferated. These structured investment vehicles (SIVs) invested in "highly rated" tranches of CDOs and leveraged them. The implosion of these funds was spectacular.

The following discussion is a simple outline of the credit arbitrage fund structure that describes the basic features. This applies to funds who do their credit research and stay away from opaque structured financial products and opaque financial institutions.

Principals establish an independent Cayman Island incorporated special purpose entity (SPE) with limited liability. The SPE engages in the activities of an investment company within proscribed parameters. A separately established "Investment Manager" conducts the investment activities of the SPE, which is a credit arbitrage fund.

The purpose of the SPE is to invest in bonds, notes, debentures, certificates of deposit, and debt securities of all kinds. Sometimes investment in credit derivatives is also possible. The SPE may enter into options, futures, and other types of hedging transactions. The SPE can raise funds and perform other incidental activities to support its investment portfolio.

Often the SPE will be a qualifying special purpose entity (QSPE) for U.S. accounting (FASB 125) purposes; that is, it will be an off—balance sheet, bankruptcy-remote entity. The SPE may have a wholly owned subsidiary, with a name along the lines of SPE Finance, Inc. (where SPE is the name given to the original Cayman SPE). This is usually a company incorporated under the laws of the state of Delaware for the sole purpose of issuing and selling debt securities as a nominee for the SPE. The Cayman SPE guarantees debt issued by SPE Finance, Inc.

The SPE typically funds itself with a euro medium-term note (EMTN) program and a U.S. euro commercial paper program. SPE Finance, Inc., will also usually have a U.S. commercial paper (CP) program and a U.S.

medium-term-note program. The Cayman SPE guarantees the obligations of SPE Finance, Inc., under the U.S. commercial paper program and the U.S. medium-term note program. The SPE may borrow and raise money in any currency and grant security over its assets to secure borrowings.

Program credit enhancement is provided by capital raised in the market. The SPE's capital will consist of "A" shares and "B" shares and capital notes denominated in a variety of currencies. The rights of the holders of the capital notes are subordinated to the rights of all other creditors, including holders of notes, on a winding up of the SPE. The economic rights of the A and the B shares are of equal rank. The returns are paid out to capital investors every six months. The returns are floating in character, and investors earn a benchmark floating rate (for example, previously LIBOR) plus a spread.

The ratio of issued and paid-up capital to investments under management is on the order of one to ten ($2 billion for $20 billion under management). Liquidity is usually obtained from liquidity facilities provided by Prime-1 (P-1) rated banks and liquid investment assets. Notes issued by these SPEs have ratings of P-1/Aaa, and CP issued by these SPEs have ratings of P-1. Any downgrade of any program rating triggers an unwind of the entire program.

The ultimate size of the asset portfolio is usually specified, and $20 billion was typical. Investments are strictly controlled with an optimization program, which constrains credit quality, maturity, portfolio diversification, asset-to-liability maturity gap, and liquidity eligibility. The SPE purchases a portfolio of high-grade assets, with an average AA credit quality. Average credit composition for the fund is approximately as follows: AAA/Aaa: 30 percent; AA/Aa: 40 percent; A/A: 20 percent; and BBB/Baa: 10 percent. The SPE is allowed to lever AA rated investments, usually up to eight times, but must use less leverage for lower-rated securities and may use more leverage for AAA assets. The SPE cannot invest in assets with a rating lower than a specified rating, usually BBB, with limited exceptions. The SPE may hold BB− /Ba3 assets if original holdings are downgraded up to a 10 percent portfolio concentration; typically, no assets with a lower rating may be held in the portfolio under any circumstances.

The vehicle funds itself to the extent possible by match funding CP and MTNs with purchased assets. It is desirable to have access to the derivatives pricing models and derivatives expertise to check value of the custom-tailored swaps (matching roll dates and so forth) required for this fund.

Distribution of the capital shares and notes has traditionally been done through a bank's capital market's sales force if the fund managers do not already have relationships with buyers. Typical buyers are capital preservation funds and high-net-worth individuals. Marketing pieces can be developed by the fund builders, and marketing sales calls are done as a joint fund/capital markets effort.

Capital markets contacts with the investment banking firms that will distribute the fund's CP and MTNs are very valuable to establish the necessary swap credit lines and distribution attention required to maintain low funding costs for the fund.

Management corporations contract with the A and the B share and capital note holder to earn a percent of the excess return above the benchmark floating rate plus some minimum number of basis points on the A and B shares and capital notes.

Investors in the A and B shares and capital notes of the SPE have no recourse to the sponsoring bank, only to the assets in the SPE. Investors in the MTNs and CP issued by the SPE also have no recourse to the sponsoring bank. Often the sponsoring bank will invest in the form of liquidity and in the shares and capital notes of the SPE, but this is not a fast rule. This is usually viewed as a strong positive signal to other potential investors, however.

The investment experience in a well-managed fund was good up to the financial crisis, but systemic risk finished most of them off. Investors in the CP and MTN issuance of the SPE received assets of the highest rating backed by a pool of well-managed and credit-enhanced collateral. The fund made no maturity, interest rate, or currency bets and invested in high-grade assets. But some of those "high grade" assets were opaque financial institutions with enormous hidden risk on their balance sheets: the banks' blind spot.

CHAPTER 8

Selected Issues: Documentation, Regulatory, Booking, & Legal

For even the simplest credit default transaction, three different jurisdictions can be involved: (1) the jurisdiction of the default protection seller, (2) the jurisdiction of the default protection buyer, and (3) the jurisdiction of the reference credit. Within each jurisdiction, different regulatory bodies may have a say in treatment of the transaction: bank regulatory authorities, insurance company regulatory bodies (for insurance company investors), the International Swaps and Derivatives Association, Inc. (ISDA), ministries of finance, tax authorities, the Bank for International Settlements (BIS), and securities firm regulatory authorities, just to name a few.

This book does not attempt to cover all of the issues involved with these transactions. It is the responsibility of the participants in these transactions to determine the documentation, regulatory, booking, and legal issues involved. But the situation is fluid. In this chapter, I highlight issues to keep in mind while investigating these transactions.

The web sites of the Bank of England, the Federal Reserve, Germany's Bundesaufsichtsamt fuer Finanzdienstleistungsaufsicht and other countries' regulators publish local regulatory guidelines for credit derivatives.

There is no substitute for good legal advice for credit derivatives documentation. There is no substitute for checking with local regulatory authorities for proper capital treatment of transactions. And there is no substitute for professional accounting and tax advice to determine the booking treatment of credit derivatives transactions.

HIDDEN COSTS IN DEFAULT LANGUAGE

Among the issues discussed earlier is the "bid/ask" of documentation. Buyers of credit default protection will attempt to put as many trigger events as possible into the credit default protection language. The ISDA master documentation allows for a variety of trigger events and provides many standard definitions.

Buyers of credit default protection want the most triggers. Sellers of credit default protection want to minimize triggers. ISDA attempted to standardize credit derivative confirmation language by issuing draft confirmations such as the International Swaps and Derivatives Association's "Confirmation of OTC Credit Swap Transaction Single Reference Entity Non-Sovereign," December 15, 1997. ISDA, revised it in 1999. It revised credit event definitions in 2003. It revised settlement protocol in 2009. It revised definitions again in 2014. No one sees unforeseeable problems but the "ISDA standard" often misses foreseeable problems. There are several examples throughout this book.

BASIS RISK: INFORMATION ASSYMETRY, DELIVERY OPTIONS AND CREDIT EVENTS

Several earlier sections of this book discussed basis risk. Sloppy documentation can create its own kind of basis risk. Another kind of basis risk has to do with acceptable delivery and with what constitutes a credit event in the first place. Although we already saw several examples of areas of concern for interpretation of a credit event, one particular type is worth revisiting.

In the fourth quarter of 2000, the credit derivatives dealer community was up in arms about credit default protection on Conseco. Banks that owned and underwrote Conseco loans included restructuring as a credit-event trigger. This was common in credit derivatives documentation. Delivery in the event of a credit event could be either a bond or a loan. This also was common in credit derivatives documentation. This is precisely why we spent so much time on the potential documentation risk of credit derivatives earlier in this book. The documentation in this transaction led to significant risk to the credit default protection providers.

A restructuring of Conseco loans by the banking community triggered a credit event, and the banking community delivered long-dated deeply discounted bonds to the credit default protection providers. The long-dated bonds were susceptible to both market risk and credit risk. Furthermore, as we discussed earlier, long-dated bonds often trade at drastically reduced prices to short-dated bonds under workout situations. The price disparity between long-dated bonds and loans is even more pronounced in these situations. The credit default protection providers had to pay the difference between par and the market price of the discounted bonds. Meanwhile, the loans, which motivated the protection purchase in the first place, were valued at a much higher price. The dealer community felt burned two ways. They felt the banking community was closer to the Conseco situation, given that they had underwritten the loans. They also felt that the banks had some control over the restructuring. Finally, by delivering the deeply discounted bonds, the banks were not acting in good faith.

There is nothing wrong with imbedding a delivery option into credit default documentation, but one should get paid for the imbedded option. That did not appear to be the case in this instance.

The credit default protection providers were surprised. I was surprised, too. I was surprised that the protection providers seemed to be unaware that they had exposed themselves to this risk. Delivery matters. If I give my counterparty the option of delivering a menu of possible choices with potentially different market values, I have just written a delivery option. This delivery option has an economic value. I do not want to give away that option for free. I am not indifferent between delivery of a bond or a loan. Often, I am not indifferent to which in a menu of bonds I'm being delivered, as we saw in the section on geared default options.

The reaction was swift, and this incident sensitized the entire dealer community. Credit default contracts are now being written excluding restructuring as a credit event. Banks hedging loans cannot use those credit default options, however. When banks buy credit default protection against their loan portfolios, they require that restructuring be specified in the credit default protection contract. The banks in the Conseco transaction that took the short-term opportunity nearly closed the door for themselves for future credit hedging transactions.

This kind of upset is good for a new market. Eventually cooler heads will prevail, and solutions and compromises to this problem will be negotiated. As of this writing, there is no standard solution. But already sound proposals are being presented to the International Swaps and Derivatives Association (ISDA).

To eliminate "gaming" from the settlement procedure, practitioners proposed language to ISDA to tighten up the definition of restructuring as a credit event. They are proposing the deletion of some of the more troublesome points in the ISDA language on restructuring and the addition of provisions to describe the limitations to what can be delivered. In the case of a credit-event triggered by a restructured loan, some practitioners are proposing either delivery of the restructured loans or cash settlement somehow tied to the perceived market value of the restructured loans. This will be difficult because the market value of restructured loans is very difficult to ascertain. One proposal calls for five quotes on loan prices. The high and the low prices would be discarded, and the price used would be the average of the remaining three loan prices. It may be difficult at times to get *five* banks to offer quotes. Another proposal would allow delivery of a floating rate note (FRN) with a maturity shorter than or equal to the final maturity of the credit derivatives contract. This is an attempt to limit market risk while capturing the credit risk. The difficulty here is that floating rate notes with the required maturity may not be available in the market.

Even delivery of the loan presents challenges. It takes time to arrange for all the required consents to a loan assignment. There is variability in the lag time between settlement of distressed loans and the trade date for a distressed loan. The Loan Syndications and Trading Association (LSTA) and ISDA have formed a joint working group to advise ISDA's credit derivative documentation group on issues that arise in connection with the physical delivery of a loan as settlement for a credit derivatives transaction.

I speculate there may be broader implications. Synthetic collateralized loan obligations (CLOs) that have this imbedded risk in the credit default documentation may have to be reexamined. This may be of particular concern to investors in the mezzanine pieces of synthetic CLOs. One might argue that since banks usually retain the equity, they would play games with the recovery values, but the above incident raises some concerns.

It seems clear that the market trend is to create clearer documentation. Lawyers can help in this process, but they cannot determine the business risks that one is willing to underwrite. There is no substitute for a good lawyer. Equally there is no substitute for business units to clearly define the risks they are willing to take for a given price and the risks they are not willing to take for a given price. In the end every risk has its price, but before one can price the risk, one must define the risk.

Do not be misled if you are told the documentation will be "standard." A close read of a document will reveal many idiosyncrasies. Users of credit derivatives have thrown in other triggers, including events leading to lack of convertibility of the currency, war, confiscation of nonlocal bank assets, and hostilities as well as broadly defined government actions.

The following language sample is typical of what a large U.S. international commercial bank will introduce as a credit event definition when it is the default protection buyer. This is adopted from the standard ISDA language from the "OTC Credit Swap Transaction Single Reference Entity Nonsovereign" draft of December 15, 1997. This is made generic for a sovereign obligation but includes triggers normally reserved for corporate debt. Just insert the particular sovereign in place of the bracket phrase [relevant government entity].

Credit Event

Each of the following shall constitute a credit event and shall apply to this transaction:

bankruptcy

credit event upon merger

cross-acceleration

cross-default

currency convertibility

downgrade

failure to pay

governmental action, including war, hostilities, and confiscation

market disruption

repudiation

restructuring

When determining the existence of occurrence of any credit event, the determination shall be made without regard to (a) any lack or alleged lack of authority or capacity of the reference entity to enter into any obligation, (b) any actual or alleged unenforceability, illegality, or invalidity with respect to any obligation, (c) the failure of the reference entity to make any payment as a result of compliance with any applicable law, order, regulation, decree, or notice, however described, or the promulgation of, or any change in, the interpretation by any court, tribunal, regulatory authority, or similar administrative or judicial body with competent or apparent jurisdiction of any applicable law, order, regulation, decree, or notice, however described, or (d) the imposition of or any change in any exchange controls, capital restrictions, or any other similar restrictions imposed by any monetary authority.

CREDIT EVENT DEFINITIONS

Bankruptcy means the reference entity or any government entity: (1) is dissolved (other than pursuant to a consolidation, amalgamation, or merger); (2) becomes insolvent or is unable to pay its debts or fails or admits in writing its inability generally to pay its debts as they become due; (3) makes a general assignment, arrangement, or composition with or for the benefit of its creditors; (4) institutes or has instituted against it a proceeding seeking a judgment of insolvency or bankruptcy or any other relief under any bankruptcy or insolvency law or other similar law affecting creditors' rights, or a petition is presented for its winding-up or liquidation, and, in the case of any such proceeding or petition instituted or presented against it, such proceeding or petition (a) results in a judgment of insolvency or bankruptcy or the entry of an order for relief or the making of an order for its winding-up or liquidation, or (b) is not dismissed, discharged, stayed, or restrained in each case within 30 days of the institution or presentation thereof; (5) has a resolution, order, or decree passed for its winding-up, official management, or liquidation (other than pursuant to a consolidation, amalgamation, or merger); (6) seeks or becomes subject to the appointment of an administrator, provisional liquidator, conservator, receiver, trustee, custodian, or other similar official for it or for all or substantially all of its assets; (7) has a secured party take possession of all or substantially all of its assets or has a distress, execution, attachment, sequestration, or other legal process levied, enforced, or sued on or against all or substantially all of its assets and such secured party maintains possession, or any such process is not dismissed, discharged, stayed, or restrained, in each case within 30 days thereafter; (8) causes or is subject to any event with respect to it, which, under the applicable laws of any jurisdiction, has an analogous effect to any of the events specified in clauses (1) to (7) (inclusive); or (9) takes any action in furtherance of, or indicating its consent to, approval of, or acquiescence in, any of the foregoing acts.

Credit Event upon Merger means the reference entity consolidates or amalgamates with, or merges with or into, or transfers all or substantially all of its assets to another entity and the creditworthiness of the resulting, surviving, or transferee entity is materially weaker than that of the reference entity immediately prior to such action.

Cross-Acceleration means the occurrence of a default, event of default, or other similar condition or event (however described), other than the failure to make any required payment, in respect of the reference entity or any government entity under one or more obligations or government obligations in an aggregate amount of not less than the default requirement that has resulted in any such obligations or government obligations becoming due and payable before they would otherwise have been due and payable, unless the reference entity or government entity shall have made all payments on the date that such obligations or government obligations became due and payable.

Cross-Default means the occurrence of a default, event of default, or other similar condition or event (however described), other than a failure to make any required payment, in respect of the reference entity or any government entity under one or more obligations or government obligations in an aggregate amount of not less than the default requirement that has resulted in any such obligations or government obligations becoming capable at such time of being declared due and payable before they would otherwise have been due and payable.

Currency Convertibility means any governmental or regulatory authority, agency, or instrumentality of the [relevant government entity], after the date hereof, (1) imposes exchange control policies or material convertibility restrictions on the [relevant domestic currency], (2) otherwise seeks to regulate the exchange rate of the [relevant domestic currency] into or for any other foreign currency including, without limitation JPY, DEM, or USD, or (3) imposes any law, rule, regulation, or policy, or official interpretation of any of the same having an effect substantially similar to the foregoing.

Downgrade means the credit rating reaches or is lower than the specified rating or the downgrade obligation is no longer rated by any rating agency.

Failure to Pay means, after giving effect to any applicable notice requirement or grace period, the failure of the reference entity or government entity to make, when due, any payment equal to or exceeding the default requirement under any obligation or government obligation.

Governmental Action means' (1) any governmental or regulatory authority, agency, or instrumentality, or any court or tribunal (a) asserts that the performance by the reference entity or any government entity of any covenant or obligation under any reference obligation or government obligation is unlawful or unenforceable against the reference entity or any government entity, or (b) declares a moratorium on the payment or performance of all or any portion of any reference obligation or government obligation, or (c) declares a general moratorium on banking activities in the [relevant government entity], or (d) asserts that the purchase or sale of any reference obligation or government obligation or the exercise of any right of a holder under any reference obligation or government obligation is unlawful or unenforceable in relation to the covenants and obligations of the reference entity or any government entity, or (e) purports to divest title to or beneficial or economic interest in any reference obligation or government obligation from any holder or group or class of holders of any reference obligation or government obligation; or (2) the occurrence of any war, insurrection, revolution, armed conflict, or outbreak or escalation of hostilities that substantially impairs the functioning of the government of, or banking activities in, the [relevant government entity].

Market Disruption means (1) trading generally shall have been suspended or materially limited in London, Tokyo, or [relevant government entity]; or (2) there shall have occurred any war, insurrection, revolution,

> or armed conflict, or outbreak or escalation of hostilities or any change in financial markets or any calamity or crisis that, in either case, is material and adverse to the reference entity or any government entity or the markets for the reference obligation or any government obligation.

> *Repudiation* means the reference entity or any government entity disaffirms, disclaims, repudiates, or rejects, in whole or in part, or challenges that validity of, any obligation or government obligation.

> *Restructuring* means a waiver, deferral, restructuring, rescheduling, standstill, obligation exchange, or other adjustment occurs with respect to any obligation or any government obligation, and the effect of such is that the terms of such obligation or government obligation are, overall, materially less favorable from a credit or risk perspective to any holder of such obligation or government obligation.

General Definitions

> *[Relevant Domestic Currency]* means the lawful currency, from time to time, of the [relevant government entity].

> *Government Entity* means the [relevant government entity], or any political subdivision or agency of the [relevant government entity], or any person controlled or supervised by and acting as an instrumentality of the government of the [relevant government entity].

> *Government Obligation* means with respect to a government entity, any obligation (whether present or future, contingent or otherwise, as principal or surety or otherwise) for the payment or repayment of money (in any currency whatsoever).

> *Reference Entity* means the issuer of the credit obligation.

> *Reference Obligation* means with respect to the reference entity, [any obligation (whether present or future, contingent or otherwise, as principal or surety or otherwise) for the payment or repayment of money]

[any obligation (whether present or future, contingent or otherwise, as principal or surety or otherwise) in respect of borrowed money] [the following obligations:] [the reference obligation(s)].

This contract throws in just about every definition. Notice that a credit default protection seller who agrees to the foregoing conditions accepts triggers that do not reflect lack of payment on the reference obligation or other financial obligations of the relevant sovereign. Lack of convertibility of the currency may not mean that the debt of the sovereign is in default. It could be a worrisome event to holders of the sovereign debt obligations, however. The same might be said for outbreak of hostilities. By these definitions, the Gulf War would have been a credit-event default trigger for U.S. government debt.

All language is negotiable, however. The default protection seller does not have to accept this language. Indeed, most of the default protection language examined in Chapter 4 was much less stringent than the foregoing language. See also the section on geared default options in Chapter 4 to review a sample of other pitfalls in term sheet and confirmation language.

We also saw earlier that credit default language often includes protection for market risk for the default protection buyer. This is usually in the form of a clause in which the default protection seller agrees to pay hedge termination costs for the default protection buyer. Strictly speaking, this is not sovereign risk at all. The hedge might be a cross-currency swap or a spot forward currency transaction. No one has forced the buyer to connect such a transaction with the reference obligation. The buyer will often ask the default protection seller for indemnification for these costs, however. The default protection seller can and should demand additional premium for this convenience.

GUARANTEES, INSURANCE, AND CREDIT DERIVATIVES

The Federal Reserve views credit default protection as a guarantee for purposes of the banking book. This means that credit default protection sold from the banking book does not have to be marked to market.

It is best not to use the word *guarantee* in a credit default swap contract.

The legal versus the regulatory interpretation can be subtle, but important. In England, for instance, a special body of rules applies to contracts of guarantees, but not all these rules will necessarily apply to credit default protection.

If credit derivatives were to be classed as insurance contracts, this could create problems in certain jurisdictions. In England, for instance, this could mean that the seller of a contract is creating a criminal offense if the seller is conducting unauthorized insurance business. The contract may be unenforceable and the buyer of the protection may have the right to recover any fees paid.

The problem is that credit default protection and convertibility protection look a lot like insurance. These contracts have many of the elements of an insurance contract. Indeed, the export finance companies refer to this protection as insurance, and private insurers write insurance contracts for this protection. Banks have long been in the legal business of providing credit guarantees, however, in the form of letters of credit (LOCs).

There are key differences between credit derivatives and insurance contracts, however. Often, even if a counterparty has not suffered a loss, a payment must be made. In the case of credit spread options, for instance, or in the case of a credit default option in which the protection buyer does not hold the reference asset, a payment is not necessarily related to an actual loss.

Law firms such as Allen & Overy in the United Kingdom have opined that credit default swaps are not insurance for purposes of U.K. law. Credit default contracts should be reviewed by legal counsel to avoid potential problems.

BOOKING ISSUES

As we saw with the first-to-default options, booking issues can be very important in the way a credit derivatives trader recognizes profitability. Further, there is no clear guidance on how credit derivatives must be booked. Several Japanese and Swiss banks sell credit default protection and do not mark these positions to market. This transaction is viewed as "bank business," as a guarantee that does not have to be marked to market. The credit default premium is taken into income as a fee, just as a fee for an LOC or an unfunded loan would be taken into income.

This treatment does not work for other banks that want to reduce "loan" exposure. Often credit default protection is traded out of a separate credit derivatives trading book. This position must be marked to market. In this case, a buyer of credit default protection, who sells protection simultaneously, wants to net off his position. Both positions must be marked to market.

Certain bank sellers of convertibility protection are also booking this protection as a country guarantee. This position is not marked to market. Other bank sellers trade this protection out of their credit derivatives trading book and must mark this position to market. As we saw in the section on convertibility pricing, marking convertibility protection to market is very difficult. Marking convertibility protection to "model" is impossible.

There is an advantage for banks and other institutions that are not required to mark their positions to market. There is a significant savings in administration and a significant savings in model booking. There is also a significant savings in time required to satisfy other bank managers that marking techniques provide reasonable, reproducible, and defensible results.

REGULATORY CAPITAL

Regulatory capital is the capital that banks must reserve against assets or against transactions. The Bank for International Settlements (BIS) in Basel sets general guideline. The guidelines have gone through several iterations: Basel I, II, and III: Check the BIS website for the most up to date guidance. As of this writing, banks use the Basel III framework. You can find current details at https://www.bis.org/bcbs/basel3.htm. Local regulators' guidance varies by country. Check local regulators' websites to see if local guidance differs from BIS guidance. The guidance that requires the most regulatory capital wins.

Regulatory capital affects banks and some of the government-sponsored export finance companies that have investment and trading portfolios. Currently, the minimum amount of capital that banks must reserve against assets is 8 percent. This minimum applies to transactions or assets that have a 100 percent BIS risk weighting. Banks will often inquire as to the BIS risk weighting of a transaction.

The reason this is important to banks, in particular, is that the risk weight affects the return on capital (ROC) calculation. This is not return on *economic* capital; it is the return on *regulatory* capital. The following example shows the ROC for a bank that holds a 100 percent risk-weighted asset. This is compared with the cash flows in which the bank holding the asset hedges the risk with a lower-credit-quality bank that has a higher funding cost. The hedging bank can choose the lower of the risk weighting of the bank counterparty or the asset on which it purchases credit default protection.

Let us reconsider our earlier example of the AAA institution holding a BBB asset and a single-A institution holding a BBB asset. If we compare an outright purchase by both banks, with the AAA bank purchasing the asset and simultaneously purchasing credit default protection from the single-A bank, the economic capital treatment for the two alternatives would be as shown in Figures 8.1 and 8.2 using hypothetical market spreads.

Often presentations and market literature will show examples such as that shown in the example in Figures 8.1 and 8.2 and include income for the invested regulatory capital. The assumption is that regulatory capital is invested in riskless market instruments such as U.S. Treasury bills (T-bills).

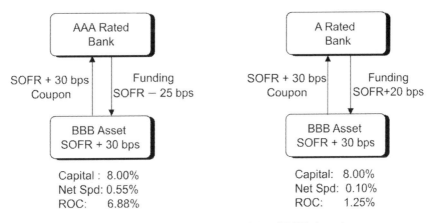

FIGURE 8.1 Cash Ownership of BBB Asset

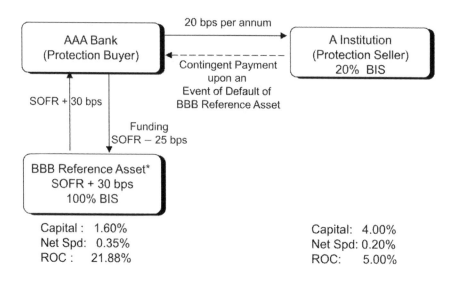

FIGURE 8.2 Regulatory Capital Effect of Credit Default Swap to Offset BBB Asset

This suggests a higher return on regulatory capital than the numbers shown in the example. I think this approach overstates return on capital because it does not take into account cost of capital. If I assume my cost of capital is the same as the return from investing in T-bills, the cost of regulatory capital and return on investment of regulatory capital nets to zero.

Using the off—balance sheet credit derivative to hedge the position of the AAA bank improves the position of the AAA bank dramatically. Not only does the AAA bank create a synthetic AA asset with a synthetic coupon of SOFR plus 10 basis points (bps), but the bank also reduces its regulatory capital requirement. Despite a lower net spread after hedging, the return on capital increases from 6.88 percent to 21.88 percent, a multiple of 3.18.

Notice that I assume that the single-A rated bank books this credit derivative as an unfunded letter of credit (LOC) to achieve a 4 percent BIS capital treatment versus an 8 percent capital reserve for the outright purchase. Nonetheless, the return for the bank with a funding cost of SOFR+20 bps is very low. This illustrates why banks with high funding costs are reaching for yield. While the return of the single-A bank is still low, the difference between owning the asset outright and taking in premium is 1.25 percent versus 5.00 percent.

This is a 400 percent improvement in the return on capital. Regulatory capital applies to the banking industry, but because banks make up most of the credit derivatives transactions, regulations that affect banks indirectly affect the entire market.

From the point of view of capital, the difficulty banks face in using credit derivatives is that there is no clear guidance on how credit derivatives should be treated for regulatory capital. As we saw in the section on first-to-default basket options in Chapter 4, the current suggested regulatory capital treatment can seem punitive. The Bank of England currently suggests that the buyer and the seller consider capital and exposure using the worst-case scenario. *Both* the buyer and the seller can't experience the worst-case scenario at the same time, however. Further, both can experience an intermediate scenario from the worst case for either of them, even in the event of default of one of the credits in the basket (which may never happen).

The current dogma on regulatory treatment gives market professionals an uneasy feeling. I often hear complaints: The regulations seem incomplete, the regulations seem arbitrary, the regulations seem unsatisfying. This is often true of new products, which are not easily pigeon-holed into existing categories.

As we saw earlier, for total return swaps (TRS), an investor bank that hedges a long position by paying the total return to a counterparty versus receiving a floating rate payment can choose the lower of the risk weight of the counterparty *or* the reference long position. In this case, the counterparty, the receiver of the total return, is a protection seller. For example, if the investor bank's reference asset is 100 percent BIS risk weighted and the counterparty is an OECD bank, the risk-based capital required for the investor bank hedging a long position is reduced from 8 percent of the principal amount to 1.6 percent of the principal amount. This is because OECD banks enjoy a 20 percent risk weighting no matter what their credit rating. Some state-sponsored finance companies, such as Finnish Export Credit and Swedish Export Credit, are also 20 percent BIS risk weighted. As we saw in the earlier examples in this section, a reduction in the required regulatory capital from 100 percent to 20 percent has an enormous impact on return on equity.

To make life even more interesting, there are anomalies in regulatory treatment in different banking jurisdictions. The Bank for International Settlements in Basel sets the guidelines for regulatory capital treatment, but these guidelines are subject to interpretation by ministries of finance and central banks in various countries. It is not uncommon to have different regulatory capital in Germany, England, and the United States for various transactions. For a time, special purpose vehicles (SPVs) collateralized with Italian government debt were interpreted by most German banks to have a 100 percent BIS risk weight, whereas the Bank of England allowed a 20 percent BIS risk weight. In the future, in the credit derivatives market, I expect to see similar anomalies, which may motivate certain types of cross-border transactions.

U.S. and European banks generally view bank debt as 20 percent BIS risk weighted and bank holding company debt as 100 percent BIS risk weighted, but that is not true everywhere. In Japan, bank holding company debt is treated as having a 20 percent BIS risk weight. From a regulatory capital view, it is more advantageous for a Japanese bank to purchase a credit-linked note from a bank holding company issuer than for a European bank to do so.

Many Japanese banks offer and document their sales of credit default protection on corporates as standby credit facilities. As an undrawn facility, it attracts only a 50 percent BIS risk weight.

In general, many OECD banks interested in reducing regulatory capital requirements are eager to buy credit protection on Brazil or Argentina while simultaneously selling credit protection on Mexico. The reason is that Brazil and Argentina, non-OECD countries, attract a 100 percent BIS risk weighting, whereas Mexico, an OECD country, attracts zero percent BIS risk capital. In general, OECD banks will be interested in reducing regulatory capital by doing business with other OECD banks. Citibank, for example, transacts credit derivatives business only with other OECD banks.

German banks attract the reference-asset BIS risk weight for writing credit default protection. This is generally true globally. What is unique, however, is that some German banks get a zero percent BIS capital treatment for writing credit spread options. In other words, there is a tremendous capital advantage to selling credit protection in the form of a credit spread option rather than as a credit default swap.

Just as some German banks put zero percent capital behind credit spread options, other European banks have received internal bank approval to put zero percent capital behind investment-grade referenced credit default options on the theory that they have an extremely low probability of exercise. The logic behind this treatment is that a credit default swap or a credit default option is the same as a very deep out-of-the-money option. *The option is worthless in normal trading conditions.* The credit default option creates an exposure only in the event of a default event. For the case of an investment-grade asset, the low probability of default makes the option nearly worthless. This argument is not as good, however, for noninvestment-grade product or for first-to-default baskets of investment-grade product where the cumulative probability of default can be quite high.

The U.S. Federal Reserve opinion on this topic is clear. If a U.S. bank buys credit default protection from another bank, the buyer of the credit default protection may choose the lower of the risk weight of the reference asset *or* the risk weight of the bank protection seller. For example, if a U.S. bank purchases credit default protection on a United Mexican States bond with a zero percent risk weight from an OECD country bank with a 20 percent risk weight, the U.S. bank can choose to use a zero percent risk weight for the transaction. In the case where the total return swap creates an unhedged long position, this bank must use the risk weighting of the reference credit issuer. The Federal Reserve's treatment is outlined in its opinion letter SR 9617 dated August 12, 1996. This document is available on the Internet at <vvww.bogirb.fed.US\boarddocs\SRLETTERS>.

Although most regulators agree that the U.S. Federal Reserve guidelines make sense, the regulations for a given jurisdiction may be different; and until there is official clarification, many banks will use the most conservative approach.

Hedge funds, which are 100 percent risk weighted, often receive the total return in a swap. Hedge funds typically put 10 percent collateral up front and use a total return swap as a synthetic financing to enjoy the leverage provided by many bank counterparties. Most jurisdictions allow for a reduction in required risk capital equal to the amount of cash or cash-equivalent collateral posted in a swap. A hedge fund that posts 10 percent cash collateral would therefore have a 90 percent risk weight.

Notice that the risk capital treatments discussed here apply to the case in which the reference asset credit default protection or the reference asset for the TRS matches the asset being hedged. This is not always the case, however. If the reference asset and the asset being hedged are obligations of the same legal entity and have the same level of seniority in bankruptcy and same maturity, the Federal Reserve considers the asset 100 percent hedged. In the case where the reference asset differs from the hedged asset, the transactions must be linked internally for documentation purposes. Further, the regulatory capital treatment is unclear. If a bank can demonstrate a high correlation between the credit derivative reference asset and the asset being hedged, the bank may treat the asset as hedged. But what degree of correlation and what evidence are suitable for regulatory purposes? There is no clear guidance on this issue, and it is a good idea to get a separate opinion memo from the relevant regulatory body so that the hedge treatment is not disallowed at a later date.

Regulatory treatment also varies depending on whether a credit default swap is held on the banking book or on the trading book. The Bank of England is now leaning toward holding credit default swaps on the trading book. Instruments held in the banking book get 8 percent of the notional value held against them. Instruments held in the trading book usually attract between 0.25 percent and 1.6 percent of the notional value as capital held against assets.

The Federal Reserve's guidelines state that if a credit derivative is held in the trading book, the capital requirements will be the same as for other derivatives in the trading book. Banks can use internal models to determine regulatory capital requirements and to add on capital to account for counterparty risk. The trick is to classify credit derivatives as eligible for booking in the trading book. Consider a credit default swap that uses a letter of credit as a reference asset. If a bank receives a premium for providing credit default protection on the LOC and agrees to take delivery of the LOC if it is funded, can this credit default swap be booked in the trading book? If a default event occurs, it appears an LOC would be a banking book asset. The same logic seems to apply for a credit default swap on a loan. Wouldn't the credit default swap booking depend on the type of reference asset? The regulatory agencies are still grappling with definitions of credit derivatives and have not yet dealt with all the implications of the various types of credit derivatives and reference assets.

These ambiguities make the credit derivatives market ripe for trades based on regulatory capital treatment arbitrage. In principle, there is nothing wrong with this. This is regulatory capital *avoidance,* not regulatory capital *evasion.* This is the same concept as exploiting cross-border or home jurisdiction tax rules for tax avoidance, which is legal, as opposed to tax evasion, which is illegal. As more banks become clear on how to exploit these differences, the market will see an upsurge in regulatory capital-based transactions.

I am usually in favor of improving balance sheet performance on a regulatory capital basis, but there is an important caveat. Notice that regulatory capital treatment has very little to do with the credit quality of the counterparty. The sovereign debt of Mexico, rated Bat, has a zero percent risk weight, as does the debt of the United States, which is rated Aaa. The debt of General Re, rated Aaa, gets a 100 percent risk weight. This doesn't make much sense, but those are the rules. Whenever regulatory rules depart from pure economics, there are ways to use them to one's advantage. One can manipulate the balance sheet to show improved performance according to the rules. This is a double-edged sword, however. When transactions are done to optimize performance according to arbitrary regulations, noneconomic transactions may occur. Transactions that cosmetically improve performance in this fashion may put an institution at greater credit risk. This is not always true, but the temptation exists. In my experience, whenever the temptation exists, someone succumbs.

These differences in regulatory capital will bias banks to behave differently toward the credit derivatives market. Keeping track of these regulatory differences will also give an edge to banks that take the time to understand which transactions have the most value to their counterparties.

BOOKING IN NONBANK ENTITIES

Because U.S. banks cannot book high-yield securities on the bank balance sheet, many banks have set up special purpose vehicles or commercial paper (CP) conduits in which to purchase assets. These vehicles can also receive the total return on a TRS without attracting adverse BIS capital treatment. The primary motivation for most banks in setting up these conduits is to avoid high capital treatment charges. Another motive is to book cash assets or to receive the total return on certain assets that normally cannot be booked on the bank balance sheet. In the United States, this helps banks avoid complications of the Glass-Steagall Act—a U.S. federal law that prohibits banks from underwriting or trading corporate bonds (among other restrictions).

The challenge that many banks face is that many banks do not want these vehicles as counterparties. Unless there is an explicit guarantee by a bank for these vehicles, the credit worthiness of the vehicle is usually a negative question mark.

SELECTED CROSS-BORDER ISSUES

Selling securities cross-border poses special problems. Tax and legal issues can arise, which are not easy to foresee in advance. The markets can pose myriad questions: Does a credit-linked note linked to default of a country that normally withholds tax to the investor create a withholding tax on the credit-linked note's interest income? Can European transactions be subjected to value-added tax? Does the local-language newspaper in the Philippines qualify as a financial news source? Will global firms have the resources to track local-language financial publications or, for that matter, local English-language publications in each of the venues in which it deals?

If prospectuses and indenture agreements for hard-currency sovereign debt are not carefully read, other problems may occur. Some sovereign reference bonds may not pay off in hard currency in the event of default. What happens if a credit default contract is poorly crafted? What if the reference asset does not necessarily pay off in a hard currency, but the credit default swap contract references only USD prices—how is the currency exchange rate and currency convertibility handled?

If there is a change of government in the country of a bank guarantor, will these contracts continue to be legal and enforceable? Would you consider buying credit default protection from an Iraqi bank or, for that matter, from an Iranian bank?

These questions and others like them are still under active discussion. There is no substitute for the services of a good international law firm and tax firm to protect the interests of both parties in a contract.

BANK BEST PRACTICES

So, you want to be a contender? You realize that your bank's major risk is credit risk. What does it take to catapult your bank into the top tier of credit mangers? What sort of infrastructure do you need to build? Although the final execution will vary, based on a bank's regulatory, accounting, and tax constraints, the most successful credit management operations exhibit a common pattern. It may be helpful to look at what others have found to be a reasonable approach.

The first step is to find people at the top of the bank who have their lights switched on. This is critical. The global banking community is stuffed with complacent, inert, self-indulgent managers whose most obvious talent is providing support for the other members of their internal politburo. Hard work is a distant bad memory to these people. You will have trouble getting this type of person to read a well-written proposal, much less take the time to understand it. Banks are not pure meritocracies. Political connections often matter more than the merits of your program.

Sometimes the program sponsor is only one powerful person at the executive-committee level or on the board of directors. This person must have the ear of the chief executive officer (CEO) and influence within the bank. If the CEO is the only sponsor, a bank may not be able to get this program off the ground, because CEOs—even the competent ones—tend to have short attention spans.

You will also need a critical mass of key professionals committed to changing your bank's old paradigm for managing credit risk. The following sections will help you draw conclusions about the number and qualifications of the people required. The global banking community is experiencing a widening expertise gulf that got worse in 2000. Talented credit professionals frustrated with the lack of expertise and support at their legacy institutions have been migrating to banks promising them support for their initiatives. The smarter banks are getting smarter.

Enterprise-Wide Transfer Pricing

To successfully manage credit risk on an enterprise-wide basis, you will require new tools, several new credit products, and a unified strategic approach. Your goal is to create a credit risk transfer-pricing unit for the bank. Your driver for rationalization of pricing is value at risk for credit. This requires the coordination of multiple areas within the bank: the loan portfolio/investment book, treasury, accounting, legal, tax, compliance, risk management, credit officers, quantitative research, systems, trading, structuring, and the executive committee.

The overlay for the credit risk transfer pricing is the investment portfolio or the loan portfolio. Most banks do not do a rigorous analysis for pricing credit risk for loans. They usually do an even worse job of pricing the imbedded options often written into loan agreements. Once a bank gets the knack of pricing credit risk, questions regarding the rationale behind loan syndication and loan inventory come next. Prepare to make people uncomfortable. Buy a dog—you will need a friend.

Most banks do not mark their loan portfolios to market. It is not a requirement for banks. The theory was that loans would be held to maturity, and banks would take all the credit risk. Regulators and banks understand the folly of that thinking. There comes a point when the risk does not justify the reward and you want to get out of what has evolved into a bad deal. This scenario is obvious to everyone. What is less obvious is when a deal is new or appears fine. Banks are less willing to put these deals under the microscope and to second-guess existing pricing.

When I first wrote this in 1998, J.P. Morgan marked its loan portfolio to market and attempted to put a price on credit risk everywhere in the bank, no matter where it occurred. Other banks in the United States grudgingly recognized that J.P. Morgan was doing the right thing. It is also the inconvenient thing. By setting a high standard and sticking to it, J.P. Morgan might have forced other banks to live up to this standard. Several of the top U.S. banks were a couple of years behind J.P. Morgan and would not be able to meet this standard in the year 2001 or even 2002. But standards can slip anywhere as we saw in the section in Chapter 3 about J.P. Morgan's "London Whale" and admitted wrongdoing around fake prices.

Even at its best, it wasn't clear whether J.P. Morgan rigorously priced embedded options in loan documentation, however. For instance, I cited an earlier example of a two-year loan that can extend an additional year after one year has passed. The loan with an original maturity of two years becomes a three-year loan. Usually there is some hand waving and a number of basis points is assigned as the value, but banks rarely use option models to price this loan option. There are obvious market and credit price issues with this sort of structure. One day everyone may rigorously price these risks using some form of consistent analytical framework.

As we saw earlier, measuring credit exposure both on a departmental and an enterprise-wide basis is crucial to the ultimate objective. Your bank will require global credit monitoring and global credit limits of various sorts. The price of credit risk does not matter if you cannot measure the risk in the first place. Often a merger of large banks will set the merged institution back at least two years. The most underestimated cost of a merger is the time, people, effort, software, and hardware it will take to successfully integrate information-reporting systems for a merged bank. Most banks are not very good at it on a stand-alone basis. Once two large banks merge, they completely lose the plot.

In Chapter 2, we discussed the general approach for pricing credit exposure. You may wish to use much more complicated models to determine your credit exposures. While using complicated models may force you to make estimates for data, it may give your management the comfort that you are using a consistent and defensible approach. There is merit in that, and models combined with common sense and experience can help you organize your entire pricing approach.

Once you have sorted out your credit exposures, you will need a credit value-at-risk (VAR) model. The challenge with all the models is not the model itself but the *data*. Correlations, recovery values, default rates, and credit migration rates are based on often-limited data, especially for credits outside the United States.

If you have gotten this far, you will want to price the credit risk. The key work on fair-value models evolved because of demand on the trading side, not the credit portfolio side, of financial institutions. You will need to manage the credit risks and market risks in traditional lending products in a manner similar to the way you manage exposures in a market-making activity. This requires the use of a fair-value model, even though banks do not reflect changes in the fair value of loans and lending commitment products in earnings reports or on the balance sheet. The effects of market conditions and events are more readily evident with a fair-value model, and this leads to better decision making and diversification.

While I made the claim that the trading books price their risks, it is not strictly true. For instance, most banks do not calculate a credit valuation adjustment for interest rate swaps and other types of interest rate derivatives. The theory was that the credit risk in the swap market was the average credit risk of the major interest rate swap market makers. This market hallucination usually puts the implied credit risk at a strong single A or a weak AA risk. Therefore, dealers never rigorously priced the credit risk to their interest rate swap counterparties. When banks do business with lower-rated corporations, they usually deal with the question of credit risk with a generalized program of limiting transaction maturity, periodic mark-to-market, mutual midmarket puts, collateral, or a combination of all the former. Very highly rated banks and sovereigns will often request collateral from lower-rated banks. This may give credit managers comfort, but it is not the same as actually pricing the risk of the credit exposure.

Sometimes a bank will act as an intermediary for another bank and charge a small fee. If a bank does not have a credit line, it will purchase protection in the event that this swap counterparty defaults and the protection buyer is owed money on the swap. The protection provider "stands in the middle," or acts as intermediary, in the swap transaction. These generally—but not always—involve small fees, and these small fees are not rigorously priced, and sometimes aren't even marked to market as required.

There is inconsistency even in the trading area of banks and financial institutions. To correct for this, a bank might make a valuation adjustment for this credit risk. This valuation adjustment is simply the estimate of credit loss using the derivatives portfolio exposure profile and market prices for credit risk based on spreads for credit derivatives, asset swaps, and bonds.

All these models have their challenges and are cumbersome to use. There is no substitute for common sense, quantitative skill, and good judgment in evaluating inputs and results. There is also no substitute for observing market credit spreads. You will need market prices in various markets, including credit derivatives, asset swaps, and bonds. To improve return on equity (ROE), you will eventually want to move credit risks off the investment book and into the trading or flow book.

Structured Credit Products

Banks use securitizations with imbedded credit derivatives and along with name-specific credit default swaps to reduce credit risk in their credit investment portfolios. Credit derivatives are the key tool of the credit transformation strategy. Banks need the ability to contemplate structures where every tranche is a derivative, so they need credit-derivatives expertise in both their investment and trading areas. These products enable a bank to reduce credit risk and total capital used for credit activities.

Banks need multiple tools that include a variety of hedging choices in addition to diversification of the credit portfolio. Hedging rather than diversification is sometimes the better answer to mitigate credit risk. This may sound like a surprising statement. Diversification is often used to justify higher exposure to new credit risks, but diversification is not a guarantee against loss, only against losing everything at once.

Banks can begin employing some of these strategies even before they measure the fair value of the entire credit portfolio. In general, the credit management books can be broken into four groups, with the investment book as the driving force. A general schematic might look as follows:

Investment Book		
Structuring	Flow Book	Exotics Book
Synthetic CLOs	Single CDs	Super Senior Risk
Synthetic CDOs	TRORS	Baskets
Conduits	Asset Swaps	Basis Risk
Credit-Linked Notes	Balance Sheet Trades	Correlation Risk
Securitization	Credit Spreads	Convertibility Risk

Although you may not participate in all of these products, the successful banks participate in structuring, flow products, and exotic products in various forms. Distribution efforts are usually organized to support this effort to get synergy and cross-product selling.

The credit trading area often becomes a centralized source of market intelligence. *The spread is where the spread is because that's where the market says it is.* There is no substitute for market intelligence, and most banks are very weak in this area. Banks should set up a credit trading area and should transact credit derivatives, asset swaps, and tranches of structured deals for profit, not just to lay off their own credit risk. This desk should also keep data of credit spreads in the bond markets. A bank will usually see a price move in credit derivatives before the cash market. Credit derivatives are often a leading indicator of bad news. The inherent leverage of a CDS gives investors and incentive to watch for credit risk.

Banks sometimes provide flexibility for deal approvals via an issuer risk matrix available to all trading books. This avoids the problem of seeking internal approvals (inaction by committee) for each deal and satisfies the need to transact swiftly and to position credits. Capital allocation is rationalized.

Trading desks are often authorized to trade if they are within limits for investment-grade deals. Authority to book noninvestment-grade deals may require a separate area with special approvals, if it is done at all. Alternatively, some banks coordinate with emerging-markets trading desks to share their lines and to make some profit accommodation for the joint nature of the business.

Most credit trading desks can price tranches of credit risk using models. The models may vary from department to department within a bank, and will vary between banks. They sometimes create tranches from credit derivatives indexes, take on basis risk and hedge out the portion of the indexes they do not sell.

The preceding list is not exhaustive; it is only meant to highlight the concept of active credit products trading. The portfolio area, the structuring desk, and the credit trading areas are symbiotic. The portfolio group needs to hedge credit risks and components of portfolio structures. The trading desk needs the credit lines of the bank. That requires the blessing and sponsorship of the portfolio area.

Banks are in the business of taking credit risk. They are natural providers of protection. As a result, they can become natural sellers of credit risk as their lines become full, while their appetite to do profitable business with a counterparty continues. Project finance creates an ongoing need to lay off global credit risk. Banks will exploit the potential advantages of trading credit lines with each other. The U.S. market, with its broad number of regional banks, the strong presence of cash-rich banks eager for U.S. credits, its single currency, and its relatively long history of credit data, is still the largest interbank-credit-line trading market in the world.

The nonstandardization of documentation, evolving economies, and evolving legal and regulatory environments in these countries will create a continued strong demand for credit products and continued confusion in pricing and documentation issues for future.

The bank strategy is to improve return on assets (ROA) and return on equity (ROE) on both economic and regulatory bases. Once a bank prices and mitigates credit risk, each incremental deal comes under the spotlight of opportunity cost. That is the blessing and the bane of credit risk pricing. If you free up a line, what is the return on capital of an alternative deal? The next best deal may be a loan, or it may even be a credit derivative.

CHAPTER 9

What's Next?

PAST IS PROLOGUE

Abraham Lincoln was elected President of the United States on November 1860. President James Buchanan, a Southern Democrat, transferred power to the Northern Republican on March 4, 1861. On April 14, 1861, the South's General Beauregard at Fort Moultrie fired his guns on Fort Sumter, forcing commanding Union officer Major Robert Anderson to evacuate. From 1861 to 1866, the North and South engaged in brutal combat, losing an estimated 750 thousand men. The American Civil War was the cause of the largest number of military casualties in U.S. history.

Just before Howell Cobb, then President James Buchanan's Treasury of the Secretary, left Washington D.C., the U.S. Treasury sold $20 million of United States five percent bonds at a price of 105 to Wall Street firms. When the war broke out, the economy was in turmoil. Seventy five percent of the buyer Wall Street firms defaulted on their obligations to purchase the Treasury bonds. The government had no means to force them to make good. At the time, there were no credit default swaps on Wall Street firms with which to hedge against the debacle.

The metaphorical Treasury box was near empty. Interest payments on outstanding debt was coming due. A default would have been disastrous to the young USA's credit. The Treasury begged Wall Street for—and got— an emergency loan at twelve percent interest.

The Lincoln Administration appointed Salmon Portland Chase, a

Democrat, to the position of Treasury Secretary. Chase tried to raise $20 million, offering six percent interest until 1884. He accepted all bids at a price of 94 and above, but he still had a large unsold balance. Anglo American Henry Clews, co-founder of Livermore, Clews, and Company, formed a consortium, took the night train to Washington D.C., and made Treasury Secretary Chase a direct bid to purchase the entire unsold balance at Chase's price of 94.

Chase thought the talk of war was a tempest in a teapot. Encouraged by Clews's proposal, Chase hesitated, saying he wanted to reoffer the bonds to rejected bidders to give them the option of buying at 94. He told Clews to come back the following morning.

The delay was an illuminating one for Clews. That night, he conferred with power brokers in Washington D.C. He learned of war preparations on both sides and of the resolve to fight to win. The following morning, Clews told Chase that U.S. Treasury bonds would plummet in price. Henry Clews was under no obligation to persist with his bid, so he withdrew it. Treasury Secretary Chase responded: "Oh, certainly, but I think you are making a mistake, for the war will be over in sixty days, and these bonds will go to par." Shortly thereafter, the bonds sank to 84.

Our media lionizes Treasury Secretaries as if they can foresee the future. No one can. Sometimes they make mistakes, and sometimes those mistakes are whoppers.

Lord Salisbury, then styled Robert Cecil, made a speech to the British Parliament wherein he asserted: "[T]he Northern States of America never can be our sure friends…when the war began [the Southern States] at once recurred to England as their natural ally."

The British Empire was then the world's superpower. Great Britain's pound sterling was the world's reserve currency. The Rothschild family held great influence over a European banking empire. They were doubtful about the USA's prospects. International banks would not lend the U.S. Treasury a shilling.

But the USA did not default. Secretary Chase later admitted that he had Henry Clews and Jay Cooke to thank for helping him raise money for the North's expensive war effort. Their firms stepped up to subsequently sell two series of bonds.

In the 20th century, the USA became the world's superpower and grew to become the largest economy in the world. In 1944, the U.S. dollar become the world's reserve currency. The ability to print one's own currency to pay off national and international debt is a huge advantage. But it does not come without a cost, and nothing lasts forever, especially if one makes all the wrong moves.

THE BIG COVID-19 SHORTS

Since the first quarter of 2020, we've damaged the global economy with lockdowns and restrictions in reaction to the COVID-19 virus that originated in a lab in Wuhan, China. Our reaction may have been more extreme than it otherwise would have been due to the Chinese Communist Party's (CCP) lies. The CCP initially claimed the virus was not transmitted human-to-human. The CCP allowed infected people to board airplanes and other public transportation. Countries scrambled for reliable data about patient zero, the asymptomatic period, the contagion rate, mortality rates, illness rates and severity by demographic, treatments, and vaccines.

The U.S. stock market started falling mid-February through March 20, 2020. Bill Ackman of Pershing Square had hedged his equity portfolio by buying credit default protection on credit indexes. His analysis showed that credit spreads were near all-time tight levels on various investment grade and high yield companies, after he adjusted companies near default. Ackman disclosed his hedges on March 3, 2020.

Ackman's trade was the opposite strategy to J.P. Morgan's infamous London Whale trade. It was also the opposite of AIG's strategy of picking up nickels in front of a steamroller. Ackman's downside was limited. Credit spreads cannot tighten to zero, and spreads were already very tight. Premiums and commissions cost Pershing Square $27 million. When credit spreads widened, Ackman's proceeds were $2.6 billion. The trade left Pershing Square's portfolio a little better than even. Unlike many, Ackman's portfolio did not have a net loss, and his shorts gave him a cash war chest with which to buy depressed equities.

Boaz Weinstein, head of Sabra Capital, had made similar bets that credit spreads were too tight. His $2.2 billion of assets under management had an 82% gain as of March 20, 2022.

Fundamental credit analysis allowed both hedge fund managers to initiate leveraged hedges that served their portfolios well.

REPRESENTATIVE THOMAS MASSIE'S TRUTH BOMB

In March 2020, Representative Thomas Massie (Republican, Kentucky), single handedly forced members of the U.S. Congress's House of Representative to fulfill their Constitutional obligation and return to Washington D.C. for an in-person vote an unprecedented $2.2 trillion stimulus bill. His fellow Congressman had wanted to vote remotely claiming COVID-19 as the excuse. Massie pointed out that service workers throughout the USA were on the job, and it was their Constitutional obligation to return. President Trump vilified Representative Massie for doing the right thing, falsely claiming Massie would delay the vote.

Massie succeeded in forcing a quorum to return to D.C. But the Democrat Speaker of the House, Nancy Pelosi, and Republican House Minority Leader, Representative Kevin McCarthy (Republican, California), blocked a recorded vote so that the public will never know the names of their "representatives" who voted for this package. Representative Massie, of course, voted "Nay!" The bill was dubbed a coronavirus relief package. But do you know who was most relieved? Banks.

Most Americans did not realize that banks had a severe liquidity crunch in mid-September 2019. Short-term repo rates soared. The Fed accepted "high quality capital" in exchange for cash. The Fed injected more than $230 billion into the banking system—expanding money supply—to forestall disaster. Yet the banks needed even more liquidity.

The March 2020 bill was perversely named the CARES Act. Massie explained that if this money were applied to relieve the 150 million locked down American workers, each would receive checks for $13,333. Instead, the money was funneled through banks and financial institutions. American workers received checks for $1,200.

COVID-19 was the excuse for spending that shattered every U.S. record. Moreover, no matter how much the Treasury uses interest rate

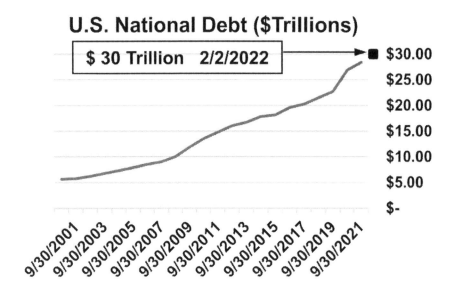

FIGURE 9.1 United States National Debt

manipulation, inflation, and other gimmicks, taxpayers are on the hook for all of it.

On March 29, 2020, Massie tweeted: "The stimulus package that just passed is the biggest wealth transfer from common folks to the super-rich (Wall Street and bankers) in the history of mankind. Done in the name of a virus with $1,200 checks as the cheese in the trap. This will be obvious in short order."

On April 24, 2020, Congress passed the "Paycheck Protection Program and Health Care Enhancement Act." It appropriated $483 billion. The idea was to provide loans to stressed small businesses. Banks, of course, administered the program in exchange for fees. The loans helped some businesses, but confusion and abuse were rampant. Controls were an afterthought.

On December 28, 2020, the $920 billion Consolidated Appropriations Act was signed into law. Workers received a $600 stimulus check. The bill appropriated money to supplement unemployment benefits.

The American Rescue Plan passed in March 2021. Another $1.9 trillion. It included $1,400 stimulus checks and billions for vaccine distribution. (See Appendix II for my impressions on the huge impact of these programs on the U.S. money supply.)

No matter how one tries to unpack the numbers, this is an enormous increase in the supply of U.S. dollars. Inflation soared to 5.35% in December 2021, and kept climbing. In January 2022, inflation rose to an annual rate of 7.5%, a 40 year high. Meanwhile, consumer prices for energy, food, and fuel have climbed well beyond 7.5%. Consumers have seen increases of 25-30%. As usual, the average taxpayer has been gored.

How long will it take to render the U.S. dollar worthless? It seems the U.S. Treasury is trying to find out.

In 2021, household debt in the USA jumped the most since 2007. Debt rose by over $1 trillion from $14.56 trillion to $15.56 trillion. The debt is perilous for many, because wages lag far behind inflation.

U.S. GDP was $23.99 trillion, for the 4th quarter of 2021, a growth rate of 6.9%. Unemployment is 4%. U.S. National Debt reached $30 trillion on February 2, 2022. (See Figure 9.1.) We don't have the full first quarter numbers for 2002 yet, but the debt to GDP ratio is at all-time highs.

"CORRUPTION-TO-PRODUCTION RATIO" IS TOO HIGH

No one knows how our current crisis plays out. But what I've christened the "Corruption-to-Production Ratio" is too high. A low ratio encourages a nation's growth and prosperity. A high ratio destabilizes a nation's economy. The dilution in the gravitas of our "leadership" is dismaying. Citizens so far remain silent as our language is tortured. Mid-wits revel in Topsyturveydom. Compare the USA's founding documents and speeches with the drivel that comes from most in Washington D.C. today. It is illuminating. More than half of the members of Congress are millionaires and many did not get the money honestly or ethically. In contrast, in 2020, approximately 8% of Americans were millionaires.

The Fed ballooned the nation's debt with no strategy to grow GDP. Historically, sovereigns have chosen the following methods to get themselves out of debt trouble:

- Grow miraculously
- Ban overseas investments
- Force banks to hold government debt
- Default on politically cloutless and foreign unfriendlies.
- Debase the currency and allow inflation
- Impose negative real interest rates

Of these choices, I far prefer growth. The USA has spurred growth in the past. Under the McKinley presidency, the USA imposed measures including protective tariffs designed to encourage the manufacture of goods capable of being made in the USA. Economists claimed that retaliatory tariffs would cripple U.S. exports. But they were wrong. Foreign countries demanded U.S. made goods, even when they were more expensive. Foreign countries perceived U.S. goods as higher quality. Exports soared. We might try to stimulate the U.S. economy again in a similar fashion:

A Proposed "Marshall Plan" for the USA

- Rebuild the USA's internal supply chain
- Have goods made in America with American labor
- Impose protective tariffs
- Invest in productive assets and services

A WILD RIDE

The previous observations are not meant to be a rigorous economic analysis. The following are possible scenarios, not to be taken as investment advice. No one can predict the future.

The Fed's policy of money printing, low nominal interest rates, and negative real interest rates will lead to higher inflation. The Fed seems afraid to raise rates lest it crashes the stock market. Cash holders will be poorer. Investors will bid up real assets: houses, oil, art, factories, equipment, automobiles, commodities, and precious metals, including gold. Gold

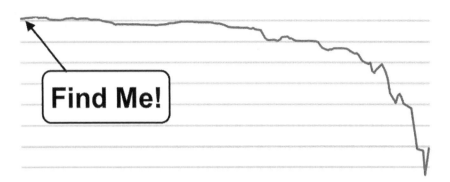

FIGURE 9.2 Fixed income price pattern of fraud-plagued "assets."

holders might recall that President Franklin Delano Roosevelt made gold ownership illegal. You cannot rule out anything.

The Fed will eventually raise rates to prevent hyperinflation if it hasn't already lost control. For that scenario, shorting Treasuries, perhaps going long puts or buying an ETF that is short long-term treasuries might be your course of action. You might consider cyclical stocks which tend not to get hurt by higher interest rates.

To paraphrase Margo Channing, "Fasten your seatbelts, you're in for a bumpy ride." It is impossible to time the market. If we have another market crisis, recall that assets exhibit strong correlations with high volatility when market makers panic.

There may be "big short" opportunities. The housing market has just had a huge price run-up. Car prices have soared. Subprime auto loan games have flourished. Those looking for fast large bonuses tend to manufacture shoddy securitizations.

If you randomly sample a portfolio of loans and see red flags, remember it is best to short overvalued securitizations early. When you short par bonds (whether they are synthetic or cash), they are not likely to rise much if at all, and they are very likely to plummet (See Figure 9.2).

Enjoy the ride.

.

APPENDIX I

SIMPLIFIED VALUE-AT-RISK CALCULATION

Consider the following equation where σ is the standard deviation, and ρ is the correlation between the assets. Correlation is simply the dimensionless (scaled) form of covariance, the degree to which assets tend to move together.

$$\text{Risk} = \sigma_{X+Y} = \sqrt{\sigma_X^2 + \sigma_Y^2 + 2\rho\sigma_X\sigma_Y}$$

The portfolio expected return is:

$$E(R) = \omega r_A + (1 - \omega) r_B$$

where $r =$ return on the assets
                        $\omega =$ the asset weighting

In this case, the assets are equally weighted. Let us assume Asset X has an expected return of 10 percent and a variance of 0.04. Asset Y has an expected return of 15 percent and a variance of 0.05. We will also assume that the covariance of the assets, or correlation, is 0.03.

The expected return of the portfolio is calculated as follows and expressed as a percentage:

$$(0.5 \times 0.10) + (0.5 \times 0.15) = 0.125 \text{ or } 12.5\%$$

The two-asset portfolio variance =
$$(0.5^2 \times 0.04) + (0.5^2 \times 0.05) + 2(0.5)(0.5)(0.03) = 0.0375.$$

The standard deviation of the variance, or volatility of our two-asset portfolio, is expressed as a percentage. (I will round to one decimal point for this example.)

$$\text{Volatility} = (0.0375)^{1/2} = 0.1936 \text{ or } 19.4\%$$

For the normal distribution, the value at risk (VAR) at the 99 percent confidence interval uses the z value for the one percent tail for a normal distribution of 2.58 standard deviations from the mean. In this case, the one percent tail is $2.58 \times 0.1936 = 0.4994$ away from the mean. So, the level of value at risk is calculated as follows based on the portfolio returns, the confidence interval, a normal distribution, and the standard deviation or portfolio volatility:

$$\text{Value-at-Risk} = 0.125 - 0.4994 = -0.374$$

There is a one percent chance the portfolio will lose more than 37.4%.

We want to minimize the volatility of the losses, thus minimizing the volatility of the expected return. How much will the portfolio volatility decline if we add a third asset?

To make this easy to see, let us create a three-asset portfolio where each asset has equal weight. The third asset, Asset Z, has an expected return of 12.5%, identical to the expected return we calculated above for the two-asset portfolio to make it easier to see the effect. The variance of asset Z is 0.0375, identical to the variance of our two-asset portfolio.

But the *covariance* of the three-asset portfolio is 0.1. It is lower than for the two-asset portfolio because the three-asset portfolio is theoretically more diversified. The expected return of the portfolio is:

$$\frac{(0.10 + 0.15 + 0.125)}{3} = 0.125 \text{ or } 12.5\%$$

The portfolio variance $= (\omega_x^2 \times \sigma_x^2) + (\omega_y^2 \times \sigma_y^2) + (\omega_z^2 \times \sigma_z^2) + (3 \times \omega_x \times \omega_y \times \omega_z \times \text{Cov}_{xyz})$

or

$[(0.33)^2 \times 0.04] + [(0.33)^2 \times 0.05] + [(0.33)^2 \times 0.0375] + (3 \times 0.33 \times 0.33$ v 0.33 v $0.01) = 0.0153$

The volatility of the portfolio is the square root of the variance or 0.1237, and it is expressed as in percentage terms as 12.4%. The one percent tail is 2.58 v 0.1237 = 0.3191 away from the expected return, or the mean. The level of value-at-risk or VAR is 0.125 – 0.3191 = 0.194. This means that at the 99 percent confidence interval, there is a one percent chance the portfolio will lose more than 19.4 percent as shown in Figure 1.7.

When we added the third asset, volatility dropped from 19.4% to 12.4% versus the two-asset portfolio. The value-at-risk declined at the 99% confidence interval. With the two-asset portfolio, at the 99% confidence interval, there was a one percent chance the portfolio would lose more than 37.4%; the model shows the three-asset portfolio has a one percent chance the portfolio will lose more than 19.4%.

APPENDIX II

U.S. DOLLAR MONEY SUPPLY: M1 AND M2

The following observations are not meant to be a rigorous money supply analysis. The Fed recently changed the definitions of M1 and M2 (see below). The Fed does not provide transparency or granularity of data. It is impossible to compare current money supply data with the data prior to the definition changes in May 2020. I will leave it to you to speculate as to why the Fed would make it more difficult to retrospectively compare data. But I offer these observations to provoke thought on the massive expansion of U.S. money supply which has led to roaring inflation.

The M1 money supply includes the most liquid forms of money: coins and currency in circulation, demand deposits (checking accounts), other checkable deposits (OCDs) such as demand deposits at thrifts, and traveler's checks. On April 24, 2020, regulations changed. Savings deposits and money market deposit accounts—both formerly reported as components of M2 (we will discuss M2 in a moment)—were made as liquid as checking accounts. After May 2020, savings deposits and OCDs ceased to be separately reported and were included in M1 as "other liquid deposits." As I mentioned earlier, it is not possible to reconstruct and compare the current M1 money supply with the pre-May 2020 M1 money supply.

On March 1, 2020, M1 was $4.28 trillion. On April 1, 2020, M1 soared $490 billion to $4.77 trillion (old reporting method). M1 (old definition) rose $490 billion from March 1 to April 1, 2020. On May 1, 2020, using the new reporting methodology, M1 was $16.26 trillion. Between May 1, 2020, and December 1, 2021, M1 soared $4.29 trillion to $20.55 trillion. (See Figure 9.1.)

One might argue that the rapid growth in M1 after May 1, 2020, was due to including components of M2 in M1, but the data suggests that isn't the case. Let's take a look at M2. On March 1, 2020, M2 was $16.01 trillion. On April 1, 2020, it was $17.04 trillion. On May 1, 2020, it was $17.89 trillion. Between May 1, 2020, and December 1, 2021, M2 soared to $21.638 trillion. M2 rose $3.75 trillion from May 1, 2020, to Dec 1, 2021. This was half the time for the last leap of this amount (roughly July 2018 to March 2020). (See Figure 10.2.) The growth pace doubled.

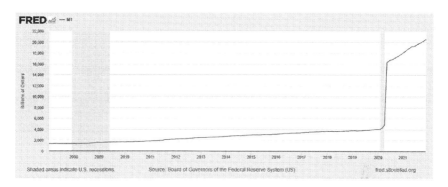

The definition of M1 is the sum of "(1) currency outside the U.S. Treasury, Federal Reserve Banks, and the vaults of depository institutions; (2) demand deposits at commercial banks (excluding those amounts held by depository institutions, the U.S. government, and foreign banks and official institutions) less cash items in the process of collection and Federal Reserve float; and [Before May 2020] (3) other checkable deposits (OCDs), consisting of negotiable order of withdrawal, or NOW, and automatic transfer service, or ATS, accounts at depository institutions, share draft accounts at credit unions, and demand deposits at thrift institutions.

[After May 2020] (3) other liquid deposits, consisting of OCDs and savings deposits (including money market deposit accounts). Seasonally adjusted M1 is constructed by summing currency, demand deposits, and OCDs (before May 2020) or other liquid deposits (beginning May 2020), each seasonally adjusted separately."

Source: Board of Governors of the Federal Reserve System (US), M1 [M1SL], retrieved from FRED, Federal Reserve Bank of St. Louis; https://fred.stlouisfed.org/series/M1SL, February 14, 2022

FIGURE 10.1 (Appendix II) Graph of M1 Money Supply January 1, 2007 to December 1, 2021.

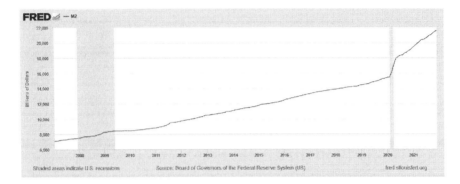

"Before May 2020, M2 consists of M1 plus (1) savings deposits (including money market deposit accounts); (2) small-denomination time deposits (time deposits in amounts of less than $100,000) less individual retirement account (IRA) and Keogh balances at depository institutions; and (3) balances in retail money market funds (MMFs) less IRA and Keogh balances at MMFs.

Beginning May 2020, M2 consists of M1 plus (1) small-denomination time deposits (time deposits in amounts of less than $100,000) less IRA and Keogh balances at depository institutions; and (2) balances in retail MMFs less IRA and Keogh balances at MMFs. Seasonally adjusted M2 is constructed by summing savings deposits (before May 2020), small-denomination time deposits, and retail MMFs, each seasonally adjusted separately, and adding this result to seasonally adjusted M1."

Source: Board of Governors of the Federal Reserve System (US), M1 [M1SL], retrieved from FRED, Federal Reserve Bank of St. Louis; https://fred.stlouisfed.org/series/M1SL, February 15, 2022

FIGURE 10.2 (Appendix II) Graph of M2 Money Supply January 1, 2007 to December 1, 2021.

*Selected Bibliography

AIG, "Residential Mortgage Presentation (Financial Figures are as of June 30, 2007)." AIG, 9 August 2007.

Arlidge, John, "I'm doing 'God's work. Meet Mr Goldman Sachs." *Sunday Times*, 8 November 2009.

Black, William K., *The Best Way to Rob a Bank Is to Own One: How Corporate Executives and Politicians Looted the S&L Industry*. University of Texas Press, 2005.

Clews, Henry. *Twenty-Eight Years in Wall Street*. J.S. Ogilvie Publishing Company, New York, 1887.

CFTC Press Release r6737-13, "CFTC Files and Settles Charges Against JPMorgan Chase Bank, N. A., for Violating Prohibition on Manipulative Conduct in Connection with 'London Whale' Swaps Trades." 16 October 2013. 1887.

Efrati, Amin and Plevin, Liam. "SEC, Justice Scrutinize AIG on Swaps Accounting." *The Wall Street Journal*, 6 June 2008.

Federal Reserve Economic Data, St. Louis Fed. "What's behind the recent surge in the M1 money supply?" The FRED Blog, 11 January 2021.

Forgey, Quint. "Both parties pile on Massie after effort to force recorded vote flops." *Politico.com* (web), 27 March 2020.

Freifeld, Karen, et al., "JPMorgan agrees $13 billion settlement with U.S. over bad mortgages." Reuters, 13 November 2013.

Gugliotta, Guy. "New Estimate Raises Civil War Death Toll." *The New York Times*, 2 April 2012.

Guildford, Gwynn. "Inflation Speeds to 40-Year High.' *The Wall Street Journal*, 11 February 2022.

Hiltzik, Michael, "What Jamie Dimon didn't tell you on 'Meet the Press'," *The Los Angeles Times*, May 14, 2012.

Hoffman, Liz. "Ackman's Pandemic Bets Pay Off Big." *The Wall Street Journal*, 1 February 2022.

Kaptur, Marcy Special Order on MF Global read into the Congressional Record. [Congressional Record Volume 157, Number 192 (Wednesday, December 14, 2011) [House] [Pages H8962-H8965] From the Congressional Record Online through the Government Publishing Office

Kopecki, Dawn, "J.P. Morgan Pays $920 Million to Settle London Whale Probes." Bloomberg News, 19 September 2013.)

Mollenkamp, Carrick and Ng, Serena. "Senate's Goldman Sachs Probe Shows Toxic Magnification." *The Wall Street Journal*, 2 May 2010. Web.

Morrison & Foerster LLP, Attorneys for the Chapter 11 Trustee, 2013, "Report of Investigation of Louis J. Freeh, Chapter 11 Trustee of MF Global Holdings Ltd., *et al.*," *In re MF Global Holdings Ltd., et al.*, Debtors, United States Bankruptcy Court for the Southern District of New York, Case No. 11-15059 (MG)." 4 April 2013.

Office of the Special Inspector General For the Troubled Asset Relief Program, "Factors Affecting Efforts to Limit Payments to AIG Counterparties." (SIGTARP-10-003), 17 November 2009.

Reilly, David. "In Subprime, AIG Sees Small Risk; Others See More." *The Wall Street Journal*, 13 August 2007. {Tavakoli's challenge of A.I.G.'s claim of zero accounting losses on credit derivatives linked to so-called super senior tranches of collateralized debt obligations backed by mezzanine tranches of CDOs backed by subprime collateral.}

Stempel, Jonathan "Corzine, others settle MF Global lawsuit for $64.5 million." *Reuters*, 7 July 2015. (Corzine faced civil lawsuits, not a criminal indictment.)

Securities and Exchange Commission, "J. P. Morgan to Pay $152.6 Million to Settle SEC Charges of Misleading Investors in CDO Tied to Housing Market (2011-131)." 21 June 21 2011.

Securities and Exchange Commission, (Press Release) "JPMorgan Admits to Widespread Recordkeeping Failures and Agrees to Pay $125 Million Penalty to Resolve SEC Charges." December 17, 2021. [Pertains to J.P. Morgan Securities LLC (JPMS), a broker-dealer subsidiary of

JPMorgan Chase & Co. JPMorgan "acknowledged its conduct violated the federal securities laws."]

Sloan, Allan. "Junk mortgages under the microscope." *Fortune*, 16 October 2007.

Sloan, Allan. "Where's the outrage over Goldman Sachs's other mortgage foray?" *Fortune*, 4 May 2010.Sloan, Allan. "Goldman Sachs' House of Junk," Fortune, 12 April 2016.

Tavakoli, Janet. "CDO Evolution Creates New World of Risk." *GARP Risk Review*, Nov/Dec 2003, Issue 15.

Tavakoli, Janet. "The Elusive Income of Synthetic CDOs." *Journal of Structured Finance*, Winter 2006, Volume 11, Number 4.

Teitelbaum, Richard and Son, Hugh. "New York Fed's Secret Choice to Pay for [Credit Default} Swaps Hits Taxpayers." *Bloomberg News*, October 27, 2009.

Timiraos, Nick. "March 2020: How The Fed Averted Economic Disaster." *The Wall Street Journal*, 19-20 February 2022.

U.S. Senate Committee on Homeland Security and Governmental Affairs. (111 second session S. Rpt. 674, vol. 4 of 5). Senators Carl Levin and Tom Corburn, M.D., Staff Report, "WALL STREET AND THE FINANCIAL CRISIS: Anatomy of a Financial Collapse." released in conjunction with the Permanent Subcommittee on Investigations April 27, 2010 (updated April 13, 2011) Hearing.

U.S. Senate Committee on Homeland Security and Governmental Affairs. (113 S. Rpt. 96, vol. 1). Senators Carl Levin and John McCain, Staff Report, "J.P. Morgan Chase Whale Trades: A Case History of Derivatives Risks and Abuses." released in conjunction with the Permanent Subcommittee on Investigations March 15, 2013, Hearing.

U. S. Senate Committee on Homeland Security and Government Affairs. Senators Carl Levin and John McCain, Staff Report, "Abuse of Structured Financial Products: Misusing Basket Options to Avoid Taxes and Leverage Limits." Washington: Government Printing Office, released in conjunction with the Permanent Subcommittee on Investigations July 22, 2014, Hearing.

Zuckerman, Gregory, and Burne, Katy. "London Whale' Rattles Debt Market." *The Wall Street Journal*, 6 April 2012.

INDEX

Made in the USA
Monee, IL
04 April 2022